Java™ Servlet Programming

THE JAVA™ SERIES

Exploring Java™

Java™ Threads

Java™ Network Programming

Java™ Virtual Machine

Java™ AWT Reference

Java™ Language Reference

Java™ Fundamental Classes Reference

Database Programming with JDBC™ and Java™

Java™ Distributed Computing

Developing Java Beans™

Java™ Security

Java™ Cryptography

Java™ Swing

Java™ Servlet Programming

Also from O'Reilly

Java™ in a Nutshell

Java™ in a Nutshell, Deluxe Edition

Java™ Examples in a Nutshell

Java™ Servlet Programming

Jason Hunter
with William Crawford

Beijing · Cambridge · Farnham · Köln · Paris · Sebastopol · Taipei · Tokyo

Java™ Servlet Programming

by Jason Hunter with William Crawford

Copyright © 1998 O'Reilly & Associates, Inc. All rights reserved.
Printed in the United States of America.

Published by O'Reilly & Associates, Inc., 101 Morris Street, Sebastopol, CA 95472.

Editor: Paula Ferguson

Production Editor: Paula Carroll

Editorial and Production Services: Benchmark Productions, Inc.

Printing History:

        October 1998:   First Edition

This book is printed on acid-free paper with 85% recycled content, 15% post-consumer waste. O'Reilly & Associates is committed to using paper with the highest recycled content available consistent with high quality.

ISBN: 1-56592-391-X   [7/99]

Table of Contents

Preface

In late 1996, Java on the server side was coming on strong. Several major software vendors were marketing technologies specifically aimed at helping server-side Java developers do their jobs more efficiently. Most of these products provided a prebuilt infrastructure that could lift the developer's attention from the raw socket level into the more productive application level. For example, Netscape introduced something it named "server-side applets"; the World Wide Web Consortium included extensible modules called "resources" with its Java-based Jigsaw web server; and with its WebSite server, O'Reilly Software promoted the use of a technology it (only coincidentally) dubbed "servlets." The drawback: each of these technologies was tied to a particular server and designed for very specific tasks.

Then, in early 1997, JavaSoft (a company that has since been reintegrated into Sun Microsystems as the Java Software division) finalized Java servlets. This action consolidated the scattered technologies into a single, standard, generic mechanism for developing modular server-side Java code. Servlets were designed to work with both Java-based and non-Java-based servers. Support for servlets has since been implemented in nearly every web server, from Apache to Zeus, and in many non-web servers as well.

Servlets have been quick to gain acceptance because, unlike many new technologies that must first explain the problem or task they were created to solve, servlets are a clear solution to a well-recognized and widespread need: generating dynamic web content. From corporations down to individual web programmers, people who struggled with the maintenance and performance problems of CGI-based web programming are turning to servlets for their power, portability, and efficiency. Others, who were perhaps intimidated by CGI programming's apparent reliance on manual HTTP communication and the Perl and C languages, are looking to servlets as a manageable first step into the world of web programming.

This book explains everything you need to know about Java servlet programming. The first five chapters cover the basics: what servlets are, what they do, and how they work. The following eight chapters are where the true meat is—they explore the things you are likely to do with servlets. You'll find numerous examples, several suggestions, a few warnings, and even a couple of true hacks that somehow made it past technical review.

We cover Version 2.0 of the Servlet API, which was introduced as part of the Java Web Server 1.1 in December 1997 and clarified by the release of the Java Servlet Development Kit 2.0 in April 1998. Changes in the API from Version 1.0, finalized in June 1997, are noted throughout the text.

Audience

Is this book for you? It is if you're interested in extending the functionality of a server—such as extending a web server to generate dynamic content. Specifically, this book was written to help:

CGI programmers
> CGI is a popular but somewhat crude method of extending the functionality of a web server. Servlets provide an elegant, efficient alternative.

NSAPI, ISAPI, ASP, and Server-Side JavaScript programmers
> Each of these technologies can be used as a CGI alternative, but each has limitations regarding portability, security, and/or performance. Servlets tend to excel in each of these areas.

Java applet programmers
> It has always been difficult for an applet to talk to a server. Servlets make it easier by giving the applet an easy-to-connect-to, Java-based agent on the server.

Authors of web pages with server-side includes
> Pages that use server-side includes to call CGI programs can use <SERVLET> tags to add content more efficiently to a page.

Authors of web pages with different appearances
> By this we mean pages that must be available in different languages, have to be converted for transmission over a low-bandwidth connection, or need to be modified in some manner before they are sent to the client. Servlets provide something called servlet chaining that can be used for processing of this type. Each servlet in a servlet chain knows how to catch, process, and return a specific kind of content. Thus, servlets can be linked together to do language translation, change large color images to small black-and-white ones, convert images in esoteric formats to standard GIF or JPEG images, or nearly anything else you can think of.

What You Need to Know

When we first started writing this book, we found to our surprise that one of the hardest things was determining what to assume about you, the reader. Are you familiar with Java? Have you done CGI or other web application programming before? Or are you getting your feet wet with servlets? Do you understand HTTP and HTML, or do those acronyms seem perfectly interchangeable? No matter what experience level we imagined, it was sure to be too simplistic for some and too advanced for others.

In the end, this book was written with the notion that it should contain predominantly original material: it could leave out exhaustive descriptions of topics and concepts that are well described online or in other books. Scattered throughout the text, you'll find several references to these external sources of information.

Of course, external references only get you so far. This book expects you are comfortable with the Java programming language and basic object-oriented programming techniques. If you are coming to servlets from another language, we suggest you prepare yourself by reading a book on general Java programming, such as *Exploring Java*, by Patrick Niemeyer and Joshua Peck (O'Reilly). You may want to skim quickly the sections on applets and AWT (graphical) programming and spend extra time on network and multithreaded programming. If you want to get started with servlets right away and learn Java as you go, we suggest you read this book with a copy of *Java in a Nutshell*, by David Flanagan (O'Reilly), or another Java reference book, at your side.

This book does *not* assume you have extensive experience with web programming, HTTP, and HTML. But neither does it provide a full introduction to or exhaustive description of these technologies. We'll cover the basics necessary for effective servlet development and leave the finer points (such as a complete list of HTML tags and HTTP 1.1 headers) to other sources.

About the Examples

In this book you'll find nearly 100 servlet examples. The code for these servlets is all contained within the text, but you may prefer to download the examples rather than type them in by hand. You can find the code online and packaged for download at *http://www.oreilly.com/catalog/jservlet/*. You can also see many of the servlets in action at *http://www.servlets.com.*

All the examples have been tested using Sun's Java Web Server 1.1.1, running in the Java Virtual Machine (JVM) bundled with the Java Development Kit (JDK) 1.1.5, on both Windows and Unix. A few examples require alternate configurations, and this has been noted in the text. The Java Web Server is free for education use and has a 30-day trial period for all other use. You can download a copy from *http://java.sun.com/products*. The Java Development Kit is freely downloadable from *http://java.sun.com/products/jdk* or, for educational use, from *http://www.sun.com/products-n-solutions/edu/java/*. The Java Servlet Development Kit (JSDK) is available separately from the JDK; you can find it at *http://java.sun.com/products/servlet/*.

This book also contains a set of utility classes—they are used by the servlet examples, and you may find them helpful for your own general-purpose servlet development. These classes are contained in the `com.oreilly.servlet` package. Among other things, there are classes to help servlets parse parameters, handle file uploads, generate multipart responses (server push), negotiate locales for internationalization, return files, manage socket connections, and act as RMI servers. There's even a class to help applets communicate with servlets. The source code for the `com.oreilly.servlet` package is contained within the text; the latest version is also available online (with *javadoc* documentation) from *http://www.oreilly.com/catalog/jservlet/* and *http://www.servlets.com*.

Organization

This book consists of 13 chapters and 5 appendices, as follows:

Chapter 1, *Introduction*
> Explains the role and advantage of Java servlets in web application development.

Chapter 2, *HTTP Servlet Basics*
> Provides a quick introduction to the things an HTTP servlet can do: page generation, server-side includes, servlet chaining, and JavaServer Pages.

Chapter 3, *The Servlet Life Cycle*
> Explains the details of how and when a servlet is loaded, how and when it is executed, how threads are managed, and how to handle the synchronization issues in a multithreaded system. Persistent state capabilities are also covered.

Chapter 4, *Retrieving Information*
> Introduces the most common methods a servlet uses to receive information—about the client, the server, the client's request, and itself.

Chapter 5, *Sending HTML Information*
> Describes how a servlet can generate HTML, return errors and other status codes, redirect requests, write data to the server log, and send custom HTTP header information.

Chapter 6, *Sending Multimedia Content*
> Looks at some of the interesting things a servlet can return: dynamically generated images, compressed content, and multipart responses.

Chapter 7, *Session Tracking*

Shows how to build a sense of state on top of the stateless HTTP protocol. The first half of the chapter demonstrates the traditional session-tracking techniques used by CGI developers; the second half shows how to use the built-in support for session tracking in the Servlet API.

Chapter 8, *Security*

Explains the security issues involved with distributed computing and demonstrates how to maintain security with servlets.

Chapter 9, *Database Connectivity*

Shows how servlets can be used for high-performance web-database connectivity.

Chapter 10, *Applet-Servlet Communication*

Describes how servlets can be of use to applet developers who need to communicate with the server.

Chapter 11, *Interservlet Communication*

Discusses why servlets need to communicate with each other and how it can be accomplished.

Chapter 12, *Internationalization*

Shows how a servlet can generate multilingual content.

Chapter 13, *Odds and Ends*

Presents a junk drawer full of useful servlet examples and tips that don't really belong anywhere else.

Appendix A, *Servlet API Quick Reference*

Contains a full description of the classes, methods, and variables in the `javax.servlet` package.

Appendix B, *HTTP Servlet API Quick Reference*

Contains a full description of the classes, methods, and variables in the `javax.servlet.http` package.

Appendix C, *HTTP Status Codes*

Lists the status codes specified by HTTP, along with the mnemonic constants used by servlets.

Appendix D, *Character Entities*

Lists the character entities defined in HTML, along with their equivalent Unicode escape values.

Appendix E, *Charsets*

Lists the suggested charsets servlets may use to generate content in several different languages.

Please feel free to read the chapters of this book in whatever order you like. Reading straight through from front to back ensures that you won't encounter any surprises, as efforts have been taken to avoid forward references. If you want to skip around, however, you can do so easily enough, especially after Chapter 5—the rest of the chapters all tend to stand alone. One last suggestion: read the "Debugging" section of Chapter 13 if at any time you find a piece of code that doesn't work as expected.

Conventions Used in This Book

Italic is used for:

- Pathnames, filenames, and program names
- New terms where they are defined
- Internet addresses, such as domain names and URLs

Boldface is used for:

- Particular keys on a computer keyboard
- Names of user interface buttons and menus

`Constant Width` is used for:

- Anything that appears literally in a Java program, including keywords, data types, constants, method names, variables, class names, and interface names
- Command lines and options that should be typed verbatim on the screen
- All Java code listings
- HTML documents, tags, and attributes

`Constant Width Italic` is used for:

- General placeholders that indicate that an item is replaced by some actual value in your own program

Request for Comments

Please help us to improve future editions of this book by reporting any errors, inaccuracies, bugs, misleading or confusing statements, and plain old typos that you find anywhere in this book. Email your bug reports and comments to us at: *bookquestions@oreilly.com.* (Before sending a bug report, however, you may want to check for an errata list at *http://www.oreilly.com/catalog/jservlet/* to see if the bug has already been submitted.)

Please also let us know what we can do to make this book more useful to you. We take your comments seriously and will try to incorporate reasonable suggestions into future editions.

Acknowledgments

The authors would like to say a big thank you to the book's technical reviewers, whose constructive criticism has done much to improve this work: Mike Slinn, Mike Hogarth, James Duncan Davidson, Dan Pritchett, Dave McMurdie, and Rob Clark. We're still in shock that it took one reviewer just three days to read what took us a full year to write!

Jason Hunter

In a sense, this book began March 20, 1997, at the Computer Literacy bookstore in San Jose, California. There—after a hilarious talk by Larry Wall and Randall Schwartz, where Larry explained how he manages to automate his house using Perl—I met the esteemed Tim O'Reilly for the first time. I introduced myself and brazenly told him that some day (far in the future, I thought) I had plans to write an O'Reilly book. I felt like I was telling Steven Spielberg I planned to star in one of his movies. To my complete and utter surprise, Tim replied, "On what topic?" So began the roller coaster ride that resulted in this book.

There have been several high points I fondly remember: meeting my editor (cool, she's young, too!), signing the official contract (did you know that all of O'Reilly's official paper has animals on it?), writing the first sentence (over and over), printing the first chapter (and having it look just like an O'Reilly book), and then watching as the printouts piled higher and higher, until eventually there was nothing more to write (well, except the acknowledgments).

There have been a fair number of trying times as well. At one point, when the book was about half finished, I realized the Servlet API was changing faster than I could keep up. I believe in the saying, "If at first you don't succeed, ask for help," so after a quick talent search I asked William Crawford, who was already working on *Java Enterprise in a Nutshell*, if he could help speed the book to completion. He graciously agreed and in the end wrote two chapters, as well as portions of the appendices.

There are many others who have helped in the writing of this book, both directly and indirectly. I'd like to say thank you to Paula Ferguson, the book's editor, and Mike Loukides, the Java series editor, for their efforts to ensure (and improve) the quality of this book. And to Tim O'Reilly for giving me the chance to fulfill a dream.

Thanks also to my managers at Silicon Graphics, Kathy Tansill and Walt Johnson, for providing me with more encouragement and flexibility than I had any right to expect.

I can't say thank you enough to the engineers at Sun who were tremendously helpful in answering questions, keeping me updated on changes in the Servlet API, and promptly fixing almost every bug I reported: James Duncan Davidson (who looks the spitting image of James Gosling), Jim Driscoll, Rob Clark, and Dave Brownell.

Thanks also to the members of the *jserv-interest* mailing list, whose questions and answers have shaped the content of this book; Will Ramey, an old friend who didn't let friendship blind his critical eye; Mike Engber, the man to whom I turned when I had run out of elegant workarounds and was ready to accept the crazy things he comes up with; Dave Vandegrift, the first person to read many of the chapters; Bill Day, author of *Java Media Players*, who helped intangibly by going through the book writing process in parallel with me; Michael O'Connell and Jill Steinberg, editors at *JavaWorld*, where I did my first professional writing; Doug Young, who shared with me the tricks he learned writing seven technical books of his own; and Shoji Kuwabara, Mieko Aono, Song Yung, Matthew Kim, and Alexandr Pashintsev for their help translating "Hello World" for Chapter 12.

Finally, thanks to Mom and Dad, for their love and support and for the time they spent long ago teaching me the basics of writing. And a special thanks to my girlfriend, Kristi Taylor, who made the small time away from work a pleasure.

And Grandpa, I wish you could have seen this.

Jason Hunter
July 1998

William Crawford

First and foremost, thanks to Shelley Norton, Dr. Isaac Kohane, Dr. James Fackler, and Dr. Richard Kitz (plus a supporting cast whose contributions were invaluable), whose assistance and early support have made everything since possible. Also, to Martin Streeter of Invantage, Inc., for his support during this project.

Without Rob Leith, Roger Stacey, and Fred Strebeigh, I would probably still be stuck in the passive voice. Dale Dougherty offered me money in exchange for words, a twist of events that I still haven't gotten over. Andy Kwak, Joel Pomerantz, and Matthew Proto, brave souls all, were willing to read drafts and listen to complaints at one o'clock in the morning.

And, of course, to Mom and Dad for their years of support, and to my sister Faith for (usually) letting me get away with being a nerd.

William Crawford
July 1998

1

Introduction

The rise of server-side Java applications is one of the latest and most exciting trends in Java programming. The Java language was originally intended for use in small, embedded devices. It was first hyped as a language for developing elaborate client-side web content in the form of applets. Until recently, Java's potential as a server-side development platform had been sadly overlooked. Now, Java is coming into its own as a language ideally suited for server-side development.

Businesses in particular have been quick to recognize Java's potential on the server—Java is inherently suited for large client/server applications. The cross-platform nature of Java is extremely useful for organizations that have a heterogeneous collection of servers running various flavors of the Unix and Windows operating systems. Java's modern, object-oriented, memory-protected design allows developers to cut development cycles and increase reliability. In addition, Java's built-in support for networking and enterprise APIs provides access to legacy data, easing the transition from older client/server systems.

Java servlets are a key component of server-side Java development. A servlet is a small, pluggable extension to a server that enhances the server's functionality. Servlets allow developers to extend and customize any Java-enabled server—a web server, a mail server, an application server, or any custom server—with a hitherto unknown degree of portability, flexibility, and ease. But before we go into any more detail, let's put things into perspective.

History of Web Applications

While servlets can be used to extend the functionality of any Java-enabled server, today they are most often used to extend web servers, providing a powerful, efficient replacement for CGI scripts. When you use a servlet to create dynamic content for a web page or otherwise extend the functionality of a web server, you are in effect creating a *web application*. While a web page merely displays static content and lets the user navigate through that content, a web application provides a more interactive experience. A web application can be as simple as a keyword search on a document archive or as complex as an electronic storefront. Web applications are being deployed on the Internet and on corporate intranets and extranets, where they have the potential to increase productivity and change the way that companies, large and small, do business.

To understand the power of servlets, we need to step back and look at some of the other approaches that can be used to create web applications.

Common Gateway Interface

The Common Gateway Interface, normally referred to as CGI, was one of the first practical techniques for creating dynamic content. With CGI, a web server passes certain requests to an external program. The output of this program is then sent to the client in place of a static file. The advent of CGI made it possible to implement all sorts of new functionality in web pages, and CGI quickly became a de facto standard, implemented on dozens of web servers.

It's interesting to note that the ability of CGI programs to create dynamic web pages is a side effect of its intended purpose: to define a standard method for an information server to talk with external applications. This origin explains why CGI has perhaps the worst life cycle imaginable. When a server receives a request that accesses a CGI program, it must create a new process to run the CGI program and then pass to it, via environment variables and standard input, every bit of information that might be necessary to generate a response. Creating a process for every such request requires time and significant server resources, which limits the number of requests a server can handle concurrently. Figure 1-1 shows the CGI life cycle.

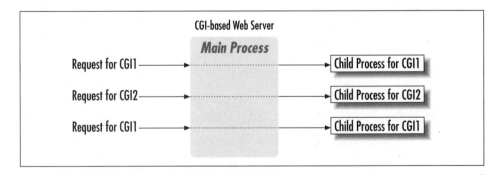

Figure 1-1. The CGI life cycle

Even though a CGI program can be written in almost any language, the Perl programming language has become the predominant choice. Its advanced text-processing capabilities are a big help in managing the details of the CGI interface. Writing a CGI script in Perl gives it a semblance of platform independence, but it also requires that each request start a separate Perl interpreter, which takes even more time and requires extra resources.

Another often-overlooked problem with CGI is that a CGI program cannot interact with the web server or take advantage of the server's abilities once it begins execution because it is running in a separate process. For example, a CGI script cannot write to the server's log file.

For more information on CGI programming, see *CGI Programming on the World Wide Web* by Shishir Gundavaram (O'Reilly).

FastCGI

A company named Open Market developed an alternative to standard CGI named FastCGI. In many ways, FastCGI works just like CGI—the important difference is that FastCGI creates a single persistent process for each FastCGI program, as shown in Figure 1-2. This eliminates the need to create a new process for each request.

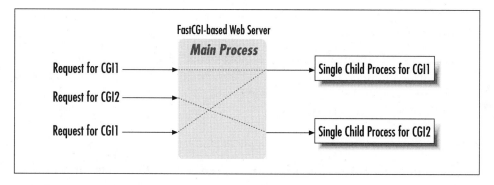

Figure 1-2. The FastCGI life cycle

Although FastCGI is a step in the right direction, it still has a problem with process proliferation: there is at least one process for each FastCGI program. If a FastCGI program is to handle concurrent requests, it needs a pool of processes, one per request. Considering that each process may be executing a Perl interpreter, this approach does not scale as well as you might hope. (Although, to its credit, FastCGI can distribute its processes across multiple servers.) Another problem with FastCGI is that it does nothing to help the FastCGI program more closely interact with the server. As of this writing, the FastCGI approach has not been implemented by some of the more popular servers, including Microsoft's Internet Information Server. Finally, FastCGI programs are only as portable as the language in which they're written.

For more information on FastCGI, see *http://www.fastcgi.com/*.

mod_perl

If you are using the Apache web server, another option for improving CGI performance is using *mod_perl*. *mod_perl* is a module for the Apache server that embeds a copy of the Perl interpreter into the Apache *httpd* executable, providing complete access to Perl functionality within Apache. The effect is that your CGI scripts are precompiled by the server and executed without forking, thus running much more quickly and efficiently. For more information on *mod_perl*, see *http://perl.apache.org/*.

PerlEx

PerlEx, developed by ActiveState, improves the performance of CGI scripts written in Perl that run on Windows NT web servers (Microsoft's Internet Information Server, O'Reilly's WebSite Professional, and Netscape's FastTrack Server and Enterprise Server). PerlEx uses the web server's native API to achieve its performance gains. For more information, see *http://www.activestate.com/plex/*.

Other Solutions

CGI/Perl has the advantage of being a more-or-less platform-independent way to produce dynamic web content. Other well-known technologies for creating web applications, such as ASP and server-side JavaScript, are proprietary solutions that work only with certain web servers.

Server Extension APIs

Several companies have created proprietary server extension APIs for their web servers. For example, Netscape provides an internal API called NSAPI (now becoming WAI) and Microsoft provides ISAPI. Using one of these APIs, you can write server extensions that enhance or change the base functionality of the server, allowing the server to handle tasks that were once relegated to external CGI programs. As you can see in Figure 1-3, server extensions exist within the main process of a web server.

Because server-specific APIs use linked C or C++ code, server extensions can run extremely fast and make full use of the server's resources. Server extensions, however, are not a perfect solution by any means. Besides being difficult to develop and maintain, they pose significant security and reliability hazards: a

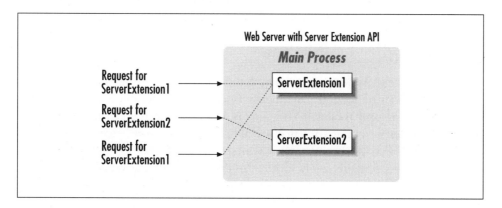

Figure 1-3. The server extension life cycle

crashed server extension can bring down the entire server. And, of course, proprietary server extensions are inextricably tied to the server API for which they were
written—and often tied to a particular operating system as well.

Active Server Pages

Microsoft has developed a technique for generating dynamic web content called
Active Server Pages, or sometimes just ASP. With ASP, an HTML page on the web
server can contain snippets of embedded code (usually VBScript or JScript—
although it's possible to use nearly any language). This code is read and executed
by the web server before it sends the page to the client. ASP is optimized for generating small portions of dynamic content.

Support for ASP is built into Microsoft Internet Information Server Version 3.0
and above, available for free from *http://www.microsoft.com/iis*. Support for other
web servers is available as a commercial product from Chili!Soft at
http://www.chilisoft.com.

For more information on programming Active Server Pages, see *http://www.
microsoft.com/workshop/server/default.asp* and *http://www.activeserverpages.com/.*

Server-side JavaScript

Netscape too has a technique for server-side scripting, which it calls server-side
JavaScript, or SSJS for short. Like ASP, SSJS allows snippets of code to be
embedded in HTML pages to generate dynamic web content. The difference is
that SSJS uses JavaScript as the scripting language. With SSJS, web pages are
precompiled to improve performance.

Support for server-side JavaScript is available only with Netscape FastTrack Server
and Enterprise Server Version 2.0 and above.

For more information on programming with server-side JavaScript, see *http://developer.netscape.com/tech/javascript/ssjs/ssjs.html.*

Java Servlets

Enter Java servlets. As was said earlier, a servlet is a generic server extension—a Java class that can be loaded dynamically to expand the functionality of a server. Servlets are commonly used with web servers, where they can take the place of CGI scripts. A servlet is similar to a proprietary server extension, except that it runs inside a Java Virtual Machine (JVM) on the server (see Figure 1-4), so it is safe and portable. Servlets operate solely within the domain of the server: unlike applets, they do not require support for Java in the web browser.

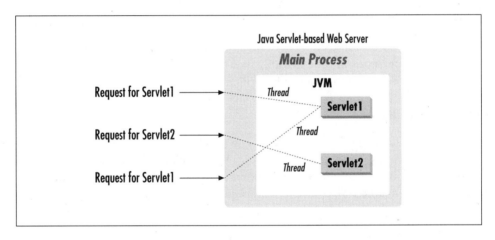

Figure 1-4. The servlet life cycle

Unlike CGI and FastCGI, which use multiple processes to handle separate programs and/or separate requests, servlets are all handled by separate threads within the web server process. This means that servlets are also efficient and scalable. Because servlets run within the web server, they can interact very closely with the server to do things that are not possible with CGI scripts.

Another advantage of servlets is that they are portable: both across operating systems as we are used to with Java and also across web servers. As you'll see shortly, all of the major web servers support servlets. We believe that Java servlets offer the best possible platform for web application development, and we'll have much more to say about this later in the chapter.

Although servlets are most commonly used as a replacement for CGI scripts on a web server, they can extend any sort of server. Imagine, for example, a Java-based FTP server that handles each command with a separate servlet. New commands can be added by simply plugging in new servlets. Or, imagine a mail server that allows servlets to extend its functionality, perhaps by performing a virus scan on all attached documents or handling mail filtering tasks.

This book emphasizes the use of servlets as a replacement for CGI programs. We believe that, at least in the near term, most servlet developers will design and deploy servlets for use with HTTP servers. In the long term, however, other uses are likely to catch on, so this book takes pains to point out what functionality is applicable to generic servlets and what applies only to HTTP servlets. Whatever you hope to do with servlets, this book can help you with your task.

Support for Servlets

Like Java itself, servlets were designed for portability. Servlets are supported on all platforms that support Java, and servlets work with all the major web servers.[*] Java servlets, as defined by the Java Software division of Sun Microsystems (formerly known as JavaSoft), are the first standard extension to Java. This means that servlets are officially blessed by Sun and are part of the Java language, but they are not part of the core Java API. Therefore, although they may work with any Java Virtual Machine (JVM), servlet classes need not be bundled with all JVMs. More information about the Java Extension Framework is available at *http//java.sun.com/ products/jdk/1.2/docs/guide/extensions.*

To make it easy for you to develop servlets, Sun has made publicly available a set of classes that provide basic servlet support. The `javax.servlet` and `javax.servlet.http` packages constitute this Servlet API. Version 2.0 of these classes comes bundled with the Java Servlet Development Kit (JSDK) for use with the Java Development Kit version 1.1 and above; the JDSK is available for download from *http://java.sun.com/products/servlet/.*[†]

Many web server vendors have incorporated these classes into their servers to provide servlet support, and several have also provided additional functionality. Sun's Java Web Server, for instance, includes a proprietary interface to the server's security features.

It doesn't much matter where you get the servlet classes, as long as you have them on your system, since you need them to compile your servlets. In addition to the servlet classes, you need a servlet engine, so that you can test and deploy your servlets. Your

---

[*] Note that several web server vendors have their own server-side Java implementations, some of which have also been given the name "servlets". These are generally incompatible with Java servlets as defined by Sun. Most of these vendors are converting their Java support to standard servlets, or are introducing standard servlet support in parallel, to allow backward compatibility.

[†] At one point it was planned the contents of the JSDK would come bundled as part of JDK 1.2. However, it was later decided to keep the servlet classes separate from the JDK, to better allow for timely revisions and corrections to the JSDK.

choice of servlet engine depends in part on the web server(s) you are running. There are three flavors of servlet engines: standalone, add-on, and embeddable.

Standalone Servlet Engines

A standalone engine is a server that includes built-in support for servlets. Such an engine has the advantage that everything works right out of the box. One disadvantage, however, is that you have to wait for a new release of the web server to get the latest servlet support. Because servlets are still fairly new, this sort of server is still a bit of a rarity. As the various vendors upgrade their web servers, we expect that many of the servers will provide built-in support for servlets.

Standalone engines in web servers include the following:

- Sun's Java Web Server (formerly called "Jeeves"), unofficially considered the reference implementation for how a servlet engine should support servlets. Written entirely in Java (except for two native code libraries that enhance its functionality but are not needed). See *http://java.sun.com/products/*.

- The World Wide Web Consortium's Jigsaw Server, freely available and also written entirely in Java. See *http://www.w3.org/Jigsaw*.

- O'Reilly's WebSite Professional (Version 2.1 and later), the first server not written in Java to provide built-in servlet support. See *http://website.oreilly.com*.

- Netscape's Enterprise Server (Version 3.51 and later), the most popular web server to provide built-in servlet support. Unfortunately, Version 3.51 supports only the early Servlet API 1.0 and suffers from a number of bugs so significant it's almost unusable. For the time being, use an add-on servlet engine with Netscape servers instead. See *http://home.netscape.com/download*.

- Lotus's Domino Go Webserver (Version 4.6 and later), another popular web server with built-in servlet support. Version 4.6.x supports only the early Servlet API 1.0; however, Lotus claims to be replacing its proprietary GWAPI server extension technology with Java servlets, so it's likely that future versions of the Domino Go Webserver will include robust servlet support. See *http://www.lotus.com/dominogowebserver/*.

Application servers are a fertile new area of development. An application server offers server-side support for developing enterprise-based applications. Here are two application servers that include servlet engines:

- WebLogic's Tengah Application Server, a high-end server written entirely in Java. See *http://www.weblogic.com/products/tengahindex.html*.

- ATG's Dynamo Application Server 3, another high-end server written entirely in Java. See *http://www.atg.com/*.

Add-on Servlet Engines

An add-on servlet engine functions as a plug-in to an existing server—it adds servlet support to a server that was not originally designed with servlets in mind. Add-on servlet engines have been written for many servers including Apache, Netscape's FastTrack Server and Enterprise Server, Microsoft's Internet Information Server and Personal Web Server, O'Reilly's WebSite, Lotus Domino's Go Webserver, StarNine's WebSTAR, and Apple's AppleShare IP. This type of engine acts as a stopgap solution until a future server release incorporates servlet support. A plug-in also can be used with a server that provides a poor or outdated servlet implementation.

Add-on servlet engines include these:

- The Java-Apache project's JServ module, a freely available servlet engine that adds servlet support to the extremely popular Apache server. See *http://java.apache.org/*.

- Live Software's JRun, a freely available plug-in designed to support the full Servlet API on all the popular web servers on all the popular operating systems. The latest version even features a basic web server for development purposes. See *http://www.livesoftware.com/products/jrun/*.

- IBM's WebSphere Application Server (formerly known as ServletExpress), a plug-in that is being called an application server. It is designed to support the full Servlet API on several popular web servers on several popular operating systems. See *http://www.software.ibm.com/webservers/*.

- New Atlanta's ServletExec, a plug-in designed to support the full Servlet API on several web servers on several operating systems. See *http://www.newatlanta.com/*.

- Gefion Software's WAICoolRunner, a freely available plug-in that supports most of the Servlet API on Netscape's FastTrack Server and Enterprise Server versions 3.x and later, written in Java using Netscape's WAI interface. See *http://www.gefionsoftware.com/WAICoolRunner/*.

- Unicom's Servlet CGI Development Kit, a freely available framework that supports servlets on top of CGI. What it lacks in efficiency it makes up for in ubiquity. See *http://www.unicom.net/java/*.

Embeddable Servlet Engines

An embeddable engine is generally a lightweight servlet deployment platform that can be embedded in another application. That application becomes the true server.

Embeddable servlet engines include the following:

- Sun's JavaServer Engine, a high-quality, high-end framework for designing and building Java servers. Sun's Java Web Server and IBM's WebSphere Application Server were built using the Java Server Engine. See *http://java.sun.com/products/javaserverengine/*.

- Jef Poskanzer's Acme.Serve, a freely available, simple web server that runs servlets "more or less compatible" with the Servlet API. See *http://www.acme.com/java/software/Package-Acme.Serve.html*.

- Paralogic's WebCore, a freely available but unsupported embeddable web server, written entirely in Java. It incorporates parts of Acme.Serve. See *http://www.paralogic.com/webcore/*.

- Anders Kristensen's Nexus Web Server, a freely available servlet runner that implements most of the Servlet API and can be easily embedded in Java applications. See *http://www-uk.hpl.hp.com/people/ak/java/nexus/*.

Additional Thoughts

Before proceeding, we feel obliged to point out that not all servlet engines are created equal. So, before you choose a servlet engine (and possibly a server) with which to deploy your servlets, take it out for a test drive. Kick its tires a little. Check the mailing lists. Always verify that your servlets behave as they do in the Java Web Server implementation. With servlets, you don't have to worry about the lowest-common-denominator implementation, so you should pick a servlet engine that has the functionality that you want.

For a complete, up-to-date list of available servlet engines, see the official list maintained by Sun at:

http://jserv.java.sun.com/products/java-server/servlets/environments.html

The Power of Servlets

So far, we have portrayed servlets as an alternative to other dynamic web content technologies, but we haven't really explained why we think you should use them. What makes servlets a viable choice for web development? We believe that servlets offer a number of advantages over other approaches, including: portability, power, efficiency, endurance, safety, elegance, integration, extensibility, and flexibility. Let's examine each in turn.

Portability

Because servlets are written in Java and conform to a well-defined and widely accepted API, they are highly portable across operating systems and across server implementations. You can develop a servlet on a Windows NT machine running the Java Web Server and later deploy it effortlessly on a high-end Unix server running Apache. With servlets, you can truly "write once, serve everywhere."

Servlet portability is not the stumbling block it so often is with applets, for two reasons. First, servlet portability is not mandatory. Unlike applets, which have to be tested on all possible client platforms, servlets have to work only on the server machines that you are using for development and deployment. Unless you are in the business of selling your servlets, you don't have to worry about complete portability. Second, servlets avoid the most error-prone and inconsistently implemented portion of the Java language: the Abstract Windowing Toolkit (AWT) that forms the basis of Java graphical user interfaces.

Power

Servlets can harness the full power of the core Java APIs: networking and URL access, multithreading, image manipulation, data compression, database connectivity, internationalization, remote method invocation (RMI), CORBA connectivity, and object serialization, among others. If you want to write a web application that allows employees to query a corporate legacy database, you can take advantage of all of the Java Enterprise APIs in doing so. Or, if you need to create a web-based directory lookup application, you can make use of the JNDI API.

As a servlet author, you can also pick and choose from a plethora of third-party Java classes and JavaBeans components. In the future, you'll even be able to use newly introduced Enterprise JavaBeans components. Today, servlets can use third-party code to handle tasks such as regular expression searching, data charting, advanced database access, and advanced networking.

Servlets are also well suited for enabling client/server communication. With a Java-based applet and a Java-based servlet, you can use RMI and object serialization to handle client/server communication, which means that you can leverage the same custom code on the client as on the server. Using CGI for the same purpose is much more complicated, as you have to develop your own custom protocol to handle the communication.

Efficiency and Endurance

Servlet invocation is highly efficient. Once a servlet is loaded, it generally remains in the server's memory as a single object instance. Thereafter, the server invokes the servlet to handle a request using a simple, lightweight method invocation. Unlike with CGI, there's no process to spawn or interpreter to invoke, so the servlet can begin handling the request almost immediately. Multiple, concurrent requests are handled by separate threads, so servlets are highly scalable.

Servlets, in general, are naturally enduring objects. Because a servlet stays in the server's memory as a single object instance, it automatically maintains its state and can hold on to external resources, such as database connections, that may otherwise take several seconds to establish.

Safety

Servlets support safe programming practices on a number of levels. Because they are written in Java, servlets inherit the strong type safety of the Java language. In addition, the Servlet API is implemented to be type-safe. While most values in a CGI program, including a numeric item like a server port number, are treated as strings, values are manipulated by the Servlet API using their native types, so a server port number is represented as an integer. Java's automatic garbage collection and lack of pointers mean that servlets are generally safe from memory management problems like dangling pointers, invalid pointer references, and memory leaks.

Servlets can handle errors safely, due to Java's exception-handling mechanism. If a servlet divides by zero or performs some other illegal operation, it throws an exception that can be safely caught and handled by the server, which can politely log the error and apologize to the user. If a C++-based server extension were to make the same mistake, it could potentially crash the server.

A server can further protect itself from servlets through the use of a Java security manager. A server can execute its servlets under the watch of a strict security manager that, for example, enforces a security policy designed to prevent a malicious or poorly written servlet from damaging the server file system.

Elegance

The elegance of servlet code is striking. Servlet code is clean, object oriented, modular, and amazingly simple. One reason for this simplicity is the Servlet API itself, which includes methods and classes to handle many of the routine chores of servlet development. Even advanced operations, like cookie handling and session tracking, are abstracted into convenient classes. A few more advanced but still common tasks were left out of the API, and, in those places, we have tried to step in and provide a set of helpful classes in the `com.oreilly.servlet` package.

Integration

Servlets are tightly integrated with the server. This integration allows a servlet to cooperate with the server in ways that a CGI program cannot. For example, a servlet can use the server to translate file paths, perform logging, check authorization, perform MIME type mapping, and, in some cases, even add users to the server's user database. Server-specific extensions can do much of this, but the process is usually much more complex and error-prone.

Extensibility and Flexibility

The Servlet API is designed to be easily extensible. As it stands today, the API includes classes that are optimized for HTTP servlets. But at a later date, it could be extended and optimized for another type of servlets, either by Sun or by a third party. It is also possible that its support for HTTP servlets could be further enhanced.

Servlets are also quite flexible. As you'll see in the next chapter, an HTTP servlet can be used to generate a complete web page; it can be added to a static page using a <SERVLET> tag in what's known as a server-side include; and it can be used in cooperation with any number of other servlets to filter content in something called a servlet chain. In addition, just before this book went to press, Sun introduced JavaServer Pages, which offer a way to write snippets of servlet code directly within a static HTML page, using a syntax that is curiously similar to Microsoft's Active Server Pages (ASP). Who knows what they (or you) will come up with next.

2

HTTP Servlet Basics

This chapter provides a quick introduction to some of the things an HTTP servlet can do. For example, an HTTP servlet can generate an HTML page, either when the servlet is accessed explicitly by name, by following a hypertext link, or as the result of a form submission. An HTTP servlet can also be embedded inside an HTML page, where it functions as a server-side include. Servlets can be chained together to produce complex effects—one common use of this technique is for filtering content. Finally, snippets of servlet code can be embedded directly in HTML pages using a new technique called JavaServer Pages.

Although the code for each of the examples in this chapter is available for download (as described in the Preface), we would suggest that for these first examples you deny yourself the convenience of the Internet and type in the examples. It should help the concepts seep into your brain.

Don't be alarmed if we seem to skim lightly over some topics in this chapter. Servlets are powerful and, at times, complicated. The point here is to give you a general overview of how things work, before jumping in and overwhelming you with all of the details. By the end of this book, we promise that you'll be able to write servlets that do everything but make tea.

HTTP Basics

Before we can even show you a simple HTTP servlet, we need to make sure that you have a basic understanding of how the protocol behind the Web, HTTP, works. If you're an experienced CGI programmer (or if you've done any serious server-side web programming), you can safely skip this section. Better yet, you might skim it to refresh your memory about the finer points of the GET and POST methods. If you are new to the world of server-side web programming, however, you should read this material carefully, as the rest of the book is going to assume that you understand HTTP. For a more thorough discussion of HTTP and its methods, see *Web Client Programming* by Clinton Wong (O'Reilly).

Requests, Responses, and Headers

HTTP is a simple, stateless protocol. A client, such as a web browser, makes a request, the web server responds, and the transaction is done. When the client sends a request, the first thing it specifies is an HTTP command, called a *method*, that tells the server the type of action it wants performed. This first line of the request also specifies the address of a document (a URL) and the version of the HTTP protocol it is using. For example:

```
GET /intro.html HTTP/1.0
```

This request uses the GET method to ask for the document named *intro.html*, using HTTP Version 1.0. After sending the request, the client can send optional header information to tell the server extra information about the request, such as what software the client is running and what content types it understands. This information doesn't directly pertain to what was requested, but it could be used by the server in generating its response. Here are some sample request headers:

```
User-Agent: Mozilla/4.0 (compatible; MSIE 4.0; Windows 95)
Accept: image/gif, image/jpeg, text/*, */*
```

The User-Agent header provides information about the client software, while the Accept header specifies the media (MIME) types that the client prefers to accept. (We'll talk more about request headers in the context of servlets in Chapter 4, *Retrieving Information.*) After the headers, the client sends a blank line, to indicate the end of the header section. The client can also send additional data, if appropriate for the method being used, as it is with the POST method that we'll discuss shortly. If the request doesn't send any data, it ends with an empty line.

After the client sends the request, the server processes it and sends back a response. The first line of the response is a status line that specifies the version of the HTTP protocol the server is using, a status code, and a description of the status code. For example:

```
HTTP/1.0 200 OK
```

This status line includes a status code of 200, which indicates that the request was successful, hence the description "OK". Another common status code is 404, with the description "Not Found"—as you can guess, this means that the requested document was not found. Chapter 5, *Sending HTML Information*, discusses common status codes and how you can use them in servlets, while Appendix C, *HTTP Status Codes*, provides a complete list of HTTP status codes.

After the status line, the server sends response headers that tell the client things
like what software the server is running and the content type of the server's
response. For example:

```
Date: Saturday, 23-May-98 03:25:12 GMT
Server: JavaWebServer/1.1.1
MIME-version: 1.0
Content-type: text/html
Content-length: 1029
Last-modified: Thursday, 7-May-98 12:15:35 GMT
```

The `Server` header provides information about the server software, while the
`Content-type` header specifies the MIME type of the data included with the
response. (We'll also talk more about response headers in Chapter 5.) The server
sends a blank line after the headers, to conclude the header section. If the request
was successful, the requested data is then sent as part of the response. Otherwise,
the response may contain human-readable data that explains why the server
couldn't fulfill the request.

GET and POST

When a client connects to a server and makes an HTTP request, the request can
be of several different types, called methods. The most frequently used methods
are GET and POST. Put simply, the GET method is designed for getting information (a document, a chart, or the results from a database query), while the POST
method is designed for posting information (a credit card number, some new
chart data, or information that is to be stored in a database). To use a bulletin
board analogy, GET is for reading and POST is for tacking up new material.

The GET method, although it's designed for reading information, can include as
part of the request some of its own information that better describes what to get—
such as an x, y scale for a dynamically created chart. This information is passed as a
sequence of characters appended to the request URL in what's called a *query string*.
Placing the extra information in the URL in this way allows the page to be bookmarked or emailed like any other. Because GET requests theoretically shouldn't
need to send large amounts of information, some servers limit the length of URLs
and query strings to about 240 characters.

The POST method uses a different technique to send information to the server
because in some cases it may need to send megabytes of information. A POST
request passes all its data, of unlimited length, directly over the socket connection
as part of its HTTP request body. The exchange is invisible to the client. The URL
doesn't change at all. Consequently, POST requests cannot be bookmarked or
emailed or, in some cases, even reloaded. That's by design—information sent to
the server, such as your credit card number, should be sent only once.

In practice, the use of GET and POST has strayed from the original intent. It's common for long parameterized requests for information to use POST instead of GET to work around problems with overly-long URLs. It's also common for simple forms that upload information to use GET because, well—why not, it works! Generally, this isn't much of a problem. Just remember that GET requests, because they can be bookmarked so easily, should not be allowed to cause damage for which the client could be held responsible. In other words, GET requests should not be used to place an order, update a database, or take an explicit client action in any way.

Other Methods

In addition to GET and POST, there are several other lesser-used HTTP methods. There's the HEAD method, which is sent by a client when it wants to see only the headers of the response, to determine the document's size, modification time, or general availability. There's also PUT, to place documents directly on the server, and DELETE, to do just the opposite. These last two aren't widely supported due to complicated policy issues. The TRACE method is used as a debugging aid—it returns to the client the exact contents of its request. Finally, the OPTIONS method can be used to ask the server which methods it supports or what options are available for a particular resource on the server.

The Servlet API

Now that you have a basic understanding of HTTP, we can move on and talk about the Servlet API that you'll be using to create HTTP servlets, or any kind of servlets, for that matter. Servlets use classes and interfaces from two packages: `javax.servlet` and `javax.servlet.http`. The `javax.servlet` package contains classes to support generic, protocol-independent servlets. These classes are extended by the classes in the `javax.servlet.http` package to add HTTP-specific functionality. The top-level package name is `javax` instead of the familiar `java`, to indicate that the Servlet API is a standard extension.

Every servlet must implement the `javax.servlet.Servlet` interface. Most servlets implement it by extending one of two special classes: `javax.servlet.GenericServlet` or `javax.servlet.http.HttpServlet`. A protocol-independent servlet should subclass `GenericServlet`, while an HTTP servlet should subclass `HttpServlet`, which is itself a subclass of `GenericServlet` with added HTTP-specific functionality.

Unlike a regular Java program, and just like an applet, a servlet does not have a `main()` method. Instead, certain methods of a servlet are invoked by the server in the process of handling requests. Each time the server dispatches a request to a servlet, it invokes the servlet's `service()` method.

A generic servlet should override its `service()` method to handle requests as appropriate for the servlet. The `service()` method accepts two parameters: a request object and a response object. The request object tells the servlet about the request, while the response object is used to return a response. Figure 2-1 shows how a generic servlet handles requests.

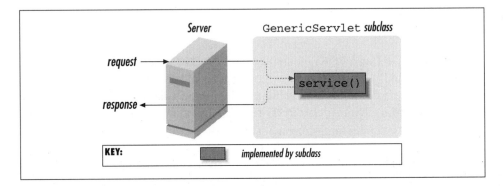

Figure 2-1. A generic servlet handling a request

In contrast, an HTTP servlet usually does not override the `service()` method. Instead, it overrides `doGet()` to handle GET requests and `doPost()` to handle POST requests. An HTTP servlet can override either or both of these methods, depending on the type of requests it needs to handle. The `service()` method of `HttpServlet` handles the setup and dispatching to all the `doXXX()` methods, which is why it usually should not be overridden. Figure 2-2 shows how an HTTP servlet handles GET and POST requests.

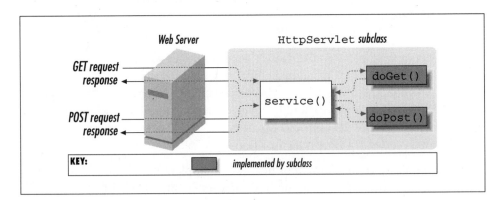

Figure 2-2. An HTTP servlet handling GET and POST requests

An HTTP servlet can override the doPut() and doDelete() methods to handle PUT and DELETE requests, respectively. However, HTTP servlets generally don't touch doHead(), doTrace(), or doOptions(). For these, the default implementations are almost always sufficient.

The remainder in the javax.servlet and javax.servlet.http packages are largely support classes. For example, the ServletRequest and ServletResponse classes in javax.servlet provide access to generic server requests and responses, while HttpServletRequest and HttpServletResponse in javax.servlet.http provide access to HTTP requests and responses. The javax.servlet.http package also contains an HttpSession class that provides built-in session tracking functionality and a Cookie class that allows you to quickly set up and process HTTP cookies.

Page Generation

The most basic type of HTTP servlet generates a full HTML page. Such a servlet has access to the same information usually sent to a CGI script, plus a bit more. A servlet that generates an HTML page can be used for all the tasks where CGI is used currently, such as for processing HTML forms, producing reports from a database, taking orders, checking identities, and so forth.

Writing Hello World

Example 2-1 shows an HTTP servlet that generates a complete HTML page. To keep things as simple as possible, this servlet just says "Hello World" every time it is accessed via a web browser.*

Example 2-1. A servlet that prints "Hello World"

```
import java.io.*;
import javax.servlet.*;
import javax.servlet.http.*;

public class HelloWorld extends HttpServlet {

  public void doGet(HttpServletRequest req, HttpServletResponse res)
                              throws ServletException, IOException {

    res.setContentType("text/html");
    PrintWriter out = res.getWriter();
```

---

* Fun trivia: the first instance of a documented "Hello World" program appeared in *A Tutorial Introduction to the Language B*, written by Brian Kernighan in 1973. For those too young to remember, B was a precursor to C. You can find more information on the B programming language and a link to the tutorial at *http://cm.bell-labs.com/who/dmr/bintro.html.*

Example 2-1. A servlet that prints "Hello World" (continued)

```
    out.println("<HTML>");
    out.println("<HEAD><TITLE>Hello World</TITLE></HEAD>");
    out.println("<BODY>");
    out.println("<BIG>Hello World</BIG>");
    out.println("</BODY></HTML>");
  }
}
```

This servlet extends the HttpServlet class and overloads the doGet() method inherited from it. Each time the web server receives a GET request for this servlet, the server invokes this doGet() method, passing it an HttpServletRequest object and an HttpServletResponse object.

The HttpServletRequest represents the client's request. This object gives a servlet access to information about the client, the parameters for this request, the HTTP headers passed along with the request, and so forth. Chapter 4 explains the full capabilities of the request object. For this example, we can completely ignore it. After all, this servlet is going to say "Hello World" no matter what the request!

The HttpServletResponse represents the servlet's response. A servlet can use this object to return data to the client. This data can be of any content type, though the type should be specified as part of the response. A servlet can also use this object to set HTTP response headers. Chapter 5 and Chapter 6, *Sending Multimedia Content*, explain everything a servlet can do as part of its response.

Our servlet first uses the setContentType() method of the response object to set the content type of its response to "text/html", the standard MIME content type for HTML pages. Then, it uses the getWriter() method to retrieve a PrintWriter, the international-friendly counterpart to a PrintStream. PrintWriter converts Java's Unicode characters to a locale-specific encoding. For an English locale, it behaves same as a PrintStream. Finally, the servlet uses this PrintWriter to send its "Hello World" HTML to the client.

That's it! That's all the code needed to say hello to everyone who "surfs" to our servlet.

Running Hello World

When developing servlets you need two things: the Servlet API class files, which are used for compiling, and a servlet engine such as a web server, which is used for deployment. To obtain the Servlet API class files, you have several options:

- Install the Java Servlet Development Kit (JSDK), available for free at *http://java.sun.com/products/servlet/*. JSDK Version 2.0 contains the class files for the Servlet API 2.0, along with their source code and a simple web server that acts as a servlet engine for HTTP servlets. It works with JDK 1.1 and later. (Note that the JSDK is the Servlet API reference implementation, and as such its version number determines the Servlet API version number.)

- Install one of the many full-featured servlet engines, each of which typically bundles the Servlet API class files.

There are dozens of servlet engines available for servlet deployment, several of which are listed in Chapter 1, *Introduction*. Why not use the servlet engine included in JSDK 2.0? Because that servlet engine is bare-bones simple. It implements the Servlet API 2.0 and nothing more. Features like robust session tracking, server-side includes, servlet chaining, and JavaServer Pages have been left out because they are technically not part of the Servlet API. For these features, you need to use a full-fledged servlet engine like the Java Web Server or one of its competitors.

So, what do we do with our code to make it run in a web server? Well, it depends on your web server. The examples in this book use Sun's Java Web Server 1.1.1, unofficially considered the reference implementation for how a web server should support servlets. It's free for educational use and has a 30-day trial period for all other use. You can download a copy from *http://java.sun.com/products* or, for educational use, *http://www.sun.com/products-n-solutions/edu/java/*. The Java Web Server includes plenty of documentation explaining the use of the server, so while we discuss the general concepts involved with managing the server, we're leaving the details to Sun's documentation. If you choose to use another web server, these examples *should* work for you, but we cannot make any guarantees.

If you are using the Java Web Server, you should put the source code for the servlet in the *server_root/servlets* directory (where *server_root* is the directory where you installed your server). This is the standard location for servlet class files. Once you have the "Hello World" source code in the right location, you need to compile it. The standard *javac* compiler (or your favorite graphical Java development environment) can do the job. Just be sure you have the `javax.servlet` and `javax.servlet.http` packages in your classpath. With the Java Web Server, all you have to do is include *server_root/lib/jws.jar* (or a future equivalent) somewhere in your classpath.

Now that you have your first servlet compiled, there is nothing more to do but start your server and access the servlet! Starting the server is easy. Look for the *httpd* script (or *httpd.exe* program under Windows) in the *server_root/bin* directory. This should start your server if you're running under Solaris or Windows. On other operating systems, or if you want to use your own Java Runtime Environment (JRE), you'll need to use *httpd.nojre*. In the default configuration, the server listens on port 8080.

There are several ways to access a servlet. For this example, we'll do it by explicitly accessing a URL with */servlet/* prepended to the servlet's class name.[*] You can enter this URL in your favorite browser: *http://server:8080/servlet/HelloWorld*. Replace *server* with the name of your server machine or with *localhost* if the server is on your local machine. You should see a page similar to the one shown in Figure 2-3.

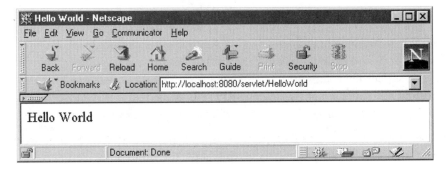

Figure 2-3. The Hello World servlet

If the servlet were part of a package, it would need to be placed in *server_root/servlets/package/name* and referred to with the URL *http://server:8080/servlet/package.name.HelloWorld*.

An alternate way to refer to a servlet is by its *registered name*. This does not have to be the same as its class name, although it can be. With the Java Web Server, you register servlets via the JavaServer Administration Tool, an administration applet that manages the server, usually available at *http://server:9090/*. Choose to manage the **Web Service**, go to the **Servlets** section, and then **Add** a new servlet. Here you can specify the name of the new servlet and the class associated with that name (on some servers the class can be an HTTP URL from which the servlet class file will be automatically loaded). If we choose the name "hi" for our `HelloWorld` servlet, we can then access it at the URL *http://server:8080/servlet/hi*. You may wonder why anyone would bother adding a servlet to her server. The short answer appropriate for Chapter 2 is that it allows the server to remember things about the servlet and give it special treatment.

A third way to access a servlet is through a *servlet alias*. The URL of a servlet alias looks like any other URL. The only difference is that the server has been told that the URL should be handled by a particular servlet. For example, we can choose to have *http://server:8080/hello.html* invoke the `HelloWorld` servlet. Using aliases in this way can help hide a site's use of servlets; it lets a servlet seamlessly replace an

---

[*] Beware, servlets are placed in a *servlets* (plural) directory but are invoked with a *servlet* (singular) tag. If you think about it, this makes a certain amount of sense, as servlets go in the *servlets* directory while a single servlet is referenced with the *servlet* tag.

existing page at any given URL. To create a servlet alias, choose to manage the **Web Service**, go to the **Setup** section, choose **Servlet Aliases**, and then **Add** the alias.

Handling Form Data

The "Hello World" servlet is not very exciting, so let's try something slightly more ambitious. This time we'll create a servlet that greets the user by name. It's not hard. First, we need an HTML form that asks the user for his or her name. The following page should suffice:

```
<HTML>
<HEAD>
<TITLE>Introductions</TITLE>
</HEAD>
<BODY>
<FORM METHOD=GET ACTION="/servlet/Hello">
If you don't mind me asking, what is your name?
<INPUT TYPE=TEXT NAME="name"><P>
<INPUT TYPE=SUBMIT>
</FORM>
</BODY>
</HTML>
```

Figure 2-4 shows how this page appears to the user.

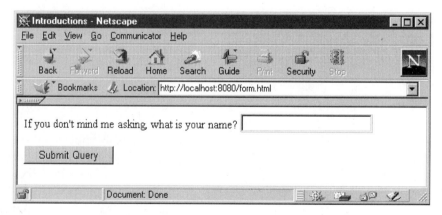

Figure 2-4. An HTML form

When the user submits this form, his name is sent to the `Hello` servlet because we've set the `ACTION` attribute to point to the servlet. The form is using the GET method, so any data is appended to the request URL as a query string. For example, if the user enters the name "Inigo Montoya," the request URL is *http://server:8080/servlet/Hello?name=Inigo+Montoya*. The space in the name is specially encoded as a plus sign by the browser because URLs cannot contain spaces.

A servlet's `HttpServletRequest` object gives it access to the form data in its query string. Example 2-2 shows a modified version of our `Hello` servlet that uses its request object to read the "name" parameter.

Example 2-2. A servlet that knows to whom it's saying hello

```
import java.io.*;
import javax.servlet.*;
import javax.servlet.http.*;

public class Hello extends HttpServlet {

  public void doGet(HttpServletRequest req, HttpServletResponse res)
                              throws ServletException, IOException {

    res.setContentType("text/html");
    PrintWriter out = res.getWriter();

    String name = req.getParameter("name");
    out.println("<HTML>");
    out.println("<HEAD><TITLE>Hello, " + name + "</TITLE></HEAD>");
    out.println("<BODY>");
    out.println("Hello, " + name);
    out.println("</BODY></HTML>");
  }

  public String getServletInfo() {
    return "A servlet that knows the name of the person to whom it's" +
           "saying hello";
  }
}
```

This servlet is nearly identical to the `HelloWorld` servlet. The most important change is that it now calls `req.getParameter("name")` to find out the name of the user and that it then prints this name instead of the harshly impersonal (not to mention overly broad) "World". The `getParameter()` method gives a servlet access to the parameters in its query string. It returns the parameter's decoded value or `null` if the parameter was not specified. If the parameter was sent but without a value, as in the case of an empty form field, `getParameter()` returns the empty string.

This servlet also adds a `getServletInfo()` method. A servlet can override this method to return descriptive information about itself, such as its purpose, author, version, and/or copyright. It's akin to an applet's `getAppletInfo()`. The method is used primarily for putting explanatory information into a web server administration tool. You'll notice we won't bother to include it in future examples because it is clutter for learning.

The servlet's output looks something like what is shown in Figure 2-5.

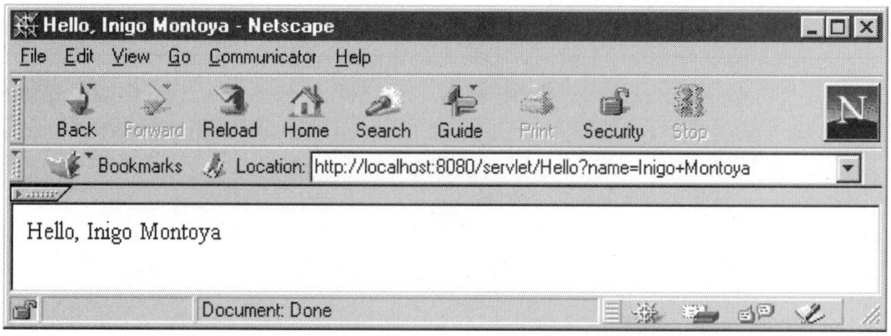

Figure 2-5. The Hello servlet using form data

Handling POST Requests

You've now seen two servlets that implement the doGet() method. Now let's change our Hello servlet so that it can handle POST requests as well. Because we want the same behavior with POST as we had for GET, we can simply dispatch all POST requests to the doGet() method with the following code:

```
public void doPost(HttpServletRequest req, HttpServletResponse res)
                              throws ServletException, IOException {
  doGet(req, res);
}
```

Now the Hello servlet can handle form submissions that use the POST method:

```
<FORM METHOD=POST ACTION="/servlet/Hello">
```

In general, it is best if a servlet implements either doGet() or doPost(). Deciding which to implement depends on what sort of requests the servlet needs to be able to handle, as discussed earlier. The code you write to implement the methods is almost identical. The major difference is that doPost() has the added ability to accept large amounts of input.

You may be wondering what would have happened had the Hello servlet been accessed with a POST request before we implemented doPost(). The default behavior inherited from HttpServlet for both doGet() and doPost() is to return an error to the client saying the requested URL does not support that method.

Handling HEAD Requests

A bit of under-the-covers magic makes it trivial to handle HEAD requests (sent by a client when it wants to see only the headers of the response). There is no

doHead() method to write. Any servlet that subclasses HttpServlet and implements the doGet() method automatically supports HEAD requests.

Here's how it works. The service() method of the HttpServlet identifies
HEAD requests and treats them specially. It constructs a modified HttpServlet-
Response object and passes it, along with an unchanged request, to the doGet()
method. The doGet() method proceeds as normal, but only the headers it sets are
returned to the client. The special response object effectively suppresses all body
output.[*] Figure 2-6 shows how an HTTP servlet handles HEAD requests.

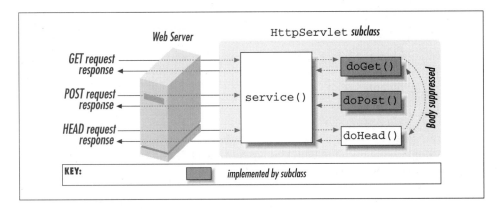

Figure 2-6. An HTTP servlet handling a HEAD request

Although this strategy is convenient, you can sometimes improve performance by
detecting HEAD requests in the doGet() method, so that it can return early,
before wasting cycles writing output that no one will see. Example 2-3 uses the
request's getMethod() method to implement this strategy (more properly called
a hack) in our Hello servlet.

Example 2-3. The Hello servlet modified to return quickly in response to HEAD requests

```
import java.io.*;
import javax.servlet.*;
import javax.servlet.http.*;

public class Hello extends HttpServlet {

  public void doGet(HttpServletRequest req, HttpServletResponse res)
                              throws ServletException, IOException {

    // Set the Content-Type header
    res.setContentType("text/html");
```

---

[*] Jason is proud to report that Sun added this feature in response to comments he made during beta
testing.

Example 2-3. The Hello servlet modified to return quickly in response to HEAD requests (continued)

```
    // Return early if this is a HEAD
    if (req.getMethod().equals("HEAD")) return;

    // Proceed otherwise
    PrintWriter out = res.getWriter();
    String name = req.getParameter("name");
    out.println("<HTML>");
    out.println("<HEAD><TITLE>Hello, " + name + "</TITLE></HEAD>");
    out.println("<BODY>");
    out.println("Hello, " + name);
    out.println("</BODY></HTML>");
  }
}
```

Notice that we set the `Content-Type` header, even if we are dealing with a HEAD request. Headers such as these are returned to the client. Some header values, such as `Content-Length`, may not be available until the response has already been calculated. If you want to be accurate in returning these header values, the effectiveness of this shortcut is limited.

Make sure that you end the request handling with a `return` statement. Do not call `System.exit()`. If you do, you risk exiting the web server.

Server-Side Includes

All the servlets you've seen so far generate full HTML pages. If this were all that servlets could do, it would still be plenty. Servlets, however, can also be embedded inside HTML pages with something called *server-side include (SSI)* functionality.

In many servers that support servlets, a page can be preprocessed by the server to include output from servlets at certain points inside the page. The tags used for a server-side include look similar to those used for applets:[*]

```
<SERVLET CODE=ServletName CODEBASE=http://server:port/dir
        initParam1=initValue1 initParam2=initValue2>
<PARAM NAME=param1 VALUE=value1>
<PARAM NAME=param2 VALUE=value2>
    If you see this text, it means that the web server
    providing this page does not support the SERVLET tag.
</SERVLET>
```

---

[*] Currently, the <SERVLET> tag syntax varies across server implementations. This section describes the syntax appropriate for the Java Web Server.

The CODE attribute specifies the class name or registered name of the servlet to invoke. The CODEBASE attribute is optional. It can refer to a remote location from which the servlet should be loaded. Without a CODEBASE attribute, the servlet is assumed to be local.

Any number of parameters may be passed to the servlet using the <PARAM> tag. The servlet can retrieve the parameter values using the getParameter() method of ServletRequest. Any number of initialization (init) parameters may also be passed to the servlet appended to the end of the <SERVLET> tag. We'll cover init parameters in Chapter 3, *The Servlet Life Cycle.*

A server that supports SSI detects the <SERVLET> tag in the process of returning the page and substitutes in its place the output from the servlet (as shown in Figure 2-7). The server does not parse every page it returns, just those that are specially tagged. The Java Web Server, by default, parses only pages with an *.shtml* extension. Note that with the <SERVLET> tag, unlike the <APPLET> tag, the client browser never sees anything between <SERVLET> and </SERVLET> unless the server does not support SSI, in which case the client receives the content, ignores the unrecognized tags, and displays the descriptive text.

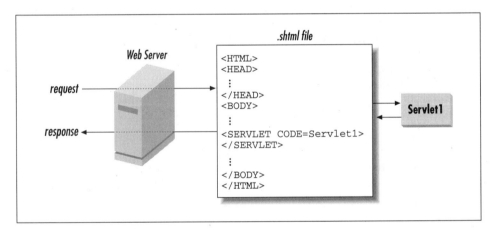

Figure 2-7. Server-side include expansion

Writing a Server-Side Include

Server-side includes are useful when a page is primarily static but contains a few distinct dynamic portions. For a simple example, let's assume we have several pages that need to display the current time. As an extra challenge, let's assume that sometimes we need the current time in time zones other than our own.

The problem is easy with server-side includes. Each page can be written as a static HTML page with one or more SSI directives that call Java code to provide the times. The HTML could look something like this, saved to a file with an *.shtml* extension:

```
<HTML>
<HEAD><TITLE>Times!</TITLE></HEAD>
<BODY>
The current time here is:
<SERVLET CODE=CurrentTime>
</SERVLET>
<P>
The current time in London is:
<SERVLET CODE=CurrentTime>
<PARAM NAME=zone VALUE=GMT>
</SERVLET>
<P>
And the current time in New York is:
<SERVLET CODE=CurrentTime>
<PARAM NAME=zone VALUE=EST>
</SERVLET>
<P>
</BODY>
</HTML>
```

The servlet named `CurrentTime` can be plugged into any page that needs a time display. The name can be either the servlet's class name or its registered name. The servlet code is shown in Example 2-4.

Example 2-4. A server-side include that prints the current time

```
import java.io.*;
import java.text.*;
import java.util.*;
import javax.servlet.*;
import javax.servlet.http.*;

public class CurrentTime extends HttpServlet {

  public void doGet(HttpServletRequest req, HttpServletResponse res)
                             throws ServletException, IOException {

    PrintWriter out = res.getWriter();

    Date date = new Date();
    DateFormat df = DateFormat.getInstance();

    String zone = req.getParameter("zone");
    if (zone != null) {
      TimeZone tz = TimeZone.getTimeZone(zone);
      df.setTimeZone(tz);
    }
```

Example 2-4. A server-side include that prints the current time (continued)

```
    out.println(df.format(date));
  }
}
```

The `CurrentTime` servlet looks strikingly similar to the `Hello` servlet. This is not a coincidence. There is no real difference between a servlet that handles full-page GET requests and one that is embedded in a page, except that embedded servlets have limited response capabilities. For example, an embedded servlet cannot set HTTP headers.

The only method `CurrentTime` implements is the `doGet()` method. All SSI serv-lets use either `doGet()` or `service()` to handle requests. Inside the method, the servlet first retrieves its `PrintWriter`.[*] This early retrieval is perhaps unnecessary; it could be retrieved as late as the next to last line. Still, we recommend fetching it first thing. It will save time later when you find you need to begin sending output sooner than you expected.

Then the servlet gets the current `Date` and a `DateFormat` instance with which to display the time. This servlet's ability to hop time zones is based on functionality in `DateFormat`. The servlet simply tells the `DateFormat` which time zone to use, and the date is displayed appropriately.

The time zone is specified by the `<PARAM>` tag in the HTML file. The servlet gains access to this parameter with the `getParameter()` method of `HttpServletRe-quest`. This technique is identical to the one we used to retrieve form data. The servlet uses the value of the "zone" parameter to create a `TimeZone` object that can be passed to the `DateFormat` object. If the "zone" parameter is not specified, as is the case with the first SSI example on our page, `getParameter()` returns `null` and the `DateFormat` uses the default time zone. Finally, the servlet outputs the `String` created when the `DateFormat` object formats the current date. The output of the HTML page is shown in Figure 2-8.

Servlet Chaining and Filters

Now you've seen how an individual servlet can create content by generating a full page or by being used in a server-side include. Servlets can also cooperate to create content in a process called *servlet chaining*.

---

[*] The Java Web Server 1.1.1 has a bug where the `PrintWriter` returned by the `getWriter()` method of `ServletRequest` does not generate output for a servlet used as a server side include. This means that to run the SSI examples shown in the book you need to use another servlet engine; or you can change the examples to manually create a `PrintWriter` as follows: `PrintWriter out = new Print-Writer(res.getOutputStream(), true);`

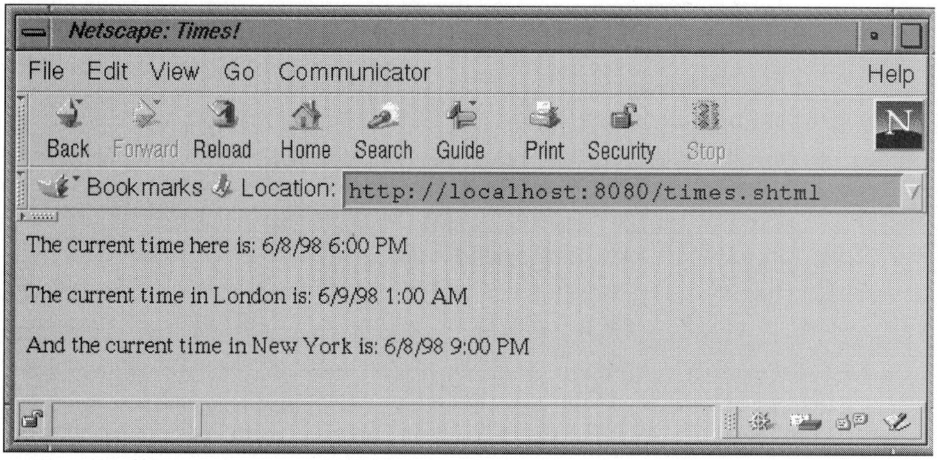

Figure 2-8. At the beep the current time will be...

In many servers that support servlets, a request can be handled by a sequence of servlets. The request from the client browser is sent to the first servlet in the chain. The response from the last servlet in the chain is returned to the browser. In between, the output from each servlet is passed (piped) as input to the next servlet, so each servlet in the chain has the option to change or extend the content, as shown in Figure 2-9.[*]

There are two common ways to trigger a chain of servlets for an incoming request. First, you can tell the server that certain URLs should be handled by an explicitly specified chain. Or, you can tell the server to send all output of a particular content type through a specified servlet before it is returned to the client, effectively creating a chain on the fly. When a servlet converts one type of content into another, the technique is called *filtering*.

Servlet chaining can change the way you think about web content creation. Here are some of the things you can do with it:

Quickly change the appearance of a page, a group of pages, or a type of content.
    For example, you can improve your site by suppressing all <BLINK> tags from the pages of your server, as shown in the next example. You can speak to those who don't understand English by dynamically translating the text from your pages to the language read by the client. You can suppress certain words that you don't want everyone to read, be they the seven dirty words or words not

---

[*] A web server could implement servlet chaining differently than described here. There is no reason the initial content must come from a servlet. It could come from a static file fetched with built-in server code or even from a CGI script. The Java Web Server does not have to make this distinction because all its requests are handled by servlets.

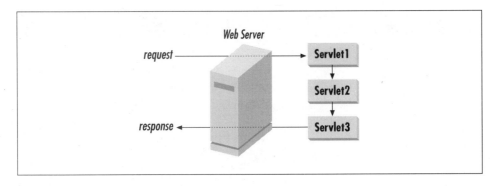

Figure 2-9. Servlet chaining

everyone knows already, like the unreleased name of your secret project. You could also suppress entire pages in which these words appear. You can enhance certain words on your site, so that an online news magazine could have a servlet detect the name of any Fortune 1000 companies and automatically make each company name a link to its home page.

Take a kernel of content and display it in special formats.

For example, you can embed custom tags in your page and have a servlet replace them with HTML content. Imagine an <SQL> tag whose query contents are executed against a database and whose results are placed in an HTML table. This is, in fact, similar to how the Java Web Server supports the <SERVLET> tag.

Support esoteric data types.

For example, you can serve unsupported image types with a filter that converts nonstandard image types to GIF or JPEG.

You may be asking yourself, why you would want to use a servlet chain when you could instead write a script that edits the files in place—especially when there is an additional amount of overhead for each servlet involved in handling a request? The answer is that servlet chains have a threefold advantage:

- They can easily be undone, so when users riot against your tyranny of removing their <BLINK> freedom, you can quickly reverse the change and appease the masses.

- They handle dynamically created content, so you can trust that your restrictions are maintained, your special tags are replaced, and your dynamically converted PostScript images are properly displayed, even in the output of a servlet (or a CGI script).

- They handle the content of the future, so you don't have to run your script every time new content is added.

Creating a Servlet Chain

Our first servlet chain example removes <BLINK> tags from HTML pages. If you're not familiar with the <BLINK> tag, be thankful. It is a tag recognized by many browsers in which any text between the <BLINK> and </BLINK> tags becomes a flashing distraction. Sure, it's a useful feature when used sparingly. The problem is that many page authors use it far too often. It has become the joke of HTML.

Example 2-5 shows a servlet that can be used in a servlet chain to remove the <BLINK> tag from all of our server's static HTML pages, all its dynamically created HTML pages, and all the pages added to it in the future. This servlet introduces the getReader() and getContentType() methods.

Example 2-5. A servlet that removes the <BLINK> tag from HTML pages

```
import java.io.*;
import javax.servlet.*;
import javax.servlet.http.*;

public class Deblink extends HttpServlet {

  public void doGet(HttpServletRequest req, HttpServletResponse res)
                            throws ServletException, IOException {

    String contentType = req.getContentType();  // get the incoming type
    if (contentType == null) return;  // nothing incoming, nothing to do
    res.setContentType(contentType);  // set outgoing type to be incoming type

    PrintWriter out = res.getWriter();

    BufferedReader in = req.getReader();

    String line = null;
    while ((line = in.readLine()) != null) {
      line = replace(line, "<BLINK>", "");
      line = replace(line, "</BLINK>", "");
      out.println(line);
    }
  }

  public void doPost(HttpServletRequest req, HttpServletResponse res)
                            throws ServletException, IOException {
    doGet(req, res);
  }

  private String replace(String line, String oldString, String newString) {
    int index = 0;
    while ((index = line.indexOf(oldString, index)) >= 0) {
      // Replace the old string with the new string (inefficiently)
```

Example 2-5. A servlet that removes the <BLINK> tag from HTML pages (continued)

```
      line = line.substring(0, index) +
             newString +
             line.substring(index + oldString.length());
      index += newString.length();
    }
    return line;
  }
}
```

This servlet overrides both the doGet() and doPost() methods. This allows it to work in chains that handle either type of request. The doGet() method contains the core logic, while doPost() simply dispatches to doGet(), using the same technique as the Hello example.

Inside doGet(), the servlet first fetches its print writer. Next, the servlet calls req.getContentType() to find out the content type of the data it is receiving. It sets its output type to match, or if getContentType() returned null, it realizes there is no incoming data to deblink and simply returns. To read the incoming data, the servlet fetches a BufferedReader with a call to req.getReader(). The reader contains the HTML output from the previous servlet in the chain. As the servlet reads each line, it removes any instance of <BLINK> or </BLINK> with a call to replace() and then returns the line to the client (or perhaps to another servlet in the chain). Note that the replacement is case-sensitive and inefficient; a solution to this problem that uses regular expressions is included in Chapter 13, *Odds and Ends*.

A more robust version of this servlet would retrieve the incoming HTTP headers and pass on the appropriate headers to the client (or to the next servlet in the chain). Chapter 4 and Chapter 5 explain the handling and use of HTTP headers. There's no need to worry about it now, as the headers aren't useful for simple tasks like the one we are doing here.

Running Deblink

If you're using the Java Web Server, before running Deblink you have to first tell the web server you want servlet chains enabled. Go to managing the **Web Service**, go to the **Setup** section, select **Site**, and then select **Options**. Here you can turn servlet chaining on. By default it's turned off to improve performance.

As we said before, there are two ways to trigger a servlet chain. A chain can be explicitly specified for certain requests, or it can be created on the fly when one servlet returns a content type that another servlet is registered to handle. We'll use both techniques to run Deblink.

First, we'll explicitly specify that all files with a name matching the wildcard pattern *.*html* should be handled by the `file` servlet followed by the `Deblink` servlet. The `file` servlet is a core Java Web Server servlet used to retrieve files. Normally it is the only servlet invoked to return an HTML file. But here, we're going to pass its output to `Deblink` before returning the HTML to the client. Go back to managing the **Web Service**, go to the **Setup** section, and select **Servlet Aliases**. Here you will see which servlets are invoked for different kinds of URLs, as shown in Figure 2-10.

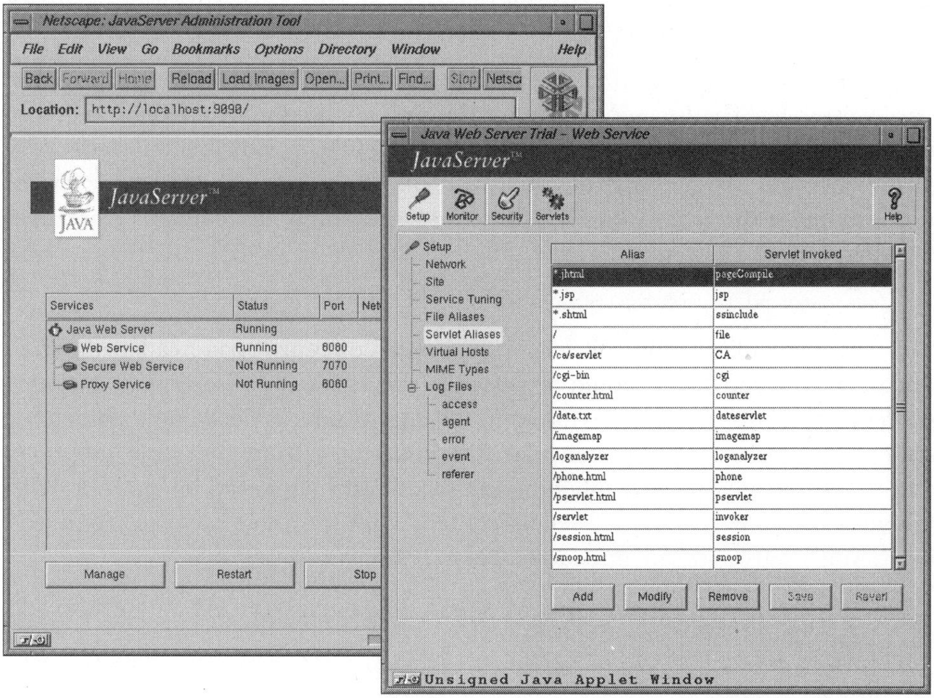

Figure 2-10. Standard servlet aliases

These mappings provide some insight into how the Java Web Server uses its core servlets. You can see / invokes `file`, *.*shtml* invokes `ssinclude`, and */servlet* invokes `invoker`. The most specific wildcard pattern is used, which is why */servlet* uses the `invoker` servlet to launch a servlet instead of using the `file` servlet to return a file. You can change the default aliases or add new aliases. For example, changing the */servlet* prefix would change the URL used to access servlets. Right now, we're interested in adding another alias. You should add an alias that specifies that *.*html* invokes `file,Deblink`. After making this change, any file ending in *.html* is retrieved by the `file` servlet and passed to `Deblink`.

Try it yourself. Create a *blinky.html* file in **server_root/public_html** that is sprinkled with a few blink tags and try surfing to *http://server:8080/blinky.html*. If everything's set up right, all evidence of the blink tags is removed.

The Loophole

This technique has one large loophole: not all HTML comes from files with the *.html* extension. For example, HTML can come from a file with the *.htm* extension or from some dynamically created HTML. We can work around multiple file extensions with more aliases. This, however, still doesn't catch dynamic content. We need our second technique for creating a servlet chain to plug that hole.

We really want to specify that all `text/html` content should pass through the `Deblink` servlet. The JavaServer Administration Tool does not yet include a graphical way to do this. Instead, we can make the change with a simple edit of a properties file. The properties file can be found at *server_root/properties/server/javawebserver/webpageservice/mimeservlets.properties*. It contains directives like this:

```
java-internal/parsed-html=ssinclude
```

This directive indicates that all responses with a `Content-Type` header of `java-internal/parsed-html` should be passed to the `ssinclude` (server-side include) servlet. Why is this necessary? Without it, the `ssinclude` servlet would handle only static files with the *.shtml* extension. It would suffer from the same loophole: dynamically created pages containing the `<SERVLET>` tag would be ignored. With this directive, any servlet can set its content type to `java-internal/parsed-html`, which causes the `ssinclude` servlet to handle its output.

To specify that all `text/html` content is passed through `Deblink`, we need to add our own directive:

```
text/html=Deblink
```

You need to restart your server before this change can take effect.

After making this change, all HTML content served by the server has its `<BLINK>` tags removed.[*] Try it yourself! Change your `HelloWorld` servlet to `<BLINK>` its message and watch the `Deblink` servlet silently remove all evidence of the deed.

---

[*] Unfortunately, some servers (including the Java Web Server 1.1.1) have a bug where they are too smart for their own good. They literally feed all `text/html` content to the `Deblink` servlet—even the `text/html` content being output by the `Deblink` servlet itself! In other words, every HTML page is deblinked forever (or until the client stops the request, whichever comes first).

JavaServer Pages

Just as this book was going to press, Sun announced a new way to use servlets, called JavaServer Pages (commonly, but not officially, referred to as JSP). JSP's functionality and syntax bear a remarkable resemblance to Active Server Pages (ASP).

JSP operates in many ways like server-side includes. The main difference is that instead of embedding a <SERVLET> tag in an HTML page, JSP embeds actual snippets of servlet code. It's an attempt by Sun to separate content from presentation, more convenient than server-side includes for pages that have chunks of dynamic content intermingled with static content in several different places.

Just like server-side includes and servlet chaining, JSP doesn't require any changes to the Servlet API. But it does require special support in your web server. This support is not included in the Java Web Server 1.1.1 (the unofficially considered reference servlet engine against which this book is written), but it's expected to be introduced in the next version of the Java Web Server, probably 1.2, and in other servlet engines as they keep pace.

Note that the following tutorial is based on the JavaServer Pages draft specification, version 0.91. You may notice small changes in the final specification.

Using JavaServer Pages

At its most basic, JSP allows for the direct insertion of servlet code into an otherwise static HTML file. Each block of servlet code (called a *scriptlet*) is surrounded by a leading <% tag and a closing %> tag.[*] For convenience, a scriptlet can use four predefined variables:

request
   The servlet request, an `HttpServletRequest` object

response
   The servlet response, an `HttpServletResponse` object

out
   The output writer, a `PrintWriter` object

in
   The input reader, a `BufferedReader` object

Example 2-6 shows a simple JSP page that says "Hello" in a manner similar to Example 2-2, though with a lot less code. It makes use of the predefined request and out variables.

---

[*] An earlier technology, called Page Compilation, uses <JAVA> and </JAVA> tags and a different internal syntax. Page Compilation has been deprecated in favor of JavaServer Pages.

If you have a server that supports JavaServer Pages and want to test this page, you should place the file under the server's document root (probably *server_ root/public_html*) and save it with a special extension. By default, this extension for JSP pages is *.jsp*. Assuming you have saved the page as *hello1.jsp*, you can then access it at the URL *http://server:port/hello1.jsp*. A screen shot is shown in Figure 2-11.

Example 2-6. Saying Hello with JSP

```
<HTML>
<HEAD><TITLE>Hello</TITLE></HEAD>
<BODY>
<H1>
<%
if (request.getParameter("name") == null) {
    out.println("Hello World");
}
else {
  out.println("Hello, " + request.getParameter("name"));
}
%>
</H1>
</BODY></HTML>
```

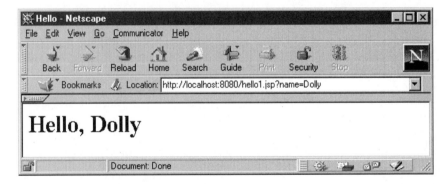

Figure 2-11. Saying Hello using JavaServer Pages

Behind the Scenes

How does JSP work? Behind the scenes, the server automatically creates, compiles, loads, and runs a special servlet to generate the page's content, as shown in Figure 2-12. You can think of this special servlet as a background, workhorse servlet. The static portions of the HTML page are generated by the workhorse servlet using the equivalent of `out.println()` calls, while the dynamic portions are included directly. For example, the servlet shown in Example 2-7 might be the background workhorse for *hello1.jsp.*[*]

Example 2-7. The workhorse servlet for hello1.jsp

```
import java.io.*;
import javax.servlet.*;
import javax.servlet.http.*;

public class _hello1_xjsp extends HttpServlet {

  public void service(HttpServletRequest request, HttpServletResponse response)
                              throws ServletException, IOException {
    response.setContentType("text/html");
    PrintWriter out = response.getWriter();
    BufferedReader in = request.getReader();

    out.println("<HTML>");
    out.println("<HEAD><TITLE>Hello</TITLE></HEAD>");
    out.println("<BODY>");
    out.println("<H1>");
    if (request.getParameter("name") == null) {
      out.println("Hello World");
    }
    else {
      out.println("Hello, " + request.getParameter("name"));
    }
    out.println("</H1>"
    out.println("</BODY></HTML>"
  }
}
```

The first time you access a JSP page, you may notice that it takes a short time to respond. This is the time necessary for the server to create and compile the background servlet. Subsequent requests should be as fast as ever because the server can reuse the servlet. The one exception is when the *.jsp* file changes, in which case the server notices and recompiles a new background servlet. If there's ever an error in compiling, you can expect the server to somehow report the problem, usually in the page returned to the client.

---

[*] If you're interested in seeing the true servlet source code for a JSP page, poke around the directories under your server root. After all, the server needs to save the Java source code somewhere before compiling it! If you find the true servlet source, you're likely to see that it is far more complicated and convoluted than what is shown here.

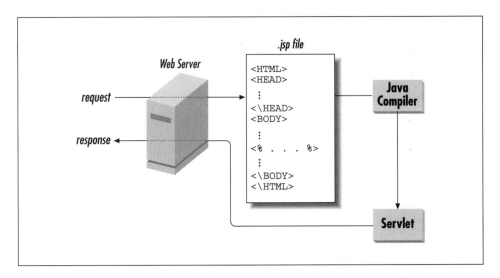

Figure 2-12. Generating JavaServer Pages

Expressions and Directives

In addition to scriptlets, JavaServer Pages allow the use of *expressions* and *directives*. A JSP expression begins with <%= and ends with %>. Any Java expression between the two tags is evaluated, the result is converted to a String, and the text is included directly in the page. This technique eliminates the clutter of an out.println() call. For example, <%= foo %> includes the value of the foo variable.

A JSP directive begins with <%@ and ends with %>. A directive allows a JSP page to control certain aspects of its workhorse servlet. Directives can be used to have the workhorse servlet set its content type, import a package, extend a different super-class, implement an interface, and handle either GET or POST requests. A directive can even specify the use of a non-Java scripting language.

In between the directive tags certain key variables can be assigned values using the following syntax:

```
<%@ varname = "value" %>
```

Here are the six variables you can set:

content_type
     Specifies the content type of the generated page. For example:

```
<%@ content_type = "text/plain" %>
```

The default content type is "text/html".

`import`

Specifies a list of classes the servlet should import. Multiple classes can be given in a comma-separated list or given through multiple `import` directives. For example:

```
<%@ import = "java.io.*,java.util.Hashtable" %>
```

`extends`

Specifies the superclass the servlet should extend. For example:

```
<%@ extends = "CustomHttpServletSuperclass" %>
```

The default superclass is `HttpServlet`.

`implements`

Specifies a list of interfaces the servlet should implement. Multiple interfaces can be given in a comma-separated list or given through multiple import directives. For example:

```
<%@ implements = "Serializable" %>
```

The default behavior is to not implement anything.

`method`

Specifies the servlet method that should contain the generated code and handle client requests. The default is "`service`", which handles all requests. For example:

```
<%@ method = "doPost" %>
```

`language`

Specifies the scripting language used by the back-end. The default language is "`java`". Some servers can choose to allow other languages. For example:

```
<%@ language = "java" %>
```

Example 2-8 shows a revised version of the Hello page that uses JSP expressions and directives. It uses a method directive to indicate it should handle POST requests, and it uses an expression to simplify its display of the `name` parameter.

Example 2-8. Saying Hello using JSP expressions and directives

```
<%@ method = "doPost" %>
<HTML>
<HEAD><TITLE>Hello</TITLE></HEAD>
<BODY>
<H1>
<% if (request.getParameter("name") == null) { %>
Hello World
<% } else { %>
Hello, <%= request.getParameter("name") %>
<% } %>
</H1>
</BODY></HTML>
```

The background workhorse servlet for this JSP page should look nearly identical to Example 2-7, with the only difference that this servlet implements `doPost()` instead of `service()`.

Declarations

Sometimes it's necessary for a JSP page to define methods and nonlocal variables in its workhorse servlet. For this there is a construct called a JSP *declaration.*

A declaration begins with a `<SCRIPT RUNAT="server">` tag and ends with a `</SCRIPT>` tag. In between the tags, you can include any servlet code that should be placed outside the servlet's service method. Example 2-9 demonstrates this with a JSP page that uses a declaration to define the `getName()` method.

Example 2-9. Saying Hello using a JSP declaration

```
<HTML>
<HEAD><TITLE>Hello</TITLE></HEAD>
<BODY>
<H1>
Hello, <%= getName(request) %>
</H1>
</BODY>
</HTML>

<SCRIPT RUNAT="server">
private static final String DEFAULT_NAME = "World";

private String getName(HttpServletRequest req) {
  String name = req.getParameter("name");
  if (name == null)
    return DEFAULT_NAME;
  else
    return name;
}
</SCRIPT>
```

The background servlet created to generate this page might look like the servlet shown in Example 2-10.

Example 2-10. The workhorse servlet for a JSP page with a declaration

```
import java.io.*;
import javax.servlet.*;
import javax.servlet.http.*;

public class _hello3_xjsp extends HttpServlet {

  public void service(HttpServletRequest request, HttpServletResponse response)
```

Example 2-10. The workhorse servlet for a JSP page with a declaration (continued)

```
                                    throws ServletException, IOException {
    response.setContentType("text/html");
    PrintWriter out = response.getWriter();
    BufferedReader in = request.getReader();

    out.println("<HTML>");
    out.println("<HEAD><TITLE>Hello</TITLE></HEAD>");
    out.println("<BODY>");
    out.println("<H1>");
    out.println("Hello, " + getName(request));
    out.println("</H1>");
    out.println("</BODY></HTML>");
  }

  private static final String DEFAULT_NAME = "World";

  private String getName(HttpServletRequest req) {
    String name = req.getParameter("name");
    if (name == null)
      return DEFAULT_NAME;
    else
      return name;
  }
}
```

JavaServer Pages and JavaBeans

One of the most interesting and powerful ways to use JavaServer Pages is in cooperation with JavaBeans components. JavaBeans are reusable Java classes whose methods and variables follow specific naming conventions to give them added abilities. They can be embedded directly in a JSP page using <BEAN> tags. A JavaBean component can perform a well-defined task (execute database queries, connect to a mail server, maintain information about the client, etc.) and make its resulting information available to the JSP page through simple accessor methods.[*]

The difference between a JavaBeans component embedded in a JSP page and a normal third-party class used by the generated servlet is that the web server can give JavaBeans special treatment. For example, a server can automatically set a bean's properties (instance variables) using the parameter values in the client's request. In other words, if the request includes a name parameter and the server detects through introspection (a technique in which the methods and variables of a Java class can be programatically determined at runtime) that the bean has a

---

[*] For more information on JavaBeans, see *http://java.sun.com/bean/* and the book *Developing Java Beans* by Robert Englander (O'Reilly).

name property and a setName(String name) method, the server can automatically call setName() with the value of the name parameter. There's no need for getParameter().

A bean can also have its scope managed automatically by the server. A bean can be assigned to a specific request (where it is used once and destroyed or recycled) or to a client session (where it's automatically made available every time the same client reconnects). Sessions and session tracking are covered in depth in Chapter 7, *Session Tracking*.

A bean can even be implemented as a servlet! If the server detects that a bean implements the javax.servlet.Servlet interface (either directly or by extending GenericServlet or HttpServlet), it will call the bean's service() method once for each request and the bean's init() method when the bean is first created. The utility of this functionality is debatable, but it can be used by beans that need to prepare somehow before handling requests.

Beans are embedded in a JSP page using the <BEAN> tag. It has the following syntax:

```
<BEAN NAME="lookup name" VARNAME="alternate variable name"
 TYPE="class or interface name" INTROSPECT="{yes|no}" BEANNAME="file name"
 CREATE="{yes|no}" SCOPE="{request|session}">
<PARAM property1=value1 property2=value2>
</BEAN>
```

You can set the following attributes of the <BEAN> tag:

NAME

Specifies the name of the bean. This is the key under which the bean is saved if its scope extends across requests. If a bean instance saved under this name already exists in the current scope, that instance is used with this page. For example:

NAME="userPreferences"

VARNAME

Specifies the variable name of the bean. This is the name used by the page to refer to the bean and invoke its methods. For example:

VARNAME="prefs"

If not given, the variable name of the bean is set to the value of its name attribute.

TYPE

Specifies the name of the bean's class or interface type. For example:

TYPE="UserPreferencesBean"

The type defaults to java.lang.Object.

INTROSPECT

Specifies if the server should set the bean's properties using the parameter values in the client's request. Its value must be "yes" or "no". The default is "yes".

BEANNAME

Specifies the serialized file or class file that contains the bean, used when first creating the bean. This is an optional attribute. For example:

```
BEANNAME="hellobean.ser"
```

CREATE

Specifies if the bean should be created if it doesn't already exist. Its value must be "yes" or "no". The default is "yes". If create is set to "no" and a preexisting instance isn't found, an error is returned to the client.

SCOPE

Specifies if the bean should be assigned to a specific request (where it is used once and destroyed or recycled) or to a client session (where it's automatically made available every time the same client reconnects, within a certain time frame). Its value must be "request" or "session". The default is "request".

Parameters can be passed to a bean as a list using a <PARAM> tags placed between the opening <BEAN> tag and the closing </BEAN> tag. The parameter values are used to set the bean's properties using introspection.

Example 2-11 demonstrates the use of a JavaBeans component with a JSP page; it says Hello with the help of a HelloBean.

Example 2-11. Saying Hello using a JavaBean

```
<%@ import = "HelloBean" %>

<BEAN NAME="hello" TYPE="HelloBean"
 INTROSPECT="yes" CREATE="yes" SCOPE="request">
</BEAN>

<HTML>
<HEAD><TITLE>Hello</TITLE></HEAD>
<BODY>
<H1>
Hello, <%= hello.getName() %>
</H1>
</BODY>
</HTML>
```

As you can see, using a JavaBeans component with JavaServer Pages greatly reduces the amount of code necessary in the page. This allows a clean separation of content (the functionality the bean provides) from presentation (the HTML structure of the page). By using a well-defined API to interact with the bean, even nonprogrammers can write JSP pages.

The code for `HelloBean` is shown in Example 2-12. Its class file should be placed in the server's classpath (something like *server_root/classes*, although for the Java Web Server you need to first create this directory).

Example 2-12. The HelloBean class

```
public class HelloBean {

  private String name = "World";

  public void setName(String name) {
    this.name = name;
  }

  public String getName() {
    return name;
  }
}
```

This is about as simple a bean as you'll ever see. It has a single `name` property that is set using `setName()` and retrieved using `getName()`. The default value of `name` is "`World`", but when a request comes in that includes a `NAME` parameter, the property is set automatically by the server with a call to `setName()`. To test the mechanism, try browsing to *http://server:port/hellobean.jsp*. You should see something similar to the screen shot in Figure 2-13.

Figure 2-13. Saying Hello using JavaServer pages in cooperation with a JavaBeans component

Moving On

We realize this chapter has been a whirlwind introduction to HTTP servlets. By now, we hope you have a sense of the different ways you can use servlets to handle a variety of web development tasks. Of course, servlets can do far more than say "Hello World," tell the time, and remove <BLINK> tags. Now that you've got your feet wet, we can dive into the details and move on to more interesting applications.

3

The Servlet Life Cycle

The servlet life cycle is one of the most exciting features of servlets. This life cycle is a powerful hybrid of the life cycles used in CGI programming and lower-level NSAPI and ISAPI programming, as discussed in Chapter 1, *Introduction*.

The Servlet Alternative

The servlet life cycle allows servlet engines to address both the performance and resource problems of CGI and the security concerns of low-level server API programming. A servlet engine may execute all its servlets in a single Java virtual machine (JVM). Because they are in the same JVM, servlets can efficiently share data with each other, yet they are prevented by the Java language from accessing one another's private data. Servlets may also be allowed to persist between requests as object instances, taking up far less memory than full-fledged processes.

Before we proceed too far, you should know that the servlet life cycle is highly flexible. Servers have significant leeway in how they choose to support servlets. The only hard and fast rule is that a servlet engine must conform to the following life cycle contract:

1. Create and initialize the servlet.

2. Handle zero or more service calls from clients.

3. Destroy the servlet and then garbage collect it.

It's perfectly legal for a servlet to be loaded, created, and instantiated in its own JVM, only to be destroyed and garbage collected without handling any client requests or after handling just one request. Any servlet engine that makes this a habit, however, probably won't last long on the open market. In this chapter we describe the most common and most sensible life cycle implementations for HTTP servlets.

A Single Java Virtual Machine

Most servlet engines want to execute all servlets in a single JVM. Where that JVM itself executes can differ depending on the server, though. With a server written in Java, such as the Java Web Server, the server itself can execute inside a JVM right alongside its servlets.

With a single-process, multithreaded web server written in another language, the JVM can often be embedded inside the server process. Having the JVM be part of the server process maximizes performance because a servlet becomes, in a sense, just another low-level server API extension. Such a server can invoke a servlet with a lightweight context switch and can provide information about requests through direct method invocations.

A multiprocess web server (which runs several processes to handle requests) doesn't really have the choice to embed a JVM directly in its process because there is no one process. This kind of server usually runs an external JVM that its processes can share. With this approach, each servlet access involves a heavy-weight context switch reminiscent of FastCGI. All the servlets, however, still share the same external process.

Fortunately, from the perspective of the servlet (and thus from your perspective, as a servlet author), the server's implementation doesn't really matter because the server always behaves the same way.

Instance Persistence

We said above that servlets persist between requests as object instances. In other words, at the time the code for a servlet is loaded, the server creates a single class instance. That single instance handles every request made of the servlet. This improves performance in three ways:

- It keeps the memory footprint small.

- It eliminates the object creation overhead that would otherwise be necessary to create a new servlet object. A servlet can be already loaded in a virtual machine when a request comes in, letting it begin executing right away.

- It enables persistence. A servlet can have already loaded anything it's likely to need during the handling of a request. For example, a database connection can be opened once and used repeatedly thereafter. It can even be used by a group of servlets. Another example is a shopping cart servlet that loads in memory the price list along with information about its recently connected clients. Yet another servlet may choose to cache entire pages of output to save time if it receives the same request again.

Not only do servlets persist between requests, but so do any threads created by servlets. This perhaps isn't useful for the run-of-the-mill servlet, but it opens up some interesting possibilities. Consider the situation where one background thread performs some calculation while other threads display the latest results. It's quite similar to an animation applet where one thread changes the picture and another one paints the display.

A Simple Counter

To demonstrate the servlet life cycle, we'll begin with a simple example. Example 3-1 shows a servlet that counts and displays the number of times it has been accessed. For simplicity's sake, it outputs plain text.

Example 3-1. A simple counter

```
import java.io.*;
import javax.servlet.*;
import javax.servlet.http.*;

public class SimpleCounter extends HttpServlet {

  int count = 0;

  public void doGet(HttpServletRequest req, HttpServletResponse res)
                             throws ServletException, IOException {
    res.setContentType("text/plain");
    PrintWriter out = res.getWriter();
    count++;
    out.println("Since loading, this servlet has been accessed " +
             count + " times.");
  }
}
```

The code is simple—it just prints and increments the instance variable named count—but it shows the power of persistence. When the server loads this servlet, the server creates a single instance to handle every request made of the servlet. That's why this code can be so simple. The same instance variables exist between invocations and for all invocations.

A Simple Synchronized Counter

From the servlet-developer's perspective, each client is another thread that calls the servlet via the service(), doGet(), or doPost() methods, as shown in Figure 3-1.[*]

---

[*] Does it seem confusing how one servlet instance can handle multiple requests at the same time? If so, it's probably because when we picture an executing program we often see object instances performing the work, invoking each other's methods and so on. But, although this model works for simple cases, it's not how things actually work. In reality, all real work is done by threads. The object instances are nothing more than data structures manipulated by the threads. Therefore, if there are two threads running, it's entirely possible that both are using the same object at the same time.

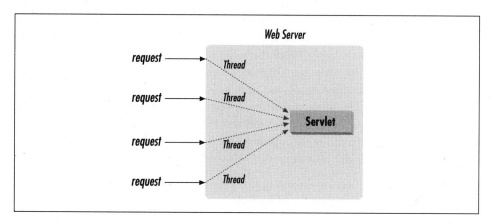

Figure 3-1. Many threads, one servlet instance

If your servlets only read from the request, write to the response, and save information in local variables (that is, variables declared within a method), you needn't
worry about the interaction among these threads. Once any information is saved
in nonlocal variables (that is, variables declared within a class but outside any
specific method), however, you must be aware that each of these client threads has
the ability to manipulate a servlet's nonlocal variables. Without precautions, this
may result in data corruption and inconsistencies. For example, the Simple-
Counter servlet makes a false assumption that the counter incrementation and
output occur atomically (immediately after one another, uninterrupted). It's
possible that if two requests are made to SimpleCounter around the same time,
each will print the same value for count. How? Imagine that one thread increments the count and just afterward, before the first thread prints the count, the
second thread also increments the count. Each thread will print the same count
value, after effectively increasing its value by 2.[*] The order of execution goes something like this

```
count++          // Thread 1
count++          // Thread 2
out.println      // Thread 1
out.println      // Thread 2
```

Now, in this case, the inconsistency is obviously not a problem, but many other
servlets have more serious opportunities for errors. To prevent these types of problems and the inconsistencies that come with them, we can add one or more
synchronized blocks to the code. Anything inside a synchronized block or a

---

[*] Odd factoid: if count were a 64-bit long instead of a 32-bit int, it would be theoretically possible for
the increment to be only half performed at the time it is interrupted by another thread. This is because
Java uses a 32-bit wide stack.

synchronized method is guaranteed not to be executed concurrently by another thread. Before any thread begins to execute synchronized code, it must obtain a *monitor* (lock) on a specified class. If another thread already has that monitor—because it is already executing the same synchronized block or some other block with the same monitor—the first thread must wait. All this is handled by the language itself, so it's very easy to use. Synchronization, however, should be used only when necessary. On some platforms, it requires a fair amount of overhead to obtain the monitor each time a synchronized block is entered. More importantly, during the time one thread is executing synchronized code, the other threads may be blocked waiting for the monitor to be released.

For `SimpleCounter`, we have four options to deal with this potential problem. First, we could add the keyword `synchronized` to the `doGet()` signature:

```
public synchronized void doGet(HttpServletRequest req,
                               HttpServletResponse res)
```

This guarantees consistency by synchronizing the entire method, using the servlet class as the monitor. In general, though, this is not the right approach because it means the servlet can handle only one GET request at a time.

Our second option is to synchronize just the two lines we want to execute atomically:

```
PrintWriter out = res.getWriter();
synchronized(this) {
  count++;
  out.println("Since loading, this servlet has been accessed " +
              count + " times.");
}
```

This approach works better because it limits the amount of time this servlet spends in its synchronized block, while accomplishing the same goal of a consistent count. Of course, for this simple example, it isn't much different than the first option.

Our third option is to create a synchronized block that performs all the work that needs to be done serially, then use the results outside the synchronized block. For our counter servlet, we can increment the count in a synchronized block, save the incremented value to a local variable (a variable declared inside a method), then print the value of the local variable outside the synchronized block:

```
PrintWriter out = res.getWriter();
int local_count;
synchronized(this) {
  local_count = ++count;
}
out.println("Since loading, this servlet has been accessed " +
            local_count + " times.");
```

This change shrinks the synchronized block to be as small as possible, while still maintaining a consistent count.

Our last option is to decide that we are willing to suffer the consequences of ignoring synchronization issues. Sometimes the consequences are quite acceptable. For this example, ignoring synchronization means that some clients may receive a count that's a bit off. Not a big deal, really. If this servlet were supposed to return unique numbers, however, it would be a different story.

Although it's not possible with this example, an option that exists for other servlets is to change instance variables into local variables. Local variables are not available to other threads and thus don't need to be carefully protected from corruption. At the same time, however, local variables are not persistent between requests, so we can't use them to store the persistent state of our counter.

A Holistic Counter

Now, the "one instance per servlet" model is a bit of a gloss-over. The truth is that each registered name for a servlet (but not each alias) is associated with one instance of the servlet. The name used to access the servlet determines which instance handles the request. This makes sense because the impression to the client should be that differently named servlets operate independently. The separate instances are also a requirement for servlets that accept initialization parameters, as discussed later in this chapter.

Our `SimpleCounter` example uses the `count` instance variable to track the number of times it has been accessed. If, instead, it needed to track the count for all instances (and thus all registered aliases), it can in some cases use a class, or static, variable. These variables are shared across all instances of a class. Example 3-2 demonstrates with a servlet that counts three things: the times it has been accessed, the number of instances created by the server (one per name), and the total times all of them have been accessed.

Example 3-2. A more holistic counter

```
import java.io.*;
import java.util.*;
import javax.servlet.*;
import javax.servlet.http.*;

public class HolisticCounter extends HttpServlet {

  static int classCount = 0;  // shared by all instances
  int count = 0;              // separate for each servlet
  static Hashtable instances = new Hashtable();  // also shared
```

Example 3-2. A more holistic counter (continued)

```
public void doGet(HttpServletRequest req, HttpServletResponse res)
                          throws ServletException, IOException {
  res.setContentType("text/plain");
  PrintWriter out = res.getWriter();

  count++;
  out.println("Since loading, this servlet instance has been accessed " +
              count + " times.");

  // Keep track of the instance count by putting a reference to this
  // instance in a Hashtable. Duplicate entries are ignored.
  // The size() method returns the number of unique instances stored.
  instances.put(this, this);
  out.println("There are currently " +
              instances.size() + " instances.");

  classCount++;
  out.println("Across all instances, this servlet class has been " +
              "accessed " + classCount + " times.");
  }
}
```

This `HolisticCounter` tracks its own access count with the `count` instance variable, the shared count with the `classCount` class variable, and the number of instances with the `instances` hashtable (another shared resource that must be a class variable). Sample output is shown in Figure 3-2.

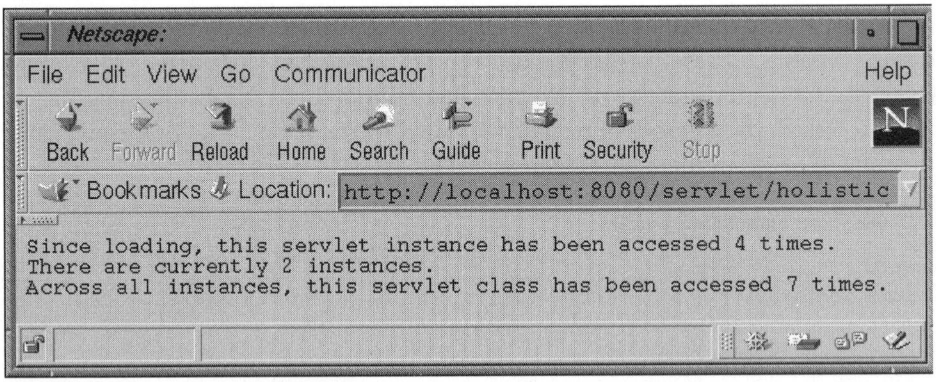

Figure 3-2. Output from HolisticCounter

Servlet Reloading

If you tried using these counters for yourself, you may have noticed that any time you recompiled one, its count automatically began again at 1. Trust us—it's not a bug, it's a feature. Most servers automatically reload a servlet after its class file (under the default servlet directory, such as *server_root/servlets*) changes. It's an on-the-fly upgrade procedure that greatly speeds up the development-test cycle— and allows for long server uptimes.

Servlet reloading may appear to be a simple feature, but it's actually quite a trick— and requires quite a hack. `ClassLoader` objects are designed to load a class just once. To get around this limitation and load servlets again and again, servers use custom class loaders that load servlets from the default servlets directory. This explains why the servlet classes are found in *server_root/servlets*, even though that directory doesn't appear in the server's classpath.

When a server dispatches a request to a servlet, it first checks if the servlet's class file has changed on disk. If it has changed, the server abandons the class loader used to load the old version and creates a new instance of the custom class loader to load the new version. Old servlet versions can stay in memory indefinitely (and, in fact, other classes can still hold references to the old servlet instances, causing odd side effects, as explained in Chapter 11, *Interservlet Communication*), but the old versions are not used to handle any more requests.

Servlet reloading is *not* performed for classes found in the server's classpath (such as *server_root/classes*) because those classes are loaded by the core, primordial class loader. These classes are loaded once and retained in memory even when their class files change.

It's generally best to put servlet support classes (such as the utility classes in `com.oreilly.servlet`) somewhere in the server's classpath (such as *server_root/classes*) where they don't get reloaded. The reason is that support classes are not nicely reloaded like servlets. A support class, placed in the default servlets directory and accessed by a servlet, is loaded by the same class loader instance that loaded the servlet. It doesn't get its own class loader instance. Consequently, if the support class is recompiled but the servlet referring to it isn't, nothing happens. The server checks only the timestamp on servlet class files.[*]

A frequently used trick to improve performance is to place servlets in the default servlet directory during development and move them to the server's classpath for

---

[*] For the daredevils out there, here's a stunt you can try to force a support class reload. Put the support class in the servlet directory. Then convince the server it needs to reload the servlet that uses the support class (recompile it or use the Unix utility *touch*). The class loader that reloads the servlet should also load the new version of the support class.

deployment. Having them out of the default directory eliminates the needless timestamp comparison for each request.

Init and Destroy

Just like applets, servlets can define `init()` and `destroy()` methods. A servlet's `init(ServletConfig)` method is called by the server immediately after the server constructs the servlet's instance. Depending on the server and its configuration, this can be at any of these times:

- When the server starts

- When the servlet is first requested, just before the `service()` method is invoked

- At the request of the server administrator

In any case, `init()` is guaranteed to be called before the servlet handles its first request.

The `init()` method is typically used to perform servlet initialization—creating or loading objects that are used by the servlet in the handling of its requests. Why not use a constructor instead? Well, in JDK 1.0 (for which servlets were originally written), constructors for dynamically loaded Java classes (such as servlets) couldn't accept arguments. So, in order to provide a new servlet any information about itself and its environment, a server had to call a servlet's `init()` method and pass along an object that implements the `ServletConfig` interface. Also, Java doesn't allow interfaces to declare constructors. This means that the `javax.servlet.Servlet` interface cannot declare a constructor that accepts a `ServletConfig` parameter. It has to declare another method, like `init()`. It's still possible, of course, for you to define constructors for your servlets, but in the constructor you don't have access to the `ServletConfig` object or the ability to throw a `ServletException`.

This `ServletConfig` object supplies a servlet with information about its initialization (init) parameters. These parameters are given to the servlet itself and are not associated with any single request. They can specify initial values, such as where a counter should begin counting, or default values, perhaps a template to use when not specified by the request. In the Java Web Server, init parameters for a servlet are usually set during the registration process. See Figure 3-3.

Other servers set init parameters in different ways. Sometimes it involves editing a configuration file. One creative technique you can use with the Java Web Server, but currently by no other servers, is to treat servlets as JavaBeans. Such servlets can be loaded from serialized files or have their init properties set automatically by the

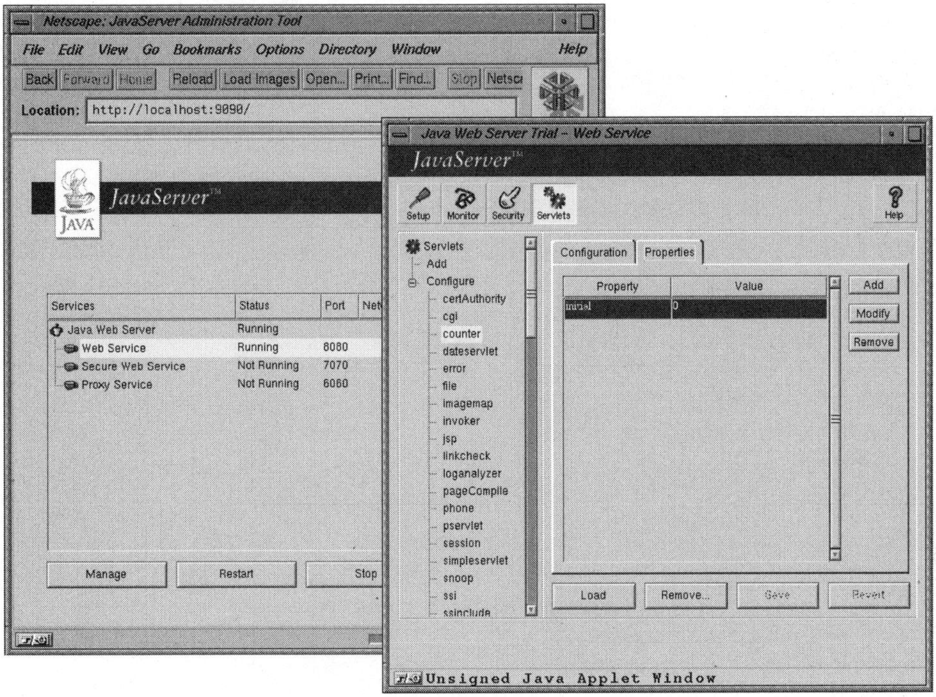

Figure 3-3. Setting init parameters in the Java Web Server

server at load time using introspection. See the Java Web Server documentation for more information.

The `ServletConfig` object also holds a reference to a `ServletContext` object that a servlet may use to investigate its environment. See Chapter 4, *Retrieving Information*, for a full discussion of this ability.

The server calls a servlet's `destroy()` method when the servlet is about to be unloaded. In the `destroy()` method, a servlet should free any resources it has acquired that will not be garbage collected. The `destroy()` method also gives a servlet a chance to write out its unsaved cached information or any persistent information that should be read during the next call to `init()`.

A Counter with Init

Init parameters can be used for anything. In general, they specify initial values or default values for servlet variables, or they tell a servlet how to customize its behavior in some way. Example 3-3 extends our `SimpleCounter` example to read an init parameter (named `initial`) that stores the initial value for our counter.

Example 3-3. A counter that reads init parameters

```
import java.io.*;
import javax.servlet.*;
import javax.servlet.http.*;

public class InitCounter extends HttpServlet {

  int count;

  public void init(ServletConfig config) throws ServletException {
    super.init(config);
    String initial = config.getInitParameter("initial");
    try {
      count = Integer.parseInt(initial);
    }
    catch (NumberFormatException e) {
      count = 0;
    }
  }

  public void doGet(HttpServletRequest req, HttpServletResponse res)
                          throws ServletException, IOException {
    res.setContentType("text/plain");
    PrintWriter out = res.getWriter();
    count++;
    out.println("Since loading (and with a possible initialization");
    out.println("parameter figured in), this servlet has been accessed");
    out.println(count + " times.");
  }
}
```

The init() method accepts an object that implements the ServletConfig interface. It uses the config object's getInitParameter() method to get the value for the init parameter named initial. This method takes the name of the parameter as a String and returns the value as a String. There is no way to get the value as any other type. This servlet therefore converts the String value to an int or, if there's a problem, defaults to a value of 0.

Take special note that the first thing the init() method does is call super.init(config). *Every servlet's init() method must do this!*

Why must the init() method call super.init(config)? The reason is that a servlet is passed its ServletConfig instance in its init() method, but not in any other method. This could cause a problem for a servlet that needs to access its config object outside of init(). Calling super.init(config) solves this problem by invoking the init() method of GenericServlet, which saves a reference to the config object for future use.

So, how does a servlet make use of this saved reference? By invoking methods on itself. The `GenericServlet` class itself implements the `ServletConfig` interface, using the saved config object in the implementation. In other words, after the call to `super.init(config)`, a servlet can invoke its own `getInitParameter()` method. That means we could replace the following call:

```
String initial = config.getInitParameter("initial");
```

with:

```
String initial = getInitParameter("initial");
```

This second style works even outside of the `init()` method. Just remember, without the call to `super.init(config)` in the `init()` method, any call to the `GenericServlet`'s implementation of `getInitParameter()` or any other `ServletConfig` methods will throw a `NullPointerException`. So, let us say it again: *every servlet's init() method should call super.init(config) as its first action.* The only reason not to is if the servlet directly implements the `javax.servlet.Servlet` interface, where there is no `super.init()`.

A Counter with Init and Destroy

Up until now, the counter examples have demonstrated how servlet state persists between accesses. This solves only part of the problem. Every time the server is shut down or the servlet is reloaded, the count begins again. What we really want is persistence across loads—a counter that doesn't have to start over.

The `init()` and `destroy()` pair can accomplish this. Example 3-4 further extends the `InitCounter` example, giving the servlet the ability to save its state in `destroy()` and load the state again in `init()`. To keep things simple, assume this servlet is not registered and is accessed only as *http://server:port/servlet/InitDestroyCounter.* If it were registered under different names, it would have to save a separate state for each name.

Example 3-4. A fully persistent counter

```
import java.io.*;
import javax.servlet.*;
import javax.servlet.http.*;

public class InitDestroyCounter extends HttpServlet {

  int count;

  public void init(ServletConfig config) throws ServletException {
    // Always call super.init(config) first  (servlet mantra #1)
    super.init(config);
```

Example 3-4. A fully persistent counter (continued)

```
    // Try to load the initial count from our saved persistent state
    try {
      FileReader fileReader = new FileReader("InitDestroyCounter.initial");
      BufferedReader bufferedReader = new BufferedReader(fileReader);
      String initial = bufferedReader.readLine();
      count = Integer.parseInt(initial);
      return;
    }
    catch (FileNotFoundException ignored) { }  // no saved state
    catch (IOException ignored) { }            // problem during read
    catch (NumberFormatException ignored) { }  // corrupt saved state

    // No luck with the saved state, check for an init parameter
    String initial = getInitParameter("initial");
    try {
      count = Integer.parseInt(initial);
      return;
    }
    catch (NumberFormatException ignored) { }  // null or non-integer value

    // Default to an initial count of "0"
    count = 0;
  }

  public void doGet(HttpServletRequest req, HttpServletResponse res)
                              throws ServletException, IOException {
    res.setContentType("text/plain");
    PrintWriter out = res.getWriter();
    count++;
    out.println("Since the beginning, this servlet has been accessed " +
                count + " times.");
  }

  public void destroy() {
    saveState();
  }

  public void saveState() {
    // Try to save the accumulated count
    try {
      FileWriter fileWriter = new FileWriter("InitDestroyCounter.initial");
      String initial = Integer.toString(count);
      fileWriter.write(initial, 0, initial.length());
      fileWriter.close();
      return;
    }
    catch (IOException e) {  // problem during write
      // Log the exception. See Chapter 5.
```

Example 3-4. A fully persistent counter (continued)

```
      }
   }
}
```

Each time this servlet is about to be unloaded, it saves its state in a file named *Init-DestroyCounter.initial.* In the absence of a supplied path, the file is saved in the server process' current directory, usually the *server_root.*[*] This file contains a single integer, saved as a string, that represents the latest count.

Each time the servlet is loaded, it tries to read the saved count from the file. If, for some reason, the read fails (as it does the first time the servlet runs because the file doesn't yet exist), the servlet checks if an init parameter specifies the starting count. If that too fails, it starts fresh with zero. You can never be too careful in `init()` methods.

Servlets can save their state in many different ways. Some may use a custom file format, as was done here. Others may save their state as serialized Java objects or put it into a database. Some may even perform journaling, a technique common to databases and tape backups, where the servlet's full state is saved infrequently while a journal file stores incremental updates as things change. Which method a servlet should use depends on the situation. In any case, you should always be watchful that the state being saved isn't undergoing any change in the background.

Right now you're probably asking yourself "What happens if the server crashes?" It's a good question. The answer is that the `destroy()` method will not be called.[†] This doesn't cause a problem for `destroy()` methods that only have to free resources; a rebooted server does that job just as well (if not better). But it does cause a problem for a servlet that needs to save its state in its `destroy()` method. For these servlets, the only guaranteed solution is to save state more often. A servlet may choose to save its state after handling each request, such as a "chess server" servlet should do, so that even if the server is restarted, the game can resume with the latest board position. Other servlets may need to save state only after some important value has changed—a "shopping cart" servlet needs to save its state only when a customer adds or removes an item from her cart. Last, for some servlets, it's fine to lose a bit of the recent state changes. These servlets can save state after some set number of requests. For example, in our `InitDestroyCounter` example, it

---

[*] The exact location of the current user directory can be found using `System.getProperty("user.dir")`.

[†] Unless you're so unlucky that your server crashes while in the `destroy()` method. In that case, you may be left with a partially-written state file—garbage written on top of your previous state. To be perfectly safe, a servlet should save its state to a temporary file and then copy that file on top of the official state file in one command.

should be satisfactory to save state every 10 accesses. To implement this, we can add the following line at the end of doGet():

```
if (count % 10 == 0) saveState();
```

Does this addition make you cringe? It should. Think about synchronization issues. We've opened up the possibility for data loss if saveState() is executed by two threads at the same time and the possibility for saveState() not to be called at all if count is incremented by several threads in a row before the check. Note that this possibility did not exist when saveState() was called only from the destroy() method: the destroy() method is called just once per servlet instance. Now that saveState() is called in the doGet() method, however, we need to reconsider. If by some chance this servlet is accessed so frequently that it has more than 10 concurrently executing threads, it's likely that two servlets (10 requests apart) will be in saveState() at the same time. This may result in a corrupted data file. It's also possible the two threads will increment count before either thread notices it was time to call saveState(). The fix is easy: move the count check into the synchronized block where count is incremented:

```
int local_count;
synchronized(this) {
  local_count = ++count;
  if (count % 10 == 0) saveState();
}
out.println("Since loading, this servlet has been accessed " +
            local_count + " times.");
```

The moral of the story is harder: always be vigilant to protect servlet code from multithreaded access problems.

Even though this series of counter examples demonstrates the servlet life cycle, the counters themselves aren't particularly useful because they count only the number of times they themselves have been accessed. You can find two truly useful counters—that count accesses to other pages—in the next chapter.

Single-Thread Model

Although it is standard to have one servlet instance per registered servlet name, it is possible for a servlet to elect instead to have a pool of instances created for each of its names, all sharing the duty of handling requests. Such servlets indicate this desire by implementing the javax.servlet.SingleThreadModel interface. This is an empty, tag interface that defines no methods or variables and serves only to flag the servlet as wanting the alternate life cycle.

A server that loads a SingleThreadModel servlet must guarantee, according to the Servlet API documentation, "that no two threads will execute concurrently the service method of that servlet." To accomplish this, each thread uses a free servlet instance from the pool, as shown in Figure 3-4. Thus, any servlet implementing `SingleThreadModel` can be considered thread safe and isn't required to synchronize access to its instance variables.

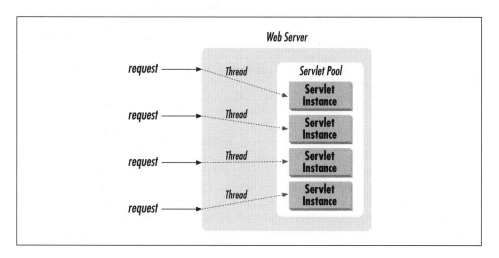

Figure 3-4. The Single Thread Model

Such a life cycle is pointless for a counter or other servlet application that requires central state maintenance. The life cycle can be useful, however, in avoiding synchronization while still performing efficient request handling.

For example, a servlet that connects to a database sometimes needs to perform several database commands atomically as part of a single transaction. Normally, this would require the servlet to synchronize around the database commands (letting it manage just one request at a time) or to manage a pool of database connections where it can "check out" and "check in" connections (letting it support multiple concurrent requests). By instead implementing `SingleThread-Model` and having one "connection" instance variable per servlet, a servlet can easily handle concurrent requests by letting its server manage the servlet instance pool (which doubles as a connection pool). The skeleton code is shown in Example 3-5.

Example 3-5. Handling database connections using SingleThreadModel

```
import java.io.*;
import java.sql.*;
import java.util.*;
import javax.servlet.*;
import javax.servlet.http.*;
```

Example 3-5. Handling database connections using SingleThreadModel (continued)

```
public class SingleThreadConnection extends HttpServlet
                                implements SingleThreadModel {

  Connection con = null;  // database connection, one per pooled servlet instance

  public void init(ServletConfig config) throws ServletException {
    super.init(config);

    // Establish the connection for this instance
    con = establishConnection();
    con.setAutoCommit(false);
  }

  public void doGet(HttpServletRequest req, HttpServletResponse res)
                          throws ServletException, IOException {
    res.setContentType("text/plain");
    PrintWriter out = res.getWriter();

    // Use the connection uniquely assigned to this instance
    Statement stmt = con.createStatement();

    // Update the database any number of ways

    // Commit the transaction
    con.commit();
  }

  public void destroy() {
    if (con != null) con.close();
  }

  private Connection establishConnection() {
    // Not implemented. See Chapter 9.
  }
}
```

Background Processing

Servlets can do more than simply persist between accesses. They can also *execute* between accesses. Any thread started by a servlet can continue executing even after the response has been sent. This ability proves most useful for long-running tasks whose incremental results should be made available to multiple clients. A background thread started in `init()` performs continuous work while request-handling threads display the current status with `doGet()`. It's a similar technique to that used in animation applets, where one thread changes the picture and another paints the display.

Example 3-6 shows a servlet that searches for prime numbers above one quadrillion. It starts with such a large number to make the calculation slow enough to adequately demonstrate caching effects—something we need for the next section. The algorithm it uses couldn't be simpler: it selects odd-numbered candidates and attempts to divide them by every odd integer between 3 and their square root. If none of the integers evenly divides the candidate, it is declared prime.

Example 3-6. On the hunt for primes

```java
import java.io.*;
import java.util.*;
import javax.servlet.*;
import javax.servlet.http.*;

public class PrimeSearcher extends HttpServlet implements Runnable {

  long lastprime = 0;                        // last prime found
  Date lastprimeModified = new Date();       // when it was found
  Thread searcher;                           // background search thread

  public void init(ServletConfig config) throws ServletException {
    super.init(config);                      // always!
    searcher = new Thread(this);
    searcher.setPriority(Thread.MIN_PRIORITY);  // be a good citizen
    searcher.start();
  }

  public void run() {
    //                    QTTTBBBMMMTTTOOO
    long candidate = 1000000000000001L;  // one quadrillion and one

    // Begin loop searching for primes
    while (true) {                       // search forever
      if (isPrime(candidate)) {
        lastprime = candidate;           // new prime
        lastprimeModified = new Date();  // new "prime time"
      }
      candidate += 2;                    // evens aren't prime

      // Between candidates take a 0.2 second break.
      // Another way to be a good citizen with system resources.
      try {
        searcher.sleep(200);
      }
      catch (InterruptedException ignored) { }
    }
  }

  private static boolean isPrime(long candidate) {
```

Example 3-6. On the hunt for primes (continued)

```
    // Try dividing the number by all odd numbers between 3 and its sqrt
    double sqrt = Math.sqrt(candidate);
    for (long i = 3; i <= sqrt; i += 2) {
      if (candidate % i == 0) return false;  // found a factor
    }

    // Wasn't evenly divisible, so it's prime
    return true;
  }

  public void doGet(HttpServletRequest req, HttpServletResponse res)
                             throws ServletException, IOException {
    res.setContentType("text/plain");
    PrintWriter out = res.getWriter();
    if (lastprime == 0) {
      out.println("Still searching for first prime...");
    }
    else {
      out.println("The last prime discovered was " + lastprime);
      out.println(" at " + lastprimeModified);
    }
  }

  public void destroy() {
    searcher.stop();
  }
}
```

The searcher thread begins its search in the `init()` method. Its latest find is saved in `lastprime`, along with the time it was found in in `lastprimeModified`. Each time a client accesses the servlet, the `doGet()` method reports the largest prime found so far and the time it was found. The searcher runs independently of client accesses; even if no one accesses the servlet it continues to find primes silently. If several clients access the servlet at the same time, they all see the same current status.

Notice that the `destroy()` method stops the searcher thread.[*] This is very important! If a servlet does not stop its background threads, they continue to run until the virtual machine exits. Even when a servlet is reloaded (either explicitly or because its class file changed), its threads won't be stopped. Instead, it's likely that

---

[*] Stopping threads using the `stop()` method as shown here is deprecated in JDK 1.2 in favor of a safer flag-based system, where a thread must periodically examine a "flag" variable to determine when it should stop, at which point it can clean up and return from its `run()` method. See the JDK documentation for details. Example source code can be found in an article titled "Scott's Solutions: Programming with threads in Java 1.2", written by Scott Oaks for Java Report Online, found at *http://www.sigs.com/jro/features/9711/oaks.html.*

the new servlet will create extra copies of the background threads. And, at least with the Java Web Server, even explicitly restarting the web server service doesn't stop background threads because the Java Web Server virtual machine continues its execution.

Last Modified Times

By now, we're sure you've learned that servlets handle `GET` requests with the `doGet()` method. And that's almost true. The full truth is that not every request really needs to invoke `doGet()`. For example, a web browser that repeatedly accesses `PrimeSearcher` should need to call `doGet()` only after the searcher thread has found a new prime. Until that time, any call to `doGet()` just generates the same page the user has already seen, a page probably stored in the browser's cache. What's really needed is a way for a servlet to report when its output has changed. That's where the `getLastModified()` method comes in.

Most web servers, when they return a document, include as part of their response a `Last-Modified` header. An example `Last-Modified` header value might be:

```
Tue, 06-May-98 15:41:02 GMT
```

This header tells the client the time the page was last changed. That information alone is only marginally interesting, but it proves useful when a browser reloads a page.

Most web browsers, when they reload a page, include in their request an `If-Modified-Since` header. Its structure is identical to the `Last-Modified` header:

```
Tue, 06-May-98 15:41:02 GMT
```

This header tells the server the `Last-Modified` time of the page when it was last downloaded by the browser. The server can read this header and determine if the file has changed since the given time. If the file has changed, the server must send the newer content. If the file hasn't changed, the server can reply with a simple, short response that tells the browser the page has not changed and it is sufficient to redisplay the cached version of the document. For those familiar with the details of HTTP, this response is the 304 "Not Modified" status code.

This technique works great for static pages: the server can use the file system to find out when any file was last modified. For dynamically generated content, though, such as that returned by servlets, the server needs some extra help. By itself, the best the server can do is play it safe and assume the content changes with every access, effectively eliminating the usefulness of the `Last-Modified` and `If-Modified-Since` headers.

The extra help a servlet can provide is implementing the `getLastModified()` method. A servlet should implement this method to return the time it last changed its output. Servers call this method at two times. The first time the server calls it is when it returns a response, so that it can set the response's `Last-Modified` header. The second time occurs in handling `GET` requests that include the `If-Modified-Since` header (usually reloads), so it can intelligently determine how to respond. If the time returned by `getLastModified()` is equal to or earlier than the time sent in the `If-Modified-Since` header, the server returns the "Not Modified" status code. Otherwise, the server calls `doGet()` and returns the servlet's output.[*]

Some servlets may find it difficult to determine their last modified time. For these situations, it's often best to use the "play it safe" default behavior. Many servlets, however, should have little or no problem. Consider a "bulletin board" servlet where people post carpool openings or the need for racquetball partners. It can record and return when the bulletin board's contents were last changed. Even if the same servlet manages several bulletin boards, it can return a different modified time depending on the board given in the parameters of the request. Here's a `getLastModified()` method for our `PrimeSearcher` example that returns when the last prime was found.

```
public long getLastModified(HttpServletRequest req) {
  return lastprimeModified.getTime() / 1000 * 1000;
}
```

Notice that this method returns a `long` value that represents the time as a number of milliseconds since midnight, January 1, 1970, GMT. This is the same representation used internally by Java to store time values. Thus, the servlet uses the `getTime()` method to retrieve `lastprimeModified` as a `long`.

Before returning this time value, the servlet rounds it down to the nearest second by dividing by 1000 and then multiplying by 1000. All times returned by `getLast-Modified()` should be rounded down like this. The reason is that the `Last-Modified` and `If-Modified-Since` headers are given to the nearest second. If `getLastModified()` returns the same time but with a higher resolution, it may erroneously appear to be a few milliseconds later than the time given by `If-Modified-Since`. For example, let's assume `PrimeSearcher` found a prime exactly 869127442359 milliseconds since the beginning of the Disco Decade. This fact is told to the browser, but only to the nearest second:

```
Thu, 17-Jul-97 09:17:22 GMT
```

---

[*] A servlet can directly set its `Last-Modified` header inside `doGet()`, using techniques discussed in Chapter 5, *Sending HTML Information*. However, by the time the header is set inside `doGet()`, it's too late to decide whether or not to call `doGet()`.

Now let's assume that the user reloads the page and the browser tells the server, via the If-Modified-Since header, the time it believes its cached page was last modified:

```
Thu, 17-Jul-97 09:17:22 GMT
```

Some servers have been known to receive this time, convert it to exactly 869127442000 milliseconds, find that this time is 359 milliseconds earlier than the time returned by getLastModified(), and falsely assume that the servlet's content has changed. This is why, to play it safe, getLastModified() should always round down to the nearest thousand milliseconds.

The HttpServletRequest object is passed to getLastModified() in case the servlet needs to base its results on information specific to the particular request. The generic bulletin board servlet can make use of this to determine which board was being requested, for example.

4

Retrieving Information

To build a successful web application, you often need to know a lot about the environment in which it is running. You may need to find out about the server that is executing your servlets or the specifics of the client that is sending requests. And no matter what kind of environment the application is running in, you most certainly need information about the requests that the application is handling.

Servlets have a number of methods available to gain access to this information. For the most part, each method returns one specific result. If you compare this to the way environment variables are used to pass a CGI program its information, the servlet approach has several advantages:

- Stronger type checking. In other words, more help from the compiler in catching errors. A CGI program uses one function to retrieve its environment variables. Many errors cannot be found until they cause runtime problems. Let's look at how both a CGI program and a servlet find the port on which its server is running.

A CGI script written in Perl calls:

```
$port = $ENV{'SERVER_PORT'};
```

where $port is an untyped variable. A CGI program written in C calls:

```
char *port = getenv("SERVER_PORT");
```

where port is a pointer to a character string. The chance for accidental errors is high. The environment variable name could be misspelled (it happens often enough) or the data type might not match what the environment variable returns.

A servlet, on the other hand, calls:

```
int port = req.getServerPort()
```

This eliminates a lot of accidental errors because the compiler can guarantee there are no misspellings and each return type is as it should be.

- Delayed calculation. When a server launches a CGI program, the value for each and every environment variable must be precalculated and passed, whether the CGI program uses it or not. A server launching a servlet has the option to improve performance by delaying these calculations and performing them on demand as needed.

- More interaction with the server. Once a CGI program begins execution, it is untethered from its server. The only communication path available to the program is its standard output. A servlet, however, can work with the server. As discussed in the last chapter, a servlet operates either within the server (when possible) or as a connected process outside the server (when necessary). Using this connectivity, a servlet can make ad hoc requests for calculated information that only the server can provide. For example, a servlet can have its server do arbitrary path translations, taking into consideration the server's aliases and virtual paths.

If you're coming to servlets from CGI, Table 4-1 is a "cheat sheet" you can use for your migration. It lists each CGI environment variable and the corresponding HTTP servlet method.

Table 4-1. CGI Environment Variables and the Corresponding Servlet Methods

CGI Environment Variable	HTTP Servlet Method
SERVER_NAME	req.getServerName()
SERVER_SOFTWARE	getServletContext().getServerInfo()
SERVER_PROTOCOL	req.getProtocol()
SERVER_PORT	req.getServerPort()
REQUEST_METHOD	req.getMethod()
PATH_INFO	req.getPathInfo()
PATH_TRANSLATED	req.getPathTranslated()
SCRIPT_NAME	req.getServletPath()
DOCUMENT_ROOT	req.getRealPath("/")
QUERY_STRING	req.getQueryString()
REMOTE_HOST	req.getRemoteHost()
REMOTE_ADDR	req.getRemoteAddr()
AUTH_TYPE	req.getAuthType()
REMOTE_USER	req.getRemoteUser()
CONTENT_TYPE	req.getContentType()
CONTENT_LENGTH	req.getContentLength()
HTTP_ACCEPT	req.getHeader("Accept")

Table 4-1. CGI Environment Variables and the Corresponding Servlet Methods (continued)

CGI Environment Variable	HTTP Servlet Method
HTTP_USER_AGENT	req.getHeader("User-Agent")
HTTP_REFERER	req.getHeader("Referer")

In the rest of this chapter, we'll see how and when to use these methods—and several other methods that have no CGI counterparts. Along the way, we'll put the methods to use in some real servlets.

Initialization Parameters

Each registered servlet name can have specific initialization (init) parameters associated with it. Init parameters are available to the servlet at any time; they are often used in init() to set initial or default values for a servlet or to customize the servlet's behavior in some way. Init parameters are more fully explained in Chapter 3, *The Servlet Life Cycle.*

Getting an Init Parameter

A servlet uses the getInitParameter() method to get access to its init parameters:

```
public String ServletConfig.getInitParameter(String name)
```

This method returns the value of the named init parameter or null if it does not exist. The return value is always a single String. It is up to the servlet to interpret the value.

The GenericServlet class implements the ServletConfig interface and thus provides direct access to the getInitParameter() method.[*] The method is usually called like this:

```
public void init(ServletConfig config) throws ServletException {
   super.init(config);
   String greeting = getInitParameter("greeting");
}
```

A servlet that needs to establish a connection to a database can use its init parameters to define the details of the connection. We can assume a custom establishConnection() method to abstract away the details of JDBC, as shown in Example 4-1.

---

[*] The servlet must call super.init(config) in its init() method to get this functionality.

Example 4-1. Using init parameters to establish a database connection

```
java.sql.Connection con = null;

public void init(ServletConfig config) throws ServletException {
  super.init(config);

  String host = getInitParameter("host");
  int port = Integer.parseInt(getInitParameter("port"));
  String db = getInitParameter("db");
  String user = getInitParameter("user");
  String password = getInitParameter("password");
  String proxy = getInitParameter("proxy");

  con = establishConnection(host, port, db, user, password, proxy);
}
```

Getting Init Parameter Names

A servlet can examine all its init parameters using `getInitParameterNames()`:

```
public Enumeration ServletConfig.getInitParameterNames()
```

This method returns the names of all the servlet's init parameters as an **Enumeration** of **String** objects or an empty **Enumeration** if no parameters exist. It's most often used for debugging.

The `GenericServlet` class also makes this method directly available to servlets. Example 4-2 shows a servlet that prints the name and value for all of its init parameters.

Example 4-2. Getting init parameter names

```
import java.io.*;
import java.util.*;
import javax.servlet.*;

public class InitSnoop extends GenericServlet {

  // No init() method needed

  public void service(ServletRequest req, ServletResponse res)
                          throws ServletException, IOException {
    res.setContentType("text/plain");
    PrintWriter out = res.getWriter();

    out.println("Init Parameters:");
    Enumeration enum = getInitParameterNames();
    while (enum.hasMoreElements()) {
      String name = (String) enum.nextElement();
```

Example 4-2. Getting init parameter names (continued)

```
        out.println(name + ": " + getInitParameter(name));
      }
    }
}
```

Notice that this servlet directly subclasses `GenericServlet`, showing that init parameters are available to servlets that aren't HTTP servlets. A generic servlet can be used in a web server even though it lacks any support for HTTP-specific functionality.

Unfortunately, there's no server-independent way for a servlet to ask for its registered name or its class file location. This information may be added in a future version of the Servlet API. Until then, although it's not pretty, this information can be passed using init parameters where necessary. Also, some servers—including the Java Web Server—provide a back door whereby a servlet can get its registered name. If a servlet defines a method with the following signature, the server calls it and passes it the servlet's registered name at initialization:

```
    public void setServletName(String name);
```

The servlet can save the passed-in name and use it later. You'll notice this back door was built without changing the Servlet API, a necessary requirement because, by the time it was added, the Servlet API 2.0 had already been frozen.

The Server

A servlet can find out much about the server in which it is executing. It can learn the hostname, listening port, and server software, among other things. A servlet can display this information to a client, use it to customize its behavior based on a particular server package, or even use it to explicitly restrict the machines on which the servlet will run.

Getting Information About the Server

There are four methods that a servlet can use to learn about its server: two that are called using the `ServletRequest` object passed to the servlet and two that are called from the `ServletContext` object in which the servlet is executing. A servlet can get the name of the server and the port number for a particular request with `getServerName()` and `getServerPort()`, respectively:

```
    public String ServletRequest.getServerName()
    public int ServletRequest.getServerPort()
```

These methods are attributes of `ServletRequest` because the values can change for different requests if the server has more than one name (a technique called

virtual hosting). The returned name might be something like "www.serv-
lets.com" while the returned port might be something like "8080".

The getServerInfo() and getAttribute() methods of ServletContext
provide information about the server software and its attributes:

```
public String ServletContext.getServerInfo()
public Object ServletContext.getAttribute(String name)
```

getServerInfo() returns the name and version of the server software, separated
by a slash. The string returned might be something like "JavaWeb-
Server/1.1.1". getAttribute() returns the value of the named server
attribute as an Object or null if the attribute does not exist. The attributes are
server-dependent. You can think of this method as a back door through which a
servlet can get extra information about its server. Attribute names should follow
the same convention as package names. The package names java.* and javax.*
are reserved for use by the Java Software division of Sun Microsystems (formerly
known as JavaSoft), and com.sun.* is reserved for use by Sun Microsystems. See
your server's documentation for a list of its attributes. Because these methods are
attributes of ServletContext in which the servlet is executing, you have to call
them through that object:

```
String serverInfo = getServletContext().getServerInfo();
```

The most straightforward use of information about the server is an "About This
Server" servlet, as shown in Example 4-3.

Example 4-3. Snooping the server

```
import java.io.*;
import java.util.*;
import javax.servlet.*;

public class ServerSnoop extends GenericServlet {

  public void service(ServletRequest req, ServletResponse res)
                            throws ServletException, IOException {
    res.setContentType("text/plain");
    PrintWriter out = res.getWriter();

    out.println("req.getServerName(): " + req.getServerName());
    out.println("req.getServerPort(): " + req.getServerPort());
    out.println("getServletContext().getServerInfo(): " +
                getServletContext().getServerInfo());
    out.println("getServerInfo() name: " +
                getServerInfoName(getServletContext().getServerInfo()));
    out.println("getServerInfo() version: " +
                getServerInfoVersion(getServletContext().getServerInfo()));
    out.println("getServletContext().getAttribute(\"attribute\"): " +
```

Example 4-3. Snooping the server (continued)

```
                    getServletContext().getAttribute("attribute"));
  }

  private String getServerInfoName(String serverInfo) {
    int slash = serverInfo.indexOf('/');
    if (slash == -1) return serverInfo;
    else return serverInfo.substring(0, slash);
  }

  private String getServerInfoVersion(String serverInfo) {
    int slash = serverInfo.indexOf('/');
    if (slash == -1) return null;
    else return serverInfo.substring(slash + 1);
  }
}
```

This servlet also directly subclasses `GenericServlet`, demonstrating that all the information about a server is available to servlets of any type. The servlet outputs simple raw text. When accessed, this servlet prints something like:

```
req.getServerName(): localhost
req.getServerPort(): 8080
getServletContext().getServerInfo(): JavaWebServer/1.1.1
getServerInfo() name: JavaWebServer
getServerInfo() version: 1.1.1
getServletContext().getAttribute("attribute"): null
```

Unfortunately, there is no server-independent way to determine the server's root directory, referred to in this book as *server_root*. However, some servers— including the Java Web Server—save the server's root directory name in the `server.root` system property, where it can be retrieved using `System.getProperty("server.root")`.

Locking a Servlet to a Server

This server information can be put to more productive uses. Let's assume you've written a servlet and you don't want it running just anywhere. Perhaps you want to sell it and, to limit the chance of unauthorized copying, you want to lock the servlet to your customer's machine with a software license. Or, alternatively, you've written a license generator as a servlet and want to make sure it works only behind your firewall. This can be done relatively easily because a servlet has instant access to the information about its server.

Example 4-4 shows a servlet that locks itself to a particular server IP address and port number. It requires an init parameter key that is appropriate for its server IP address and port before it unlocks itself and handles a request. If it does not receive the appropriate key, it refuses to continue. The algorithm used to map the key to the IP address and port (and vice-versa) must be secure.

Example 4-4. A servlet locked to a server

```
import java.io.*;
import java.net.*;
import java.util.*;
import javax.servlet.*;

public class KeyedServerLock extends GenericServlet {

  // This servlet has no class or instance variables
  // associated with the locking, so as to simplify
  // synchronization issues.

  public void service(ServletRequest req, ServletResponse res)
                          throws ServletException, IOException {
    res.setContentType("text/plain");
    PrintWriter out = res.getWriter();

    // The piracy check shouldn't be done in init
    // because name/port are part of request.
    String key = getInitParameter("key");
    String host = req.getServerName();
    int port = req.getServerPort();

    // Check if the init parameter "key" unlocks this server.
    if (! keyFitsServer(key, host, port)) {
      // Explain, condemn, threaten, etc.
      out.println("Pirated!");
    }
    else {
      // Give 'em the goods
      out.println("valid");
      // etc...
    }
  }


  // This method contains the algorithm used to match a key with
  // a server host and port. This example implementation is extremely
  // weak and should not be used by commercial sites.
  //
  private boolean keyFitsServer(String key, String host, int port) {

    if (key == null) return false;

    long numericKey = 0;
    try {
```

Example 4-4. A servlet locked to a server (continued)

```
          numericKey = Long.parseLong(key);
      }
      catch (NumberFormatException e) {
        return false;
      }

      // The key must be a 64-bit number equal to the logical not (~)
      // of the 32-bit IP address concatenated with the 32-bit port number.

      byte hostIP[];
      try {
        hostIP = InetAddress.getByName(host).getAddress();
      }
      catch (UnknownHostException e) {
        return false;
      }

      // Get the 32-bit IP address
      long servercode = 0;
      for (int i = 0; i < 4; i++) {
        servercode <<= 8;
        servercode |= (hostIP[i] & 255);
      }

      // Concatentate the 32-bit port number
      servercode <<= 32;
      servercode |= port;

      // Logical not
      long accesscode = ~numericKey;

      // The moment of truth: Does the key match?
      return (servercode == accesscode);
    }
}
```

This servlet refuses to perform unless given the correct key. To really make it
secure, however, the simple `keyFitsServer()` logic should be replaced with a
strong algorithm and the whole servlet should be run through an obfuscator to
prevent decompiling. Example 4-8 later in this chapter provides the code used to
generate keys. If you try this servlet yourself, it's best if you access the server with
its actual name, rather than *localhost*, so the servlet can determine the web server's
true name and IP address.

The Client

For each request, a servlet has the ability to find out about the client machine and, for pages requiring authentication, about the actual user. This information can be used for logging access data, associating information with individual users, or restricting access to certain clients.

Getting Information About the Client Machine

A servlet can use `getRemoteAddr()` and `getRemoteHost()` to retrieve the IP address and hostname of the client machine, respectively:

```
public String ServletRequest.getRemoteAddr()
public String ServletRequest.getRemoteHost()
```

Both values are returned as `String` objects. The information comes from the socket that connects the server to the client, so the remote address and hostname may be that of a proxy server. An example remote address might be `"192.26.80.118"` while an example remote host might be `"dist.engr. sgi.com"`.

The IP address or remote hostname can be converted to a `java.net.InetAddress` object using `InetAddress.getByName()`:

```
InetAddress remoteInetAddress = InetAddress.getByName(req.getRemoteAddr());
```

Restricting Access to the United States and Canada

Due to the United States government's policy restricting the export of strong encryption outside the United States and Canada, some web sites must be careful about who they let download certain software. Servlets, with their ability to find out about the client machine, are well suited to enforce this restriction. These servlets can check the client machine and provide links for download only if the client appears to be coming from inside the United States or Canada. Example 4-5 gives an example.

Example 4-5. Can they be trusted?

```
import java.io.*;
import java.net.*;
import java.util.*;
import javax.servlet.*;
import javax.servlet.http.*;

public class ExportRestriction extends HttpServlet {

  public void doGet(HttpServletRequest req, HttpServletResponse res)
```

Example 4-5. Can they be trusted? (continued)

```
                          throws ServletException, IOException {
  res.setContentType("text/html");
  PrintWriter out = res.getWriter();

  // ...Some introductory HTML...

  // Get the client's hostname
  String remoteHost = req.getRemoteHost();

  // See if the client is allowed
  if (! isHostAllowed(remoteHost)) {
    out.println("Access <BLINK>denied</BLINK>");  // filter out the blink!
  }
  else {
    out.println("Access granted");
    // Display download links, etc...
  }
}

// We assume hosts ending with .com, .edu, .net, .org,
// .gov, .mil, .us, and .ca are legal even though this is an
// over-simplification now that .com, .net, and .org have
// become global top-level domains. We also assume
// clients without a domain name are local and that
// local is allowed. (After all, if local isn't allowed
// you would have to be outside the United States and Canada -- so
// why would you be using this servlet?)
private boolean isHostAllowed(String host) {
  return (host.endsWith(".com") ||
          host.endsWith(".edu") ||
          host.endsWith(".net") ||
          host.endsWith(".org") ||
          host.endsWith(".gov") ||
          host.endsWith(".mil") ||
          host.endsWith(".us") ||
          host.endsWith(".ca") ||
          (host.indexOf('.') == -1));  // no domain, assume OK
  }
}
```

This servlet gets the client hostname with a call to `req.getRemoteHost()` and, based on its suffix, decides if the client came from inside or outside the United States and Canada. Of course, be sure to get high-priced legal counsel before making any cryptographic code available for download.

Getting Information About the User

What do you do when you need to restrict access to some of your web pages but want to have a bit more control over the restriction than this "continent by continent" approach? Say, for example, you publish an online magazine and want only paid subscribers to read the articles. Well (prepare yourself), you don't need servlets to do this.

Nearly every HTTP server has a built-in capability to restrict access to some or all of its pages to a given set of registered users. How you set up restricted access depends on the server, but here's how it works mechanically. The first time a browser attempts to access one of these pages, the HTTP server replies that it needs special user authentication. When the browser receives this response, it usually pops open a window asking the user for a name and password appropriate for the page, as shown in Figure 4-1.

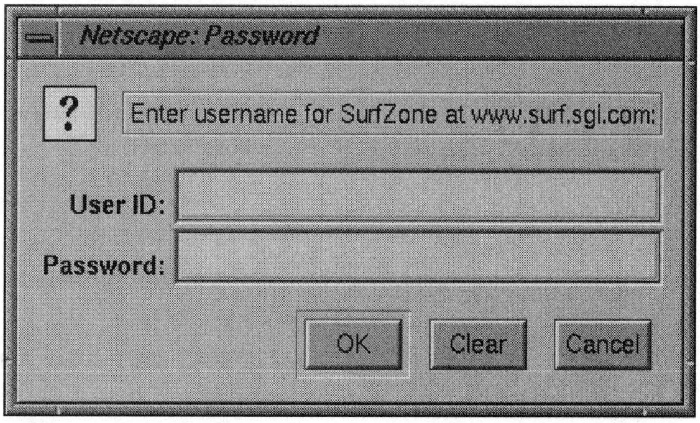

Figure 4-1. Please log in

Once the user enters his information, the browser again attempts to access the page, this time attaching the user's name and password along with the request. If the server accepts the name/password pair, it happily handles the request. If, on the other hand, the server doesn't accept the name/password pair, the browser is again denied and the user swears under his breath about forgetting yet another password.

How does this involves servlets? When access to a servlet has been restricted by the server, the servlet can get the name of the user that was accepted by the server, using the getRemoteUser() method:

```
public String HttpServletRequest.getRemoteUser()
```

Note that this information is retrieved from the servlet's `HttpServletRequest` object, the HTTP-specific subclass of `ServletRequest`. This method returns the name of the user making the request as a `String` or `null` if access to the servlet was not restricted. There is no comparable method to get the remote user's password (although it can be manually determined, as shown in Example 8-2). An example remote user might be `"jhunter"`.

A servlet can also use the `getAuthType()` method to find out what type of authorization was used:

```
public String HttpServletRequest.getAuthType()
```

This method returns the type of authorization used or `null` if access to the servlet was not restricted. The most common authorization types are `"BASIC"` and `"DIGEST"`.

By the time the servlet calls `getRemoteUser()`, the server has already determined that the user is authorized to invoke the servlet, but that doesn't mean the remote user's name is worthless. The servlet could perform a second authorization check, more restrictive and dynamic than the server's. For example, it could return sensitive information about someone only if that person made the request, or it could enforce a rule that each user can make only 10 accesses per day.[*]

Then again, the client's name can simply tell the servlet who is accessing it. After all, the remote host is not necessarily unique to one user. Unix servers often host hundreds of users, and gateway proxies can act on behalf of thousands. But bear in mind that access to the client's name comes with a price. Every user must be registered with your server and, before accessing your site, must enter his name and password. Generally speaking, authentication should not be used just so a servlet can know to whom it is talking. Chapter 7, *Session Tracking*, describes some better, lower-maintenance techniques for knowing about users. However, if a servlet is already protected and has the name easily available, the servlet might as well use it.

With the remote user's name, a servlet can save information about each client. Over the long term, it can remember each individual's preferences. For the short term, it can remember the series of pages viewed by the client and use them to add a sense of state to a stateless HTTP protocol. The session tracking tricks from Chapter 7 may be unnecessary if the servlet already knows the name of the client user.

---

[*] Want to know how to say "Access Denied" for the eleventh access? It's in the next chapter.

A Personalized Welcome

A simple servlet that uses getRemoteUser() can greet its clients by name and remember when each last logged in, as shown in Example 4-6.

Example 4-6. Hey, I remember you!

```
import java.io.*;
import java.util.*;
import javax.servlet.*;
import javax.servlet.http.*;

public class PersonalizedWelcome extends HttpServlet {

  Hashtable accesses = new Hashtable();

  public void doGet(HttpServletRequest req, HttpServletResponse res)
                            throws ServletException, IOException {
    res.setContentType("text/html");
    PrintWriter out = res.getWriter();

    // ...Some introductory HTML...

    String remoteUser = req.getRemoteUser();

    if (remoteUser == null) {
      out.println("Welcome!");
    }
    else {
      out.println("Welcome, " + remoteUser + "!");
      Date lastAccess = (Date) accesses.get(remoteUser);
      if (lastAccess == null) {
        out.println("This is your first visit!");
      }
      else {
        out.println("Your last visit was " + accesses.get(remoteUser));
      }

      if (remoteUser.equals("PROFESSOR FALKEN")) {
        out.println("Shall we play a game?");
      }

      accesses.put(remoteUser, new Date());
    }

    // ...Continue handling the request...
  }
}
```

This servlet uses a `Hashtable` to save the last access time for each remote user. The first thing it does for each request is greet the person by name and tell him the time of his last visit. Then it records the time of this visit, for use next time. After that, it continues handling the request.

The Request

We've seen how the servlet finds out about the server and about the client. Now it's time to move on to the really important stuff: how a servlet finds out what the client wants.

Request Parameters

Each access to a servlet can have any number of request parameters associated with it. These parameters are typically name/value pairs that tell the servlet any extra information it needs to handle the request. Please don't confuse these request parameters with init parameters, which are associated with the servlet itself.

An HTTP servlet gets its request parameters as part of its query string (for GET requests) or as encoded post data (for POST requests). A servlet used as a server-side include has its parameters supplied by <PARAM> tags. Other types of servlets can receive their parameters in other ways.

Fortunately, even though a servlet can receive parameters in a number of different ways, every servlet retrieves its parameters the same way, using `getParameter()` and `getParameterValues()`:

```
public String ServletRequest.getParameter(String name)
public String[] ServletRequest.getParameterValues(String name)
```

`getParameter()` returns the value of the named parameter as a `String` or `null` if the parameter was not specified.[*] The value is guaranteed to be in its normal, decoded form. If the parameter has multiple values, the value returned is server-dependent. If there's any chance a parameter could have more than one value, you should use the `getParameterValues()` method instead. This method returns all the values of the named parameter as an array of `String` objects or `null` if the parameter was not specified. A single value is returned in an array of length 1.

One word of warning: if the parameter information came in as encoded POST data, it may not be available if the POST data has already been read manually using the

---

[*] The `getParameter()` method was deprecated in the Java Web Server 1.1 in favor of `getParameter-Values()`. However, after quite a lot of public protest, Sun took `getParameter()` off the deprecation list in the final release of Servlet API 2.0. It was the first Java method to be undeprecated!

getReader() or getInputStream() method of ServletRequest (because POST data can be read only once).

The possible uses for request parameters are unlimited. They are a general-purpose way to tell a servlet what to do, how to do it, or both. For a simple example, let's look at how a dictionary servlet might use getParameter() to find out the word it needs to look up.

An HTML file could contain this form asking the user for a word to look up:

```
<FORM METHOD=GET ACTION="/servlet/Dictionary">
Word to look up: <INPUT TYPE=TEXT NAME="word"><P>
Another word? <INPUT TYPE=TEXT NAME="word"><P>
<INPUT TYPE=SUBMIT><P>
</FORM>
```

Or the HTML file could contain this server-side include:

```
<SERVLET CODE=Dictionary>
<PARAM NAME=word VALUE=obfuscate>
<PARAM NAME=word VALUE=onomatopoeia>
</SERVLET>
```

No matter what the HTML looks like or whether the servlet handles GET requests, POST requests, or server-side include requests or is part of a filter chain, you can use code like the following to retrieve the servlet's parameters:

```
String word = req.getParameter("word");
String definition = getDefinition(word);
out.println(word + ": " + definition);
```

While this code works fine, it can handle only one word per request. To handle multiple values for word, the servlet can use the getParameterValues() method instead:

```
String[] words = req.getParameterValues("word");
if (words != null) {
  for (int i = 0; i < words.length; i++) {
    String definition = getDefinition(words[i]);
    out.println(words[i] + ": " + definition);
    out.println("<HR>");
  }
}
```

In addition to getting parameter values, a servlet can access parameter names using getParameterNames():

```
public Enumeration ServletRequest.getParameterNames()
```

This method returns all the parameter names as an `Enumeration` of `String` object or an empty `Enumeration` if the servlet has no parameters. The method is most often used for debugging.

Finally, a servlet can retrieve the raw query string of the request with `getQueryString()`:

```
public String ServletRequest.getQueryString()
```

This method returns the raw query string (encoded GET parameter information) of the request or `null` if there was no query string. This low-level information is rarely useful for handling form data. It's best for handling a single unnamed value, as in `"/servlet/Sqrt?576"`, where the returned query string is `"576"`.

Example 4-7 shows the use of these methods with a servlet that prints its query string, then prints the name and value for all its parameters.

Example 4-7. Snooping parameters

```java
import java.io.*;
import java.util.*;
import javax.servlet.*;
import javax.servlet.http.*;

public class ParameterSnoop extends HttpServlet {

  public void doGet(HttpServletRequest req, HttpServletResponse res)
                            throws ServletException, IOException {
    res.setContentType("text/plain");
    PrintWriter out = res.getWriter();

    out.println("Query String:");
    out.println(req.getQueryString());
    out.println();

    out.println("Request Parameters:");
    Enumeration enum = req.getParameterNames();
    while (enum.hasMoreElements()) {
      String name = (String) enum.nextElement();
      String values[] = req.getParameterValues(name);
      if (values != null) {
        for (int i = 0; i < values.length; i++) {
          out.println(name + " (" + i + "): " + values[i]);
        }
      }
    }
  }
}
```

This servlet's output is shown in Figure 4-2.

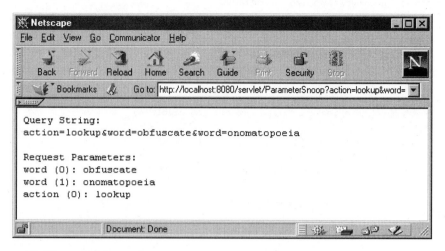

Figure 4-2. The snooped parameters

Generating a License Key

Now we're ready to write a servlet that generates a `KeyedServerLock` license key for any given host and port number. A key from this servlet can be used to unlock the `KeyedServerLock` servlet. So, how will this servlet know the host and port number of the servlet it needs to unlock? Why, with request parameters, of course. Example 4-8 shows the code.

Example 4-8. Unlocking KeyedServerLock

```
import java.io.*;
import java.net.*;
import java.util.*;
import javax.servlet.*;
import javax.servlet.http.*;

public class KeyedServerUnlock extends HttpServlet {

  public void doGet(HttpServletRequest req, HttpServletResponse res)
                          throws ServletException, IOException {
    PrintWriter out = res.getWriter();

    // Get the host and port
    String host = req.getParameter("host");
    String port = req.getParameter("port");

    // Convert the port to an integer
    int numericPort;
    try {
      numericPort = Integer.parseInt(port);
```

Example 4-8. Unlocking KeyedServerLock (continued)

```
  }
  catch (NumberFormatException e) {
    numericPort = 80;  // default
  }


  // Generate and print the key
  // Any KeyGenerationException is caught and displayed
  try {
    long key = generateKey(host, numericPort);
    out.println(host + ":" + numericPort + " has the key " + key);
  }
  catch (KeyGenerationException e) {
    out.println("Could not generate key: " + e.getMessage());
  }
}


// This method contains the algorithm used to match a key with
// a server host and port. This example implementation is extremely
// weak and should not be used by commercial sites.
//
// Throws a KeyGenerationException because anything more specific
// would be tied to the chosen algorithm.
//
private long generateKey(String host, int port) throws KeyGenerationException {

  // The key must be a 64-bit number equal to the logical not (~)
  // of the 32-bit IP address concatenated by the 32-bit port number.

  byte hostIP[];
  try {
    hostIP = InetAddress.getByName(host).getAddress();
  }
  catch (UnknownHostException e) {
    throw new KeyGenerationException(e.getMessage());
  }

  // Get the 32-bit IP address
  long servercode = 0;
  for (int i = 0; i < 4; i++) {
    servercode <<= 8;
    servercode |= (hostIP[i] & 255);
  }

  // Concatentate the 32-bit port number
  servercode <<= 32;
  servercode |= port;

  // The key is the logical not
```

Example 4-8. Unlocking KeyedServerLock (continued)

```
    return ~servercode;
  }
}

class KeyGenerationException extends Exception {

  public KeyGenerationException() {
    super();
  }

  public KeyGenerationException(String msg) {
    super(msg);
  }
}
```

This servlet can either generate a full page (for handling GET requests) or act as a server-side include.

Path Information

In addition to parameters, an HTTP request can include something called "extra path information" or a "virtual path." In general, this extra path information is used to indicate a file on the server that the servlet should use for something. This path information is encoded in the URL of an HTTP request. An example URL looks like this:

```
http://server:port/servlet/ViewFile/index.html
```

This invokes the `ViewFile` servlet, passing `"/index.html"` as extra path information. A servlet can access this path information, and it can also translate the `"/index.html"` string into the real path of the *index.html* file. What is the real path of `"/index.html"`? It's the full file system path to the file—what the server would return if the client asked for `"/index.html"` directly. This probably turns out to be *document_root/index.html*, but, of course, the server could have special aliasing that changes this.

Besides being specified explicitly in a URL, this extra path information can also be encoded in the `ACTION` parameter of an HTML form:

```
<FORM METHOD=GET ACTION="/servlet/Dictionary/dict/definitions.txt">
Word to look up: <INPUT TYPE=TEXT NAME="word"><P>
<INPUT TYPE=SUBMIT><P>
</FORM>
```

This form invokes the `Dictionary` servlet to handle its submissions and passes the `Dictionary` the extra path information `"/dict/definitions.txt"`. The `Dictionary` servlet can then know to look up word definitions using the *definitions.txt* file, the same file the client would see if it requested `"/dict/definitions.txt"`, probably *server_root/public_html/dict/definitions.txt*.

Why Extra Path Information?

Why does HTTP have special support for extra path information? Isn't it enough to pass the servlet a `path` parameter? The answer is yes. Servlets don't need the special support, but CGI programs do.

A CGI program cannot interact with its server during execution, so it has no way to receive a `path` parameter, let alone ask the server to map it to a real file system location. The server has to somehow translate the path *before* invoking the CGI program. This is why there needs to be support for special "extra path information." Servers know to pretranslate this extra path and send the translation to the CGI program as an environment variable. It's a fairly elegant workaround to a shortcoming in CGI.

Of course, just because servlets don't need the special handling of "extra path information," it doesn't mean they shouldn't use it. It provides a simple, convenient way to attach a path along with a request.

Getting path information

A servlet can use the `getPathInfo()` method to get extra path information:

```
public String HttpServletRequest.getPathInfo()
```

This method returns the extra path information associated with the request or `null` if none was given. An example path is `"/dict/definitions.txt"`. The path information by itself, however, is only marginally useful. A servlet usually needs to know the actual file system location of the file given in the path info, which is where `getPathTranslated()` comes in:

```
public String HttpServletRequest.getPathTranslated()
```

This method returns the extra path information translated to a real file system path or `null` if there is no extra path information. The returned path does not necessarily point to an existing file or directory. An example translated path is `"C:\JavaWebServer1.1.1\public_html\dict\definitions.txt"`.

Example 4-9 shows a servlet that uses these two methods to print the extra path information it receives and the resulting translation to a real path.

Example 4-9. Showing where the path leads

```
import java.io.*;
import java.util.*;
import javax.servlet.*;
import javax.servlet.http.*;

public class FileLocation extends HttpServlet {

  public void doGet(HttpServletRequest req, HttpServletResponse res)
                           throws ServletException, IOException {
    res.setContentType("text/plain");
    PrintWriter out = res.getWriter();

    if (req.getPathInfo() != null) {
      out.println("The file \"" + req.getPathInfo() + "\"");
      out.println("Is stored at \"" + req.getPathTranslated() + "\"");
    }
  }
}
```

Some example output of this servlet might be:

```
The file "/index.html"
Is stored at "/usr/JavaWebServer1.1.1/public_html/index.html"
```

Ad hoc path translations

Sometimes a servlet needs to translate a path that wasn't passed in as extra path information. You can use the `getRealPath()` method for this task:

```
public String ServletRequest.getRealPath(String path)
```

This method returns the real path of any given "virtual path" or `null` if the translation cannot be performed. If the given path is `"/"`, the method returns the document root (the place where documents are stored) for the server. If the given path is `getPathInfo()`, the method returns the same real path as would be returned by `getPathTranslated()`. This method can be used by generic servlets as well as HTTP servlets. There is no CGI counterpart.

Getting MIME types

Once a servlet has the path to a file, it often needs to discover the type of the file. Use `getMimeType()` to do this:

```
public String ServletContext.getMimeType(String file)
```

This method returns the MIME type of the given file or `null` if it isn't known. Some implementations return `"text/plain"` if the given file doesn't exist. Common MIME types are `"text/html"`, `"text/plain"`, `"image/gif"`, and `"image/jpeg"`.

The following code fragment finds the MIME type of the extra path information:

```
String type = getServletContext().getMimeType(req.getPathTranslated())
```

Serving Files

The Java Web Server itself uses servlets to handle every request. Besides being a showcase for the ability of servlets, this gives the server a modular design that allows the wholesale replacement of certain aspects of its functionality. For example, all files are served by the `com.sun.server.http.FileServlet` servlet, registered under the name `file` and charged with the responsibility to handle the `"/"` alias (meaning it's the default handler for requests). But there's nothing to say that Sun's `FileServlet` cannot be replaced. In fact, it can be, either by registering another servlet under the name `file` or by changing the `"/"` alias to use another servlet. Furthermore, it's not all that hard to write a replacement for `file`, using the methods we've just seen.

Example 4-10 shows a `ViewFile` servlet that uses the `getPathTranslated()` and `getMimeType()` methods to return whatever file is given by the extra path information.

Example 4-10. Dynamically returning static files

```
import java.io.*;
import java.util.*;
import javax.servlet.*;
import javax.servlet.http.*;

import com.oreilly.servlet.ServletUtils;

public class ViewFile extends HttpServlet {

  public void doGet(HttpServletRequest req, HttpServletResponse res)
                          throws ServletException, IOException {
    // Use a ServletOutputStream because we may pass binary information
    ServletOutputStream out = res.getOutputStream();

    // Get the file to view
    String file = req.getPathTranslated();

    // No file, nothing to view
    if (file == null) {
      out.println("No file to view");
```

Example 4-10. Dynamically returning static files (continued)

```
    return;
  }


  // Get and set the type of the file
  String contentType = getServletContext().getMimeType(file);
  res.setContentType(contentType);

  // Return the file
  try {
    ServletUtils.returnFile(file, out);
  }
  catch (FileNotFoundException e) {
    out.println("File not found");
  }
  catch (IOException e) {
    out.println("Problem sending file: " + e.getMessage());
  }
 }
}
```

This servlet first uses `getPathTranslated()` to get the name of file it needs to display. Then it uses `getMimeType()` to find the content type of this file and sets the response content type to match. Last, it returns the file using the `return-File()` method found in the `com.oreilly.servlet.ServletUtils` utility class:

```
// Send the contents of the file to the output stream
public static void returnFile(String filename, OutputStream out)
                        throws FileNotFoundException, IOException {
  // A FileInputStream is for bytes
  FileInputStream fis = null;
  try {
    fis = new FileInputStream(filename);
    byte[] buf = new byte[4 * 1024];  // 4K buffer
    int bytesRead;
    while ((bytesRead = fis.read(buf)) != -1) {
      out.write(buf, 0, bytesRead);
    }
  }
  finally {
    if (fis != null) fis.close();
  }
}
```

The servlet's error handling is basic—it returns a page that describes the error. This is acceptable for our simple example (and really more than many programs seem capable of), but we'll learn a better way using status codes in the next chapter.

This servlet can be used directly with a URL like this.

```
http://server:port/servlet/ViewFile/index.html
```

Or, if you use it as a replacement for the `"file"` servlet, it is automatically invoked even for a URL like this.

```
http://server:port/index.html
```

Just beware that this servlet is a "proof of concept" example and does not have the full functionality of the `com.sun.server.http.FileServlet` servlet.

Determining What Was Requested

A servlet can use several methods to find out exactly what file or servlet the client requested. After all, only the most conceited servlet would always assume itself to be the direct target of a request. A servlet may be nothing more than a single link in a long servlet chain.

No method directly returns the original Uniform Resource Locator (URL) used by the client to make a request. The `javax.servlet.http.HttpUtils` class, however, provides a `getRequestURL()` method that does about the same thing:[*]

```
public static StringBuffer HttpUtils.getRequestURL(HttpServletRequest req)
```

This method reconstructs the request URL based on information available in the `HttpServletRequest` object. It returns a `StringBuffer` that includes the scheme (such as HTTP), server name, server port, and extra path information. The reconstructed URL should look almost identical to the URL used by the client. Differences between the original and reconstructed URLs should be minor (that is, a space encoded by the client as `"%20"` might be encoded by the server as a `"+"`). Because this method returns a `StringBuffer`, the request URL can be modified efficiently (for example, by appending query parameters). This method is often used for creating redirect messages and reporting errors.

Most of the time, however, a servlet doesn't really need the request URL. It just needs the request URI, which is returned by `getRequestURI()`:

```
public String HttpServletRequest.getRequestURI()
```

This method returns the Universal Resource Identifier (URI) of the request. For normal HTTP servlets, a request URI can be thought of as a URL minus the

---

[*] Why isn't there a method that directly returns the original URL shown in the browser? Because the browser never sends the full URL. The port number, for example, is used by the client to make its HTTP connection, but it isn't included in the request made to the web server answering on that port.

scheme, host, port, and query string, but including any extra path information.[*]
Table 4-2 shows the request URIs for several request URLs.

Table 4-2. URLs and Their URIs

Request URL	Its URI Component
http://server:port/servlet/Classname	*/servlet/Classname*
http://server:port/servlet/registeredName	*/servlet/registeredName*
http://server:port/servlet/Classname?var=val	*/servlet/Classname* [a]
http://server:port/servlet/Classname/pathinfo	*/servlet/Classname/pathinfo*
http://server:port/servlet/Classname/pathinfo?var=val	*/servlet/Classname/pathinfo*
http://server:port/ssi.shtml (SSI)	*/ssi.shtml*
http://server:port/alias.html (alias to a servlet)	*/alias.html*

[a] Several servlet engines (including the Java Web Server 1.1.1) have a bug where `getRequestURI()` erroneously includes the query string. The JSDK 2.0 servlet runner behaves correctly.

For servlets in a chain, the request URI is always that of the first servlet in the chain.

In some situations it is enough for a servlet to know the servlet name under which it was invoked. You can retrieve this information with `getServletPath()`:

```
public String HttpServletRequest.getServletPath()
```

This method returns the part of the URI that refers to the servlet being invoked or `null` if the URI does not directly point to a servlet. The servlet path does not include extra path information. Table 4-3 shows the servlet names for several request URLs.

Table 4-3. URLs and Their Servlet Paths

Request URL	Its Servlet Path
http://server:port/servlet/Classname	*/servlet/Classname*
http://server:port/servlet/registeredName	*/servlet/registeredName*
http://server:port/servlet/Classname?var=val	*/servlet/Classname*
http://server:port/servlet/Classname/pathinfo	*/servlet/Classname*
http://server:port/servlet/Classname/pathinfo?var=val	*/servlet/Classname*
http://server:port/ssi.shtml (SSI)	`null`
http://server:port/alias.html (alias to a servlet)	*/alias.html*

---

[*] Technically, what is referred to here as a request URI could more formally be called a "request URL path". This is because a URI is, in the most precise sense, a general purpose identifier for a resource. A URL is one type of URI; a URN (Uniform Resource Name) is another. For more information on URIs, URLs, and URNs, see RFC 1630 at *http://www.ietf.org/rfc/rfc1630.txt*.

For servlets in a filter chain, the servlet path is always the same as the path of the first servlet in the chain. If the request URI does not point at a servlet, `getServlet-Path()` returns `null`. It does not matter that a servlet (such as the `file` servlet) may have handled the request behind the scenes or that the request eventually ended up in a servlet.

For example, if the client requests the page */index.html* and the content goes through the `Deblink` servlet from Chapter 2, *HTTP Servlet Basics,* the `Deblink` servlet has a `null` servlet path—the original request was for a static file, not a servlet. If, however, the client requests */alias.html*—which is a direct alias to a servlet—both that servlet and the `Deblink` servlet have a servlet path of */alias.html.*

A servlet invoked as a server-side include behaves similarly. If it is embedded in a static file, it too has a `null` servlet path. The only way for it to have a non-`null` servlet path is if it is part of a servlet chain started by a servlet.

An Improved Counter

We can make use of the request URI information to improve our counter servlet. The counter example from Chapter 3 could count only its own accesses. A real counter has to be able to count accesses to pages other than itself. There are two elegant ways to accomplish this: use the counter as an SSI servlet embedded in a page or use the counter in a servlet chain where it can replace any instances of the `<COUNT>` tag with the appropriate number. For each approach, a servlet can use the `getRequestURI()` method to associate a separate count with each requested URI.

Example 4-11 shows a `GenericCounter` servlet superclass that knows how to manage a hashtable that stores counts for different URIs. Example 4-12 and Example 4-13 show servlets that subclass `GenericCounter` to act as a server-side include counter and a chain-based counter, respectively.[*]

Example 4-11. A generic counter superclass

```
import java.io.*;
import java.util.*;
import javax.servlet.*;
import javax.servlet.http.*;

public class GenericCounter extends HttpServlet {

  private Hashtable counts = new Hashtable();

  public void init(ServletConfig config) throws ServletException {
    // Always call super.init(config) first
    super.init(config);
```

Example 4-11. A generic counter superclass (continued)

```java
    // Try to load the initial page counts from the saved persistent state
    try {
      FileReader fileReader = new FileReader(getClass().getName() + ".counts");
      BufferedReader bufferedReader = new BufferedReader(fileReader);
      String line = null;
      String uri = null;
      String count = null;
      int[] holder = null;  // holder for the count, to make it an object
      while ((line = bufferedReader.readLine()) != null) {
        StringTokenizer tokenizer = new StringTokenizer(line);
        if (tokenizer.countTokens() < 2) continue;  // bogus line
        uri = tokenizer.nextToken();
        count = tokenizer.nextToken();
        // Store the uri/count pair in the counts hashtable
        // The count is saved as an int[1] to make it an "object"
        try {
          holder = new int[1];
          holder[0] = Integer.parseInt(count);
          counts.put(uri, holder);
        }
        catch (NumberFormatException e) { }  // bogus line
      }
    }
    catch (FileNotFoundException e) { }  // no saved state
    catch (IOException e) { }            // problem during read
  }

  // Increment and return the count for the given URI
  public int incrementAndGetCount(String uri) {
    int[] holder = (int[])counts.get(uri);
    if (holder == null) {
      // Initialize the count to 0
      holder = new int[1];
      holder[0] = 0;
      counts.put(uri, holder); // save the holder
    }
    holder[0]++;                     // increment
    return holder[0];
  }

  public void destroy() {
    // Try to save the accumulated count
```

---

* For Example 4-12, please note that the Java Web Server 1.1.1 has a bug where the PrintWriter returned by getWriter() doesn't generate output for servlets used as server side includes. See to Chapter 2 for more information.

Example 4-11. A generic counter superclass (continued)

```
    try {
      FileWriter fileWriter = new FileWriter(getClass().getName() + ".counts");
      BufferedWriter bufferedWriter = new BufferedWriter(fileWriter);
      Enumeration keys = counts.keys();
      Enumeration elements = counts.elements();
      String output = null;
      while (keys.hasMoreElements() && elements.hasMoreElements()) {
        bufferedWriter.write(keys.nextElement() + " " +
                             elements.nextElement() + "\n");
      }
      bufferedWriter.close();
      fileWriter.close();
      return;
    }
    catch (IOException e) { }  // problem during write
  }
}
```

Example 4-12. A server-side include counter

```
import java.io.*;
import javax.servlet.*;
import javax.servlet.http.*;

public class SSICounter extends GenericCounter {

  public void doGet(HttpServletRequest req, HttpServletResponse res)
                              throws ServletException, IOException {
    PrintWriter out = res.getWriter();

    // Fetch the page we're on.
    String uri = req.getRequestURI();

    // Get and increment the count for that page
    int count = incrementAndGetCount(uri);

    // Fulfull our purpose: print the count
    out.println(count);
  }
}
```

Example 4-13. A chain-based counter that replaces <COUNT> with the hit count

```
import java.io.*;
import javax.servlet.*;
import javax.servlet.http.*;

public class ChainCounter extends GenericCounter {
```

Example 4-13. A chain-based counter that replaces <COUNT> with the hit count (continued)

```java
public void doGet(HttpServletRequest req, HttpServletResponse res)
                            throws ServletException, IOException {

    String contentType = req.getContentType();
    res.setContentType(contentType);

    PrintWriter out = res.getWriter();

    // Fetch the page we're on.
    String uri = req.getRequestURI();

    // Get and increment the count
    int count = incrementAndGetCount(uri);

    // Prepare to read the input
    BufferedReader reader = req.getReader();

    String line = null;
    while ((line = reader.readLine()) != null) {
      line = replace(line, "<COUNT>", "" + count);  // case sensitive
      out.println(line);
    }
  }

  public void doPost(HttpServletRequest req, HttpServletResponse res)
                             throws ServletException, IOException {
    doGet(req, res);
  }

  private String replace(String line, String oldString, String newString) {
    int index = 0;
    while ((index = line.indexOf(oldString, index)) >= 0) {
      line = line.substring(0, index) +
             newString +
             line.substring(index + oldString.length());
      index += newString.length();
    }
    return line;
  }
}
```

How It Was Requested

Besides knowing *what* was requested, a servlet has several ways of finding out details about *how* it was requested. The getScheme() method returns the scheme used to make this request:

```java
public String ServletRequest.getScheme()
```

Examples include "http", "https", and "ftp", as well as the newer Java-specific schemes "jdbc" and "rmi". There is no direct CGI counterpart (though some CGI implementations have a SERVER_URL variable that includes the scheme). For HTTP servlets, this method indicates whether the request was made over a secure connection using the Secure Sockets Layer (SSL), as indicated by the scheme "https", or if it was an insecure request, as indicated by the scheme "http".

The getProtocol() method returns the protocol and version number used to make the request:

```
public String ServletRequest.getProtocol()
```

The protocol and version number are separated by a slash. The method returns null if no protocol could be determined. For HTTP servlets, the protocol is usually vHTTP/1.0v or vHTTP/1.1". HTTP servlets can use the protocol version to determine if it's okay with the client to use the new features in HTTP Version 1.1.

To find out what method was used for a request, a servlet uses getMethod():

```
public String HttpServletRequest.getMethod()
```

This method returns the HTTP method used to make the request. Examples include "GET", "POST", and "HEAD". The service() method of the Http-Servlet implementation uses this method in its dispatching of requests.

Request Headers

HTTP requests and responses can have a number of associated HTTP "headers". These headers provide some extra information about the request (or response). The HTTP Version 1.0 protocol defines literally dozens of possible headers; the HTTP Version 1.1 protocol includes even more. A description of all the headers extends beyond the scope of this book; we discuss only the headers most often accessed by servlets. For a full list of HTTP headers and their uses, we recommend *Web Client Programming* by Clinton Wong (O'Reilly) or *Webmaster in a Nutshell* by Stephen Spainhour and Valerie Quercia (O'Reilly).

A servlet rarely needs to read the HTTP headers accompanying a request. Many of the headers associated with a request are handled by the server itself. Take, for example, how a server restricts access to its documents. The server uses HTTP headers, and servlets need not know the details. When a server receives a request for a restricted page, it checks that the request includes an appropriate Authorization header that contains a valid username and a password. If it doesn't, the server itself issues a response containing a WWW-Authenticate header, to tell the browser its access to a resource was denied. When the client sends a request that includes the proper `Authorization` header, the server grants the access and gives any servlet invoked access to the user's name via the `getRemoteUser()` call.

Other headers are used by servlets, but indirectly. A good example is the `Last-Modified` and `If-Last-Modified` pair discussed in Chapter 3. The server itself sees the `If-Last-Modified` header and calls the servlet's `getLastModified()` method to determine how to proceed.

There are a few HTTP headers that a servlet may want to read on occasion. These are listed in Table 4-4.

Table 4-4. Useful HTTP Request Headers

Header	**Usage**
`Accept`	Specifies the media (MIME) types the client prefers to accept, separated by commas.[a] Each media type is divided into a type and subtype given as *type/subtype*. An asterisk (`*`) wildcard is allowed for the subtype (*type*/`*`) or for both the type and subtype (`*/*`). For example: `Accept: image/gif, image/jpeg, text/*, */*` A servlet can use this header to help determine what type of content to return. If this header is not passed as part of the request, the servlet can assume the client accepts all media types.

`User-Agent`	Gives information about the client software. The format of the returned string is relatively free form, but it often includes the browser name and version as well as information about the machine on which it is running. Netscape 3.01 on an SGI Indy running IRIX 6.2 reports:
	`User-Agent: Mozilla/3.01SC-SGI (X11; I; IRIX 6.2 IP22)`
	Microsoft Internet Explorer 4.0 running on a Windows 95 machine reports:
	`User-Agent: Mozilla/4.0 (compatible; MSIE 4.0; Windows 95)`
	A servlet can use this header to keep statistics or to customize its response based on browser type.

`Referer`	Gives the URL of the document that refers to the requested URL (that is, the document that contains the link the client followed to access this document).[b] For example: `Referer: http://www.gamelan.com/pages/Gamelan.sites.home.html` A servlet can use this header to keep statistics or, if there's some error in the request, to keep track of the documents with errors.
`Authorization`	Provides the client's authorization to access the requested URI, including a username and password encoded in Base64. Servlets can use this for custom authorization, as discussed in Chapter 8, *Security*.

[a] Some older browsers send a separate `Accept` header for each media type. This can confuse some servlet engines, including the Java Web Server.

[b] The properly-spelled `Referrer` header gives you nothing.

Accessing header values

HTTP header values are accessed through the `HttpServletRequest` object. A
header value can be retrieved as a `String`, a `long` (representing a `Date`), or an
`int`, using `getHeader()`, `getDateHeader()`, and `getIntHeader()`, respectively:

```
public String HttpServletRequest.getHeader(String name)
public long HttpServletRequest.getDateHeader(String name)
public int HttpServletRequest.getIntHeader(String name)
```

`getHeader()` returns the value of the named header as a `String` or `null` if the
header was not sent as part of the request. The name is case insensitive, as it is for
all these methods. Headers of all types can be retrieved with this method.

`getDateHeader()` returns the value of the named header as a `long` (representing a `Date`) that specifies the number of milliseconds since the epoch) or `-1` if
the header was not sent as part of the request. This method throws an `Ille-
galArgumentException` when called on a header whose value cannot be
converted to a `Date`. The method is useful for handling headers like `Last-Modi-
fied` and `If-Modified-Since`.

`getIntHeader()` returns the value of the named header as an `int` or `-1` if the
header was not sent as part of the request. This method throws a `NumberFormat-
Exception` when called on a header whose value cannot be converted to an `int`.

A servlet can also get the names of all the headers it can access using
`getHeaderNames()`:

```
public Enumeration HttpServletRequest.getHeaderNames()
```

This method returns the names of all the headers as an `Enumeration` of `String`
objects. It returns an empty `Enumeration` if there were no headers. The Servlet
API gives servlet engine implementations the right to not allow headers to be
accessed in this way, in which case this method returns `null`.

Example 4-14 demonstrates the use of these methods in a servlet that prints information about its HTTP request headers.

Example 4-14. Snooping headers

```
import java.io.*;
import java.util.*;
import javax.servlet.*;
import javax.servlet.http.*;

public class HeaderSnoop extends HttpServlet {

  public void doGet(HttpServletRequest req, HttpServletResponse res)
                      throws ServletException, IOException {
```

Example 4-14. Snooping headers (continued)

```
      res.setContentType("text/plain");
      PrintWriter out = res.getWriter();

      out.println("Request Headers:");
      out.println();
      Enumeration enum = req.getHeaderNames();
      while (enum.hasMoreElements()) {
        String name = (String) enum.nextElement();
        String value = req.getHeader(name);
        if (value != null) {
          out.println(name + ": " + value);
        }
      }
    }
}
```

Some example output from this servlet might look like this:

```
Request Headers:

Connection: Keep-Alive
If-Modified-Since: Saturday, 13-Jun-98 20:50:31 GMT; length=297
User-Agent: Mozilla/4.05 [en] (X11; I; IRIX 6.2 IP22)
Host: localhost:8080
Accept: image/gif, image/x-xbitmap, image/jpeg, image/pjpeg, image/png, */*
Accept-Language: en
Accept-Charset: iso-8859-1,*,utf-8
Cookie: jwssessionid=A3KBB1YAAAAABQDGPM5QAAA
```

Headers in servlet chains

Servlet chains add an interesting twist to how servlets handle headers. Unlike all other servlets, a servlet in the middle or at the end of a servlet chain reads header values not from the client's request, but from the previous servlet's response.

The power and flexibility of this approach comes from the fact that a servlet can intelligently process a previous servlet's output, not only in body content, but in header values. For example, it can add extra headers to the response or change the value of existing headers. It can even suppress the previous servlet's headers.

But power comes with responsibilities: unless a chained servlet specifically reads the previous servlet's response headers and sends them as part of its own response, the headers are not passed on and will not be seen by the client. A well-behaved chained servlet always passes on the previous servlet's headers, unless it has a specific reason to do otherwise.

The code shown in Example 4-15 uses getHeaderNames() in combination with getHeader() and setHeader() to pass on the headers from the previous servlet to the client (or possibly to another servlet in the chain). The only header given special treatment is the Content-Length header. This header's value reports the length of the response in bytes—a value that is likely to change during the chaining process and so not appropriate to send on. Note that you haven't seen the setHeader() method before. It can be used to, well, set a header.

Example 4-15. Passing on the headers

```
Enumeration enum = req.getHeaderNames();
if (enum != null) {  // to be safe across all implementations
  while (enum.hasMoreElements()) {
    String header = (String)enum.nextElement();
    if ("Content-Length").equalsIgnoreCase(header))
      continue;
    String value = req.getHeader(header);
    res.setHeader(header, value);
  }
}
```

An HTTP servlet designed to function in a chain should include code similar to this early on in its handling of a request, so as to pass on the appropriate headers.

Wading the Input Stream

Each request handled by a servlet has an input stream associated with it. Just as a servlet can write to a PrintWriter or OutputStream associated with its response object, it can read from a Reader or InputStream associated with its request object. The data read from the input stream can be of any content type and of any length. The input stream has three purposes:

- To pass a chained servlet the response body from the previous servlet
- To pass an HTTP servlet the content associated with a POST request
- To pass a non-HTTP servlet the raw data sent by the client

To read character data from the input stream, you should use getReader() to retrieve the input stream as a BufferedReader object:

```
public BufferedReader ServletRequest.getReader() throws IOException
```

The advantage of using a BufferedReader for reading character-based data is that it should translate charsets as appropriate. This method throws an Illegal-StateException if getInputStream() has been called before on this same request. It throws an UnsupportedEncodingException if the character encoding of the input is unsupported or unknown.

To read binary data from the input stream, use `getInputStream()` to retrieve the input stream as a `ServletInputStream` object:

```
public ServletInputStream ServletRequest.getInputStream() throws IOException
```

A `ServletInputStream` is a direct subclass of `InputStream` and can be treated as a normal `InputStream`, with the added ability to efficiently read input a line at a time into an array of bytes. The method throws an `IllegalStateException` if `getReader()` has been called before on this same request. Once you have the `ServletInputStream`, you can read a line from it using `readLine()`:

```
public int ServletInputStream.readLine(byte b[], int off, int len)
    throws IOException
```

This method reads bytes from the input stream into the `byte` array `b`, starting at an offset in the array given by `off`. It stops reading when it encounters an '\n' or when it has read `len` number of bytes. The ending '\n' character is read into the buffer as well. The method returns the number of bytes read or -1 if the end of the stream is reached.

A servlet can also check the content type and the length of the data being sent via the input stream, using `getContentType()` and `getContentLength()`, respectively:

```
public String ServletRequest.getContentType()
public int ServletRequest.getContentLength()
```

`getContentType()` returns the media type of the content being sent via the input stream or `null` if the type is not known (such as when there is no data). `getContentLength()` returns the length, in bytes, of the content being sent via the input stream or -1 if this not known.

Chaining servlets using the input stream

A servlet in a servlet chain receives its response body from the previous servlet in the chain through its input stream. This use was first shown in the `Deblink` servlet in Chapter 2, *HTTP Servlet Basics*. The pertinent section is shown again here:

```
String contentType = req.getContentType();  // get the incoming type
if (contentType == null) return;  // nothing incoming, nothing to do
res.setContentType(contentType);  // set outgoing type to be incoming type

BufferedReader br = req.getReader();

String line = null;
while ((line = br.readLine()) != null) {
  line = replace(line, "<BLINK>", "");
  line = replace(line, "</BLINK>", "");
  out.println(line);
}
```

Notice the use of getContentType() to retrieve the content type of the previous servlet's output. Also notice that getContentLength() is not used. We don't need to use it because all read() and readLine() methods indicate that they have reached the end of the stream with special return values. In fact, it's better not to use getContentLength() in a servlet chain because it is unsupported in many servlet engine implementations. Presumably the reason is that the server may choose to tie the output stream of one servlet directly to the input stream of the next servlet, giving no chance to determine a total content length.

Handling POST requests using the input stream

It is a rare occurrence when a servlet handling a POST request is forced to use its input stream to access the POST data. Typically, the POST data is nothing more than encoded parameter information, which a servlet can conveniently retrieve with its getParameter() method.

A servlet can identify this type of POST request by checking the content type of the input stream. If it is of type application/x-www-form-urlencoded, the data can be retrieved with getParameter() and similar methods. Example 4-16 demonstrates a servlet that keys off the input stream's content type to handle POST requests.

Example 4-16. Reading parameters passed by POST

```
import java.io.*;
import java.util.*;
import javax.servlet.*;
import javax.servlet.http.*;

public class PostParams extends HttpServlet {

  public void doPost(HttpServletRequest req, HttpServletResponse res)
                            throws ServletException, IOException {
    res.setContentType("text/plain");
    PrintWriter out = res.getWriter();

    if ("application/x-www-form-urlencoded".equals(req.getContentType())) {
      Enumeration enum = req.getParameterNames();
      while (enum.hasMoreElements()) {
        String name = (String) enum.nextElement();
        String values[] = req.getParameterValues(name);
        if (values != null) {
          for (int i = 0; i < values.length; i++) {
            out.println(name + " (" + i + "): " + values[i]);
          }
```

Example 4-16. Reading parameters passed by POST (continued)

```
        }
      }
    }
  }
}
```

In case you were wondering, the odd arrangement of code that checks the request's content type is arranged to avoid a `NullPointerException` if the `getContentType()` call returns `null`.

A servlet may wish to call the `getContentLength()` method before calling `getParameter()` to prevent denial of service attacks. A rogue client may send an absurdly large amount of data as part of a POST request, hoping to slow the server to a crawl as the servlet's `getParameter()` method churns over the data. A servlet can use `getContentLength()` to verify that the length is reasonable, perhaps less than 4K, as a preventive measure.

Receiving files using the input stream

A servlet can also receive a file upload using its input stream. Before we see how, it's important to note that file uploading is experimental and not supported in all browsers. Netscape first supported file uploads with Netscape Navigator 3; Microsoft first supported it with Internet Explorer 4.

The full file upload specification is contained in experimental RFC 1867, available at *http://www.ietf.org/rfc/rfc1867.txt*. The short summary is that any number of files and parameters can be sent as form data in a single POST request. The POST request is formatted differently than standard `application/x-www-form-urlencoded` form data and indicates this fact by setting its content type to `multipart/form-data`.

It's fairly simple to write the client half of a file upload. The following HTML generates a form that asks for a user's name and a file to upload. Note the addition of the `ENCTYPE` attribute and the use of a `FILE` input type:

```
<FORM ACTION="/servlet/UploadTest" ENCTYPE="multipart/form-data" METHOD=POST>
What is your name? <INPUT TYPE=TEXT NAME=submitter> <BR>
Which file do you want to upload? <INPUT TYPE=FILE NAME=file> <BR>
<INPUT TYPE=SUBMIT>
</FORM>
```

A user receiving this form sees a page that looks something like Figure 4-3. A filename can be entered in the text area, or it can be selected by browsing. After selection, the user submits the form as usual.

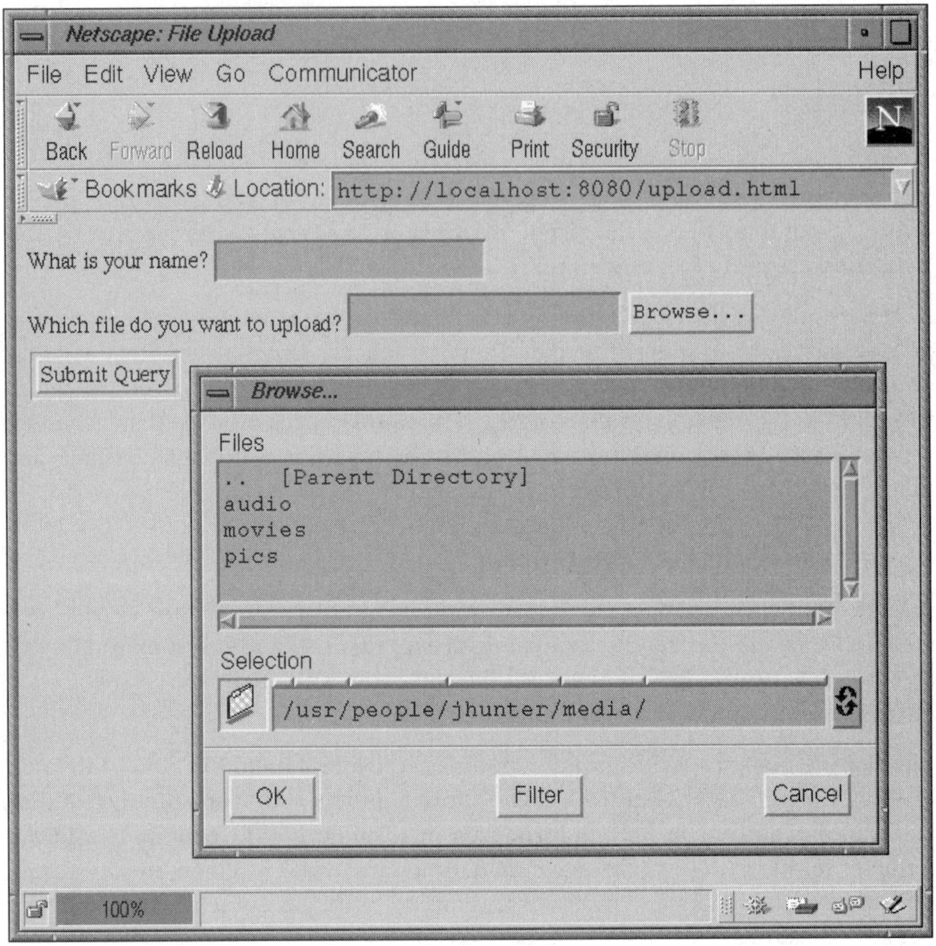

Figure 4-3. Choosing a file to upload

The server's responsibilities during a file upload are slightly more complicated. From the receiving servlet's perspective, the submission is nothing more than a raw data stream in its input stream—a data stream formatted according to the multipart/form-data content type given in RFC 1867. The Servlet API, lamentably, provides no methods to aid in the parsing of the data. To simplify your life (and ours since we don't want to explain RFC 1867), Jason has written a utility class that does the work for you. It's named MultipartRequest and is shown in Example 4-18 later in this section.

MultipartRequest wraps around a ServletRequest and presents a simple API to the servlet programmer. The class has two constructors:

```
public MultipartRequest(ServletRequest request, String saveDirectory,
                        int maxPostSize) throws IOException
public MultipartRequest(ServletRequest request,
                        String saveDirectory) throws IOException
```

Each of these methods creates a new `MultipartRequest` object to handle the specified request, saving any uploaded files to `saveDirectory`. Both constructors actually parse the `multipart/form-data` content and throw an `IOException` if there's any problem. The constructor that takes a `maxPostSize` parameter also throws an `IOException` if the uploaded content is larger than `maxPostSize`. The second constructor assumes a default `maxPostSize` of 1 MB.

The `MultipartRequest` class has six public methods that let you get at information about the request. You'll notice that many of these methods are modeled after `ServletRequest` methods. Use `getParameterNamess()` to retrieve the names of all the request parameters:

```
public Enumeration MultipartRequest.getParameterNames()
```

This method returns the names of all the parameters as an `Enumeration` of `String` objects or an empty `Enumeration` if there are no parameters.

To get the value of a named parameter, use `getParameter()`:

```
public String MultipartRequest.getParameter(String name)
```

This method returns the value of the named parameter as a `String` or `null` if the parameter was not given. The value is guaranteed to be in its normal, decoded form. If the parameter has multiple values, only the last one is returned.

Use `getFileNames()` to get a list of all the uploaded files:

```
public Enumeration MultipartRequest.getFileNames()
```

This method returns the names of all the uploaded files as an `Enumeration` of `String` objects, or an empty `Enumeration` if there are no uploaded files. Note that each filename is the name specified by the HTML form's `name` attribute, not by the user. Once you have the name of a file, you can get its file system name using `getFilesystemName()`:

```
public String MultipartRequest.getFilesystemName(String name)
```

This method returns the file system name of the specified file or `null` if the file was not included in the upload. A file system name is the name specified by the user. It is also the name under which the file is actually saved. You can get the content type of the file with `getContentType()`:

```
public String MultipartRequest.getContentType(String name)
```

This method returns the content type of the specified file (as supplied by the client browser) or null if the file was not included in the upload. Finally, you can get a java.io.File object for the file with getFile():

```
public File MultipartRequest.getFile(String name)
```

This method returns a File object for the specified file saved on the server's file system or null if the file was not included in the upload.

Example 4-17 shows how a servlet uses MultipartRequest. The servlet does nothing but display the statistics for what was uploaded. Notice that it does not delete the files it saves.

Example 4-17. Handling a file upload

```
import java.io.*;
import java.util.*;
import javax.servlet.*;
import javax.servlet.http.*;

import com.oreilly.servlet.MultipartRequest;

public class UploadTest extends HttpServlet {

  public void doPost(HttpServletRequest req, HttpServletResponse res)
                            throws ServletException, IOException {
    res.setContentType("text/html");
    PrintWriter out = res.getWriter();

    try {
      // Blindly take it on faith this is a multipart/form-data request

      // Construct a MultipartRequest to help read the information.
      // Pass in the request, a directory to save files to, and the
      // maximum POST size we should attempt to handle.
      // Here we (rudely) write to the server root and impose 5 Meg limit.
      MultipartRequest multi =
        new MultipartRequest(req, ".", 5 * 1024 * 1024);

      out.println("<HTML>");
      out.println("<HEAD><TITLE>UploadTest</TITLE></HEAD>");
      out.println("<BODY>");
      out.println("<H1>UploadTest</H1>");

      // Print the parameters we received
      out.println("<H3>Params:</H3>");
      out.println("<PRE>");
      Enumeration params = multi.getParameterNames();
```

Example 4-17. Handling a file upload (continued)

```
      while (params.hasMoreElements()) {
        String name = (String)params.nextElement();
        String value = multi.getParameter(name);
        out.println(name + " = " + value);
      }
      out.println("</PRE>");

      // Show which files we received
      out.println("<H3>Files:</H3>");
      out.println("<PRE>");
      Enumeration files = multi.getFileNames();
      while (files.hasMoreElements()) {
        String name = (String)files.nextElement();
        String filename = multi.getFilesystemName(name);
        String type = multi.getContentType(name);
        File f = multi.getFile(name);
        out.println("name: " + name);
        out.println("filename: " + filename);
        out.println("type: " + type);
        if (f != null) {
          out.println("length: " + f.length());
          out.println();
        }
        out.println("</PRE>");
      }
    }
    catch (Exception e) {
      out.println("<PRE>");
      e.printStackTrace(out);
      out.println("</PRE>");
    }
    out.println("</BODY></HTML>");
  }
}
```

The servlet passes its request object to the `MultipartRequest` constructor, along with a directory relative to the server root where the uploaded files are to be saved (because large files may not fit in memory) and a maximum POST size of 5 MB. The servlet then uses `MultipartRequest` to iterate over the parameters that were sent. Notice that the `MultipartRequest` API for handling parameters matches that of `ServletRequest`. Finally, the servlet uses its `MultipartRequest` to iterate over the files that were sent. For each file, it gets the file's name (as specified on the form), file system name (as specified by the user), and content type. It also gets a `File` reference and uses it to display the length of the saved file. If there are any problems, the servlet reports the exception to the user.

Example 4-18 shows the code for `MultipartRequest`. This class could be written more elegantly using a regular expression library, as discussed in Chapter 13, *Odds and Ends*; however, not doing so allows this class to be self-contained and works just as well. We aren't going to elaborate on the class here—you should read the comments if you want to understand everything that is going on. This class uses some of the techniques that we've covered in this chapter, so it is a good review of the material. You should also feel free to skip this example for now and come back to it later if you'd like.

Example 4-18. The MultipartRequest class

```
package com.oreilly.servlet;

import java.io.*;
import java.util.*;
import javax.servlet.*;

public class MultipartRequest {

  private static final int DEFAULT_MAX_POST_SIZE = 1024 * 1024;  // 1 Meg

  private ServletRequest req;
  private File dir;
  private int maxSize;

  private Hashtable parameters = new Hashtable();  // name - value
  private Hashtable files = new Hashtable();        // name - UploadedFile

  public MultipartRequest(ServletRequest request,
                          String saveDirectory) throws IOException {
    this(request, saveDirectory, DEFAULT_MAX_POST_SIZE);
  }

  public MultipartRequest(ServletRequest request,
                          String saveDirectory,
                          int maxPostSize) throws IOException {
    // Sanity check values
    if (request == null)
      throw new IllegalArgumentException("request cannot be null");
    if (saveDirectory == null)
      throw new IllegalArgumentException("saveDirectory cannot be null");
    if (maxPostSize <= 0) {
      throw new IllegalArgumentException("maxPostSize must be positive");
    }

    // Save the request, dir, and max size
    req = request;
    dir = new File(saveDirectory);
```

Example 4-18. The MultipartRequest class (continued)

```
    maxSize = maxPostSize;

    // Check saveDirectory is truly a directory
    if (!dir.isDirectory())
      throw new IllegalArgumentException("Not a directory: " + saveDirectory);

    // Check saveDirectory is writable
    if (!dir.canWrite())
      throw new IllegalArgumentException("Not writable: " + saveDirectory);

    // Now parse the request saving data to "parameters" and "files";
    // write the file contents to the saveDirectory
    readRequest();
  }

  public Enumeration getParameterNames() {
    return parameters.keys();
  }

  public Enumeration getFileNames() {
    return files.keys();
  }

  public String getParameter(String name) {
    try {
      String param = (String)parameters.get(name);
      if (param.equals("")) return null;
      return param;
    }
    catch (Exception e) {
      return null;
    }
  }

  public String getFilesystemName(String name) {
    try {
      UploadedFile file = (UploadedFile)files.get(name);
      return file.getFilesystemName();  // may be null
    }
    catch (Exception e) {
      return null;
    }
  }

  public String getContentType(String name) {
    try {
      UploadedFile file = (UploadedFile)files.get(name);
      return file.getContentType();  // may be null
```

Example 4-18. The MultipartRequest class (continued)

```
    }
    catch (Exception e) {
      return null;
    }
  }

  public File getFile(String name) {
    try {
      UploadedFile file = (UploadedFile)files.get(name);
      return file.getFile();  // may be null
    }
    catch (Exception e) {
      return null;
    }
  }

  protected void readRequest() throws IOException {
    // Check the content type to make sure it's "multipart/form-data"
    String type = req.getContentType();
    if (type == null ||
        !type.toLowerCase().startsWith("multipart/form-data")) {
      throw new IOException("Posted content type isn't multipart/form-data");
    }

    // Check the content length to prevent denial of service attacks
    int length = req.getContentLength();
    if (length > maxSize) {
      throw new IOException("Posted content length of " + length +
                            " exceeds limit of " + maxSize);
    }

    // Get the boundary string; it's included in the content type.
    // Should look something like "-----------------------12012133613061"
    String boundary = extractBoundary(type);
    if (boundary == null) {
      throw new IOException("Separation boundary was not specified");
    }

    // Construct the special input stream we'll read from
    MultipartInputStreamHandler in =
        new MultipartInputStreamHandler(req.getInputStream(), boundary, length);

    // Read the first line, should be the first boundary
    String line = in.readLine();
    if (line == null) {
      throw new IOException("Corrupt form data: premature ending");
    }
```

Example 4-18. The MultipartRequest class (continued)

```
    // Verify that the line is the boundary
    if (!line.startsWith(boundary)) {
      throw new IOException("Corrupt form data: no leading boundary");
    }

    // Now that we're just beyond the first boundary, loop over each part
    boolean done = false;
    while (!done) {
      done = readNextPart(in, boundary);
    }
  }

  protected boolean readNextPart(MultipartInputStreamHandler in,
                               String boundary) throws IOException {
    // Read the first line, should look like this:
    // content-disposition: form-data; name="field1"; filename="file1.txt"
    String line = in.readLine();
    if (line == null) {
      // No parts left, we're done
      return true;
    }

    // Parse the content-disposition line
    String[] dispInfo = extractDispositionInfo(line);
    String disposition = dispInfo[0];
    String name = dispInfo[1];
    String filename = dispInfo[2];

    // Now onto the next line. This will either be empty
    // or contain a Content-Type and then an empty line.
    line = in.readLine();
    if (line == null) {
      // No parts left, we're done
      return true;
    }

    // Get the content type, or null if none specified
    String contentType = extractContentType(line);
    if (contentType != null) {
      // Eat the empty line
      line = in.readLine();
      if (line == null || line.length() > 0) {  // line should be empty
        throw new
          IOException("Malformed line after content type: " + line);
      }
    }
    else {
      // Assume a default content type
```

Example 4-18. The MultipartRequest class (continued)

```
        contentType = "application/octet-stream";
    }

    // Now, finally, we read the content (end after reading the boundary)
    if (filename == null) {
      // This is a parameter
      String value = readParameter(in, boundary);
      parameters.put(name, value);
    }
    else {
      // This is a file
      readAndSaveFile(in, boundary, filename);
      if (filename.equals("unknown")) {
        files.put(name, new UploadedFile(null, null, null));
      }
      else {
        files.put(name,
          new UploadedFile(dir.toString(), filename, contentType));
      }
    }
    return false;  // there's more to read
  }

  protected String readParameter(MultipartInputStreamHandler in,
                                 String boundary) throws IOException {
    StringBuffer sbuf = new StringBuffer();
    String line;

    while ((line = in.readLine()) != null) {
      if (line.startsWith(boundary)) break;
      sbuf.append(line + "\r\n");  // add the \r\n in case there are many lines
    }

    if (sbuf.length() == 0) {
      return null;  // nothing read
    }

    sbuf.setLength(sbuf.length() - 2);  // cut off the last line's \r\n
    return sbuf.toString();  // no URL decoding needed
  }

  protected void readAndSaveFile(MultipartInputStreamHandler in,
                                 String boundary,
                                 String filename) throws IOException {
    File f = new File(dir + File.separator + filename);
    FileOutputStream fos = new FileOutputStream(f);
    BufferedOutputStream out = new BufferedOutputStream(fos, 8 * 1024); // 8K
```

Example 4-18. The MultipartRequest class (continued)

```
    byte[] bbuf = new byte[8 * 1024];   // 8K
    int result;
    String line;

    // ServletInputStream.readLine() has the annoying habit of
    // adding a \r\n to the end of the last line.
    // Since we want a byte-for-byte transfer, we have to cut those chars.
    boolean rnflag = false;
    while ((result = in.readLine(bbuf, 0, bbuf.length)) != -1) {
      // Check for boundary
      if (result > 2 && bbuf[0] == '-' && bbuf[1] == '-') { // quick pre-check
        line = new String(bbuf, 0, result, "ISO-8859-1");
        if (line.startsWith(boundary)) break;
      }
      // Are we supposed to write \r\n for the last iteration?
      if (rnflag) {
        out.write('\r'); out.write('\n');
        rnflag = false;
      }
      // Write the buffer, postpone any ending \r\n
      if (result >= 2 &&
          bbuf[result - 2] == '\r' &&
          bbuf[result - 1] == '\n') {
        out.write(bbuf, 0, result - 2);  // skip the last 2 chars
        rnflag = true;  // make a note to write them on the next iteration
      }
      else {
        out.write(bbuf, 0, result);
      }
    }
    out.flush();
    out.close();
    fos.close();
  }

  private String extractBoundary(String line) {
    int index = line.indexOf("boundary=");
    if (index == -1) {
      return null;
    }
    String boundary = line.substring(index + 9);  // 9 for "boundary="

    // The real boundary is always preceded by an extra "--"
    boundary = "--" + boundary;

    return boundary;
  }
```

Example 4-18. The MultipartRequest class (continued)

```java
private String[] extractDispositionInfo(String line) throws IOException {
  // Return the line's data as an array: disposition, name, filename
  String[] retval = new String[3];

  // Convert the line to a lowercase string without the ending \r\n
  // Keep the original line for error messages and for variable names.
  String origline = line;
  line = origline.toLowerCase();

  // Get the content disposition, should be "form-data"
  int start = line.indexOf("content-disposition: ");
  int end = line.indexOf(";");
  if (start == -1 || end == -1) {
    throw new IOException("Content disposition corrupt: " + origline);
  }
  String disposition = line.substring(start + 21, end);
  if (!disposition.equals("form-data")) {
    throw new IOException("Invalid content disposition: " + disposition);
  }

  // Get the field name
  start = line.indexOf("name=\"", end);  // start at last semicolon
  end = line.indexOf("\"", start + 7);    // skip name=\"
  if (start == -1 || end == -1) {
    throw new IOException("Content disposition corrupt: " + origline);
  }
  String name = origline.substring(start + 6, end);

  // Get the filename, if given
  String filename = null;
  start = line.indexOf("filename=\"", end + 2);  // start after name
  end = line.indexOf("\"", start + 10);           // skip filename=\"
  if (start != -1 && end != -1) {                 // note the !=
    filename = origline.substring(start + 10, end);
    // The filename may contain a full path. Cut to just the filename.
    int slash =
      Math.max(filename.lastIndexOf('/'), filename.lastIndexOf('\\'));
    if (slash > -1) {
      filename = filename.substring(slash + 1);  // past last slash
    }
    if (filename.equals("")) filename = "unknown"; // sanity check
  }

  // Return a String array: disposition, name, filename
  retval[0] = disposition;
  retval[1] = name;
  retval[2] = filename;
  return retval;
```

Example 4-18. The MultipartRequest class (continued)

```
    }

    private String extractContentType(String line) throws IOException {
      String contentType = null;

      // Convert the line to a lowercase string
      String origline = line;
      line = origline.toLowerCase();

      // Get the content type, if any
      if (line.startsWith("content-type")) {
        int start = line.indexOf(" ");
        if (start == -1) {
          throw new IOException("Content type corrupt: " + origline);
        }
        contentType = line.substring(start + 1);
      }
      else if (line.length() != 0) {  // no content type, so should be empty
        throw new IOException("Malformed line after disposition: " + origline);
      }

      return contentType;
    }
}


// A class to hold information about an uploaded file.
//
class UploadedFile {

  private String dir;
  private String filename;
  private String type;

  UploadedFile(String dir, String filename, String type) {
    this.dir = dir;
    this.filename = filename;
    this.type = type;
  }

  public String getContentType() {
    return type;
  }

  public String getFilesystemName() {
    return filename;
  }
```

Example 4-18. The MultipartRequest class (continued)

```
  public File getFile() {
    if (dir == null || filename == null) {
      return null;
    }
    else {
      return new File(dir + File.separator + filename);
    }
  }
}


// A class to aid in reading multipart/form-data from a ServletInputStream.
// It keeps track of how many bytes have been read and detects when the
// Content-Length limit has been reached. This is necessary because some
// servlet engines are slow to notice the end of stream.
//
class MultipartInputStreamHandler {

  ServletInputStream in;
  String boundary;
  int totalExpected;
  int totalRead = 0;
  byte[] buf = new byte[8 * 1024];

  public MultipartInputStreamHandler(ServletInputStream in,
                                     String boundary,
                                     int totalExpected) {
    this.in = in;
    this.boundary = boundary;
    this.totalExpected = totalExpected;
  }

  public String readLine() throws IOException {
    StringBuffer sbuf = new StringBuffer();
    int result;
    String line;

    do {
      result = this.readLine(buf, 0, buf.length);  // this.readLine() does +=
      if (result != -1) {
        sbuf.append(new String(buf, 0, result, "ISO-8859-1"));
      }
    } while (result == buf.length);  // loop only if the buffer was filled

    if (sbuf.length() == 0) {
      return null;  // nothing read, must be at the end of stream
    }
```

Example 4-18. The MultipartRequest class (continued)

```
    sbuf.setLength(sbuf.length() - 2);   // cut off the trailing \r\n
    return sbuf.toString();
  }

  public int readLine(byte b[], int off, int len) throws IOException {
    if (totalRead >= totalExpected) {
      return -1;
    }
    else {
      int result = in.readLine(b, off, len);
      if (result > 0) {
        totalRead += result;
      }
      return result;
    }
  }
}
```

Extra Attributes

Sometimes a servlet needs to know something about a request that's not available via any of the previously mentioned methods. In these cases, there is one last alternative, the `getAttribute()` method. Remember how `ServletContext` has a `getAttribute()` method that returns server-specific attributes about the server itself? `ServletRequest` also has a `getAttribute()` method:

```
    public Object ServletRequest.getAttribute(String name)
```

This method returns the value of a server-specific attribute for the request or `null` if the server does not support the named request attribute. This method allows a server to provide a servlet with custom information about a request. For example, the Java Web Server makes three attributes available: `javax.net.ssl.cipher_suite`, `javax.net.ssl.peer_certificates`, and `javax.net.ssl.session`. A servlet running in the Java Web Server can use these attributes to inspect the details of an SSL connection with the client.

Example 4-19 shows a code snippet that uses `getAttribute()` to query the server on the details of its SSL connection. Remember, these attributes are server-specific and may not be available in servers other than the Java Web Server.

Example 4-19. Getting the attributes available in the Java Web Server

```
import javax.security.cert.X509Certificate;
import javax.net.ssl.SSLSession;

out.println("<PRE>");
```

Example 4-19. Getting the attributes available in the Java Web Server (continued)

```java
// Display the cipher suite in use
String cipherSuite =
  (String) req.getAttribute("javax.net.ssl.cipher_suite");
out.println("Cipher Suite: " + cipherSuite);

// Display the client's certificates, if there are any
if (cipherSuite != null) {
  X509Certificate[] certChain =
    (X509Certificate[]) req.getAttribute("javax.net.ssl.peer_certificates");
  if (certChain != null) {
    for (int i = 0; i < certChain.length; i++) {
      out.println ("Client Certificate [" + i + "] = "
                    + certChain[i].toString());
    }
  }
}

out.println("</PRE>");
```

The servlet's output on receiving a VeriSign certificate is shown below. What it means is discussed in Chapter 8.

```
Cipher Suite:  SSL_RSA_EXPORT_WITH_RC4_40_MD5
Client Certificate [0] = [
  X.509v3 certificate,
  Subject is OID.1.2.840.113549.1.9.1=#160F6A68756E746572407367692E636F6D,
CN=Jason Hunter, OU=Digital ID Class 1 - Netscape,
OU="www.verisign.com/repository/CPS Incorp. by Ref.,LIAB.LTD(c)96",
OU=VeriSign Class 1 CA - Individual Subscriber, O="VeriSign, Inc.",
L=Internet
  Key:  algorithm = [RSA], exponent = 0x     010001, modulus =
    b35ed5e7 45fc5328 e3f5ce70 838cc25d 0a0efd41 df4d3e1b 64f70617 528546c8
    fae46995 9922a093 7a54584d d466bee7 e7b5c259 c7827489 6478e1a9 3a16d45f
  Validity until
  Issuer is OU=VeriSign Class 1 CA - Individual Subscriber, O="VeriSign,
Inc.",
    L=Internet
  Issuer signature used [MD5withRSA]
  Serial number =      20556dc0 9e31dfa4 ada6e10d 77954704
]
Client Certificate [1] = [
  X.509v3 certificate,
  Subject is OU=VeriSign Class 1 CA - Individual Subscriber, O="VeriSign,
Inc.", L=Internet
  Key:  algorithm = [RSA], exponent = 0x     010001, modulus =
    b614a6cf 4dd0050d d8ca23d0 6faab429 92638e2c f86f96d7 2e9d764b 11b1368d
    57c9c3fd 1cc6bafe 1e08ba33 ca95eabe e35bcd06 a8b7791d 442aed73 f2b15283
    68107064 91d73e6b f9f75d9d 14439b6e 97459881 47d12dcb ddbb72d7 4c3f71aa
```

```
    e240f254 39bc16ee cf7cecba db3f6c2a b316b186 129dae93 34d5b8d5 d0f73ea9
   Validity  until
   Issuer is OU=Class 1 Public Primary Certification Authority, O="VeriSign,
Inc.", C=US
   Issuer signature used [MD2withRSA]
   Serial number =      521f351d f2707e00 2bbeca59 8704d539
  ]
```

Servers are free to provide whatever attributes they choose, or even no attributes at all. The only rules are that attribute names should follow the same convention as package names, with the package names `java.*` and `javax.*` reserved for use by the Java Software division of Sun Microsystems (formerly known as JavaSoft) and `com.sun.*` reserved for use by Sun Microsystems. You should see your server's documentation for a list of its attributes. There is no `getAttributeNames()` method to help.

5

Sending HTML Information

In the previous chapter, we learned that a servlet has access to all sorts of information—information about the client, about the server, about the request, and even about itself. Now it's time to look at what a servlet can do with that information, by learning how it sets and sends information.

The chapter begins with a review of how a servlet returns a normal HTML response, fully explaining some methods we glossed over in previous examples. Next we cover how to reduce the overhead involved in returning a response by keeping alive a connection to the client. Then we explore the extra things you can do with HTML and HTTP, including using support classes to objectify the HTML output, returning errors and other status codes, sending custom header information, redirecting the request, using client pull, detecting when the user disconnects, and writing data to the server log.

The Structure of a Response

An HTTP servlet can return three kinds of things to the client: a single status code, any number of HTTP headers, and a response body. A status code is an integer value that describes, as you would expect, the status of the response. The status code can indicate success or failure, or it can tell the client software to take further action to finish the request. The numerical status code is often accompanied by a "reason phrase" that describes the status in prose better understood by a human. Usually, a status code works behind the scenes and is interpreted by the browser software. Sometimes, especially when things go wrong, a browser may show the status code to the user. The most famous status code is probably the "404 Not Found" code, sent by a web server when it cannot locate a requested URL.

We saw HTTP headers in the previous chapter when clients used them to send extra information along with a request. In this chapter, we'll see how a servlet can send HTTP headers as part of its response.

The response body is the main content of the response. For an HTML page, the response body is the HTML itself. For a graphic, the response body contains the bytes that make up the image. A response body can be of any type and of any length; the client knows what to expect by reading and interpreting the HTTP headers in the response.

A generic servlet is much simpler than an HTTP servlet—it returns only a response body to its client. It's possible, however, for a subclass of `Generic-Servlet` to present an API that divides this single response body into a more elaborate structure, giving the appearance of returning multiple items. In fact, this is exactly what HTTP servlets do. At the lowest level, a web server sends its entire response as a stream of bytes to the client. Any methods that set status codes or headers are abstractions above that.

It's important to understand this because even though a servlet programmer doesn't have to know the details of the HTTP protocol, the protocol does affect the order in which a servlet can call its methods. Specifically, the HTTP protocol specifies that the status code and headers must be sent *before* the response body. A servlet, therefore, should be careful to always set its status codes and headers before returning any of its response body. Some servers, including the Java Web Server, internally buffer some length of a servlet's response body (usually about 4K)—this allows you some freedom to set the status codes and headers even after a servlet has written a short amount of response body. However, this behavior is server implementation dependent, and as a wise servlet programmer, you'll forget all about it!

Sending a Normal Response

Let's begin our discussion of servlet responses with another look at the first servlet in this book, the `HelloWorld` servlet, shown in Example 5-1. We hope it looks a lot simpler to you now than it did back in Chapter 2, *HTTP Servlet Basics*.

Example 5-1. Hello again

```
import java.io.*;
import javax.servlet.*;
import javax.servlet.http.*;

public class HelloWorld extends HttpServlet {

  public void doGet(HttpServletRequest req, HttpServletResponse res)
```

Example 5-1. Hello again (continued)

```
                                   throws ServletException, IOException {

    res.setContentType("text/html");
    PrintWriter out = res.getWriter();

    out.println("<HTML>");
    out.println("<HEAD><TITLE>Hello World</TITLE></HEAD>");
    out.println("<BODY>");
    out.println("<BIG>Hello World</BIG>");
    out.println("</BODY></HTML>");
  }
}
```

This servlet uses two methods and a class that have been only briefly mentioned before. The setContentType() method of ServletResponse sets the content type of the response to be the specified type:

```
    public void ServletResponse.setContentType(String type)
```

In an HTTP servlet, this method sets the Content-Type HTTP header.

The getWriter() method returns a PrintWriter for writing character-based response data:

```
    public PrintWriter ServletResponse.getWriter() throws IOException
```

The writer encodes the characters according to whatever charset is given in the content type. If no charset is specified, as is generally the case, the writer uses the ISO-8859-1 (Latin-1) encoding appropriate for Western European languages. Charsets are covered in depth in Chapter 12, *Internationalization,* so for now just remember that it's good form to always set the content type before you get a PrintWriter. This method throws an IllegalStateException if getOutput-Stream() has already been called for this response; it throws an UnsupportedEncodingException if the encoding of the output stream is unsupported or unknown.

In addition to using a PrintWriter to return a response, a servlet can use a special subclass of java.io.OutputStream to write binary data—the Serv-letOutputStream, which is defined in javax.servlet. You can get a ServletOutputStream with getOutputStream():

```
    public ServletOutputStream ServletResponse.getOutputStream() throws
    IOException
```

This method returns an ServletOutputStream for writing binary (byte-at-a-time) response data. No encoding is performed. This method throws an Illegal-StateException if getWriter() has already been called for this response.

The `ServletOutputStream` class resembles the standard Java `PrintStream` class. In the Servlet API Version 1.0, this class was used for all servlet output, both textual and binary. In the Servlet API Version 2.0, however, it has been relegated to handling binary output only. As a direct subclass of `OutputStream`, it makes available the `write()`, `flush()`, and `close()` methods of the `OutputStream` class. To these it adds its own `print()` and `println()` methods for writing most of the primitive Java data types (see Appendix A, *Servlet API Quick Reference*, for a complete list). The only difference between the `ServletOutputStream` interface and that of a `PrintStream` is that the `print()` and `println()` methods of `ServletOutputStream` inexplicably cannot directly print parameters of type `Object` or `char[]`.

Using Persistent Connections

Persistent connections (sometimes called "keep-alive" connections) can be used to optimize the way servlets return content to the client. To understand how this optimization works, you first need to understand how HTTP connections work. We'll keep this at a high level and only go as low as is necessary to explain the basic idea. The details are well covered in Clinton Wong's *Web Client Programming* (O'Reilly).

When a client, such as a browser, wants to request a web document from a server, it begins by establishing a socket connection to the server. Over this connection, the client makes its request and then receives the server's response. The client indicates it has finished its request by sending a blank line; the server, in turn, indicates that the response is complete by closing the socket connection.

So far, so good. But what if the retrieved page contains <IMG> tags or <APPLET> tags that require the client to retrieve more content from the server? Well, another socket connection is used. If a page contains 10 graphics along with an applet made up of 25 classes, that's 36 connections needed to transfer the page. No wonder some people say WWW stands for the World Wide Wait! This approach is like ordering a pizza, but making a separate phone call for each topping.

A better approach is to use the same socket connection to retrieve more than one piece of a page, something called a *persistent connection*. The trick with a persistent connection is that the client and server must somehow agree on where the server's response ends and where the client's next request begins. They could try to use a token like a blank line, but what if the response itself contains a blank line? The way persistent connections work is that the server just tells the client how big the response body will be by setting the `Content-Length` header as part of the response. The client then knows that after that much response body, it has control of the socket again.

Most servers internally manage the `Content-Length` header for the static files they serve, but do not do the same for the servlets they serve. That's left to the servlets themselves. A servlet can gain the advantages of a persistent connection for its dynamic content by using the `setContentLength()` method:

```
public void ServletResponse.setContentLength(int len)
```

This method sets the length (in bytes) of the content being returned by the server. In an HTTP servlet, the method sets the HTTP `Content-Length` header. Note that using this method is optional. If you use it, however, your servlets will be able to take advantage of persistent connections when they are available. The client will also be able to display an accurate progress monitor during the download.

If you do call `setContentLength()`, there are two caveats: a servlet must call this method before sending the response body, and the given length must be exact. If it's off by even one byte, you will have problems.[*] This sounds more difficult than it really is. The trick is for a servlet to use a `ByteArrayOutputStream` to buffer the output, as shown in Example 5-2.

Example 5-2. A servlet using persistent connections

```
import java.io.*;
import javax.servlet.*;
import javax.servlet.http.*;

public class KeepAlive extends HttpServlet {

  public void doGet(HttpServletRequest req, HttpServletResponse res)
                            throws ServletException, IOException {

    res.setContentType("text/html");

    // Set up a PrintStream built around a special output stream
    ByteArrayOutputStream bytes = new ByteArrayOutputStream(1024);
    PrintWriter out = new PrintWriter(bytes, true);  // true forces flushing

    out.println("<HTML>");
    out.println("<HEAD><TITLE>Hello World</TITLE></HEAD>");
    out.println("<BODY>");
    out.println("<BIG>Hello World</BIG>");
    out.println("</BODY></HTML>");

    // Set the content length to the size of the buffer
    res.setContentLength(bytes.size());
```

---

[*] For example, with the Java Web Server, if a servlet sets the length too short, the server throws an `IOException` saying there was a "write past end of stream". If a servlet sets the length too long, the client stalls as it waits for the rest of the response.

Example 5-2. A servlet using persistent connections (continued)

```
    // Send the buffer
    bytes.writeTo(res.getOutputStream());
  }
}
```

Instead of writing to the `PrintWriter` returned by `getWriter()`, this servlet writes to a `PrintWriter` built around a `ByteArrayOutputStream`. This array grows as necessary to accommodate whatever output the servlet sends. When the servlet is ready to exit, it sets the content length to be the size of the buffer and then sends the contents of the buffer to the client. Notice that the bytes are sent using the byte-oriented `ServletOutputStream`. With this simple modification, a servlet can take advantage of a persistent connection.

It is important to note that persistent connections come with a price. Buffering all the output and sending it all in one batch requires extra memory, and it may delay the time at which a client begins receiving data. For servlets with short responses, persistent connections make sense, but for servlets with long responses, the memory overhead and delay probably outweigh the benefit of opening fewer connections.

It is also important to note that not all servers and not all clients support persistent connections. That said, it's still appropriate for a servlet to set its content length. This information will be used by those servers that support persistent connections and ignored by the others.

HTML Generation

No, "HTML Generation" is not another name for the children born in the 1980s, many of whom grew up browsing the web—although Jason and Will, saddled with the Generation X moniker, feel that would be only fair. HTML generation is an alternate way for servlets to send HTML content to clients.

So far, every example in this book has generated its HTML by hand, as one long `String` that is sent to the client. This strategy works fine for small web pages (like book examples), but it quickly becomes unwieldy for larger, more complicated pages. For that type of page, it's sometimes helpful to use an HTML generation package.

An HTML generation package provides a servlet with a set of classes that abstract away the details of HTML, in particular, the HTML tags. The level of abstraction depends on the package: some put only the thinnest veneer above the HTML tags, leaving the nitty-gritty details (such as opening and closing each HTML tag) to the programmer. Using packages such as these is similar to writing HTML by hand

and is not discussed here. Other packages elegantly abstract away the HTML speci-fication and treat HTML as just another set of Java objects. A web page is seen as an object that can contain other HTML objects (such as lists and tables) that can contain yet more HTML objects (such as list items and table cells). This object-oriented approach can greatly simplify the task of generating HTML and make a servlet easier to write, easier to maintain, and sometimes even more efficient.

Generating Hello World

Let's look at an example to see how object-oriented HTML generation works. Example 5-3 shows the ubiquitous `HelloWorld` servlet, rewritten to take advan-tage of WebLogic's htmlKona package (available for free evaluation and purchase at *http://www.weblogic.com*—you may need to poke around a bit to find it).

Example 5-3. Hello, htmlKona

```java
import java.io.*;
import javax.servlet.*;
import javax.servlet.http.*;

import weblogic.html.*;

public class HtmlKonaHello extends HttpServlet {

  public void doGet(HttpServletRequest req, HttpServletResponse res)
                            throws ServletException, IOException {

    res.setContentType("text/html");

    ServletPage page = new ServletPage();
    page.getHead().addElement(new TitleElement("Hello World"));
    page.getBody().addElement(new BigElement("Hello World!"));

    page.output(res.getOutputStream());
  }
}
```

Note how all the HTML tags have been replaced with objects. This servlet first creates a new `ServletPage` object that represents the web page it will return. Then, it adds a "Hello World" title to the page's head section and a "Hello World!" big string to its body section. Finally, the servlet outputs the page to its output stream.[*] That's how object-oriented HTML generation works: get a page object, add component objects to it, and send it to the output stream.

---

[*] We must use the `ServletOutputStream` here since htmlKona was not written to output its page to a `PrintWriter`.

One advantage of HTML generation should already be apparent: it ensures valid HTML. HTML generation eliminates the possibility for a misspelled <TITLE> open tag or a forgotten </TITLE> close tag. We'll admit it's not an advantage worth writing home about, but it is appealing to not have to remember to open and close every tag or to clutter your code with HTML. Unfortunately, object-oriented HTML has the fairly serious drawback that it can litter memory with a multitude of small objects, requiring more frequent garbage collection.

Generating a Weather Forecast

That's how HTML generation works for a simple web page. Now let's create a more complicated web page, so we can test how HTML generation scales to handle the harder challenges. Figure 5-1 shows a hypothetical web page that displays the current weather and an extended forecast, the kind you might find on Yahoo! or CNN. We've kept it simple for the sake of space, but it still includes enough components to make an interesting example.

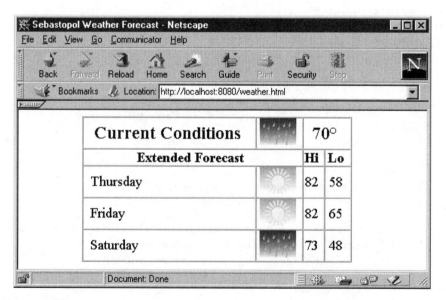

Figure 5-1. Oh, the weather outside is delightful

Imagine a servlet creating this web page. Assuming the servlet already has access to the current conditions and forecast information, how would the servlet do it? We will examine and discuss three strategies:

- Constructing the HTML by hand
- Using an HTML generator
- Using an HTML generator creatively

The first strategy, constructing the HTML by hand (Example 5-4), is the standard approach demonstrated elsewhere in this book. A servlet implemented using this strategy acts as a baseline against which we can compare the other two servlets. The second approach, using an HTML generator (Example 5-5), constructs the web page as a set of objects. This is like the HelloWorld example, just on a much larger scale. The third strategy, using an HTML generator and some creativity (Example 5-6), takes the second servlet and simplifies it by reusing objects and subclassing.

Weather forecast constructed by hand

Example 5-4 shows a servlet that creates the weather forecast page without using HTML generation, manually sending its content wrapped with almost a hundred HTML tags.

Example 5-4. Weather forecast constructed by hand

```
import java.io.*;
import java.text.*;
import java.util.*;
import javax.servlet.*;
import javax.servlet.http.*;

public class WeatherHtml extends HttpServlet {

    // Some static final variables to populate the page...
    // These would normally come from a database or
    // maybe another servlet that retrieved it as POST data.

    static final int currentTemp = 70;
    static final String currentImage = "/images/rainy.gif";
    static final String[] forecastDay = { "Thursday",
                                           "Friday",
                                           "Saturday" };
    static final String[] forecastImage = { "/images/sunny.gif",
                                             "/images/sunny.gif",
                                             "/images/rainy.gif" };
    static final int[] forecastHi = { 82, 82, 73 };
    static final int[] forecastLo = { 58, 65, 48 };

    public void doGet(HttpServletRequest req, HttpServletResponse res)
                              throws ServletException, IOException {
      res.setContentType("text/html");
      PrintWriter out = res.getWriter();

      // Set its title
      String title = "Sebastopol Weather Forecast";
      out.println("<HTML>");
```

Example 5-4. Weather forecast constructed by hand (continued)

```java
    out.println("<HEAD>");
    out.println("<TITLE>" + title + "</TITLE>");
    out.println("</HEAD>");

    // Start on the body
    out.println("<BODY>");

    // Make a centered table
    out.println("<CENTER>");
    out.println("<TABLE BORDER=1 CELLPADDING=0 CELLSPACING=0 WIDTH=70%>");

    // First row
    out.println("<TR>");
    out.println("<TD><CENTER><B>");
    out.println("<FONT SIZE=+2>Current Conditions</FONT>");
    out.println("</B></CENTER></TD>");

    out.println("<TD><CENTEr>");
    out.println("<IMG WIDTH=48 HEIGHT=35 SRC=\"" + currentImage + "\">");
    out.println("</CENTER></TD>");

    out.println("<TD COLSPAN=2><CENTER><B><FONT SIZE=+2>");
    out.println(currentTemp + "&#176;");
    out.println("</FONT></B></CENTER></TD>");
    out.println("</TR>");

    // Second row
    out.println("<TR>");
    out.println("<TD COLSPAN=2><CENTER><B><FONT SIZE=+1>");
    out.println("Extended Forecast");
    out.println("</FONT></B></CENTER></TD>");

    out.println("<TD><CENTER><B><FONT SIZE=+1>");
    out.println("Hi");
    out.println("</FONT></B></CENTER></TD>");

    out.println("<TD><CENTER><B><FONT SIZE=+1>");
    out.println("Lo");
    out.println("</FONT></B></CENTER></TD>");
    out.println("</TR>");

    // Daily forecast rows
    for (int i = 0; i < forecastDay.length; i++) {
      out.println("<TR>");
      out.println("<TD> <FONT SIZE=+1>");
      out.println(forecastDay[i]);
      out.println("</FONT></TD>");
      out.println("<TD><CENTER>");
```

Example 5-4. Weather forecast constructed by hand (continued)

```
        out.println("<IMG WIDTH=48 HEIGHT=35 SRC=\"" + forecastImage[i] + "\">");
        out.println("</CENTER></TD>");
        out.println("<TD><CENTER><FONT SIZE=+1>");
        out.println(forecastHi[i]);
        out.println("</FONT></CENTER></TD>");
        out.println("<TD><CENTER><FONT SIZE=+1>");
        out.println(forecastLo[i]);
        out.println("</FONT></CENTER></TD>");
        out.println("</TR>");
    }

    // Close the still-open tags
    out.println("</TABLE>");
    out.println("</CENTER>");
    out.println("</BODY></HTML>");
  }
}
```

This code exactly generates the weather forecast page as shown in Figure 5-1. It begins by defining `static final` variables to use as its content and proceeds to nest that content among HTML tags. This approach presents a pretty page to the end user, but it can leave the programmer counting tags and looking for the right place to put the forgotten </TD>. The approach also has limited maintainability. Pulling out one HTML tag can result in the same cascading disaster you get when you pull on a knit sweater's loose tail. And for the same reason—everything's connected. Even a change as simple as decentering the table requires a modification in the beginning of doGet() and at the end. And a whimsical change, like making the extended forecast font bold, requires more than a little concentration.

Weather forecast using HTML generation

The same servlet written using HTML generation is shown in Example 5-5.

Example 5-5. Weather forecast using HTML generation

```
import java.io.*;
import java.text.*;
import java.util.*;
import javax.servlet.*;
import javax.servlet.http.*;

import weblogic.html.*;

public class WeatherHtmlKona extends HttpServlet {

    // Some static final variables to populate the page...
    // These would normally come from a database or
```

Example 5-5. Weather forecast using HTML generation (continued)

```java
// maybe another servlet that retrieved it as POST data.

static final int currentTemp = 70;
static final String currentImage = "/images/rainy.gif";
static final String[] forecastDay = { "Thursday",
                                      "Friday",
                                      "Saturday" };
static final String[] forecastImage = { "/images/sunny.gif",
                                        "/images/sunny.gif",
                                        "/images/rainy.gif" };
static final int[] forecastHi = { 82, 82, 73 };
static final int[] forecastLo = { 58, 65, 48 };

public void doGet(HttpServletRequest req, HttpServletResponse res)
                          throws ServletException, IOException {
  res.setContentType("text/html");

  // Get a new page
  ServletPage page = new ServletPage();

  // Set its title
  String title = "Sebastopol Weather Forecast";
  page.getHead().addElement(new TitleElement(title));

  // Get the body
  HtmlContainer body = page.getBody();

  // Make a table, and add it to the body (even before it's filled)
  TableElement tab = new TableElement()
                    .setCellPadding(0)
                    .setCellSpacing(0)
                    .setBorder(1)
                    .setWidth("60%");
  body.addElement(new CenteredElement(tab));

  // Create the first row
  HtmlElement conditions = new StringElement("Current Conditions")
                          .asFontElement("+2")
                          .asBoldElement()
                          .asCenteredElement();
  HtmlElement image = new ImageElement(currentImage)
                    .setWidth(48)
                    .setHeight(35)
                    .asCenteredElement();
  HtmlElement temp = new StringElement(currentTemp + "&#176;")
                    .asFontElement("+2")
                    .asBoldElement()
```

Example 5-5. Weather forecast using HTML generation (continued)

```
                               .asCenteredElement();
    tab.addElement(new TableRowElement()
                    .addElement(new TableDataElement(conditions))
                    .addElement(new TableDataElement(image))
                    .addElement(new TableDataElement(temp)
                               .setColSpan(2)));

    // Create the second row
    HtmlElement extended = new StringElement("Extended Forecast")
                           .asFontElement("+1")
                           .asBoldElement()
                           .asCenteredElement();
    HtmlElement hi = new StringElement("Hi")
                     .asFontElement("+1")
                     .asBoldElement()
                     .asCenteredElement();
    HtmlElement lo = new StringElement("Lo")
                     .asFontElement("+1")
                     .asBoldElement()
                     .asCenteredElement();
    tab.addElement(new TableRowElement()
                    .addElement(new TableDataElement(extended)
                               .setColSpan(2))
                    .addElement(new TableDataElement(hi))
                    .addElement(new TableDataElement(lo)));

    // Create the forecast rows
    for (int i = 0; i < forecastDay.length; i++) {
      HtmlElement day = new StringElement(" " + forecastDay[i])
                        .asFontElement("+1");
      HtmlElement daypic = new ImageElement(forecastImage[i])
                           .setWidth(48)
                           .setHeight(35)
                           .asCenteredElement();
      HtmlElement dayhi = new StringElement("" + forecastHi[i])
                          .asFontElement("+1")
                          .asCenteredElement();
      HtmlElement daylo = new StringElement("" + forecastLo[i])
                          .asFontElement("+1")
                          .asCenteredElement();
      tab.addElement(new TableRowElement()
                      .addElement(new TableDataElement(day))
                      .addElement(new TableDataElement(daypic))
                      .addElement(new TableDataElement(dayhi))
                      .addElement(new TableDataElement(daylo)));
    }

    // Send the page to the response's output stream
```

Example 5-5. Weather forecast using HTML generation (continued)

```
    page.output(res.getOutputStream());
  }
}
```

The basic structure of this servlet is similar to that of the previous example. The major difference is that this servlet uses an HTML generation package to create an object-oriented representation of the web page.

A few things may look strange about this code. The most striking is its use of method chaining, where several methods are invoked on the same object with code like the following:

```
TableElement tab = new TableElement()
                    .setCellPadding(0)
                    .setCellSpacing(0);
```

The whitespace here is irrelevant. The previous code is equivalent to:

```
TableElement tab = new TableElement().setCellPadding(0).setCellSpacing(0);
```

This chaining is possible because each "set" method returns a reference to the object on which it was invoked—that reference is used to invoke the next "set" method. This trick comes in handy when using htmlKona.

You may also be wondering why so many objects are declared as `HtmlElement` objects but created as `StringElement` objects or `ImageElement` objects, as with the following code:

```
HtmlElement image = new ImageElement(currentImage)
                    .setWidth(48)
                    .setHeight(35)
                    .asCenteredElement();
```

The answer is that each "as" method returns an object of a different type than the object on which it was invoked. In the example above, the `asCenteredEle-ment()` method returns a `CenteredElement` wrapped around the original `ImageElement`. For simplicity, each HTML component can be declared to be of type `HtmlElement`, which is the superclass of all HTML objects—its actual subclass type can be changed later with ease.

Now let's look at how this servlet compares to the previous servlet. This servlet no longer has code that writes the individual HTML tags, but it replaces that code with almost as many method invocations. We don't appear to be saving any keystrokes. What using HTML generation does do is give you confidence that the page you constructed is valid. Tags cannot be forgotten or misplaced. The larger benefit comes from easier maintainability. What if your pointy-haired boss wants the table left-justified instead of centered? The change is simple. The following line:

```
body.addElement(new CenteredElement(tab));
```

changes to:

```
body.addElement(tab);
```

And what if you decide you want the forecast font to be bold? Well, it's still a lot of work. For an elegant solution to this problem, we need to look at the next servlet.

Weather forecast using HTML generation creatively

Example 5-6 (the last full weather forecast example) shows another servlet that generates the weather forecast web page. This servlet demonstrates some of HTML generation's potential by reusing objects and subclassing. This technique produces results similar to what you can achieve with Cascading Style Sheets (CSS), a recent enhancement to HTML for controlling document appearance.[*] The major advantage of HTML generation is that, because it operates entirely on the server side, it can work with all browsers. CSS only started being supported in Microsoft Internet Explorer 3 and later and Netscape Navigator 4 and later.

Example 5-6. Weather forecast using HTML generation creatively

```
import java.io.*;
import java.text.*;
import java.util.*;
import javax.servlet.*;
import javax.servlet.http.*;

import weblogic.html.*;

class CurrentStyle extends StringElement {
  CurrentStyle(String val) {
    super(new StringElement(val)
          .asFontElement("+2")
          .asBoldElement()
          .asCenteredElement());
  }
}

class ExtendedTitleStyle extends StringElement {
  ExtendedTitleStyle(String val) {
    super(new StringElement(val)
          .asFontElement("+1")
          .asBoldElement()
```

---

[*] For more information on Cascading Style Sheets, see *http://www.w3.org/Style/css*.

Example 5-6. Weather forecast using HTML generation creatively (continued)

```
            .asCenteredElement());
    }
}


class ExtendedDayStyle extends StringElement {
  ExtendedDayStyle(String val) {
    super(new StringElement(val)
          .asFontElement("+1"));
  }
}


class ExtendedTempStyle extends StringElement {
  ExtendedTempStyle(String val) {
    super(new StringElement(val)
          .asFontElement("+1")
          .asCenteredElement());
  }
}


class ImageStyle extends CenteredElement {
  ImageStyle(String src) {
    super(new ImageElement(src).setWidth(48).setHeight(35));
  }
}


public class WeatherHtmlKonaRevised extends HttpServlet {

  static final ImageStyle sunny = new ImageStyle("/images/sunny.gif");
  static final ImageStyle rainy = new ImageStyle("/images/rainy.gif");

  // Some static final variables to populate the page...
  // These would normally come from a database or
  // maybe another servlet that retrieved it as POST data.

  static final int currentTemp = 70;
  static final ImageStyle currentImage = sunny;
  static final String[] forecastDay = { "Thursday", "Friday", "Saturday" };
  static final ImageStyle[] forecastImage = { sunny, sunny, rainy };
  static final int[] forecastHi = { 82, 82, 73 };
  static final int[] forecastLo = { 58, 65, 48 };

  public void doGet(HttpServletRequest req, HttpServletResponse res)
                              throws ServletException, IOException {
    res.setContentType("text/html");

    // Get a new page
    ServletPage page = new ServletPage();
```

Example 5-6. Weather forecast using HTML generation creatively (continued)

```java
// Set its title
String title = "Sebastopol Weather Forecast";
page.getHead().addElement(new TitleElement(title));

// Get the body
HtmlContainer body = page.getBody();

// Make a table, and add it to the body (even before it's filled)
TableElement tab = new TableElement()
                    .setCellPadding(0)
                    .setCellSpacing(0)
                    .setBorder(1)
                    .setWidth("60%");
body.addElement(new CenteredElement(tab));

// Create the first row
HtmlElement conditions = new CurrentStyle("Current Conditions");
HtmlElement image = currentImage;
HtmlElement temp = new CurrentStyle(currentTemp + "&#176;"); // degree symbol
tab.addElement(new TableRowElement()
            .addElement(new TableDataElement(conditions))
            .addElement(new TableDataElement(image))
            .addElement(new TableDataElement(temp)
                    .setColSpan(2)));

// Create the second row
HtmlElement extended = new ExtendedTitleStyle("Extended Forecast");
HtmlElement hi = new ExtendedTitleStyle("Hi");
HtmlElement lo = new ExtendedTitleStyle("Lo");
tab.addElement(new TableRowElement()
            .addElement(new TableDataElement(extended)
                    .setColSpan(2))
            .addElement(new TableDataElement(hi))
            .addElement(new TableDataElement(lo)));

// Create the forecast rows
for (int i = 0; i < forecastDay.length; i++) {
  HtmlElement day = new ExtendedDayStyle(" " + forecastDay[i]);
  HtmlElement daypic = forecastImage[i];
  HtmlElement dayhi = new ExtendedTempStyle("" + forecastHi[i]);
  HtmlElement daylo = new ExtendedTempStyle("" + forecastLo[i]);
  tab.addElement(new TableRowElement()
            .addElement(new TableDataElement(day))
            .addElement(new TableDataElement(daypic))
            .addElement(new TableDataElement(dayhi))
            .addElement(new TableDataElement(daylo)));
}
```

Example 5-6. Weather forecast using HTML generation creatively (continued)

```
    // Send the page to the response's output stream
    page.output(res.getOutputStream());
  }
}
```

This servlet uses five support classes to define custom styles for portions of the generated web page. For example, `CurrentStyle` defines the font and positioning for the elements that display the current conditions, while `ImageStyle` defines the size and positioning of the forecast icons. Each support class is a subclass of `HtmlElement` (though not always directly) and can thus be treated like a first-class component on the web page.

Custom styles further abstract the HTML components on the page. What was once a `String` surrounded by HTML tags is now a high-level page component. A servlet can fill these components with content and not worry about exactly how they will be displayed. Their display is left to the style class. Should it happen that the appearance needs to be changed, such as when you decide you want the extended forecast font to be bold, the change can be done with a single modification to the appropriate style.

Subclassing also proves useful for more mundane tasks. It can be used to define basic HTML components that, for whatever reason, are not included in the HTML generation package. For example, htmlKona has no `ServletElement` class to represent an embedded `<SERVLET>` tag. This class could be written similarly to its `AppletElement` class by subclassing htmlKona's `ElementWithAttributes` class.

Notice how this servlet has changed its representation of the `sunny` and `rainy` images. The previous servlets stored these images as `String` objects representing image locations. This servlet, however, creates each one as an `ImageStyle` object with an inherent size and width. This means they can be added directly to the page, simplifying the code in which they are used. It also shows how a servlet can reuse an HTML component.

For a better demonstration of reuse, imagine the `TableElement` created by this servlet being cached and resent in response to every request. This is simple to accomplish using the techniques demonstrated in Chapter 3, *The Servlet Life Cycle*. The table could be on a page surrounded by rotating ad banners, but it can persist as an object between requests.

But what happens when the current temperature changes? Does the table have to be entirely regenerated? Not at all. Remember, the table is an object filled with other objects. All we need to do is replace the object that represents the current temperature. For our example this can be done with one line of code (note "°" is the HTML representation of the degree symbol):

```
tab.setCellAt(0, 2, new CurrentStyle(newTemp + "&#176;"));
```

The possible creative uses for object-oriented HTML generation go far beyond the techniques shown in this example. One could imagine a custom-created `Banner-Element` displayed at the top of all the servlets on a site. It could be just a predefined `ImageElement` or a conglomeration of elements. Let your imagination run wild!

HTML generation and databases

Before we conclude our discussion of HTML generation, there is one more feature to discuss: its potential close integration with a database. It's not by coincidence that WebLogic packages htmlKona with its database-centric dbKona and jdbcKona—the packages work well together. We'll leave the details to WebLogic's web site, but the general idea is that when you execute a query against a database, the returned result set can be thought of as a formatted table without a graphical representation. This result set table can be passed to the `TableElement` constructor to automatically display the query results in an HTML table on a web page.

The `TableElement` constructor also accepts `java.util.Dictionary` objects (the superclass of `java.util.Hashtable` and `java.util.Properties`). By sub-classing `TableElement`, it is possible to have it accept even more types, thus making it easy to create tables from all different kinds of data. A subclass can also give special treatment to certain types of data, perhaps converting them into hyperlinks to other queries.

Status Codes

Until now, our servlet examples have not set HTTP response status codes. We've been taking advantage of the fact that if a servlet doesn't specifically set the status code, the server steps in and sets its value to the default 200 "OK" status code. That's a useful convenience when we are returning normal successful responses. However, by using status codes, a servlet can do more with its response. For example, it can redirect a request or report a problem.

The most common status code numbers are defined as mnemonic constants (`public final static int` fields) in the `HttpServletResponse` class. A few of these are listed in Table 5-1. The full list is available in Appendix C, *HTTP Status Codes.*

Table 5-1. HTTP Status Codes

Mnemonic Constant	Code	Default Message	Meaning
SC_OK	200	OK	The client's request was successful, and the server's response contains the requested data. This is the default status code.
SC_NO_CONTENT	204	No Content	The request succeeded, but there was no new response body to return. Browsers receiving this code should retain their current document view. This is a useful code for a servlet to use when it accepts data from a form but wants the browser view to stay at the form, as it avoids the "Document contains no data" error message.
SC_MOVED_PERMANENTLY	301	Moved Perma-nently	The requested resource has permanently moved to a new location. Future references should use the new URL in requests. The new location is given by the Location header. Most browsers automatically access the new location.
SC_MOVED_TEMPORARILY	302	Moved Temporarily	The requested resource has temporarily moved to another location, but future references should still use the original URL to access the resource. The new location is given by the Location header. Most browsers automatically access the new location.
SC_UNAUTHORIZED	401	Unauthorized	The request lacked proper authorization. Used in conjunction with the WWW-Authenticate and Authorization headers.
SC_NOT_FOUND	404	Not Found	The requested resource was not found or is not available.
SC_INTERNAL_SERVER_ERROR	500	Internal Server Error	An unexpected error occurred inside the server that prevented it from fulfilling the request.

Table 5-1. HTTP Status Codes (continued)

Mnemonic Constant	Code	Default Message	Meaning
SC_NOT_ IMPLEMENTED	501	Not Implemented	The server does not support the functionality needed to fulfill the request.
SC_SERVICE_ UNAVAILABLE	503	Service Unavailable	The service (server) is temporarily unavailable but should be restored in the future. If the server knows when it will be available again, a Retry-After header may also be supplied.

Setting a Status Code

A servlet can use setStatus() to set a response status code:

```
public void HttpServletResponse.setStatus(int sc)
public void HttpServletResponse.setStatus(int sc, String sm)
```

Both of these methods set the HTTP status code to the given value. The code can be specified as a number or with one of the SC_*XXX* codes defined within Http-ServletResponse. With the single-argument version of the method, the reason phrase is set to the default message for the given status code. The two-argument version allows you to specify an alternate message. Remember, the setStatus() method should be called before your servlet returns any of its response body.

If a servlet sets a status code that indicates an error during the handling of the request, it can call sendError() instead of setStatus():

```
public void HttpServletResponse.sendError(int sc)
public void HttpServletResponse.sendError(int sc, String sm)
```

A server may give the sendError() method different treatment than setStatus(). When the two-argument version of the method is used, the status message parameter may be used to set an alternate reason phrase or it may be used directly in the body of the response, depending on the server's implementation.

Improving ViewFile Using Status Codes

So far, we haven't bothered calling any of these methods to set a response's status code. We've simply relied on the fact that the status code defaults to SC_OK. But there are times when a servlet needs to return a response that doesn't have the SC_OK status code—when the response does not contain the requested data. As an example, think back to how the ViewFile servlet in Chapter 4, *Retrieving Information*, handled the FileNotFoundException:

```
// Return the file
try {
  ServletUtils.returnFile(file, out);
}
catch (FileNotFoundException e) {
  out.println("File not found");
}
```

Without setting a status code, the best this servlet can do is write out an explanation of the problem, ironically sending the explanation as part of a page that is supposed to contain the file's contents. With status codes, however, it can do exactly what Sun's `FileServlet` does: set the response code to `SC_NOT_FOUND` to indicate that the requested file was not found and cannot be returned. Here's the improved version:

```
// Return the file
try {
  ServletUtils.returnFile(file, out);
}
catch (FileNotFoundException e) {
  res.sendError(res.SC_NOT_FOUND);
}
```

The full effect of a `sendError()` call is server dependent, but for the Java Web Server this call generates the server's own "404 Not Found" page, complete with Duke's picture (as shown in Figure 5-2). Note that this page is indistinguishable from every other Java Web Server "404 Not Found" page. The call to `sendError()` also results in a note in the server's access log that the file could not be found.

HTTP Headers

A servlet can set HTTP headers to provide extra information about its response. As we said in Chapter 4, a full discussion of all the possible HTTP 1.0 and HTTP 1.1 headers is beyond the scope of this book. Table 5-2 lists the HTTP headers that are most often set by servlets as a part of a response.

Setting an HTTP Header

The `HttpServletResponse` class provides a number of methods to assist servlets in setting HTTP response headers. Use `setHeader()` to set the value of a header:

```
public void HttpServletResponse.setHeader(String name, String value)
```

This method sets the value of the named header as a `String`. The name is case insensitive, as it is for all these methods. If the header had already been set, the new value overwrites the previous one. Headers of all types can be set with this method.

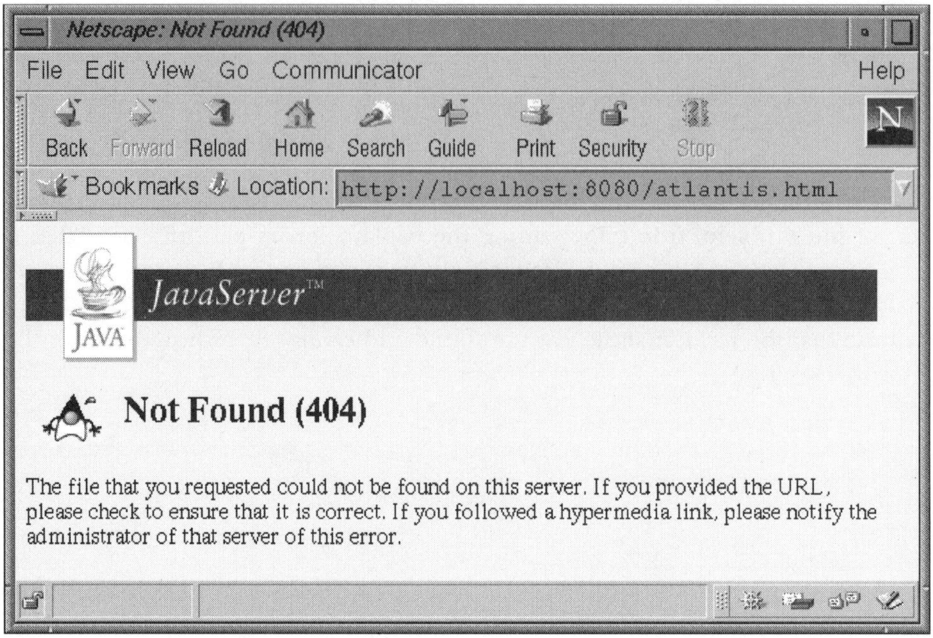

Figure 5-2. The Java Web Server "404 Not Found" page

Table 5-2. HTTP Response Headers

Header	Usage
Cache-Control	Specifies any special treatment a caching system should give to this document. The most common values are no-cache (to indicate this document should not be cached), no-store (to indicate this document should not be cached or even stored by a proxy server, usually due to its sensitive contents), and max-age=*seconds* (to indicate how long before the document should be considered stale). This header was introduced in HTTP 1.1.
Pragma	The HTTP 1.0 equivalent of Cache-control, with no-cache as its only possible value.
Connection	Used to indicate whether the server is willing to maintain an open (persistent) connection to the client. If so, its value is set to keep-alive. If not, its value is set to close. Most web servers handle this header on behalf of their servlets, automatically setting its value to keep-alive when a servlet sets its Content-Length header.
Retry-After	Specifies a time when the server can again handle requests, used with the SC_SERVICE_UNAVAILABLE status code. Its value is either an int that represents the number of seconds or a date string that represents an actual time.

Table 5-2. HTTP Response Headers (continued)

Header	Usage
Expires	Specifies a time when the document may change or when its information will become invalid. It implies that it is unlikely the document will change before that time.
Location	Specifies a new location of a document, usually used with the status codes SC_CREATED, SC_MOVED_PERMANENTLY, and SC_MOVED_TEMPORARILY. Its value must be a fully qualified URL (including "http://").
WWW-Authenticate	Specifies the authorization scheme and the realm of authorization required by the client to access the requested URL. Used with the status code SC_UNAUTHORIZED.
Content-Encoding	Specifies the scheme used to encode the response body. Possible values are gzip (or x-gzip) and compress (or x-compress). Multiple encodings should be represented as a comma-separated list in the order in which the encodings were applied to the data.

If you need to specify a time stamp for a header, you can use setDateHeader():

```
public void HttpServletResponse.setDateHeader(String name, long date)
```

This method sets the value of the named header to a particular date and time. The method accepts the date value as a long that represents the number of milliseconds since the epoch (midnight, January 1, 1970 GMT). If the header has already been set, the new value overwrites the previous one.

Finally, you can use setIntHeader() to specify an integer value for a header:

```
public void HttpServletResponse.setIntHeader(String name, int value)
```

This method sets the value of the named header as an int. If the header had already been set, the new value overwrites the previous one.

The containsHeader() method provides a way to check if a header already exists:

```
public boolean HttpServletResponse.containsHeader(String name)
```

This method returns true if the named header has already been set, false if not.

In addition, the HTML 3.2 specification defines an alternate way to set header values using the <META HTTP-EQUIV> tag inside the HTML page itself:

```
<META HTTP-EQUIV="name" CONTENT="value">
```

This tag must be sent as part of the <HEAD> section of the HTML page. This technique does not provide any special benefit to servlets; it was developed for use with static documents, which do not have access to their own headers.

Redirecting a Request

One of the useful things a servlet can do using status codes and headers is redirect a request. This is done by sending instructions for the client to use another URL in the response. Redirection is generally used when a document moves (to send the client to the new location), for load balancing (so one URL can distribute the load to several different machines), or for simple randomization (choosing a destination at random).

Example 5-7 shows a servlet that performs a random redirect, sending a client to a random site selected from its site list. Depending on the site list, a servlet like this could have many uses. As it stands now, it's just a jump-off point to a selection of cool servlet sites. With a site list containing advertising images, it can be used to select the next ad banner.

Example 5-7. Random redirector

```
import java.io.*;
import java.util.*;
import javax.servlet.*;
import javax.servlet.http.*;

public class SiteSelector extends HttpServlet {

  Vector sites = new Vector();
  Random random = new Random();

  public void init(ServletConfig config) throws ServletException {
    super.init(config);
    sites.addElement("http://www.oreilly.com/catalog/jservlet");
    sites.addElement("http://www.servlets.com");
    sites.addElement("http://jserv.java.sun.com");
    sites.addElement("http://www.servletcentral.com");
  }

  public void doGet(HttpServletRequest req, HttpServletResponse res)
                              throws ServletException, IOException {
    res.setContentType("text/html");
    PrintWriter out = res.getWriter();

    int siteIndex = Math.abs(random.nextInt()) % sites.size();
    String site = (String)sites.elementAt(siteIndex);

    res.setStatus(res.SC_MOVED_TEMPORARILY);
    res.setHeader("Location", site);
  }
}
```

The actual redirection happens in two lines:

```
res.setStatus(res.SC_MOVED_TEMPORARILY);
res.setHeader("Location", site);
```

The first line sets the status code to indicate a redirection is to take place, while the second line gives the new location. To guarantee they will work, you must call these methods before you send any output. Remember, the HTTP protocol sends status codes and headers before the content body. Also, the new site must be given as an absolute URL (for example, *http://server:port/path/file.html*). Anything less than that may confuse the client.

These two lines can be simplified to one using the `sendRedirect()` convenience method:

```
public void HttpServletResponse.sendRedirect(String location) throws
IOException
```

This method redirects the response to the specified location, automatically setting the status code and `Location` header. For our example, the two lines become simply:

```
res.sendRedirect(site);
```

Client Pull

Client pull is similar to redirection, with one major difference: the browser actually displays the content from the first page and waits some specified amount of time before retrieving and displaying the content from the next page. It's called client pull because the client is responsible for pulling the content from the next page.

Why is this useful? For two reasons. First, the content from the first page can explain to the client that the requested page has moved before the next page is automatically loaded. Second, pages can be retrieved in sequence, making it possible to present a slow-motion page animation.

Client pull information is sent to the client using the `Refresh` HTTP header. This header's value specifies the number of seconds to display the page before pulling the next one, and it optionally includes a URL string that specifies the URL from which to pull. If no URL is given, the same URL is used. Here's a call to `setHeader()` that tells the client to reload this same servlet after showing its current content for three seconds:

```
setHeader("Refresh", "3");
```

And here's a call that tells the client to display Netscape's home page after the three seconds:

```
    setHeader("Refresh", "3; URL=http://home.netscape.com");
```

Example 5-8 shows a servlet that uses client pull to display the current time, updated every 10 seconds.

Example 5-8. The current time, kept current

```
import java.io.*;
import java.util.*;
import javax.servlet.*;
import javax.servlet.http.*;

public class ClientPull extends HttpServlet {

  public void doGet(HttpServletRequest req, HttpServletResponse res)
                              throws ServletException, IOException {
    res.setContentType("text/plain");
    PrintWriter out = res.getWriter();

    res.setHeader("Refresh", "10");
    out.println(new Date().toString());
  }
}
```

This is an example of a text-based animation—we'll look at graphical animations in the next chapter. Note that the Refresh header is nonrepeating. It is not a directive to load the document repeatedly. For this example, however, the Refresh header is specified on each retrieval, creating a continuous display.

The use of client pull to retrieve a second document is shown in Example 5-9. This servlet redirects requests for one host to another host, giving an explanation to the client before the redirection.

Example 5-9. An explained host change

```
import java.io.*;
import java.util.*;
import javax.servlet.*;
import javax.servlet.http.*;

public class ClientPullMove extends HttpServlet {

  static final String NEW_HOST = "http://www.oreilly.com";

  public void doGet(HttpServletRequest req, HttpServletResponse res)
                              throws ServletException, IOException {
    res.setContentType("text/html");
    PrintWriter out = res.getWriter();

    String newLocation = NEW_HOST + req.getRequestURI();
```

Example 5-9. An explained host change (continued)

```
        res.setHeader("Refresh", "10; URL=" + newLocation);

        out.println("The requested URI has been moved to a different host.<BR>");
        out.println("Its new location is " + newLocation + "<BR>");
        out.println("Your browser will take you there in 10 seconds.");
    }
}
```

This servlet generates the new location from the requested URI, which allows it to redirect any requests made to the old server. With the Java Web Server, this servlet could be configured to handle every request, to gradually transition clients to the new location.

When Things Go Wrong

All right, let's face it. Sometimes things go wrong. Sometimes the dog bites, and sometimes the bee stings. There are any number of possible causes: bad parameters, missing resources, and (gasp!) actual bugs. The point here is that a servlet has to be prepared for problems, both expected and unexpected. There are two points of concern when things go wrong:

- Limiting damage to the server

- Properly informing the client

Because servlets are written in Java, the potential damage they can cause to their server is greatly minimized. A server can safely embed servlets (even within its process), just as a web browser can safely embed downloaded applets. This safety is built on Java's security features, including the use of protected memory, exception handling, and security managers. Java's memory protection guarantees that servlets cannot accidentally (or intentionally) access the server's internals. Java's exception handling lets a server catch every exception raised by a servlet. Even if a servlet accidentally divides by zero or calls a method on a null object, the server can continue to function. Java's security manager mechanism provides a way for servers to place untrusted servlets in a sandbox, limiting their abilities and keeping them from intentionally causing problems.

You should be aware that trusted servlets executing outside a security manager's sandbox are given abilities that could potentially cause damage to the server. For example, a servlet can overwrite the server's file space or even call `System.exit()`. It is also true that a trusted servlet should never cause damage except by accident, and it's hard to accidentally call `System.exit()`. Still, if it's a concern, even trusted servlets can be (and often are) run inside a fairly lenient but sanity-checking security manager.

Properly describing a problem to the client cannot be handled by Java language technology alone. There are many things to consider:

How much to tell the client?
> Should the servlet send a generic status code error page, a prose explanation of the problem, or (in the case of a thrown exception) a detailed stack trace? What if the servlet is supposed to return nontextual content, such as an image?

How to record the problem?
> Should it be saved to a file, written to the server log, sent to the client, or ignored?

How to recover?
> Can the same servlet instance handle subsequent requests? Or is the servlet corrupted, meaning that it needs to be reloaded?

The answers to these questions depend on the servlet and its intended use, and they should be addressed for each servlet you write on a case-by-case basis. How you handle errors is up to you and should be based on the level of reliability and robustness required for your servlet. What we'll look at next is an overview of the servlet error-handling mechanisms that you can use to implement whatever policy you select.

Status Codes

The simplest (and arguably best) way for a servlet to report an error is to use the `sendError()` method to set the appropriate 400 series or 500 series status code. For example, when the servlet is asked to return a file that does not exist, it can return `SC_NOT_FOUND`. When it is asked to do something beyond its capabilities, it can return `SC_NOT_IMPLEMENTED`. And when the entirely unexpected happens, it can return `SC_INTERNAL_SERVER_ERROR`.

By using `sendError()` to set the status code, a servlet provides the server an opportunity to give the response special treatment. For example, some servers, such as the Java Web Server, replace the servlet's response body with a server-specific page that explains the error. If the error is such that a servlet ought to provide its own explanation to the client in the response body, it can set the status code with `setStatus()` and send the appropriate body—which could be text based, a generated image, or whatever is appropriate.

A servlet must be careful to catch and handle any errors before it sends any part of its response body. As you probably recall (because we've mentioned it several times), HTTP specifies that the status code and HTTP headers must be sent before the response body. Once you've sent even one character of a response body, it may be too late to change your status code or your HTTP headers. The easy way to guarantee you don't find yourself in this "too late" situation is to send your content all at once when the servlet is done processing, using an `ByteArray-OutputStream` buffer or HTML generation package, as shown earlier in this chapter.

Logging

Servlets have the ability to write their actions and their errors to a log file using the `log()` method:

```
public void ServletContext.log(String msg)
public void ServletContext.log(Exception e, String msg)
```

The single-argument method writes the given message to a servlet log, which is usually an event log file. The two-argument version writes the given message and exception's stack trace to a servlet log. Notice the nonstandard placement of the optional `Exception` parameter as the first parameter instead of the last for this method. For both methods, the output format and location of the log are server-specific.

The `GenericServlet` class also provides a `log()` method:

```
public void GenericServlet.log(String msg)
```

This is another version of the `ServletContext` method, moved to `Generic-Servlet` for convenience. This method allows a servlet to call simply:

```
log(msg);
```

to write to the servlet log. Note, however, that `GenericServlet` does not provide the two-argument version of `log()`. The absence of this method is probably an oversight, to be rectified in a future release. For now, a servlet can perform the equivalent by calling:

```
getServletContext().log(e, msg);
```

The `log()` method aids debugging by providing a way to track a servlet's actions. It also offers a way to save a complete description of any errors encountered by the servlet. The description can be the same as the one given to the client, or it can be more exhaustive and detailed.

Now we can go back and improve `ViewFile` further, so that it uses `log()` to record on the server when requested files do not exist, while returning a simple "404 Not Found" page to the client:

```
// Return the file
try {
  ServletUtils.returnFile(file, out);
}
catch (FileNotFoundException e) {
  log("Could not find file: " + e.getMessage());
  res.sendError(res.SC_NOT_FOUND);
}
```

For more complicated errors, a servlet can log the complete stack trace, as shown here:

```
// Return the file
try {
  ServletUtils.returnFile(file, out);
}
catch (FileNotFoundException e) {
  log("Could not find file: " + e.getMessage());
  res.sendError(res.SC_NOT_FOUND);
}
catch (IOException e) {
  getServletContext().log(e, "Problem sending file");
  res.sendError(res.SC._INTERNAL_SERVER_ERROR);
}
```

Reporting

In addition to logging errors and exceptions for the server administrator, during development it's often convenient to print a full description of the problem along with a stack trace. Unfortunately, an exception cannot return its stack trace as a String it can only print its stack trace to a PrintStream or PrintWriter. To retrieve a stack trace as a String, we have to jump through a few hoops. We need to let the Exception print to a special PrintWriter built around a ByteArray-OutputStream. That ByteArrayOutputStream can catch the output and convert it to a String. The com.oreilly.servlet.ServletUtils class has a getStackTraceAsString() method that does just this:

```
public static String getStackTraceAsString(Exception e) {
  ByteArrayOutputStream bytes = new ByteArrayOutputStream();
  PrintWriter writer = new PrintWriter(bytes, true);
  e.printStackTrace(writer);
  return bytes.toString();
}
```

Here's how ViewFile can provide information that includes an IOException stack trace:

```
// Return the file
try {
```

```
    ServletUtils.returnFile(file, out);
  }
  catch (FileNotFoundException e) {
    log("Could not find file: " + e.getMessage());
    res.sendError(res.SC_NOT_FOUND);
  }
  catch (IOException e) {
    getServletContext().log(e, "Problem sending file");
    res.sendError(res.SC_INTERNAL_SERVER_ERROR,
                  ServletUtils.getStackTraceAsString(e));
  }
```

The output for a sample exception is shown in Figure 5-3.

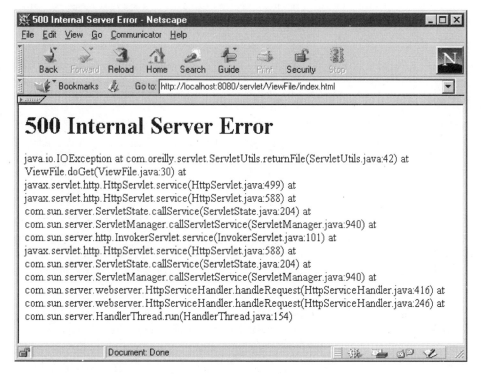

Figure 5-3. Keeping the client well informed

Exceptions

As we said before, any exception that is thrown but not caught by a servlet is caught by its server. How the server handles the exception is server-dependent: it may pass the client the message and the stack trace, or it may not. It may automatically log the exception, or it may not. It may even call destroy() on the servlet and reload it, or it may not.

Servlets designed and developed to run with a particular server can optimize for that server's behavior. A servlet designed to interoperate across several servers cannot expect any particular exception handling on the part of the server. If such a servlet requires special exception handling, it must catch its own exceptions and handle them accordingly.

There are some types of exceptions a servlet has no choice but to catch itself. A servlet can propagate to its server only those exceptions that subclass `IOException`, `ServletException`, or `RuntimeException`. The reason has to do with method signatures. The `service()` method of `Servlet` declares in its `throws` clause that it throws `IOException` and `ServletException` exceptions. For it (or the `doGet()` and `doPost()` methods it calls) to throw and not catch anything else causes a compile time error. The `RuntimeException` is a special case exception that never needs to be declared in a `throws` clause. A common example is a `NullPointerException`.

The `init()` and `destroy()` methods have their own signatures as well. The `init()` method declares that it throws only `ServletException` exceptions, and `destroy()` declares that it throws no exceptions.

`ServletException` is a subclass of `java.lang.Exception` that is specific to servlets—the class is defined in the `javax.servlet` package. This exception is thrown to indicate a general servlet problem. It has the same constructors as `java.lang.Exception`: one that takes no arguments and one that takes a single message string. Servers catching this exception may handle it any way they see fit.

The `javax.servlet` package defines one subclass of `ServletException`, `UnavailableException`, although you can, of course, add your own. This exception indicates a servlet is unavailable, either temporarily or permanently. Servers (services) that catch an `UnavailableException` are expected to behave as described in the Servlet API documentation:

> Servlets may report this exception at any time, and the network service running the servlet should behave appropriately. There are two types of unavailability, and sophisticated services will deal with these differently:
>
> *Permanent unavailability.* The servlet will not be able to handle client requests until some administrative action is taken to correct a servlet problem. For example, the servlet might be misconfigured, or the state of the servlet may be corrupted. Well written servlets will log both the error and the corrective action which an administrator must perform to let the servlet become available.
>
> *Temporary unavailability.* The servlet cannot handle requests at this moment due to a system-wide problem. For example, a third-tier server might not be accessible, or there may be insufficient memory or disk storage to handle requests. The problem may be self-correcting, such as those due to excessive load, or corrective action may need to be taken by an administrator.

Network services may safely treat both types of exceptions as "permanent," but good treatment of temporary unavailability leads to more robust network services. Specifically, requests to the servlet might be blocked (or otherwise deferred) for a servlet-suggested amount of time, rather than being rejected until the service itself restarts.

UnavailableException has two constructors:

```
javax.servlet.UnavailableException(Servlet servlet, String msg)
javax.servlet.UnavailableException(int seconds, Servlet servlet, String msg)
```

The two-argument constructor creates a new exception that indicates the given servlet is permanently unavailable, with an explanation given by msg. The three-argument version creates a new exception that indicates the given servlet is temporarily unavailable, with an explanation given by msg. The duration of its unavailability is given by seconds. This time is only an estimate. If no estimate can be made, a nonpositive value may be used. Notice the nonstandard placement of the optional seconds parameter as the first parameter instead of the last. This may be changed in an upcoming release. UnavailableException provides the isPermanent(), getServlet(), and getUnavailableSeconds() methods to retrieve information about an exception.

Knowing When No One's Listening

Sometimes clients hang up on servlets. Sure, it's rude, but it happens. Sometimes the client makes a mistake and goes to the wrong page. Sometimes the servlet takes too long to respond. Remember, all the while a servlet is preparing its response, the user is being tempted by the browser's big, glowing **Stop** button that is just begging to be pushed. You may be wondering, just what happens to the servlet once that button is pushed?

Unfortunately, a servlet is not given any immediate indication that the user has pressed the **Stop** button—there is no interrupt that tells it to stop processing. The servlet discovers the client has stopped the request only when it tries to send output to the nonexistent client, at which point an error condition occurs.

A servlet that sends information using a ServletOutputStream sees an IOException when it tries to write output. For servers that buffer their output, the IOException is thrown when the buffer fills up and its contents are flushed.

Because an IOException may be thrown any time a servlet tries to output, a well-written servlet frees its resources in a finally block. (The finally block is an optional part of a try/catch/finally construct. It comes after zero or more catch blocks, and its code is executed once regardless of how the code in the try block executes.) Here's a version of the returnFile() method from the View-

File servlet that uses a `finally` block to guarantee the closure of its
`FileInputStream`:

```
void returnFile(String filename, OutputStream out)
                        throws FileNotFoundException, IOException {
  FileInputStream fis = null;
  try {
    fis = new FileInputStream(filename);
    byte[] buf = new byte[4 * 1024];  // 4K buffer
    int bytesRead;
    while ((bytesRead = fis.read(buf)) != -1) {
      out.write(buf, 0, bytesRead);
    }
  }
  finally {
    if (fis != null) fis.close();
  }
}
```

The addition of a `finally` block does not change the fact that this method propa-
gates all exceptions to its caller, but it does guarantee that, before that
propagation, the method gets a chance to close the open `FileInputStream`.

A servlet sending character data using a `PrintWriter` doesn't get an `IOExcep-
tion` when it tries to write output, because the methods of `PrintWriter` never
throw exceptions. Instead, a servlet that sends character data has to call the
`checkError()` method of `PrintWriter`. This method flushes the output and
returns a `boolean` that indicates if there was a problem writing to the underlying
`OutputStream`. It returns `true` if the client has stopped the request.

A long-running servlet should call `checkError()` regularly to determine if it can
halt processing early. If there hasn't been any output since the last check, a servlet
can send filler content. For example:

```
out.println("<H2>Here's the solution for your differential equation:</H2>");
if (out.checkError()) return;

// Preliminary calculation here
out.print(" "); // filler content, extra whitespace is ignored in HTML
if (out.checkError()) return;

// Additional calculation here
```

It's important to note that a server is not required to throw an `IOException` or set
the error flag of the `PrinWriter` after the client disconnects. A server may elect to
let the response run to completion with its output ignored. Generally this does not
cause a problem, but it does mean that a servlet running inside such a server
should always have a set end point and should not be written to continuously loop
until the user hits **Stop**.

6

Sending Multimedia Content

Until now, every servlet we've written has returned a standard HTML page. The web consists of more than HTML, though, so in this chapter we'll look at some of the more interesting things a servlet can return. We begin with a look at why you'd want to return different MIME types and how to do it. The most common use of a different MIME type is for returning an image graphic generated by a servlet (or even by an applet embedded inside the servlet!). The chapter also explores when and how to send a compressed response and examines using multipart responses to implement server push.

Images

People are visually oriented—they like to see, not just read, their information. Consequently, it's nearly impossible to find a web site that doesn't use images in some way, and those you do find tend to look unprofessional. To cite the well-worn cliche (translated into programmer-speak), "An *image* is worth a thousand words."

Luckily, it's relatively simple for a servlet to send an image as its response. In fact, we've already seen a servlet that does just this: the `ViewFile` servlet from Chapter 4, *Retrieving Information*. As you may recall, this servlet can return any file under the server's document root. When the file happens to be an image file, it detects that fact with the `getMimeType()` method and sets its response's content type with `setContentType()` before sending the raw bytes to the client.

This technique requires that we already have the needed image files saved on disk, which isn't always the case. Often, a servlet must generate or manipulate an image before sending it to the client. Imagine, for example, a web page that contains an image of an analog clock that displays the current time. Sure, someone could save

720 images (60 minutes times 12 hours) to disk and use a servlet to dispatch the appropriate one. But that someone isn't me, and it shouldn't be you. Instead, the wise servlet programmer writes a servlet that dynamically generates the image of the clock face and its hands—or as a variant, a servlet that loads an image of the clock face and adds just the hands. And, of course, the frugal programmer also has the servlet cache the image (for about a minute) to save server cycles.

There are many other reasons you might want a servlet to return an image. By generating images, a servlet can display things such as an up-to-the-minute stock chart, the current score for a baseball game (complete with icons representing the runners on base), or a graphical representation of the Cokes left in the Coke machine. By manipulating preexisting images, a servlet can do even more. It can draw on top of them, change their color, size, or appearance, or combine several images into one.

Image Generation

Suppose you have an image as raw pixel data that you want to send to someone. How do you do it? Let's assume it's a true-color, 24-bit image (3 bytes per pixel) and that it's 100 pixels tall and 100 pixels wide. You could take the obvious approach and send it one pixel at a time, in a stream of 30,000 bytes. But is that enough? How does the receiver know what to do with the 30,000 bytes he received? The answer is that he doesn't. You also need to say that you are sending raw, true-color pixel values, that you're beginning in the upper left corner, that you're sending row by row, and that each row is 100 pixels wide. Yikes! And what if you decide to send fewer bytes by using compression? You have to say what kind of compression you are using, so the receiver can decompress the image. Suddenly this has become a complicated problem.

Fortunately this is a problem that has been solved, and solved several different ways. Each image format (GIF, JPEG, TIFF, etc.) represents one solution. Each image format defines a standard way to encode an image so that it can later be decoded for viewing or manipulation. Each encoding technique has certain advantages and limitations. For example, the compression used for GIF encoding excels at handling computer-generated images, but the GIF format is limited to just 256 colors. The compression used for JPEG encoding, on the other hand, works best on photo-realistic images that contain millions of colors, but it works so well because it uses "lossy" compression that can blur the photo's details.

Understanding image encoding helps you understand how servlets handle images. A servlet like `ViewFile` can return a preexisting image by sending its encoded representation unmodified to the client—the browser decodes the image for viewing. But a servlet that generates or modifies an image must construct an internal representation of that image, manipulate it, and then encode it, before sending it to the client.

A "Hello World" image

Example 6-1 gives a simple example of a servlet that generates and returns a GIF image. The graphic says "Hello World!", as shown in Figure 6-1.

Example 6-1. Hello World graphics

```java
import java.io.*;
import java.awt.*;
import javax.servlet.*;
import javax.servlet.http.*;

import Acme.JPM.Encoders.GifEncoder;

public class HelloWorldGraphics extends HttpServlet {

  public void doGet(HttpServletRequest req, HttpServletResponse res)
                          throws ServletException, IOException {
    ServletOutputStream out = res.getOutputStream();  // binary output!

    Frame frame = null;
    Graphics g = null;

    try {
      // Create an unshown frame
      frame = new Frame();
      frame.addNotify();

      // Get a graphics region, using the Frame
      Image image = frame.createImage(400, 60);
      g = image.getGraphics();

      // Draw "Hello World!" to the off-screen graphics context
      g.setFont(new Font("Serif", Font.ITALIC, 48));
      g.drawString("Hello World!", 10, 50);

      // Encode the off-screen image into a GIF and send it to the client
      res.setContentType("image/gif");
      GifEncoder encoder = new GifEncoder(image, out);
      encoder.encode();
    }
    finally {
      // Clean up resources
      if (g != null) g.dispose();
      if (frame != null) frame.removeNotify();
    }
```

Example 6-1. Hello World graphics (continued)

```
  }
}
```

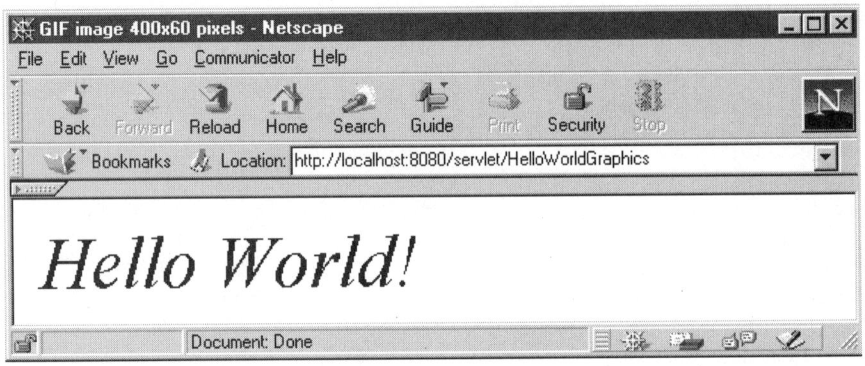

Figure 6-1. Hello World graphics

Although this servlet uses the `java.awt` package, it never actually displays a window on the server's display. Nor does it display a window on the client's display. It performs all its work in an off-screen graphics context and lets the browser display the image. The strategy is as follows: create an off-screen image, get its graphics context, draw to the graphics context, and then encode the resulting image for transmission to the client.

Obtaining an off-screen image involves jumping through several hoops. In Java, an image is represented by the `java.awt.Image` class. Unfortunately, an `Image` object cannot be instantiated directly through a constructor. It must be obtained through a factory method like the `createImage()` method of `Component` or the `getImage()` method of `Toolkit`. Because we're creating a new image, we use `createImage()`. Note that before a component can create an image, its native peer must already exist. Thus, to create our `Image` we must create a `Frame`, create the frame's peer with a call to `addNotify()`, and then use the frame to create our `Image`.[*] Once we have an image, we draw onto it using its graphics context, which can be retrieved with a call to the `getGraphics()` method of `Image`. In this example, we just draw a simple string.

After drawing into the graphics context, we call `setContentType()` to set the MIME type to `"image/gif"` since we're going to use the GIF encoding. For the examples in this chapter, we use a GIF encoder written by Jef Poskanzer. It's well

---

[*] For web servers running on Unix systems, the frame's native peer has to be created inside an X server. Thus, for optimal performance, make sure the DISPLAY environment variable (which specifies the X server to use) is unset or set to a local X server. Also make sure the web server has been granted access to the X server, which may require the use of xhost or xauth.

written and freely available with source from *http://www.acme.com.*[*] To encode the image, we create a `GifEncoder` object, passing it the image object and the `ServletOutputStream` for the servlet. When we call `encode()` on the `GifEncoder` object, the image is encoded and sent to the client.

After sending the image, the servlet does what all well-behaved servlets should do: it releases its graphical resources. These would be reclaimed automatically during garbage collection, but releasing them immediately helps on systems with limited resources. The code to release the resources is placed in a `finally` block to guarantee its execution, even when the servlet throws an exception.

A dynamically generated chart

Now let's look at a servlet that generates a more interesting image. Example 6-2 creates a bar chart that compares apples to oranges, with regard to their annual consumption. Figure 6-2 shows the results. There's little need for this chart to be dynamically generated, but it lets us get the point across without too much code. Picture in your mind's eye, if you will, that the servlet is charting up-to-the-minute stock values or the server's recent load.

Example 6-2. A chart comparing apples and oranges

```
import java.awt.*;
import java.io.*;
import javax.servlet.*;
import javax.servlet.http.*;

import Acme.JPM.Encoders.GifEncoder;

import javachart.chart.*;   // from Visual Engineering

public class SimpleChart extends HttpServlet {

  static final int WIDTH = 450;
  static final int HEIGHT = 320;

  public void doGet(HttpServletRequest req, HttpServletResponse res)
                            throws ServletException ,IOException {
    ServletOutputStream out = res.getOutputStream();

    Frame frame = null;
```

---

[*] Note that the LZW compression algorithm used for GIF encoding is protected by Unisys and IBM patents which, according to the Free Software Foundation, make it impossible to have free software that generates the GIF format. For more information, see *http://www.fsf.org/philosophy/gif.html.* Of course, a servlet can encode its Image into any image format. For web content, JPEG exists as the most likely alternative to GIF. There are JPEG encoders in JDK 1.2 and commercial products such as the JIMI product (Java Image Management Interface), available from Activated Intelligence at *http://www.activated.com.*

Example 6-2. A chart comparing apples and oranges (continued)

```
Graphics g = null;

try {
  // Create a simple chart
  BarChart chart = new BarChart("Apples and Oranges");

  // Give it a title
  chart.getBackground().setTitleFont(new Font("Serif", Font.PLAIN, 24));
  chart.getBackground().setTitleString("Comparing Apples and Oranges");

  // Show, place, and customize its legend
  chart.setLegendVisible(true);
  chart.getLegend().setLlX(0.4);   // normalized from lower left
  chart.getLegend().setLlY(0.75); // normalized from lower left
  chart.getLegend().setIconHeight(0.04);
  chart.getLegend().setIconWidth(0.04);
  chart.getLegend().setIconGap(0.02);
  chart.getLegend().setVerticalLayout(false);

  // Give it its data and labels
  double[] appleData = {950, 1005, 1210, 1165, 1255};
  chart.addDataSet("Apples", appleData);

  double[] orangeData = {1435, 1650, 1555, 1440, 1595};
  chart.addDataSet("Oranges", orangeData);

  String[] labels = {"1993", "1994", "1995", "1996", "1997"};
  chart.getXAxis().addLabels(labels);

  // Color apples red and oranges orange
  chart.getDatasets()[0].getGc().setFillColor(Color.red);
  chart.getDatasets()[1].getGc().setFillColor(Color.orange);

  // Name the axes
  chart.getXAxis().setTitleString("Year");
  chart.getYAxis().setTitleString("Tons Consumed");

  // Size it appropriately
  chart.resize(WIDTH, HEIGHT);

  // Create an unshown frame
  frame = new Frame();
  frame.addNotify();

  // Get a graphics region of appropriate size, using the Frame
  Image image = frame.createImage(WIDTH, HEIGHT);
  g = image.getGraphics();
```

Example 6-2. A chart comparing apples and oranges (continued)

```
        // Ask the chart to draw itself to the off screen graphics context
        chart.drawGraph(g);

        // Encode and return what it painted
        res.setContentType("image/gif");
        GifEncoder encoder = new GifEncoder(image, out);
        encoder.encode();
      }
      finally {
      // Clean up resources
      if (g != null) g.dispose();
      if (frame != null) frame.removeNotify();
      }
    }
  }
}
```

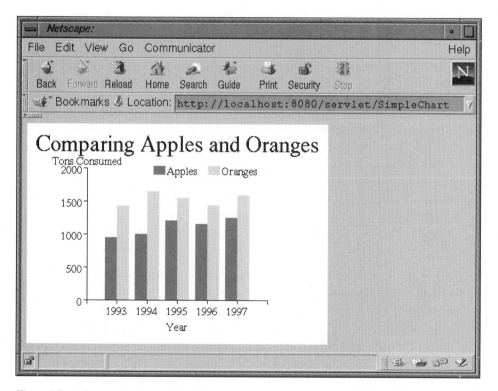

Figure 6-2. A chart comparing apples and oranges

The basics are the same: create an off-screen image and get its graphics context, draw to the graphics context, and then encode the image for transmission to the client. The difference is that this servlet constructs a `BarChart` object to do the drawing. There are more than a dozen charting packages available in Java. You can find several showcased at *http://www.gamelan.com*. The `BarChart` class from this example came from Visual Engineering's JavaChart package, available at *http://www.ve.com/javachart*. It's a commercial product, but for readers of this book they have granted free permission to use the portion of the API presented above. The JavaChart package also includes a set of free chart-generating applets that we will use later in this chapter.

Image Composition

So far, we've drawn our graphics onto empty images. In this section, we discuss how to take preexisting images and either draw on top of them or combine them to make conglomerate images. We also examine error handling in servlets that return images.

Drawing over an image

Sometimes it's useful for a servlet to draw on top of an existing image. A good example is a building locator servlet that knows where every employee sits. When queried for a specific employee, it can draw a big red dot over that employee's office.

One deceptively obvious technique for drawing over a preexisting image is to retrieve the `Image` with `Toolkit.getDefaultToolkit().getImage(image-name)`, get its graphics context with a call to the `getGraphics()` method of `Image`, and then use the returned graphics context to draw on top of the image. Unfortunately, it isn't quite that easy. The reason is that you cannot use `getGraphics()` unless the image was created with the `createImage()` method of `Component`. With the AWT, you always need to have a native peer in the background doing the actual graphics rendering.

Here's what you have to do instead: retrieve the preexisting image via the `Toolkit.getDefaultToolkit().getImage(imagename)` method and then tell it to draw itself into another graphics context created with the `createImage()` method of `Component`, as shown in the previous two examples. Now you can use that graphics context to draw on top of the original image.

Example 6-3 clarifies this technique with an example. It's a servlet that writes "CONFIDENTIAL" over every image it returns. The image name is passed to the servlet as extra path information. Some example output is shown in Figure 6-3.

Example 6-3. Drawing over an image to mark it confidential

```
import java.awt.*;
import java.io.*;
import javax.servlet.*;
import javax.servlet.http.*;

import Acme.JPM.Encoders.GifEncoder;

public class Confidentializer extends HttpServlet {

  Frame frame = null;
  Graphics g = null;

  public void init(ServletConfig config) throws ServletException {
    super.init(config);
    // Construct a reusable unshown frame
    frame = new Frame();
    frame.addNotify();
  }

  public void doGet(HttpServletRequest req, HttpServletResponse res)
                            throws ServletException, IOException {
    ServletOutputStream out = res.getOutputStream();

    try {
      // Get the image location from the path info
      String source = req.getPathTranslated();
      if (source == null) {
        throw new ServletException("Extra path information " +
                                   "must point to an image");
      }

      // Load the image (from bytes to an Image object)
      MediaTracker mt = new MediaTracker(frame);  // frame acts as ImageObserver
      Image image = Toolkit.getDefaultToolkit().getImage(source);
      mt.addImage(image, 0);
      try {
        mt.waitForAll();
      }
      catch (InterruptedException e) {
        getServletContext().log(e, "Interrupted while loading image");
        throw new ServletException(e.getMessage());
      }
```

Example 6-3. Drawing over an image to mark it confidential (continued)

```
        // Construct a matching-size off screen graphics context
        int w = image.getWidth(frame);
        int h = image.getHeight(frame);
        Image offscreen = frame.createImage(w, h);
        g = offscreen.getGraphics();

        // Draw the image to the off-screen graphics context
        g.drawImage(image, 0, 0, frame);

        // Write CONFIDENTIAL over its top
        g.setFont(new Font("Monospaced", Font.BOLD | Font.ITALIC, 30));
        g.drawString("CONFIDENTIAL", 10, 30);

        // Encode the off-screen graphics into a GIF and send it to the client
        res.setContentType("image/gif");
        GifEncoder encoder = new GifEncoder(offscreen, out);
        encoder.encode();
      }
      finally {
        // Clean up resources
        if (g != null) g.dispose();
      }
    }

    public void destroy() {
      // Clean up resources
      if (frame != null) frame.removeNotify();
    }
  }
```

You can see that this servlet performs each step exactly as described above, along with some additional housekeeping. The servlet creates its unshown Frame in its init() method. Creating the Frame once and reusing it is an optimization previously left out for the sake of clarity. For each request, the servlet begins by retrieving the name of the preexisting image from the extra path information. Then it retrieves a reference to the image with the getImage() method of Toolkit and physically loads it into memory with the help of a MediaTracker. Normally it's fine for an image to load asynchronously with its partial results painted as it loads, but in this case we paint the image just once and need to guarantee it's fully loaded beforehand. Then the servlet gets the width and height of the loaded image and creates an off-screen image to match. Finally, the big moment: the loaded image is drawn on top of the newly constructed, empty image. After that it's old hat. The servlet writes its big "CONFIDENTIAL" and encodes the image for transmission.

Figure 6-3. Drawing over an image to mark it confidential

Notice how this servlet handles error conditions by throwing exceptions and logging any errors that may interest the server administrator. When returning images, it's difficult to do much more. After all, a textual description doesn't help when a servlet is referenced in an <IMG> tag. This approach allows the server to do whatever it deems appropriate.

Combining images

A servlet can also combine images into one conglomerate image. Using this ability, a building locator servlet could display an employee's smiling face over her office, instead of a red dot. The technique used for combining images is similar to the one we used to draw over the top of an image: the appropriate images are loaded, they're drawn onto a properly created Image object, and that image is encoded for transmission.

Example 6-4 shows how to do this for a servlet that displays a hit count as a sequence of individual number images combined into one large image. Its output can be seen in Figure 6-4. The number images it uses are available at *http://www.geocities.com/SiliconValley/6742/*, along with several other styles.

Example 6-4. Combining images to form a graphical counter

```java
import java.awt.*;
import java.io.*;
import javax.servlet.*;
import javax.servlet.http.*;

import Acme.JPM.Encoders.GifEncoder;

public class GraphicalCounter extends HttpServlet {

  public static final String DIR = "/images/odometer";
  public static final String COUNT = "314159";

  public void doGet(HttpServletRequest req, HttpServletResponse res)
                             throws ServletException, IOException {
    ServletOutputStream out = res.getOutputStream();

    Frame frame = null;
    Graphics g = null;

    try {
      // Get the count to display, must be sole value in the raw query string
      // Or use the default
      String count = (String)req.getQueryString();
      if (count == null) count = COUNT;

      int countlen = count.length();
      Image images[] = new Image[countlen];

      for (int i = 0; i < countlen; i++) {
        String imageSrc =
          req.getRealPath(DIR + "/" + count.charAt(i) + ".GIF");
        images[i] = Toolkit.getDefaultToolkit().getImage(imageSrc);
      }

      // Create an unshown Frame
      frame = new Frame();
      frame.addNotify();

      // Load the images
      MediaTracker mt = new MediaTracker(frame);
      for (int i = 0; i < countlen; i++) {
        mt.addImage(images[i], i);
      }
      try {
```

Example 6-4. Combining images to form a graphical counter (continued)

```
      mt.waitForAll();
    }
    catch (InterruptedException e) {
      getServletContext().log(e, "Interrupted while loading image");
      throw new ServletException(e.getMessage());
    }

    // Check for problems loading the images
    if (mt.isErrorAny()) {
      // We had a problem, find which image(s)
      StringBuffer problemChars = new StringBuffer();
      for (int i = 0; i < countlen; i++) {
        if (mt.isErrorID(i)) {
          problemChars.append(count.charAt(i));
        }
      }
      throw new ServletException(
        "Coult not load an image for these characters: " +
        problemChars.toString());
    }

    // Get the cumulative size of the images
    int width = 0;
    int height = 0;
    for (int i = 0; i < countlen; i++) {
      width += images[i].getWidth(frame);
      height = Math.max(height, images[i].getHeight(frame));
    }

    // Get a graphics region to match, using the Frame
    Image image = frame.createImage(width, height);
    g = image.getGraphics();

    // Draw the images
    int xindex = 0;
    for (int i = 0; i < countlen; i++) {
      g.drawImage(images[i], xindex, 0, frame);
      xindex += images[i].getWidth(frame);
    }

    // Encode and return the composite
    res.setContentType("image/gif");
    GifEncoder encoder = new GifEncoder(image, out);
    encoder.encode();
  }
  finally {
    // Clean up resources
    if (g != null) g.dispose();
```

Example 6-4. Combining images to form a graphical counter (continued)

```
        if (frame != null) frame.removeNotify();
    }
  }
}
```

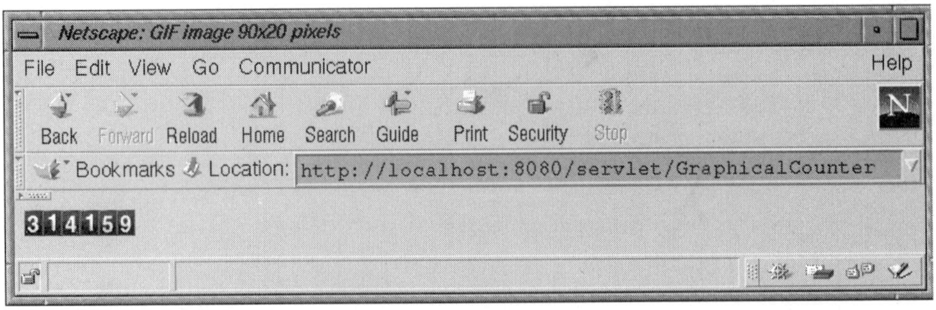

Figure 6-4. Combining images to form a graphical counter

This servlet receives the number to display by reading its raw query string. For each number in the count, it retrieves and loads the corresponding number image from the directory given by DIR. (DIR is always under the server's document root. It's given as a virtual path and translated dynamically to a real path.) Then it calculates the combined width and the maximum height of all these images and constructs an off-screen image to match. The servlet draws each number image into this off-screen image in turn from left to right. Finally, it encodes the image for transmission.

To be of practical use, this servlet must be called by another servlet that knows the hit count to be displayed. For example, it could be called by a server-side include servlet embedded in a page, using syntax like the following:

```
    <IMG SRC="/servlet/GraphicalCounter?121672">
```

This servlet handles error conditions in the same way as the previous servlet, by throwing a ServletException and leaving it to the server to behave appropriately.

Image Effects

We've seen how servlets can create and combine images. In this section, we look at how servlets can also perform special effects on images. For example, a servlet can reduce the transmission time for an image by scaling down its size before transmission. Or it can add some special shading to an image to make it resemble a pressable button. As an example, let's look at how a servlet can convert a color image to grayscale.

Converting an image to grayscale

Example 6-5 shows a servlet that converts an image to grayscale before returning it. The servlet performs this effect without ever actually creating an off-screen graphics context. Instead, it creates the image using a special `ImageFilter`. (We'd show you before and after images, but they wouldn't look very convincing in a black-and-white book.)

Example 6-5. An image effect converting an image to grayscale

```java
import java.awt.*;
import java.awt.image.*;
import java.io.*;
import javax.servlet.*;
import javax.servlet.http.*;

import Acme.JPM.Encoders.*;

public class DeColorize extends HttpServlet {

  public void doGet(HttpServletRequest req, HttpServletResponse res)
                          throws ServletException, IOException {
    res.setContentType("image/gif");
    ServletOutputStream out = res.getOutputStream();

    // Get the image location from the path info
    String source = req.getPathTranslated();
    if (source == null) {
      throw new ServletException("Extra path information " +
                                 "must point to an image");
    }

    // Construct an unshown frame
    // No addNotify() because its peer isn't needed
    Frame frame = new Frame();

    // Load the image
    Image image = Toolkit.getDefaultToolkit().getImage(source);
    MediaTracker mt = new MediaTracker(frame);
    mt.addImage(image, 0);
    try {
      mt.waitForAll();
    }
    catch (InterruptedException e) {
      getServletContext().log(e, "Interrupted while loading image");
      throw new ServletException(e.getMessage());
    }

    // Get the size of the image
```

Example 6-5. An image effect converting an image to grayscale (continued)

```
    int width = image.getWidth(frame);
    int height = image.getHeight(frame);

    // Create an image to match, run through a filter
    Image filtered = frame.createImage(
      new FilteredImageSource(image.getSource(),
                          new GrayscaleImageFilter())));

    // Encode and return the filtered image
    GifEncoder encoder = new GifEncoder(filtered, out);
    encoder.encode();
  }
}
```

Much of the code for this servlet matches that of the `Confidentializer` example. The major difference is shown here:

```
    // Create an image to match, run through a filter
    Image filtered = frame.createImage(
      new FilteredImageSource(image.getSource(),
                          new GrayscaleImageFilter())));
```

This servlet doesn't use the `createImage(int, int)` method of `Component` we've used up until now. It takes advantage of the `createImage(ImageProducer)` method of `Component` instead. The servlet creates an image producer with a `FilteredImageSource` that passes the image through an `GrayscaleImage-Filter`. This filter converts each color pixel to its grayscale counterpart. Thus, the image is converted to grayscale as it is being created. The code for the `GrayscaleImageFilter` is shown in Example 6-6.

Example 6-6. The GrayscaleImageFilter class

```
import java.awt.*;
import java.awt.image.*;

public class GrayscaleImageFilter extends RGBImageFilter {

  public GrayscaleImageFilter() {
    canFilterIndexColorModel = true;
  }

  // Convert color pixels to grayscale
  // The algorithm matches the NTSC specification
  public int filterRGB(int x, int y, int pixel) {

    // Get the average RGB intensity
    int red = (pixel & 0x00ff0000) >> 16;
    int green = (pixel & 0x0000ff00) >> 8;
```

Example 6-6. The GrayscaleImageFilter class (continued)

```
    int blue = pixel & 0x000000ff;

    int luma = (int) (0.299 * red + 0.587 * green + 0.114 * blue);

    // Return the luma value as the value for each RGB component
    // Note: Alpha (transparency) is always set to max (not transparent)
    return (0xff << 24) | (luma << 16) | (luma << 8) | luma;
  }
}
```

For each value in the colormap, this filter receives a pixel value and returns a new filtered pixel value. By setting the `canFilterIndexColorModel` variable to `true`, we signify that this filter can operate on the colormap and not on individual pixel values. The pixel value is given as a 32-bit `int`, where the first octet represents the alpha (transparency) value, the second octet the intensity of red, the third octet the intensity of green, and the fourth octet the intensity of blue. To convert a pixel value to grayscale, the red, green, and blue intensities must be set to identical values. We could average the red, green, and blue values and use that average value for each color intensity. That would convert the image to grayscale. Taking into account how people actually perceive color (and other factors), however, demands a weighted average. The 0.299, 0.587, 0.114 weighting used here matches that used by the National Television Systems Committee for black-and-white television. For more information, see Charles A. Poynton's book *A Technical Introduction to Digital Video* (Wiley) and the web site *http://www.color.org*.

Caching a converted image

The process of creating and encoding an image can be expensive, taking both time and server CPU cycles. Caching encoded images can often improve performance dramatically. Instead of doing all the work for every request, the results can be saved and resent for subsequent requests. The clock face idea that we mentioned earlier is a perfect example. The clock image needs to be created at most once per minute. Any other requests during that minute can be sent the same image. A chart for vote tabulation is another example. It can be created once and changed only as new votes come in.

For our example, let's give the `DeColorize` servlet the ability to cache the grayscale images it returns. The servlet life cycle makes this extremely simple. Our new `DeColorize` servlet saves each converted image as a byte array stored in a `Hashtable` keyed by the image name. First, our servlet needs to create a `Hashtable` instance variable. This must be declared outside `doGet()`:

```
    Hashtable gifs = new Hashtable();
```

To fill this hashtable, we need to capture the encoded graphics. So, instead of giving the GifEncoder the ServletOutputStream, we give it a ByteArrayOutputStream. Then, when we encode the image with encode(), the encoded image is stored in the ByteArrayOutputStream. Finally, we store the captured bytes in the hashtable and then write them to the ServletOutputStream to send the image to the client. Here's the new code to encode, store, and return the filtered image:

```
// Encode, store, and return the filtered image
ByteArrayOutputStream baos = new ByteArrayOutputStream();
GifEncoder encoder = new GifEncoder(filtered, baos);
encoder.encode();
gifs.put(source, baos);
baos.writeTo(out);
```

This fills the hashtable with encoded images keyed by image name. Now, earlier in the servlet, we can go directly to the cache when asked to return a previously encoded image. This code should go immediately after the code executed if source==null:

```
// Short circuit if it's been done before
if (gifs.containsKey(source)) {
    ByteArrayOutputStream baos = (ByteArrayOutputStream) gifs.get(source);
    baos.writeTo(out);
    return;
}
```

With these modifications, any image found in the cache is returned quickly, directly from memory.

Of course, caching multiple images tends to consume large amounts of memory. To cache a single image is rarely a problem, but a servlet such as this should use some method for cleaning house. For example, it could cache only the 10 most recently requested images.

Image Effects in Filter Chains

We haven't talked about filter chains yet in this chapter, but they are actually quite useful for performing image effects. If you recall, a servlet in a filter chain receives content on its input stream and sends a filtered version of that content out its output stream. In previous examples, we have always filtered textual HTML. Now we can see how to filter images in a servlet chain.

Performing special effects on an image works the same whether it happens in a filter chain or in a standard servlet. The only difference is that instead of loading the image from a file, a chained servlet receives its image as an encoded stream of bytes. Example 6-7 shows how a servlet receives an encoded stream of bytes and creates an `Image` from them. In this case, the servlet shrinks the image to one-quarter its original size.

Example 6-7. Shrinking an image using a filter chain

```
import java.awt.*;
import java.awt.image.*;
import java.io.*;
import javax.servlet.*;
import javax.servlet.http.*;

import Acme.JPM.Encoders.*;

public class ShrinkFilter extends HttpServlet {

  public void doGet(HttpServletRequest req, HttpServletResponse res)
                            throws ServletException, IOException {
    ServletOutputStream out = res.getOutputStream();

    String contentType = req.getContentType();
    if (contentType == null || !contentType.startsWith("image")) {
      throw new ServletException("Incoming content type must be \"image/*\"");
    }

    // Fetch the bytes of the incoming image
    DataInputStream in = new DataInputStream(
                      new BufferedInputStream(
                      req.getInputStream()));
    ByteArrayOutputStream baos = new ByteArrayOutputStream();
    byte[] buf = new byte[4 * 1024];  // 4K buffer
    int len;
    while ((len = in.read(buf, 0, buf.length)) != -1) {
      baos.write(buf, 0, len);
    }

    // Create an image out of them
    Image image = Toolkit.getDefaultToolkit()
                          .createImage(baos.toByteArray());

    // Construct an unshown frame
    // No addNotify() since it's peer isn't needed
    Frame frame = new Frame();

    // Load the image, so we can get a true width and height
    MediaTracker mt = new MediaTracker(frame);
    mt.addImage(image, 0);
    try {
      mt.waitForAll();
    }
```

Example 6-7. Shrinking an image using a filter chain (continued)

```
    catch (InterruptedException e) {
      getServletContext().log(e, "Interrupted while loading image");
      throw new ServletException(e.getMessage());
    }

    // Shrink the image to half its width and half its height.
    // An improved version of this servlet would receive the desired
    // ratios in its init parameters.
    // We could also resize using ReplicateScaleFilter or
    // AreaAveragingScaleFilter.
    Image shrunk = image.getScaledInstance(image.getWidth(frame) / 2,
                                           image.getHeight(frame) / 2,
                                           image.SCALE_DEFAULT);

    // Encode and return the shrunken image
    res.setContentType("image/gif");
    GifEncoder encoder = new GifEncoder(shrunk, out);
    encoder.encode();
  }
}
```

The `createImage(byte[])` method of `Toolkit` creates an `Image` from an array of bytes. The method determines the image format automatically, as long as the image is in one of the formats understood and decodable by the AWT (typically GIF, JPEG, and XBM, although it's possible to add a custom content handler).

The servlet uses the `createImage()` method to create an `Image` out of the incoming bytes. Because the `createImage()` method doesn't accept an input stream, the servlet first captures the bytes with a `ByteArrayOutputStream`. After creating the `Image`, the servlet loads it in order to get its true width and height. Then the servlet gets a scaled instance that is half as wide and half as tall, using the `getScaledInstance()` method of `Image`. Last, it encodes the image and sends it out its output stream.

Why use a filter chain to perform an image effect instead of a standard servlet? The main reason is for increased flexibility. For example, a server can be told that all the large classified images in one subdirectory should be run through a "shrink" filter and a "confidential tag" filter. Closer to reality, the server can be told that any image on the web site should be served in its "shrunken" form if the request URI begins with `"/lite"`. Another possibility is to tell the server that all images of type `image/xbm` need to be run through a basic filter that converts the XBM image into a GIF.

Are you wondering why we aren't taking advantage of object serialization to pass our image from servlet to servlet? The reason is simple: images are not `Serializ-`

able. If a servlet can guarantee that the next link in the chain is another servlet and not the client, though, then it can pass the Image more efficiently using techniques described in Chapter 11, *Interservlet Communication.*

An Image of an Embedded Applet

Now let's take a look at one of the more creative ways a servlet can generate an image: by taking a picture of an embedded applet. Applets are small Java programs that can be sent to a client for execution inside a web page—they've been used to create everything from animations to interactive programs to static charts. Here we're going to twist their use a bit. Instead of having the server send a program to the client for execution, we have it send just a picture of the program executing on the server. Now we'll admit that replacing an executing applet with an image is hardly a fair trade, but it does has its advantages. For a static, noninteractive applet, it's often more efficient to send its image than to send the code and data needed to have the client create the image itself. Plus, the image displays even for clients whose browsers don't support Java or who may have Java support disabled.

An image of a simple applet

Example 6-8 shows an applet that may look familiar to you. It's the SecondApplet example taken from David Flanagan's *Java Examples in a Nutshell* book (O'Reilly). Figure 6-5 shows its "fancy graphics."

Example 6-8. A simple applet

```java
import java.applet.*;
import java.awt.*;

public class SecondApplet extends Applet {
  static final String message = "Hello World";
  private Font font;

  // One-time initialization for the applet
  // Note: no constructor defined.
  public void init() {
    font = new Font("Helvetica", Font.BOLD, 48);
  }

  // Draw the applet whenever necessary. Do some fancy graphics.
  public void paint(Graphics g) {
    // The pink oval
    g.setColor(Color.pink);
    g.fillOval(10, 10, 330, 100);

    // The red outline. Java doesn't support wide lines, so we
    // try to simulate a 4-pixel-wide line by drawing four ovals.
```

Example 6-8. A simple applet (continued)

```
      g.setColor(Color.red);
      g.drawOval(10,10, 330, 100);
      g.drawOval(9, 9, 332, 102);
      g.drawOval(8, 8, 334, 104);
      g.drawOval(7, 7, 336, 106);

      // The text
      g.setColor(Color.black);
      g.setFont(font);
      g.drawString(message, 40, 75);
    }
}
```

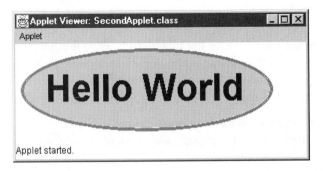

Figure 6-5. The simple applet's fancy graphics

This applet can be embedded the traditional way inside an HTML file with the <APPLET> tag:

```
<APPLET CODE="SecondApplet.class" WIDTH=500 HEIGHT=200>
</APPLET>
```

An <APPLET> tag can include a CODEBASE parameter that tells the client where to fetch the given class. Because the previous <APPLET> tag does not provide a CODE-BASE parameter, the *SecondApplet.class* file is assumed to be in the same directory as the HTML file.

This applet can also be embedded inside HTML content returned by a servlet:

```
import java.io.*;
import javax.servlet.*;
import javax.servlet.http.*;

public class SecondAppletHtml extends HttpServlet {

    public void doGet(HttpServletRequest req, HttpServletResponse res)
                                 throws ServletException, IOException {
        res.setContentType("text/html");
```

```
      PrintWriter out = res.getWriter();

      // ...
      out.println("<APPLET CODE=SecondApplet.class CODEBASE=/ " +
                  "WIDTH=500 HEIGHT=200>");
      out.println("</APPLET>");
      // ...
    }
  }
```

Notice that here the CODEBASE parameter must be supplied. If it's not given, the code base is erroneously assumed to be */servlet* or whatever other virtual path was used to launch the servlet.

Now let's look at a servlet that embeds SecondApplet inside itself and sends a picture of the applet to the client. The code is shown in Example 6-9 and its output in Figure 6-6. In order to embed an applet, a servlet needs a special Frame subclass that implements AppletContext and AppletStub. For these examples, we can use a modified version of Jef Poskanzer's Acme.MainFrame class. In addition to some minor bug fixes, the class has been modified to not call its own show() method (to keep it from actually displaying during execution) and to call the applet's init() and start() methods synchronously instead of in a separate thread (to guarantee the applet is ready when we call its paint() method). A copy of Acme.MainFrameModified is available with the book examples as described in the Preface.

Example 6-9. Embedding SecondApplet

```
import java.applet.*;
import java.awt.*;
import java.awt.image.*;
import java.io.*;
import java.net.*;
import java.util.*;
import javax.servlet.*;
import javax.servlet.http.*;

import Acme.JPM.Encoders.GifEncoder;
import Acme.MainFrameModified;

public class SecondAppletViewer extends HttpServlet {

  static final int WIDTH = 450;
  static final int HEIGHT = 320;
  static final String APPLETNAME = "SecondApplet";

  public void doGet(HttpServletRequest req, HttpServletResponse res)
                              throws ServletException, IOException {
```

Example 6-9. Embedding SecondApplet (continued)

```
ServletOutputStream out = res.getOutputStream();

MainFrameModified frame = null;
Graphics g = null;
Applet applet = null;

try {
  // Load the SecondApplet
  // Must be in the standard CLASSPATH
  try {
    applet = (Applet) Class.forName(APPLETNAME).newInstance();
  }
  catch (Exception e) {
    throw new ServletException("Could not load applet:" + e);
  }

  // Prepare the applet arguments
  String args[] = new String[1];
  args[0] = "barebones=true";   // run without a menu bar

  // Put the applet in its frame
  // addNotify() is called by MainFrameModified
  frame = new MainFrameModified(applet, args, WIDTH, HEIGHT);

  // Get a graphics region to match the applet size, using the Frame
  Image image = frame.createImage(WIDTH, HEIGHT);
  g = image.getGraphics();

  // Ask the applet to paint itself
  applet.validate();
  applet.paint(g);

  // Encode and return what it painted
  res.setContentType("image/gif");
  GifEncoder encoder = new GifEncoder(image, out);
  encoder.encode();
}
finally {
  // Clean up resources
  if (applet != null) {
    applet.stop();
    applet.destroy();
    applet.removeAll();
  }
  if (g != null) {
    g.dispose();
  }
  if (frame != null) {
```

Example 6-9. Embedding SecondApplet (continued)

```
        frame.removeAll();
        frame.removeNotify();
        frame.dispose();
      }
    }
  }
}
```

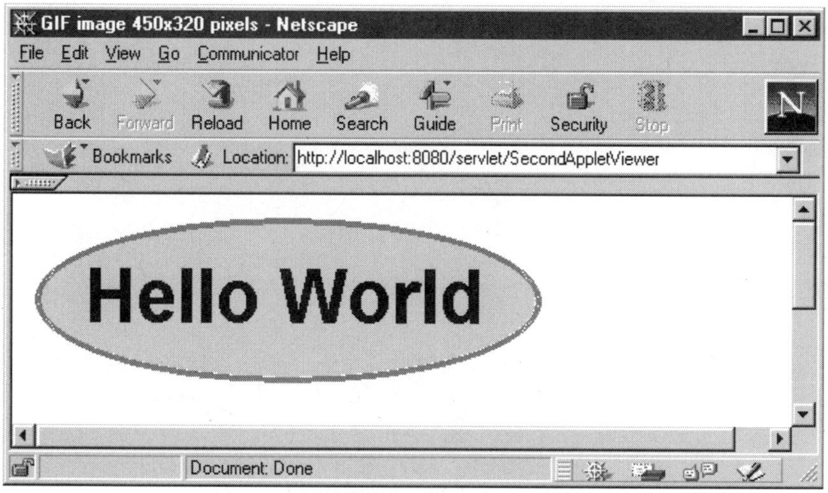

Figure 6-6. Another view of the simple applet's fancy graphics

This servlet begins by dynamically loading the SecondApplet class and creating a single instance of it. For SecondApplet to be found, it must be somewhere in the server's standard CLASSPATH which for the Java Web Server by default excludes the *server_root/servlets* directory. Then the servlet prepares the applet's arguments. These are passed to the MainFrameModified constructor as an array of "*name=value*" strings. SecondApplet takes no parameters, so this step would seem to be unnecessary. However, MainFrameModified piggy-backs into the argument list its own "barebones" argument, which we set to true to indicate it should display the applet without any special decoration. Finally, the servlet creates an appropriately sized off-screen graphics context, has the applet paint itself using that context, and encodes the image for transmission to the client.

A generic applet viewer

We can build on this example to develop a generic servlet capable of embedding and taking a picture of any applet. It can accept as request parameters the applet name, its width and height, and its parameters. Example 6-10 contains the code.

Example 6-10. A generic applet viewer

```
import java.applet.*;
import java.awt.*;
import java.awt.image.*;
import java.io.*;
import java.net.*;
import java.util.*;
import javax.servlet.*;
import javax.servlet.http.*;

import Acme.JPM.Encoders.GifEncoder;
import Acme.MainFrameModified;

public class AppletViewer extends HttpServlet {

  static final int WIDTH = 450;
  static final int HEIGHT = 320;

  public void doGet(HttpServletRequest req, HttpServletResponse res)
                              throws ServletException, IOException {
    ServletOutputStream out = res.getOutputStream();

    MainFrameModified frame = null;
    Graphics g = null;
    Applet applet = null;

    try {
      String appletParam = req.getParameter("applet");
      String widthParam = req.getParameter("width");
      String heightParam = req.getParameter("height");

      // Load the given applet
      // Must be in the standard CLASSPATH
      try {
        applet = (Applet) Class.forName(appletParam).newInstance();
      }
      catch (Exception e) {
        throw new ServletException("Could not load applet:" + e);
      }

      // Convert width/height to integers
      // Use default values if they weren't given or there's a problem
```

Example 6-10. A generic applet viewer (continued)

```java
    int width = WIDTH;
    int height = HEIGHT;
    try { width = Integer.parseInt(widthParam); }
    catch (NumberFormatException e) { /* leave as default */ }
    try { height = Integer.parseInt(heightParam); }
    catch (NumberFormatException e) { /* leave as default */ }

    // Get a list of the other parameters in a format MainFrame understands
    // (Specifically, an array of "name=value" Strings)
    Vector temp = new Vector();
    Enumeration names = req.getParameterNames();
    while (names.hasMoreElements()) {
      String name = (String) names.nextElement();
      if (name != "applet" && name != "width" && name != "height")
        temp.addElement(name + "=" + req.getParameter(name));
    }
    temp.addElement("barebones=true");  // run without a menu bar
    // Now from Vector to array
    int size = temp.size();
    String args[] = new String[size];
    for (int i = 0; i < size; i++) {
      args[i] = (String) temp.elementAt(i);
    }

    // Put the applet in its frame
    // addNotify() is called by MainFrameModified
    frame = new MainFrameModified(applet, args, width, height);

    // Get a graphics region to match the applet size, using the Frame
    Image image = frame.createImage(width, height);
    g = image.getGraphics();

    // Ask the applet to paint its children and itself
    applet.validate();
    paintContainerChildren(g, applet);
    applet.paint(g);

    // Encode and return what it painted
    res.setContentType("image/gif");
    GifEncoder encoder = new GifEncoder(image, out);
    encoder.encode();
  }
  finally {
    // Clean up resources
    if (applet != null) {
      applet.stop();
      applet.destroy();
      applet.removeAll();
```

Example 6-10. A generic applet viewer (continued)

```
      }
      if (g != null) {
        g.dispose();
      }
      if (frame != null) {
        frame.removeAll();
        frame.removeNotify();
        frame.dispose();
      }
    }
  }

  // Recursively paints all the Components of a Container.
  // It's different from paintComponents(Graphics) because
  // paintComponents(Graphics) does not paint to the passed-in
  // Graphics! It uses it only to get the clipping region.
  void paintContainerChildren(Graphics g, Container c) {
    Component[] children = c.getComponents();
    for (int i = 0; i < children.length; i++) {
      if (children[i] != null) {
        children[i].paintAll(g);  // get lightweights too
        if (children[i] instanceof Container) {
          paintContainerChildren(g, (Container)children[i]);
        }
      }
    }
  }

}
```

There are two major differences between this servlet and `SecondAppletViewer`: how it handles parameters and how it paints the applet's components. All the details, from the applet's name to its parameters, are passed to this servlet via request parameters. It receives the name of the applet as the `"applet"` parameter and its width and height as the `"width"` and `"height"` parameters; it passes all the other parameters on to the applet itself.

The painting is more radically different. This servlet uses a custom-built `paint-ContainerChildren()` utility method to paint all the components of the applet. For the servlet to call `applet.paintComponents(g)` is not sufficient because `paintComponents(g)` does not paint to the passed-in `Graphics` object! Instead, it uses the `Graphics` parameter only to get a clipping region. This servlet also uses `paintAll()` instead of `paint()`, so that it correctly paints lightweight components. Note that for this technique to work well, the embedded applet has to fully paint itself during its first `paint()` invocation. It can't display a splash screen or perform a lazy load of its images.

The `AppletViewer` servlet can replace `SecondAppletViewer`. Just invoke it with the URL *http://server:port/servlet/AppletViewer?applet=SecondApplet*. It can also replace our `SimpleChart` example. Remember when we said JavaChart includes a set of free chart-generating applets? We can use `AppletViewer` to embed any of these free applets and send the resulting chart as an image to the client. To duplicate the `SimpleChart` example requires this lengthy URL (split into separate lines for readability, probably so long that many servers won't be able to handle it):

```
http://server:port/servlet/AppletViewer?
applet=javachart.applet.columnApp&
titleFont=TimesRoman%2c24%2c0&
titleString=Comparing+Apples+And+Oranges&
xAxisTitle=Year&
yAxisTitle=Tons+Consumed&
xAxisLabels=1993%2c1994%2c1995%2c1996%2c1997&
dataset0yValues=950%2c1005%2c1210%2c1165%2c1255&
dataset1yValues=1435%2c1650%2c1555%2c1440%2c1595&
dataset0Color=red&
dataset0Name=Apples&
dataset1Color=orange&
dataset1Name=Oranges&
legendOn=yes&
legendHorizontal=true&
legendllX=0.4&
legendllY=0.75&
iconHeight=0.04&
iconWidth=0.04&
iconGap=0.02&
xAxisOptions=gridOff&
yAxisOptions=gridOff
```

The graph generated by this URL looks identical to Figure 6-2 shown earlier (with the one difference that the applet version contains a blue dot in the lower right corner that can be removed with the purchase of a JavaChart license).

Advantages and disadvantages

We think you'll agree that embedding an applet in a servlet has a certain coolness factor. But is it ever practical? Let's look over its advantages and disadvantages. First, the advantages:

It can save money.

Hey, the JavaChart applets are free, and Visual Engineering assured us that this use doesn't violate their license!

It can save download time.

Why send all the code and data needed to make an image when you can send the image itself, especially when the image can be pregenerated?

It works for every client.
It works even when the client browser doesn't support Java or has Java disabled.

However, on the downside:

It requires extra resources on the server.
Specifically it consumes CPU power and memory.

It works well for only a few applets.
Specifically it works best on static, noninteractive applets that fully paint themselves with their first `paint()` invocation.

Compressed Content

The `java.util.zip` package was introduced in JDK 1.1. This package contains classes that support reading and writing the GZIP and ZIP compression formats. Although these classes were added to support Java Archive (JAR) files, they also provide a convenient, standard way for a servlet to send compressed content.

Compressed content doesn't look any different to the end user because it's decompressed by the browser before it's displayed. Yet, while it looks the same, it can improve the end user's experience by reducing the time required to download the content from the server. For heavily compressable content such as HTML, compression can reduce transmission times by an order of magnitude. Quite a trick! Just bear in mind that to compress content dynamically forces the server to perform extra work, so any speed-up in transmission time has to be weighed against slower server performance.

By now you should be familiar with the idea that a servlet can send a `Content-Type` header as part of its response to tell the client the type of information being returned. To send compressed content, a servlet must also send a `Content-Encoding` header to tell the client the scheme by which the content has been encoded. Under the HTTP 1.0 specification, the possible encoding schemes are `gzip` (or `x-gzip`) and `compress` (or `x-compress`) for GZIP and ZIP compression formats, respectively.

Not all clients understand the `gzip` and `compress` encodings. To tell the server which encoding schemes it understands, a client may send an `Accept-Encoding` header that specifies acceptable encoding schemes as a comma-separated list. Most browsers do not yet provide this header—even those that do support compressed encodings. For now, a servlet has to decide that without the header it won't send compressed content, or it has to examine the `User-Agent` header to see if the browser is one that supports compression. Of the current popular browsers, only Netscape Navigator 3 and 4 on Unix and Microsoft Internet Explorer 4 on

Windows support GZIP encoding, and none support ZIP encoding. For more information (and a regular expression to identify GZIP-enabled browsers), see *http://www.kulturbox.de/perl/test/content-encoding-gzip/3.*

Although negotiating which compression format to use can involve a fair amount of logic, actually sending the compressed content could hardly be simpler. The servlet just wraps its standard `ServletOutputStream` with a `GZIPOutputStream` or `ZipOutputStream`. Be sure to call `out.close()` when your servlet is done writing output, so that the appropriate trailer for the compression format is written. Ah, the wonders of Java!

Example 6-11 shows the `ViewFile` servlet from Chapter 4 rewritten to send compressed content whenever possible. We'd show you a screen shot, but there's nothing new to see. As we said before, an end user cannot tell that the server sent compressed content to the browser—except perhaps with reduced download times.

Example 6-11. Sending compressed content

```
import java.io.*;
import java.util.*;
import java.util.zip.*;
import javax.servlet.*;
import javax.servlet.http.*;

import com.oreilly.servlet.ServletUtils;

public class ViewFileCompress extends HttpServlet {

  public void doGet(HttpServletRequest req, HttpServletResponse res)
                               throws ServletException, IOException {

    OutputStream out = null;

    // Select the appropriate content encoding based on the
    // client's Accept-Encoding header. Choose GZIP if the header
    // includes "gzip". Choose ZIP if the header includes "compress".
    // Choose no compression otherwise.
    String encodings = req.getHeader("Accept-Encoding");
    if (encodings != null && encodings.indexOf("gzip") != -1) {
      // Go with GZIP
      res.setHeader("Content-Encoding", "x-gzip");
      out = new GZIPOutputStream(res.getOutputStream());
    }
    else if (encodings != null && encodings.indexOf("compress") != -1) {
      // Go with ZIP
      res.setHeader("Content-Encoding", "x-compress");
      out = new ZipOutputStream(res.getOutputStream());
```

Example 6-11. Sending compressed content (continued)

```
      ((ZipOutputStream)out).putNextEntry(new ZipEntry("dummy name"));
    }
    else {
      // No compression
      out = res.getOutputStream();
    }
    res.setHeader("Vary", "Accept-Encoding");

    // Get the file to view
    String file = req.getPathTranslated();

    // No file, nothing to view
    if (file == null) {
      res.sendError(res.SC_FORBIDDEN);
      return;
    }

    // Get and set the type of the file
    String contentType = getServletContext().getMimeType(file);
    res.setContentType(contentType);

    // Return the file
    try {
      ServletUtils.returnFile(file, out);
    }
    catch (FileNotFoundException e) {
      res.sendError(res.SC_NOT_FOUND);
      return;
    }
    catch (IOException e) {
      getServletContext().log(e, "Problem sending file");
      res.sendError(res.SC_INTERNAL_SERVER_ERROR,
                    ServletUtils.getStackTraceAsString(e));
    }

    // Write the compression trailer and close the output stream
    out.close();
  }
}
```

The servlet begins by declaring a null OutputStream and then setting this
OutputStream to a GZIPOutputStream, ZipOutputStream, or ServletOutput-
Stream, depending on the received Accept-Encoding header. As it selects which
output stream to use, the servlet sets the Content-Encoding header accordingly.
When sending compressed content, this header must be set for the client to run
the appropriate decompression algorithm. The servlet also sets the Vary header to
the value Accept-Encoding to be polite and indicate to the client that the servlet

varies its output depending on the Accept-Encoding header. Most clients ignore this header.

After this early logic, the servlet can treat the output stream as just another OutputStream. It could wrap the stream with a PrintStream or PrintWriter, or it could pass it to a GifEncoder. But, no matter what it does, the servlet has to be sure to call out.close() when it's finished sending content. This call writes the appropriate trailer to the compressed stream.

There is some content that should not be compressed. For example, GIF and JPEG images are already compressed as part of their encoding, so there's no benefit in compressing them again. An improved version of the FileViewCompressed servlet would detect when it's returning an image and not bother with an attempt at further compression. Another improvement would be to rewrite this servlet as a filter—compressing whatever content is piped through it.

Server Push

Up until now, every page returned by a servlet has been just that: a page. Always one page with one content type. But why think in such limited terms? Why not have a servlet return several pages, each with a different content type, all in response to the same request? It may be hard to imagine—and sound even harder to implement—but it's actually quite easy using a technique known as *server push*.

It's called server push because the server sends, or pushes, a sequence of response pages to the client. Compare this to the client pull technique discussed in the last chapter, where it's left to the client to get, or pull, each page from the server. Although the results of each technique are similar to the end user—the appearance of a sequence of pages—the implementation details and the appropriate uses of the two techniques are quite different.

With server push, the socket connection between the client and the server remains open until the last page has been sent. This gives the server the ability to send page updates quickly and to control exactly when those updates are sent. As such, server push is ideal for pages that need frequent updates (such as rudimentary animations) or pages that need server-controlled but somewhat infrequent updates (such as live status updates). Note, however, that server push is not yet supported by Microsoft Internet Explorer, and extended use should be avoided, as it has been found to be harmful to the server's available socket count.

With client pull, the socket connection is broken after every page, so responsibility for page updates falls to the client. The client uses the Refresh header value sent by the server to determine when to perform its update, so client pull is the best choice for pages that require infrequent updates or have updates at known intervals.

Server push can come in handy for limited-length animations and for real-time status updates. For example, consider a servlet that could push the four latest satellite weather maps, creating a rudimentary animation. If you recall the PrimeSearcher servlet from Chapter 3, *The Servlet Life Cycle*, think about how we could use server push to notify a limited number of clients immediately as the servlet finds each new prime.

Example 6-12 shows a servlet that uses server push to display a countdown to a rocket launch. It begins by sending a series of pages that count down from 10 to 1. Every page replaces the previous page. When the countdown reaches 0, the servlet sends a picture of a launch. It uses the com.oreilly.servlet.MultipartResponse utility class (shown in Example 6-13) to manage the server push details.

Example 6-12. Countdown to a rocket launch

```
import java.awt.*;
import java.io.*;
import javax.servlet.*;
import javax.servlet.http.*;

import com.oreilly.servlet.MultipartResponse;
import com.oreilly.servlet.ServletUtils;

public class Countdown extends HttpServlet {

  static final String LAUNCH = "/images/launch.gif";

  public void doGet(HttpServletRequest req, HttpServletResponse res)
                          throws ServletException, IOException {
    ServletOutputStream out = res.getOutputStream();  // some binary output

    // Prepare a multipart response
    MultipartResponse multi = new MultipartResponse(res);

    // First send a countdown
    for (int i = 10; i > 0; i--) {
      multi.startResponse("text/plain");
      out.println(i + "...");
      multi.endResponse();
      try { Thread.sleep(1000); } catch (InterruptedException e) { }
    }

    // Then send the launch image
    multi.startResponse("image/gif");
    try {
```

Example 6-12. Countdown to a rocket launch (continued)

```
      ServletUtils.returnFile(req.getRealPath(LAUNCH), out);
    }
    catch (FileNotFoundException e) {
      throw new ServletException("Could not find file: " + e.getMessage());
    }

    // Don't forget to end the multipart response
    multi.finish();
  }
}
```

The `MultipartResponse` class hides most of the nasty, dirty details involved in using server push. Feel free to use it in your own servlets. It is easy to use, as you can see from the previous example.

First, create a new `MultipartResponse` object, passing it the servlet's response object. `MultipartResponse` uses the response object to fetch the servlet's output stream and to set the response's content type. Then, for each page of content, begin by calling `startResponse()` and passing in the content type for that page. Send the content for the page by writing to the output stream as usual. A call to `endResponse()` ends the page and flushes the content, so the client can see it. At this point, you can add a call to `sleep()`, or some other kind of delay, until the next page is ready for sending. The call to `endResponse()` is optional, as the `startResponse()` method knows whether the previous response was ended and ends it if necessary. You should still call `endResponse()` if there's going to be a delay between the time one response ends and the next begins. This lets the client display the latest response while it is waiting for the next one. Finally, after all the response pages have been sent, a call to the `finish()` method finishes the multipart response and sends a code telling the client there will be no more responses.

Example 6-13 contains the code for the `MultipartResponse` class.

Example 6-13. The MultipartResponse class

```
public class MultipartResponse {

  HttpServletResponse res;
  ServletOutputStream out;
  boolean endedLastResponse = true;

  public MultipartResponse(HttpServletResponse response) throws IOException {
    // Save the response object and output stream
    res = response;
    out = res.getOutputStream();

    // Set things up
```

Example 6-13. The MultipartResponse class (continued)

```
    res.setContentType("multipart/x-mixed-replace;boundary=End");
    out.println();
    out.println("--End");
  }

  public void startResponse(String contentType) throws IOException {
    // End the last response if necessary
    if (!endedLastResponse) {
      endResponse();
    }
    // Start the next one
    out.println("Content-Type: " + contentType);
    out.println();
    endedLastResponse = false;
  }

  public void endResponse() throws IOException {
    // End the last response, and flush so the client sees the content
    out.println();
    out.println("--End");
    out.flush();
    endedLastResponse = true;
  }

  public void finish() throws IOException {
    out.println("--End--");
    out.flush();
  }
}
```

7

Session Tracking

HTTP is a stateless protocol: it provides no way for a server to recognize that a sequence of requests are all from the same client. Privacy advocates may consider this a feature, but it causes problems because many web applications aren't stateless. The shopping cart application is a classic example—a client can put items in his virtual cart, accumulating them until he checks out several page requests later. Other examples include sites that offer stock brokerage services or interactive data mining.

The HTTP state problem can best be understood if you imagine an online chat forum where you are the guest of honor. Picture dozens of chat users, all conversing with you at the same time. They are asking you questions, responding to your questions, and generally making you wish you had taken that typing course back in high school. Now imagine that when each participant writes to you, the chat forum doesn't tell you who's speaking! All you see is a bunch of questions and statements mixed in with each other. In this kind of forum, the best you can do is hold simple conversations, perhaps answering direct questions. If you try to do anything more, such as ask someone a question in return, you won't necessarily know when the answer comes back. This is exactly the HTTP state problem. The HTTP server sees only a series of requests—it needs extra help to know exactly who's making a request.[*]

The solution, as you may have already guessed, is for a client to introduce itself as it makes each request. Each client needs to provide a unique identifier that lets the server identify it, or it needs to give some information that the server can use

---

[*] If you're wondering why the HTTP server can't identify the client by the connecting machine's IP address, the answer is that the reported IP address could possibly be the address of a proxy server or the address of a server machine that hosts multiple users.

to properly handle the request. To use the chat example, a participant has to begin each of his sentences with something like "Hi, I'm Jason, and ..." or "Hi, I just asked about your age, and ...". As you'll see in this chapter, there are several ways for HTTP clients to send this introductory information with each request.

The first half of the chapter explores the traditional session-tracking techniques used by CGI developers: user authorization, hidden form fields, URL rewriting, and persistent cookies. The second half of the chapter demonstrates the built-in support for session tracking in Version 2.0 of the Servlet API. This support is built on top of the traditional techniques and it greatly simplifies the task of session tracking in your servlets.

User Authorization

One way to perform session tracking is to leverage the information that comes with user authorization. We discussed user authorization back in Chapter 4, *Retrieving Information*, but, in case you've forgotten, it occurs when a web server restricts access to some of its resources to only those clients that log in using a recognized username and password. After the client logs in, the username is available to a servlet through getRemoteUser().

We can use the username to track a client session. Once a user has logged in, the browser remembers her username and resends the name and password as the user views new pages on the site. A servlet can identify the user through her username and thereby track her session. For example, if the user adds an item to her virtual shopping cart, that fact can be remembered (in a shared class or external database, perhaps) and used later by another servlet when the user goes to the checkout page.

For example, a servlet that utilizes user authorization might add an item to a user's shopping cart with code like the following:

```
String name = req.getRemoteUser();
if (name == null) {
  // Explain that the server administrator should protect this page
}
else {
  String[] items = req.getParameterValues("item");
  if (items != null) {
    for (int i = 0; i < items.length; i++) {
      addItemToCart(name, items[i]);
    }
  }
}
```

Another servlet can then retrieve the items from a user's cart with code like this:

```
String name = req.getRemoteUser();
if (name == null) {
  // Explain that the server administrator should protect this page
}
else {
  String[] items = getItemsFromCart(name);
}
```

The biggest advantage of using user authorization to perform session tracking is that it's easy to implement. Simply tell the server to protect a set of pages, and use `getRemoteUser()` to identify each client. Another advantage is that the technique works even when the user accesses your site from different machines. It also works even if the user strays from your site or exits her browser before coming back.

The biggest disadvantage of user authorization is that it requires each user to register for an account and then log in each time she starts visiting your site. Most users will tolerate registering and logging in as a necessary evil when they are accessing sensitive information, but it's overkill for simple session tracking. We clearly need a better approach to support anonymous session tracking. Another small problem with user authorization is that a user cannot simultaneously maintain more than one session at the same site.

Hidden Form Fields

One way to support anonymous session tracking is to use hidden form fields. As the name implies, these are fields added to an HTML form that are not displayed in the client's browser. They are sent back to the server when the form that contains them is submitted. You include hidden form files with HTML like this:

```
<FORM ACTION="/servlet/MovieFinder" METHOD="POST">
...
<INPUT TYPE=hidden NAME="zip" VALUE="94040">
<INPUT TYPE=hidden NAME="level" VALUE="expert">
...
</FORM>
```

In a sense, hidden form fields define constant variables for a form. To a servlet receiving a submitted form, there is no difference between a hidden field and a visible field.

With hidden form fields, we can rewrite our shopping cart servlets so that users can shop anonymously until check-out time. Example 7-1 demonstrates the technique with a servlet that displays the user's shopping cart contents and lets the

user choose to add more items or check out. An example screen for a bookworm
is shown in Figure 7-1.

Example 7-1. Session tracking using hidden form fields

```
import java.io.*;
import javax.servlet.*;
import javax.servlet.http.*;

public class ShoppingCartViewerHidden extends HttpServlet {

  public void doGet(HttpServletRequest req, HttpServletResponse res)
                              throws ServletException, IOException {
    res.setContentType("text/html");
    PrintWriter out = res.getWriter();

    out.println("<HEAD><TITLE>Current Shopping Cart Items</TITLE></HEAD>");
    out.println("<BODY>");

    // Cart items are passed in as the item parameter.
    String[] items = req.getParameterValues("item");

    // Print the current cart items.
    out.println("You currently have the following items in your cart:<BR>");
    if (items == null) {
      out.println("<B>None</B>");
    }
    else {
      out.println("<UL>");
      for (int i = 0; i < items.length; i++) {
        out.println("<LI>" + items[i]);
      }
      out.println("</UL>");
    }

    // Ask if the user wants to add more items or check out.
    // Include the current items as hidden fields so they'll be passed on.
    out.println("<FORM ACTION=\"/servlet/ShoppingCart\" METHOD=POST>");
    if (items != null) {
      for (int i = 0; i < items.length; i++) {
        out.println("<INPUT TYPE=hidden NAME=item VALUE=\"" +
          items[i] + "\">");
      }
    }
    out.println("Would you like to<BR>");
    out.println("<INPUT TYPE=submit VALUE=\" Add More Items \">");
    out.println("<INPUT TYPE=submit VALUE=\" Check Out \">");
    out.println("</FORM>");
```

Example 7-1. Session tracking using hidden form fields (continued)

```
    out.println("</BODY></HTML>");
  }
}
```

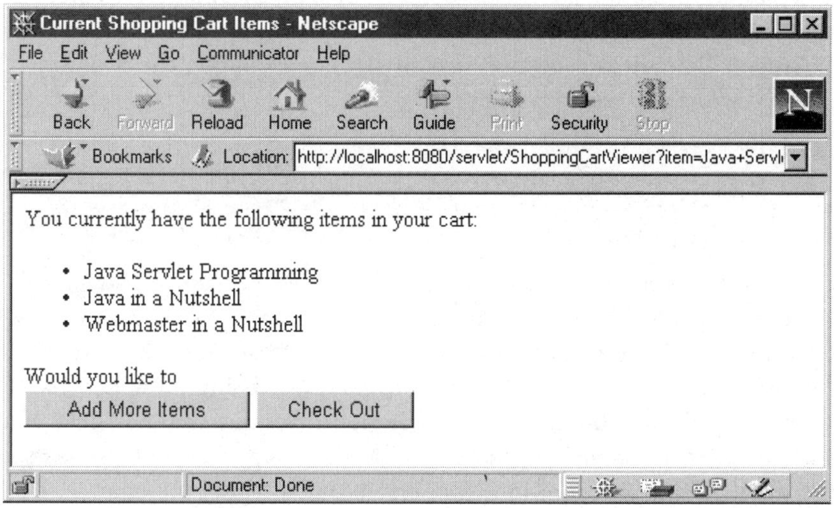

Figure 7-1. Shopping cart contents

This servlet first reads the items already in the cart using `getParameter-Values("item")`. Presumably, the `item` parameter values were sent to this servlet using hidden fields. The servlet then displays the current items to the user and asks if he wants to add more items or check out. The servlet asks its question with a form that includes hidden fields, so the form's target (the `ShoppingCart` servlet) receives the current items as part of the submission.

As more and more information is associated with a client's session, it can become burdensome to pass it all using hidden form fields. In these situations, it's possible to pass on just a unique session ID that identifies a particular client's session. That session ID can be associated with complete information about the session that is stored on the server.

The advantages of hidden form fields are their ubiquity and support for anonymity. Hidden fields are supported in all the popular browsers, they demand no special server requirements, and they can be used with clients that haven't registered or logged in. The major disadvantage with this technique, however, is that it works only for a sequence of dynamically generated forms. The technique breaks down immediately with static documents, emailed documents, bookmarked documents, and browser shutdowns.

URL Rewriting

URL rewriting is another way to support anonymous session tracking. With URL rewriting, every local URL the user might click on is dynamically modified, or rewritten, to include extra information. The extra information can be in the form of extra path information, added parameters, or some custom, server-specific URL change. Due to the limited space available in rewriting a URL, the extra information is usually limited to a unique session ID. For example, the following URLs have been rewritten to pass the session ID 123:

```
http://server:port/servlet/Rewritten                original
http://server:port/servlet/Rewritten/123            extra path information
http://server:port/servlet/Rewritten?sessionid=123  added parameter
http://server:port/servlet/Rewritten;$sessionid$123 custom change
```

Each rewriting technique has its advantages and disadvantages. Using extra path information works on all servers, and it works as a target for forms that use both the GET and POST methods. It doesn't work well if a servlet has to use the extra path information as true path information, however. Using an added parameter works on all servers too, but it fails as a target for forms that use the POST method, and it can cause parameter naming collisions. Using a custom, server-specific change works under all conditions for servers that support the change. Unfortunately, it doesn't work at all for servers that don't support the change.

Example 7-2 shows a revised version of our shopping cart viewer that uses URL rewriting in the form of extra path information to anonymously track a shopping cart.

Example 7-2. Session tracking using URL rewriting

```
import java.io.*;
import javax.servlet.*;
import javax.servlet.http.*;

public class ShoppingCartViewerRewrite extends HttpServlet {

  public void doGet(HttpServletRequest req, HttpServletResponse res)
                            throws ServletException, IOException {
    res.setContentType("text/html");
    PrintWriter out = res.getWriter();

    out.println("<HEAD><TITLE>Current Shopping Cart Items</TITLE></HEAD>");
    out.println("<BODY>");

    // Get the current session ID, or generate one if necessary
    String sessionid = req.getPathInfo();
    if (sessionid == null) {
      sessionid = generateSessionId();
```

Example 7-2. Session tracking using URL rewriting (continued)

```
    }

    // Cart items are associated with the session ID
    String[] items = getItemsFromCart(sessionid);

    // Print the current cart items.
    out.println("You currently have the following items in your cart:<BR>");
    if (items == null) {
      out.println("<B>None</B>");
    }
    else {
      out.println("<UL>");
      for (int i = 0; i < items.length; i++) {
        out.println("<LI>" + items[i]);
      }
      out.println("</UL>");
    }

    // Ask if the user wants to add more items or check out.
    // Include the session ID in the action URL.
    out.println("<FORM ACTION=\"/servlet/ShoppingCart/" + sessionid +
                "\" METHOD=POST>");
    out.println("Would you like to<BR>");
    out.println("<INPUT TYPE=submit VALUE=\" Add More Items \">");
    out.println("<INPUT TYPE=submit VALUE=\" Check Out \">");
    out.println("</FORM>");

    // Offer a help page. Include the session ID in the URL.
    out.println("For help, click <A HREF=\"/servlet/Help/" + sessionid +
                "?topic=ShoppingCartViewerRewrite\">here</A>");

    out.println("</BODY></HTML>");
  }

  private static String generateSessionId() {
    String uid = new java.rmi.server.UID().toString();  // guaranteed unique
    return java.net.URLEncoder.encode(uid);  // encode any special chars
  }

  private static String[] getItemsFromCart(String sessionid) {
    // Not implemented
  }
}
```

This servlet first tries to retrieve the current session ID using `getPathInfo()`. If a session ID is not specified, it calls `generateSessionId()` to generate a new unique session ID using an RMI class designed specifically for this. The session ID is used to fetch and display the current items in the cart. The ID is then added to the form's ACTION attribute, so it can be retrieved by the ShoppingCart servlet. The session ID is also added to a new help URL that invokes the Help servlet. This wasn't possible with hidden form fields because the Help servlet isn't the target of a form submission.

The advantages and disadvantages of URL rewriting closely match those of hidden form fields. The major difference is that URL rewriting works for all dynamically created documents, such as the Help servlet, not just forms. Plus, with the right server support, custom URL rewriting can even work for static documents. Unfortunately, actually performing the URL rewriting can be tedious.

Persistent Cookies

A fourth technique to perform session tracking involves persistent cookies. A *cookie* is a bit of information sent by a web server to a browser that can later be read back from that browser. When a browser receives a cookie, it saves the cookie and thereafter sends the cookie back to the server each time it accesses a page on that server, subject to certain rules. Because a cookie's value can uniquely identify a client, cookies are often used for session tracking.

Cookies were first introduced in Netscape Navigator. Although they were not part of the official HTTP specification, cookies quickly became a de facto standard supported in all the popular browsers including Netscape 0.94 Beta and up and Microsoft Internet Explorer 2 and up. Currently the HTTP Working Group of the Internet Engineering Task Force (IETF) is in the process of making cookies an official standard as written in RFC 2109. For more information on cookies see Netscape's Cookie Specification at *http://home.netscape.com/newsref/std/cookie_spec.html* and RFC 2109 at *http://www.ietf.org/rfc/rfc2109.txt*. Another good site is *http://www.cookiecentral.com*.

Working with Cookies

Version 2.0 of the Servlet API provides the javax.servlet.http.Cookie class for working with cookies. The HTTP header details for the cookies are handled by the Servlet API. You create a cookie with the Cookie() constructor:

```
public Cookie(String name, String value)
```

This creates a new cookie with an initial name and value. The rules for valid names and values are given in Netscape's Cookie Specification and RFC 2109.

A servlet can send a cookie to the client by passing a Cookie object to the addCookie() method of HttpServletResponse:

```
public void HttpServletResponse.addCookie(Cookie cookie)
```

This method adds the specified cookie to the response. Additional cookies can be added with subsequent calls to addCookie(). Because cookies are sent using HTTP headers, they should be added to the response before you send any content. Browsers are only required to accept 20 cookies per site, 300 total per user, and they can limit each cookie's size to 4096 bytes.

The code to set a cookie looks like this:

```
Cookie cookie = new Cookie("ID", "123");
res.addCookie(cookie);
```

A servlet retrieves cookies by calling the getCookies() method of HttpServlet-Request:

```
public Cookie[] HttpServletRequest.getCookies()
```

This method returns an array of Cookie objects that contains all the cookies sent by the browser as part of the request or null if no cookies were sent. The code to fetch cookies looks like this:

```
Cookie[] cookies = req.getCookies();
if (cookies != null) {
  for (int i = 0; i < cookies.length; i++) {
    String name = cookies[i].getName();
    String value = cookies[i].getValue();
  }
}
```

You can set a number of attributes for a cookie in addition to its name and value. The following methods are used to set these attributes. As you can see in Appendix B, *HTTP Servlet API Quick Reference*, there is a corresponding get method for each set method. The get methods are rarely used, however, because when a cookie is sent to the server, it contains only its name, value, and version.

public void Cookie.setVersion(int v)

Sets the version of a cookie. Servlets can send and receive cookies formatted to match either Netscape persistent cookies (Version 0) or the newer, somewhat experimental, RFC 2109 cookies (Version 1). Newly constructed cookies default to Version 0 to maximize interoperability.

public void Cookie.setDomain(String pattern)

Specifies a domain restriction pattern. A domain pattern specifies the servers that should see a cookie. By default, cookies are returned only to the host that saved them. Specifying a domain name pattern overrides this. The pattern must begin with a dot and must contain at least two dots. A pattern matches only one entry beyond the initial dot. For example, ".foo.com" is valid and matches *www.foo.com* and *upload.foo.com* but not *www.upload.foo.com*. For details on domain patterns, see Netscape's Cookie Specification and RFC 2109.

`public void Cookie.setMaxAge(int expiry)`

Specifies the maximum age of the cookie in seconds before it expires. A negative value indicates the default, that the cookie should expire when the browser exits. A zero value tells the browser to delete the cookie immediately.

`public void Cookie.setPath(String uri)`

Specifies a path for the cookie, which is the subset of URIs to which a cookie should be sent. By default, cookies are sent to the page that set the cookie and to all the pages in that directory or under that directory. For example, if */servlet/CookieMonster* sets a cookie, the default path is `"/servlet"`. That path indicates the cookie should be sent to */servlet/Elmo* and to */servlet/subdir/BigBird*—but not to the */Oscar.html* servlet alias or to any CGI programs under */cgi-bin*. A path set to `"/"` causes a cookie to be sent to all the pages on a server. A cookie's path must be such that it includes the servlet that set the cookie.

`public void Cookie.setSecure(boolean flag)`

Indicates whether the cookie should be sent only over a secure channel, such as SSL. By default, its value is `false`.

`public void Cookie.setComment(String comment)`

Sets the comment field of the cookie. A comment describes the intended purpose of a cookie. Web browsers may choose to display this text to the user. Comments are not supported by Version 0 cookies.

`public void Cookie.setValue(String newValue)`

Assigns a new value to a cookie. With Version 0 cookies, values should not contain the following: whitespace, brackets and parentheses, equals signs, commas, double quotes, slashes, question marks, at signs, colons, and semicolons. Empty values may not behave the same way on all browsers.

Shopping Using Persistent Cookies

Example 7-3 shows a version of our shopping cart viewer that has been modified to maintain the shopping cart using persistent cookies.

Example 7-3. Session tracking using persistent cookies

```
import java.io.*;
import javax.servlet.*;
import javax.servlet.http.*;

public class ShoppingCartViewerCookie extends HttpServlet {

  public void doGet(HttpServletRequest req, HttpServletResponse res)
                        throws ServletException, IOException {
    res.setContentType("text/html");
```

Example 7-3. Session tracking using persistent cookies (continued)

```
PrintWriter out = res.getWriter();

// Get the current session ID by searching the received cookies.
String sessionid = null;
Cookie[] cookies = req.getCookies();
if (cookies != null) {
  for (int i = 0; i < cookies.length; i++) {
    if (cookies[i].getName().equals("sessionid")) {
      sessionid = cookies[i].getValue();
      break;
    }
  }
}

// If the session ID wasn't sent, generate one.
// Then be sure to send it to the client with the response.
if (sessionid == null) {
  sessionid = generateSessionId();
  Cookie c = new Cookie("sessionid", sessionid);
  res.addCookie(c);
}

out.println("<HEAD><TITLE>Current Shopping Cart Items</TITLE></HEAD>");
out.println("<BODY>");

// Cart items are associated with the session ID
String[] items = getItemsFromCart(sessionid);

// Print the current cart items.
out.println("You currently have the following items in your cart:<BR>");
if (items == null) {
  out.println("<B>None</B>");
}
else {
  out.println("<UL>");
  for (int i = 0; i < items.length; i++) {
    out.println("<LI>" + items[i]);
  }
  out.println("</UL>");
}

// Ask if they want to add more items or check out.
out.println("<FORM ACTION=\"/servlet/ShoppingCart\" METHOD=POST>");
out.println("Would you like to<BR>");
out.println("<INPUT TYPE=submit VALUE=\" Add More Items \">");
out.println("<INPUT TYPE=submit VALUE=\" Check Out \">");
out.println("</FORM>");
```

Example 7-3. Session tracking using persistent cookies (continued)

```
    // Offer a help page.
    out.println("For help, click <A HREF=\"/servlet/Help" +
                "?topic=ShoppingCartViewerCookie\">here</A>");

    out.println("</BODY></HTML>");
  }

  private static String generateSessionId() {
    String uid = new java.rmi.server.UID().toString();  // guaranteed unique
    return java.net.URLEncoder.encode(uid);  // encode any special chars
  }

  private static String[] getItemsFromCart(String sessionid) {
    // Not implemented
  }
}
```

This servlet first tries to fetch the client's session ID by iterating through the cookies it received as part of the request. If no cookie contains a session ID, the servlet generates a new one using `generateSessionId()` and adds a cookie containing the new session ID to the response. The rest of this servlet matches the URL rewriting version, except that this version doesn't perform any rewriting.

Persistent cookies offer an elegant, efficient, easy way to implement session tracking. Cookies provide as automatic an introduction for each request as you could hope for. For each request, a cookie can automatically provide a client's session ID or perhaps a list of the client's preferences. In addition, the ability to customize cookies gives them extra power and versatility.

The biggest problem with cookies is that browsers don't always accept cookies. Sometimes this is because the browser doesn't support cookies. More often, it's because the user has specifically configured the browser to refuse cookies (out of privacy concerns, perhaps). If any of your clients might not accept cookies, you have to fall back to the solutions discussed earlier in this chapter.

The Session Tracking API

Fortunately for us servlet developers, it's not always necessary for a servlet to manage its own sessions using the techniques we have just discussed. The Servlet API provides several methods and classes specifically designed to handle session tracking on behalf of servlets. In other words, servlets have built in session tracking.[*]

---

[*] Yes, we do feel a little like the third grade teacher who taught you all the steps of long division, only to reveal later how you could use a calculator to do the same thing. But we believe, as your teacher probably did, that you better understand the concepts after first learning the traditional approach.

The Session Tracking API, as we call the portion of the Servlet API devoted to session tracking, should be supported in any web server that supports servlets. The level of support, however, depends on the server. The minimal implementation provided by the servlet classes in JSDK 2.0 manages sessions through the use of persistent cookies. A server can build on this base to provide additional features and capabilities. For example, the Java Web Server has the ability to revert to using URL rewriting when cookies fail, and it allows session objects to be written to the server's disk as memory fills up or when the server shuts down. (The items you place in the session need to implement the `Serializable` interface to take advantage of this option.) See your server's documentation for details pertaining to your server. The rest of this section describe the lowest-common-denominator functionality provided by Version 2.0 of the Servlet API.

Session-Tracking Basics

Session tracking is wonderfully elegant. Every user of a site is associated with a `javax.servlet.http.HttpSession` object that servlets can use to store or retrieve information about that user. You can save any set of arbitrary Java objects in a session object. For example, a user's session object provides a convenient location for a servlet to store the user's shopping cart contents or, as you'll see in Chapter 9, *Database Connectivity*, the user's database connection.

A servlet uses its request object's `getSession()` method to retrieve the current `HttpSession` object:

```
public HttpSession HttpServletRequest.getSession(boolean create)
```

This method returns the current session associated with the user making the request. If the user has no current valid session, this method creates one if `create` is `true` or returns `null` if `create` is `false`. To ensure the session is properly maintained, this method must be called at least once before any output is written to the response.

You can add data to an `HttpSession` object with the `putValue()` method:

```
public void HttpSession.putValue(String name, Object value)
```

This method binds the specified object value under the specified name. Any existing binding with the same name is replaced. To retrieve an object from a session, use `getValue()`:

```
public Object HttpSession.getValue(String name)
```

This methods returns the object bound under the specified name or `null` if there is no binding. You can also get the names of all of the objects bound to a session with `getValueNames()`:

```
public String[] HttpSession.getValueNames()
```

This method returns an array that contains the names of all objects bound to this session or an empty (zero length) array if there are no bindings. Finally, you can remove an object from a session with removeValue():

```
public void HttpSession.removeValue(String name)
```

This method removes the object bound to the specified name or does nothing if there is no binding. Each of these methods can throw a java.lang.Illegal-StateException if the session being accessed is invalid (we'll discuss invalid sessions in an upcoming section).

A Hit Count Using Session Tracking

Example 7-4 shows a simple servlet that uses session tracking to count the number of times a client has accessed it, as shown in Figure 7-2. The servlet also displays all the bindings for the current session, just because it can.

Example 7-4. Session tracking a hit count

```java
import java.io.*;
import javax.servlet.*;
import javax.servlet.http.*;

public class SessionTracker extends HttpServlet {

  public void doGet(HttpServletRequest req, HttpServletResponse res)
                             throws ServletException, IOException {
    res.setContentType("text/html");
    PrintWriter out = res.getWriter();

    // Get the current session object, create one if necessary
    HttpSession session = req.getSession(true);

    // Increment the hit count for this page. The value is saved
    // in this client's session under the name "tracker.count".
    Integer count = (Integer)session.getValue("tracker.count");
    if (count == null)
      count = new Integer(1);
    else
      count = new Integer(count.intValue() + 1);
    session.putValue("tracker.count", count);

    out.println("<HTML><HEAD><TITLE>SessionTracker</TITLE></HEAD>");
    out.println("<BODY><H1>Session Tracking Demo</H1>");

    // Display the hit count for this page
    out.println("You've visited this page " + count +
      ((count.intValue() == 1) ? " time." : " times."));
```

Example 7-4. Session tracking a hit count (continued)

```
    out.println("<P>");

    out.println("<H2>Here is your session data:</H2>");
    String[] names = session.getValueNames();
    for (int i = 0; i < names.length; i++) {
      out.println(names[i] + ": " + session.getValue(names[i]) + "<BR>");
    }
    out.println("</BODY></HTML>");
  }
}
```

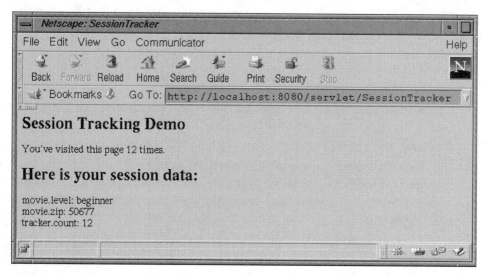

Figure 7-2. Counting client visits

This servlet first gets the HttpSession object associated with the current client. By passing true to getSession(), it asks for a session to be created if necessary. The servlet then gets the Integer object bound to the name "tracker.count". If there is no such object, the servlet starts a new count. Otherwise, it replaces the Integer with a new Integer whose value has been incremented by one. Finally, the servlet displays the current count and all the current name/value pairs in the session.

The Session Life Cycle

Sessions do not last forever. A session either expires automatically, after a set time of inactivity (for the Java Web Server the default is 30 minutes), or manually, when it is explicitly invalidated by a servlet. When a session expires (or is invalidated), the HttpSession object and the data values it contains are removed from the system.

Beware that any information saved in a user's session object is lost when the session is invalidated. If you need to retain information beyond that time, you should keep it in an external location (such as a database) and store a handle to the external data in the session object (or your own persistant cookie).

There are several methods involved in managing the session life cycle:

public boolean HttpSession.isNew()

> This method returns whether the session is new. A session is considered new if it has been created by the server but the client has not yet acknowledged joining the session. For example, if a server supports only cookie-based sessions and a client has completely disabled the use of cookies, calls to the getSession() method of HttpServletRequest always return new sessions.

public void HttpSession.invalidate()

> This method causes the session to be immediately invalidated. All objects stored in the session are unbound.

public long HttpSession.getCreationTime()

> This method returns the time at which the session was created, as a long value that represents the number of milliseconds since the epoch (midnight, January 1, 1970, GMT).

public long HttpSession.getLastAccessedTime()

> This method returns the time at which the client last sent a request associated with this session, as a long value that represents the number of milliseconds since the epoch.

Each of these methods can throw a java.lang.IllegalStateException if the session being accessed is invalid.

Manually Invalidating a Stale Session

To demonstrate these methods, Example 7-5 shows a servlet that manually invalidates a session if it is more than a day old or has been inactive for more than an hour.

Example 7-5. Invalidating a stale session

```
import java.io.*;
import java.util.*;
import javax.servlet.*;
import javax.servlet.http.*;

public class ManualInvalidate extends HttpServlet {

  public void doGet(HttpServletRequest req, HttpServletResponse res)
                              throws ServletException, IOException {
```

Example 7-5. Invalidating a stale session (continued)

```
    res.setContentType("text/html");
    PrintWriter out = res.getWriter();

    // Get the current session object, create one if necessary
    HttpSession session = req.getSession(true);

    // Invalidate the session if it's more than a day old or has been
    // inactive for more than an hour.
    if (!session.isNew()) {  // skip new sessions
      Date dayAgo = new Date(System.currentTimeMillis() - 24*60*60*1000);
      Date hourAgo = new Date(System.currentTimeMillis() - 60*60*1000);
      Date created = new Date(session.getCreationTime());
      Date accessed = new Date(session.getLastAccessedTime());

      if (created.before(dayAgo) || accessed.before(hourAgo)) {
        session.invalidate();
        session = req.getSession(true);  // get a new session
      }
    }

    // Continue processing...
  }
}
```

Putting Sessions in Context

So, how does a web server implement session tracking? When a user first accesses the site, that user is assigned a new `HttpSession` object and a unique session ID. The session ID identifies the user and is used to match the user with the `HttpSession` object in subsequent requests. Behind the scenes, the session ID is usually saved on the client in a cookie or sent as part of a rewritten URL. Other implementations, such as using SSL (Secure Sockets Layer) sessions, are also possible.

A servlet can discover a session's ID with the `getId()` method:

```
    public String HttpSession.getId()
```

This method returns the unique `String` identifier assigned to this session. For example, a Java Web Server ID might be something like HT04D1QAAAAABQDGPM5QAAA. The method throws an `IllegalStateException` if the session is invalid.

All valid sessions are grouped together in a `HttpSessionContext` object. Theoretically, a server may have multiple session contexts, although in practice most have just one. A reference to the server's `HttpSessionContext` is available via any session object's `getSessionContext()` method:

```
public HttpSessionContext HttpSession.getSessionContext()
```

This method returns the context in which the session is bound. It throws an IllegalStateException if the session is invalid.

Once you have an HttpSessionContext, it's possible to use it to examine all the currently valid sessions with the following two methods:

```
public Enumeration HttpSessionContext.getIds()
public HttpSession HttpSessionContext.getSession(String sessionId)
```

The getIds() method returns an Enumeration that contains the session IDs for all the currently valid sessions in this context or an empty Enumeration if there are no valid sessions. getSession() returns the session associated with the given session ID. The session IDs returned by getIds() should be held as a server secret because any client with knowledge of another client's session ID can, with a forged cookie or URL, join the second client's session.

Manually Invalidating All Stale Sessions

Example 7-6 demonstrates the use of these methods with a servlet that manually invalidates all the sessions on the server that are more than a day old or have been inactive more than an hour.

Example 7-6. Invalidating all stale sessions

```
import java.io.*;
import java.util.*;
import javax.servlet.*;
import javax.servlet.http.*;

public class ManualInvalidateScan extends HttpServlet {

  public void doGet(HttpServletRequest req, HttpServletResponse res)
                           throws ServletException, IOException {
    res.setContentType("text/plain");
    PrintWriter out = res.getWriter();

    // Get the current session object, create one if necessary
    HttpSession dummySession = req.getSession(true);

    // Use the session to get the session context
    HttpSessionContext context = dummySession.getSessionContext();

    // Use the session context to get a list of session IDs
    Enumeration ids = context.getIds();

    // Iterate over the session IDs checking for stale sessions
    while (ids.hasMoreElements()) {
```

Example 7-6. Invalidating all stale sessions (continued)

```
      String id = (String)ids.nextElement();
      out.println("Checking " + id + "...");
      HttpSession session = context.getSession(id);

      // Invalidate the session if it's more than a day old or has been
      // inactive for more than an hour.
      Date dayAgo = new Date(System.currentTimeMillis() - 24*60*60*1000);
      Date hourAgo = new Date(System.currentTimeMillis() - 60*60*1000);
      Date created = new Date(session.getCreationTime());
      Date accessed = new Date(session.getLastAccessedTime());

      if (created.before(dayAgo)) {
        out.println("More than a day old, invalidated!");
        session.invalidate();
      }
      else if (accessed.before(hourAgo)) {
        out.println("More than an hour inactive, invalidated!");
        session.invalidate();
      }
      else {
        out.println("Still valid.");
      }
      out.println();
    }
  }
}
```

A servlet that manually invalidates sessions according to arbitrary rules is useful on servers with limited session expiration capabilities.

Storing Session IDs

Every server that supports servlets should implement at least cookie-based session tracking, where the session ID is saved on the client in a persistent cookie. Many web servers also support session tracking based on URL rewriting, as a fallback for browsers that don't accept cookies. This requires additional help from servlets.

For a servlet to support session tracking via URL rewriting, it has to rewrite every local URL before sending it to the client. The Servlet API provides two methods to perform this encoding:

public String HttpServletResponse.encodeUrl(String url)

> This method encodes (rewrites) the specified URL to include the session ID and returns the new URL, or, if encoding is not needed or not supported, it leaves the URL unchanged. The rules used to decide when and how to encode

a URL are server-specific. All URLs emitted by a servlet should be run through this method.

public String HttpServletResponse.encodeRedirectUrl(String url)

This method encodes (rewrites) the specified URL to include the session ID and returns the new URL, or, if encoding is not needed or not supported, it leaves the URL unchanged. The rules used to decide when and how to encode a URL are server-specific. This method may use different rules than `encodeUrl()`. All URLs passed to the `sendRedirect()` method of `HttpServletResponse` should be run through this method.

Note that `encodeUrl()` and `encodeRedirectedUrl()` employ a different capitalization scheme than `getRequestURL()` and `getRequestURI()`. The following code snippet shows a servlet writing a link to itself that is encoded to contain the current session ID:

```
out.println("Click <A HREF=\"" +
            res.encodeUrl(req.getRequestURI()) + "\">here</A>");
out.println("to reload this page.");
```

On servers that don't support URL rewriting or have URL rewriting turned off, the resulting URL remains unchanged. Now here's a code snippet that shows a servlet redirecting the user to a URL encoded to contain the session ID:

```
res.sendRedirect(res.encodeRedirectUrl("/servlet/NewServlet"));
```

On servers that don't support URL rewriting or have URL rewriting turned off, the resulting URL remains unchanged.

A servlet can detect whether the session ID used to identify the current `HttpSession` object came from a cookie or from an encoded URL using the `isRequestedSessionIdFromCookie()` and `isRequestedSessionIdFromUrl()` methods:

```
public boolean HttpServletRequest.isRequestedSessionIdFromCookie()
public boolean HttpServletRequest.isRequestedSessionIdFromUrl()
```

Determining if the session ID came from another source, such as an SSL session, is not currently possible.

A requested session ID may not match the ID of the session returned by the `getSession()` method, such as when the session ID is invalid. A servlet can determine whether a requested session ID is valid using `isRequestedSessionIdValid()`:

```
public boolean HttpServletRequest.isRequestedSessionIdValid()
```

Session Snoop

The `SessionSnoop` servlet shown in Example 7-7 uses most of the methods discussed thus far in the chapter to snoop information about the current session and other sessions on the server. Figure 7-3 shows a sample of its output.

Example 7-7. Snooping session information

```java
import java.io.*;
import java.util.*;
import javax.servlet.*;
import javax.servlet.http.*;

public class SessionSnoop extends HttpServlet {

  public void doGet(HttpServletRequest req, HttpServletResponse res)
                         throws ServletException, IOException {
    res.setContentType("text/html");
    PrintWriter out = res.getWriter();

    // Get the current session object, create one if necessary
    HttpSession session = req.getSession(true);

    // Increment the hit count for this page. The value is saved
    // in this client's session under the name "snoop.count".
    Integer count = (Integer)session.getValue("snoop.count");
    if (count == null)
      count = new Integer(1);
    else
      count = new Integer(count.intValue() + 1);
    session.putValue("snoop.count", count);

    out.println("<HTML><HEAD><TITLE>SessionSnoop</TITLE></HEAD>");
    out.println("<BODY><H1>Session Snoop</H1>");

    // Display the hit count for this page
    out.println("You've visited this page " + count +
      ((count.intValue() == 1) ? " time." : " times."));

    out.println("<P>");

    out.println("<H3>Here is your saved session data:</H3>");
    String[] names = session.getValueNames();
    for (int i = 0; i < names.length; i++) {
      out.println(names[i] + ": " + session.getValue(names[i]) + "<BR>");
    }

    out.println("<H3>Here are some vital stats on your session:</H3>");
    out.println("Session id: " + session.getId() + "<BR>");
```

Example 7-7. Snooping session information (continued)

```
    out.println("New session: " + session.isNew() + "<BR>");
    out.println("Creation time: " + session.getCreationTime());
    out.println("<I>(" + new Date(session.getCreationTime()) + ")</I><BR>");
    out.println("Last access time: " + session.getLastAccessedTime());
    out.println("<I>(" + new Date(session.getLastAccessedTime()) +
                ")</I><BR>");

    out.println("Requested session ID from cookie: " +
                req.isRequestedSessionIdFromCookie() + "<BR>");
    out.println("Requested session ID from URL: " +
                req.isRequestedSessionIdFromUrl() + "<BR>");
    out.println("Requested session ID valid: " +
                req.isRequestedSessionIdValid() + "<BR>");

    out.println("<H3>Here are all the current session IDs");
    out.println("and the times they've hit this page:</H3>");
    HttpSessionContext context = session.getSessionContext();
    Enumeration ids = context.getIds();
    while (ids.hasMoreElements()) {
      String id = (String)ids.nextElement();
      out.println(id + ": ");
      HttpSession foreignSession = context.getSession(id);
      Integer foreignCount =
        (Integer)foreignSession.getValue("snoop.count");
      if (foreignCount == null)
        out.println(0);
      else
        out.println(foreignCount.toString());
      out.println("<BR>");
    }

    out.println("<H3>Test URL Rewriting</H3>");
    out.println("Click <A HREF=\"" +
                res.encodeUrl(req.getRequestURI()) + "\">here</A>");
    out.println("to test that session tracking works via URL");
    out.println("rewriting even when cookies aren't supported.");

    out.println("</BODY></HTML>");
  }
}
```

This servlet begins with the same code as the `SessionTracker` servlet shown in Example 7-4. Then it continues on to display the current session's ID, whether it is a new session, the session's creation time, and the session's last access time. Next the servlet displays whether the requested session ID (if there is one) came from a cookie or a URL and whether the requested ID is valid. Then the servlet iterates over all the currently valid session IDs, displaying the number of times they have visited

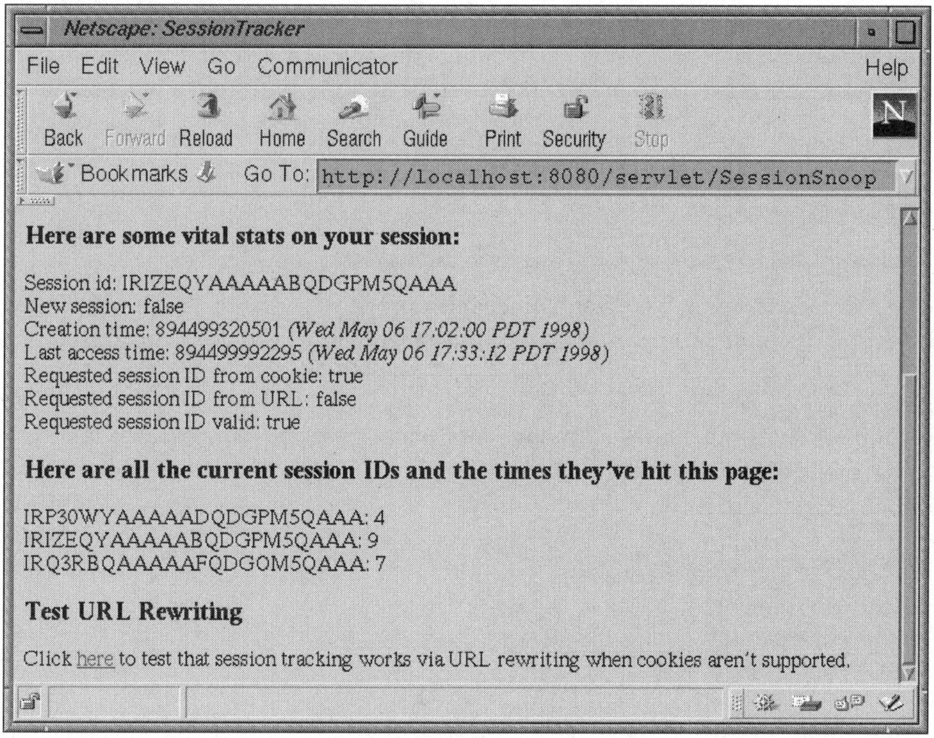
Netscape: SessionTracker
File Edit View Go Communicator Help
Back Forward Reload Home Search Guide Print Security Stop
Bookmarks Go To: http://localhost:8080/servlet/SessionSnoop
Here are some vital stats on your session:
Session id: IRIZEQYAAAAABQDGPM5QAAA
New session: false
Creation time: 894499320501 (Wed May 06 17:02:00 PDT 1998)
Last access time: 894499992295 (Wed May 06 17:33:12 PDT 1998)
Requested session ID from cookie: true
Requested session ID from URL: false
Requested session ID valid: true
Here are all the current session IDs and the times they've hit this page:
IRP30WYAAAAADQDGPM5QAAA: 4
IRIZEQYAAAAABQDGPM5QAAA: 9
IRQ3RBQAAAAAFQDGOM5QAAA: 7
Test URL Rewriting
Click here to test that session tracking works via URL rewriting when cookies aren't supported.

Figure 7-3. Example output from SessionSnoop

this page. Finally, the servlet prints an encoded URL that can be used to reload this page to test that URL rewriting works even when cookies aren't supported.

Note that installing this servlet is a security risk, as it exposes the server's session IDs—these may be used by unscrupulous clients to join other clients' sessions. The `SessionServlet` that is installed by default with the Java Web Server 1.1.x has similar behavior.

Session Binding Events

Some objects may wish to perform an action when they are bound or unbound from a session. For example, a database connection may begin a transaction when bound to a session and end the transaction when unbound. Any object that implements the `javax.servlet.http.HttpSessionBindingListener` interface is notified when it is bound or unbound from a session. The interface declares two methods, `valueBound()` and `valueUnbound()`, that must be implemented:

```
public void HttpSessionBindingListener.valueBound(
        HttpSessionBindingEvent event)
```

```
    public void HttpSessionBindingListener.valueUnbound(
            HttpSessionBindingEvent event)
```

The `valueBound()` method is called when the listener is bound into a session, and `valueUnbound()` is called when the listener is unbound from a session.

The `javax.servlet.http.HttpSessionBindingEvent` argument provides access to the name under which the object is being bound (or unbound) with the `getName()` method:

```
    public String HttpSessionBindingEvent.getName()
```

The `HttpSessionBindingEvent` object also provides access to the `HttpSession` object to which the listener is being bound (or unbound) with `getSession()`:

```
    public HttpSession HttpSessionBindingEvent.getSession()
```

Example 7-8 demonstrates the use of `HttpSessionBindingListener` and `HttpSessionBindingEvent` with a listener that logs when it is bound and unbound from a session.

Example 7-8. Tracking session binding events

```
import java.io.*;
import javax.servlet.*;
import javax.servlet.http.*;

public class SessionBindings extends HttpServlet {

  public void doGet(HttpServletRequest req, HttpServletResponse res)
                              throws ServletException, IOException {
    res.setContentType("text/plain");
    PrintWriter out = res.getWriter();

    // Get the current session object, create one if necessary
    HttpSession session = req.getSession(true);

    // Add a CustomBindingListener
    session.putValue("bindings.listener",
                new CustomBindingListener(getServletContext()));

    out.println("This page intentionally left blank");
  }
}

class CustomBindingListener implements HttpSessionBindingListener {

  // Save a ServletContext to be used for its log() method
  ServletContext context;

  public CustomBindingListener(ServletContext context) {
```

Example 7-8. Tracking session binding events (continued)

```
    this.context = context;
  }

  public void valueBound(HttpSessionBindingEvent event) {
    context.log("BOUND as " + event.getName() +
                " to " + event.getSession().getId());
  }

  public void valueUnbound(HttpSessionBindingEvent event) {
    context.log("UNBOUND as " + event.getName() +
                " from " + event.getSession().getId());
  }
}
```

Each time a `CustomBindingListener` object is bound to a session, its `value-Bound()` method is called and the event is logged. Each time it is unbound from a session, its `valueUnbound()` method is called so that event too is logged. We can observe the sequence of events by looking at the server's event log.

Let's assume that this servlet is called once, reloaded 30 seconds later, and not called again for at least a half hour. The event log would look something like this:

```
[Tue Jan 27 01:46:48 PST 1998]
  BOUND as bindings.listener to INWBUJIAAAAAHQDGPM5QAAA
[Tue Jan 27 01:47:18 PST 1998]
  UNBOUND as bindings.listener from INWBUJIAAAAAHQDGPM5QAAA
[Tue Jan 27 01:47:18 PST 1998]
  BOUND as bindings.listener to INWBUJIAAAAAHQDGPM5QAAA
[Tue Jan 27 02:17:18 PST 1998]
  UNBOUND as bindings.listener from INWBUJIAAAAAHQDGPM5QAAA
```

The first entry occurs during the first page request, when the listener is bound to the new session. The second and third entries occur during the reload, as the listener is unbound and rebound during the same `putValue()` call. The fourth entry occurs a half hour later, when the session expires and is invalidated.

Shopping Using Session Tracking

Let's end this chapter with a look at how remarkably simple our shopping cart viewer servlet becomes when we use session tracking. Example 7-9 shows the viewer saving each of the cart's items in the user's session under the name `"cart.items"`.

Example 7-9. Using the session tracking API

```
import java.io.*;
import javax.servlet.*;
```

Example 7-9. Using the session tracking API (continued)

```java
import javax.servlet.http.*;

public class ShoppingCartViewerSession extends HttpServlet {

  public void doGet(HttpServletRequest req, HttpServletResponse res)
                          throws ServletException, IOException {
    res.setContentType("text/html");
    PrintWriter out = res.getWriter();

    // Get the current session object, create one if necessary.
    HttpSession session = req.getSession(true);

    // Cart items are maintained in the session object.
    String[] items = (String[])session.getValue("cart.items");

    out.println("<HTML><HEAD><TITLE>SessionTracker</TITLE></HEAD>");
    out.println("<BODY><H1>Session Tracking Demo</H1>");

    // Print the current cart items.
    out.println("You currently have the following items in your cart:<BR>");
    if (items == null) {
      out.println("<B>None</B>");
    }
    else {
      out.println("<UL>");
      for (int i = 0; i < items.length; i++) {
        out.println("<LI>" + items[i]);
      }
      out.println("</UL>");
    }

    // Ask if they want to add more items or check out.
    out.println("<FORM ACTION=\"/servlet/ShoppingCart\" METHOD=POST>");
    out.println("Would you like to<BR>");
    out.println("<INPUT TYPE=submit VALUE=\" Add More Items \">");
    out.println("<INPUT TYPE=submit VALUE=\" Check Out \">");
    out.println("</FORM>");

    // Offer a help page. Encode it as necessary.
    out.println("For help, click <A HREF=\"" +
                res.encodeUrl("/servlet/Help?topic=ShoppingCartViewer") +
                "\">here</A>");

    out.println("</BODY></HTML>");
  }
}
```

8

Security

So far we have imagined that our servlets exist in a perfect world, where everyone is trustworthy and nobody locks their doors at night. Sadly, that's a 1950s fantasy world: the truth is that the Internet has its share of fiendish rogues. As companies place more and more emphasis on online commerce and begin to load their Intranets with sensitive information, security has become one of the most important topics in web programming.

Security is the science of keeping sensitive information in the hands of authorized users. On the web, this boils down to three important issues:

Authentication
> Being able to verify the identities of the parties involved

Confidentiality
> Ensuring that only the parties involved can understand the communication

Integrity
> Being able to verify that the content of the communication is not changed during transmission

A client wants to be sure that it is talking to a legitimate server (authentication), and it also want to be sure that any information it transmits, such as credit card numbers, is not subject to eavesdropping (confidentiality). The server is also concerned with authentication and confidentiality. If a company is selling a service or providing sensitive information to its own employees, it has a vested interest in making sure that nobody but an authorized user can access it. And both sides need integrity to make sure that whatever information they send gets to the other party unaltered.

Authentication, confidentiality, and integrity are all linked by digital certificate technology. Digital certificates allow web servers and clients to use advanced cryptographic techniques to handle identification and encryption in a secure manner. Thanks to Java's built-in support for digital certificates, servlets are an excellent platform for deploying secure web applications that use digital certificate technology. We'll be taking a closer look at them later.

Security is also about making sure that crackers can't gain access to the sensitive data on your web server. Because Java was designed from the ground up as a secure, network-oriented language, it is possible to leverage the built-in security features and make sure that server add-ons from third parties are almost as safe as the ones you write yourself.

This chapter introduces the basics of web security and digital certificate technology in the context of using servlets. It also discusses how to maintain the security of your web server when running servlets from untrusted third-parties. You'll notice that this chapter takes a higher-level approach and shows fewer examples than previous chapters. The reason is that many of the topics in this chapter require web server-specific administration to implement. The servlets just tag along for the ride.

Finally, a note of caution. We are just a couple of servlet programmers, and we disclaim all responsibility for any security-related incidents that might result from following our advice. For a much more complete overview of web security technology and procedures, see *Web Security & Commerce* by Simson Garfinkel with Gene Spafford (O'Reilly). Of course, they probably won't accept responsibility either.

HTTP Authentication

As we discussed briefly in Chapter 4, *Retrieving Information*, the HTTP protocol provides built-in authentication support—called basic authentication—based on a simple challenge/response, username/password model. With this technique, the web server maintains a database of usernames and passwords and identifies certain resources (files, directories, servlets, etc.) as protected. When a user requests access to a protected resource, the server responds with a request for the client's username and password. At this point, the browser usually pops up a dialog box where the user enters the information, and that input is sent back to the server as part of a second authorized request. If the submitted username and password match the information in the server's database, access is granted. The whole authentication process is handled by the server itself.

Basic authentication is very weak. It provides no confidentiality, no integrity, and only the most basic authentication. The problem is that passwords are transmitted over the network, thinly disguised by a well-known and easily reversed Base64 encoding. Anyone monitoring the TCP/IP data stream has full and immediate access to all the information being exchanged, including the username and password. Plus, passwords are often stored on the server in clear text, making them vulnerable to anyone cracking into the server's file system. While it's certainly better than nothing, sites that rely exclusively on basic authentication cannot be considered really secure.

Digest authentication is a variation on the basic authentication scheme. Instead of transmitting a password over the network directly, a digest of the password is used instead. The digest is produced by taking a hash (using the very secure MD5 encryption algorithm) of the username, password, URI, HTTP request method, and a randomly generated "nonce" value provided by the server. Both sides of the transaction know the password and use it to compute digests. If the digests match, access is granted. Transactions are thus somewhat more secure than they would be otherwise because digests are valid for only a single URI request and nonce value. The server, however, must still maintain a database of the original passwords. And, as of this writing, digest authentication is not supported by very many browsers.

The moral of the story is that HTTP authentication can be useful in low-security environments. For example, a site that charges for access to content—say, an online newspaper—is more concerned with ease of use and administration than lock-tight security, so HTTP authentication is often sufficient.

Retrieving Authentication Information

A server can retrieve information about the server's authentication using two methods introduced in Chapter 4: getRemoteUser() and getAuthType(). Example 8-1 shows a simple servlet that tells the client its name and what kind of authentication has been performed (basic, digest, or some alternative). To see this servlet in action, you should install it in your web server and protect it with a basic or digest security scheme. Because web server implementations vary, you'll need to check your server documentation for the specifics on how to set this up.

Example 8-1. Snooping the authorization information

```
import java.io.*;
import javax.servlet.*;
import javax.servlet.http.*;

public class AuthorizationSnoop extends HttpServlet {

  public void doGet(HttpServletRequest req, HttpServletResponse res)
                            throws ServletException, IOException {
    res.setContentType("text/html");
    PrintWriter out = res.getWriter();

    out.println("<HTML><HEAD><TITLE>Authorization Snoop</TITLE></HEAD><BODY>");
```

Example 8-1. Snooping the authorization information (continued)

```
        out.println("<H1>This is a password protected resource</H1>");
        out.println("<PRE>");
        out.println("User Name: " + req.getRemoteUser());
        out.println("Authorization Type: " + req.getAuthType());
        out.println("</PRE>");
        out.println("</BODY></HTML>");
    }
}
```

Custom Authorization

Normally, client authentication is handled by the web server. The server administrator tells the server which resources are to be restricted to which users, and
information about those users (such as their passwords) is somehow made available to the server.

This is often good enough, but sometimes the desired security policy cannot be
implemented by the server. Maybe the user list needs to be stored in a format that
is not readable by the server. Or maybe you want any username to be allowed, as
long as it is given with the appropriate "skeleton key" password. To handle these
situations, we can use servlets. A servlet can be implemented so that it learns about
users from a specially formatted file or a relational database; it can also be written
to enforce any security policy you like. Such a servlet can even add, remove, or
manipulate user entries—something that isn't supported directly in the Servlet
API, except through proprietary server extensions.[*]

A servlet uses status codes and HTTP headers to manage its own security policy.
The servlet receives encoded authorization credentials in the Authorization
header. If it chooses to deny those credentials, it does so by sending the SC_UNAU-
THORIZED status code and a WWW-Authenticate header that describes the desired
credentials. A web server normally handles these details without involving its servlets, but for a servlet to do its own authorization, it must handle these details itself,
while the server is told *not* to restrict access to the servlet.

The Authorization header, if sent by the client, contains the client's username
and password. With the basic authorization scheme, the Authorization header
contains the string of "*username:password*" encoded in Base64. For example,

---

[*] Sadly, getAuthType() and getRemoteUser() are the only security-related methods supported in the
core Servlet API. This is because different web servers implement different types of security, making a
server-independent API difficult to develop. Individual servers and servlet implementations are free to
provide their own customized user management routines. The Java Web Server, for example, provides
servlets with programmatic access to its security and authentication systems using classes in the
com.sun.server.* packages. Servlets written to these APIs are, of course, non-portable.

the username of "webmaster" with the password "try2gueSS" is sent in an Authorization header with the value:

```
BASIC d2ViBWFzdGVyOnRyeTJndWVTUw
```

If a servlet needs to, it can send an WWW-Authenticate header to tell the client the authorization scheme and the realm against which users will be verified. A realm is simply a collection of user accounts and protected resources. For example, to tell the client to use basic authorization for the realm "Admin", the WWW-Authenticate header is:

```
BASIC realm="Admin"
```

Example 8-2 shows a servlet that performs custom authorization, receiving an Authorization header and sending the SC_UNAUTHORIZED status code and WWW-Authenticate header when necessary. The servlet restricts access to its "top-secret stuff" to those users (and passwords) it recognizes in its user list. For this example, the list is kept in a simple Hashtable and its contents are hard-coded; this would, of course, be replaced with some other mechanism, such as an external relational database, for a production servlet.

To retrieve the Base64-encoded username and password, the servlet needs to use a Base64 decoder. Fortunately, there are several freely available decoders. For this servlet, we have chosen to use the sun.misc.BASE64Decoder class that accompanies the JDK. Being in the sun.* hierarchy means it's unsupported and subject to change, but it also means it's probably already on your system. You can find the details of Base64 encoding in RFC 1521 at *http://www.ietf.org/rfc/rfc1521.txt*.

Example 8-2. Security in a servlet

```java
import java.io.*;
import java.util.*;
import javax.servlet.*;
import javax.servlet.http.*;

public class CustomAuth extends HttpServlet {

  Hashtable users = new Hashtable();

  public void init(ServletConfig config) throws ServletException {
    super.init(config);
    users.put("Wallace:cheese",      "allowed");
    users.put("Gromit:sheepnapper", "allowed");
    users.put("Penguin:evil",        "allowed");
  }

  public void doGet(HttpServletRequest req, HttpServletResponse res)
                      throws ServletException, IOException {
```

Example 8-2. Security in a servlet (continued)

```
    res.setContentType("text/plain");
    PrintWriter out = res.getWriter();

    // Get Authorization header
    String auth = req.getHeader("Authorization");

    // Do we allow that user?
    if (!allowUser(auth)) {
      // Not allowed, so report he's unauthorized
      res.sendError(res.SC_UNAUTHORIZED);
      res.setHeader("WWW-Authenticate", "BASIC realm=\"users\"");
      // Could offer to add him to the allowed user list
    }
    else {
      // Allowed, so show him the secret stuff
      out.println("Top-secret stuff");
    }
  }

  // This method checks the user information sent in the Authorization
  // header against the database of users maintained in the users Hashtable.
  protected boolean allowUser(String auth) throws IOException {
    if (auth == null) return false;  // no auth

    if (!auth.toUpperCase().startsWith("BASIC "))
      return false;  // we only do BASIC

    // Get encoded user and password, comes after "BASIC "
    String userpassEncoded = auth.substring(6);

    // Decode it, using any base 64 decoder
    sun.misc.BASE64Decoder dec = new sun.misc.BASE64Decoder();
    String userpassDecoded = new String(dec.decodeBuffer(userpassEncoded));

    // Check our user list to see if that user and password are "allowed"
    if ("allowed".equals(users.get(userpassDecoded)))
      return true;
    else
      return false;
  }
}
```

Although the web server is told to grant any client access to this servlet, the servlet sends its top-secret output only to those users it recognizes. With a few modifications, it could allow any user with a trusted skeleton password. Or, like anonymous FTP, it could allow the `"anonymous"` username with any email address given as the password.

Custom authorization can be used for more than restricting access to a single servlet. Were we to add this logic to our ViewFile servlet, we could implement a custom access policy for an entire set of files. Were we to create a special subclass of HttpServlet and add this logic to that, we could easily restrict access to every servlet derived from that subclass. Our point is this: with custom authorization, the security policy limitations of the server do not limit the possible security policy implementations of its servlets.

Form-based Custom Authorization

Servlets can also perform custom authorization without relying on HTTP authorization, by using HTML forms and session tracking instead. It's a bit more effort to give users a well-designed, descriptive, and friendly login page. For example, imagine you're developing an online banking site. Would you rather let the browser present a generic prompt for username and password or provide your customers with a custom login form that politely asks for specific banking credentials, as shown in Figure 8-1?

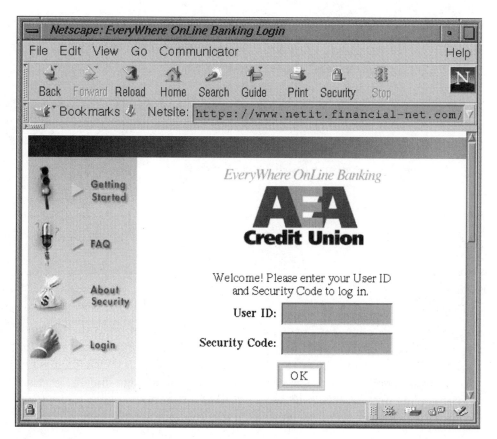

Figure 8-1. An online banking login screen

Many banks and other online services have chosen to use form-based custom authorization. Implementing such a system is relatively straightforward with servlets. First, we need the login page. It can be written like any other HTML form. Example 8-3 shows a sample *login.html* file that generates the form shown in Figure 8-2.

Example 8-3. The login.html file

```
<HTML>
<TITLE>Login</TITLE>
<BODY>
<FORM ACTION=/servlet/LoginHandler METHOD=POST>
<CENTER>
<TABLE BORDER=0>
<TR><TD COLSPAN=2>
<P ALIGN=center>
Welcome!  Please enter your Name<br>
 and Password to log in.
</TD></TR>

<TR><TD>
<P ALIGN=right><B>Name:</B>
</TD>
<TD>
<P><INPUT TYPE=text NAME="name" VALUE="" SIZE=15>
</TD></TR>

<TR><TD>
<P ALIGN=right><B>Password:</B>
</TD>
<TD>
<P><INPUT TYPE=password NAME="passwd" VALUE="" SIZE=15>
</TD></TR>

<TR><TD COLSPAN=2>
<CENTER>
<INPUT TYPE=submit VALUE="  OK   ">
</CENTER>
</TD></TR>
</TABLE>
</BODY></HTML>
```

This form asks the client for her name and password, then submits the information to the LoginHandler servlet that validates the login. We'll see the code for LoginHandler soon, but first we should ask ourselves, "When is the client going to see this login page?" It's clear she can browse to this login page directly, perhaps following a link on the site's front page. But what if she tries to access a protected resource directly without first logging in? In that case, she should be redirected to

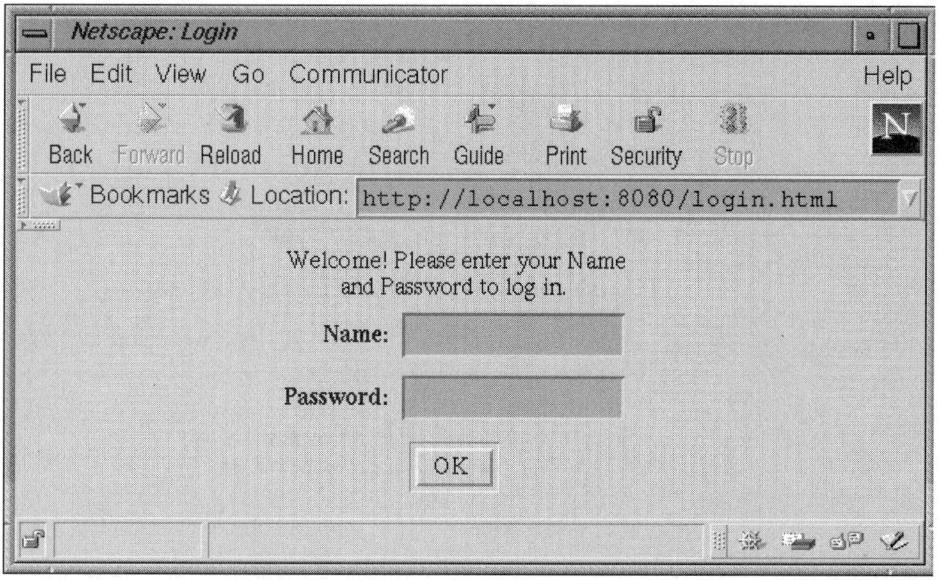

Figure 8-2. A friendly login form

this login page and, after a successful login, be redirected back to the original target. The process should work as seamlessly as having the browser pop open a window—except in this case the site pops open an intermediary page.

Example 8-4 shows a servlet that implements this redirection behavior. It outputs its secret data only if the client's session object indicates she has already logged in. If she hasn't logged in, the servlet saves the request URL in her session for later use, and then redirects her to the login page for validation.

Example 8-4. A protected resource

```
import java.io.*;
import java.util.*;
import javax.servlet.*;
import javax.servlet.http.*;

public class ProtectedResource extends HttpServlet {

  public void doGet(HttpServletRequest req, HttpServletResponse res)
                          throws ServletException, IOException {
    res.setContentType("text/plain");
    PrintWriter out = res.getWriter();

    // Get the session
    HttpSession session = req.getSession(true);
```

Example 8-4. A protected resource (continued)

```
    // Does the session indicate this user already logged in?
    Object done = session.getValue("logon.isDone");  // marker object
    if (done == null) {
      // No logon.isDone means he hasn't logged in.
      // Save the request URL as the true target and redirect to the login page.
      session.putValue("login.target",
                        HttpUtils.getRequestURL(req).toString());
      res.sendRedirect(req.getScheme() + "://" +
                        req.getServerName() + ":" + req.getServerPort() +
                        "/login.html");
      return;
    }

    // If we get here, the user has logged in and can see the goods
    out.println("Unpublished O'Reilly book manuscripts await you!");
  }
}
```

This servlet sees if the client has already logged in by checking her session for an object with the name `"logon.isDone"`. If such an object exists, the servlet knows that the client has already logged in and therefore allows her to see the secret goods. If it doesn't exist, the client must not have logged in, so the servlet saves the request URL under the name `"login.target"`, and then redirects the client to the login page. Under form-based custom authorization, all protected resources (or the servlets that serve them) have to implement this behavior. Subclassing, or the use of a utility class, can simplify this task.

Now for the login handler. After the client enters her information on the login form, the data is posted to the `LoginHandler` servlet shown in Example 8-5. This servlet checks the username and password for validity. If the client fails the check, she is told that access is denied. If the client passes, that fact is recorded in her session object and she is immediately redirected to the original target.

Example 8-5. Handling a login

```
import java.io.*;
import java.util.*;
import javax.servlet.*;
import javax.servlet.http.*;

public class LoginHandler extends HttpServlet {

  public void doPost(HttpServletRequest req, HttpServletResponse res)
                                throws ServletException, IOException {
    res.setContentType("text/html");
    PrintWriter out = res.getWriter();
```

Example 8-5. Handling a login (continued)

```
    // Get the user's name and password
    String name = req.getParameter("name");
    String passwd = req.getParameter("passwd");

    // Check the name and password for validity
    if (!allowUser(name, passwd)) {
      out.println("<HTML><HEAD><TITLE>Access Denied</TITLE></HEAD>");
      out.println("<BODY>Your login and password are invalid.<BR>");
      out.println("You may want to <A HREF=\"/login.html\">try again</A>");
      out.println("</BODY></HTML>");
    }
    else {
      // Valid login. Make a note in the session object.
      HttpSession session = req.getSession(true);
      session.putValue("logon.isDone", name);  // just a marker object

      // Try redirecting the client to the page he first tried to access
      try {
        String target = (String) session.getValue("login.target");
        if (target != null)
          res.sendRedirect(target);
        return;
      }
      catch (Exception ignored) { }

      // Couldn't redirect to the target. Redirect to the site's home page.
      res.sendRedirect(req.getScheme() + "://" +
                       req.getServerName() + ":" + req.getServerPort());
    }
  }

  protected boolean allowUser(String user, String passwd) {
    return true;  // trust everyone
  }
}
```

The actual validity check in this servlet is quite simple: it assumes any username and password are valid. That keeps things simple, so we can concentrate on how the servlet behaves when the login is successful. The servlet saves the user's name (any old object will do) in the client's session under the name "logon.isDone", as a marker that tells all protected resources this client is okay. It then redirects the client to the original target saved as "login.target", seamlessly sending her where she wanted to go in the first place. If that fails for some reason, the servlet redirects the user to the site's home page.

Digital Certificates

Real applications require a higher level of security than basic and digest authentication provide. They also need guaranteed confidentiality and integrity, as well as more reliable authentication. Digital certificate technology provides this.

The key concept is public key cryptography. In a public key cryptographic system, each participant has two keys that are used to encrypt or decrypt information. One is the public key, which is distributed freely. The other is a private key, which is kept secret. The keys are related, but one can not be derived from the other. To demonstrate, assume Jason wants to send a secret message to Will. He finds Will's public key and uses it to encrypt the message. When Will gets the message, he uses his private key to decrypt it. Anyone intercepting the message in transit is confronted with indecipherable gibberish.

Public key encryption schemes have been around for several years and are quite well developed. Most are based on the patented RSA algorithm developed by Ron Rivest, Adi Shamir, and Leonard Adelman. RSA uses very large prime numbers to generate a pair of asymmetric keys (i.e., each key can decode messages encoded with the other). Individual keys come in varying lengths, usually expressed in terms of the number of bits that make up the key. 1024- or 2048-bit keys are adequate for secure RSA communications.

Because keys are so large, it is not practical for a user to type one into her web brower for each request. Instead, keys are stored on disk in the form of digital certificates. Digital certificates can be generated by software like Phil Zimmerman's PGP package, or they can be issued by a third party. The certificate files themselves can be loaded by most security-aware applications, such as servers, browsers, and email software.

Public key cryptography solves the confidentiality problem because the communication is encrypted. It also solves the integrity problem: Will knows that the message he received was not tampered with since it decodes properly. So far, though, it does not provide any authentication. Will has no idea whether Jason actually sent the message. This is where digital signatures come into play. Because public and private keys are asymmetric, Jason can first use his private key to encode a message and then use Will's public key to encode it again. When Will gets the message, he decodes it first with his private key, and then with Jason's public key. Because only Jason can encode messages with his private key—messages that can be decoded only with his public key—Will knows that the message was truly sent by Jason.

This is different from simpler symmetric key systems, where a single key is used for encoding and decoding. While asymmetric keys have the significant advantage of allowing secure communication without ever requiring a secure channel, they have the disadvantage of requiring much more computational muscle. As a compromise, many encryption systems use asymmetric public and private keys to identify each other and then confidentially exchange a separate symmetric key for encrypting the actual exchange. The symmetric key is usually based on DES (Data Encryption Standard).

U.S. government restrictions currently limit symmetric key size to 56 bits (about 72 quadrillion possible keys). Messages encrypted with a 56-bit key are difficult to decode, but by no means impossible—large networks have been used to decode such messages within a matter of days. With the United States, however, many systems use 128-bit DES keys (about 3.40282×10^{38} possible keys). Because there is no know way to decode a DES-encrypted message short of brute-force trial and error, messages sent using large keys are very, very secure.

This leaves one final problem—how does one user know that another user is who she says she is? Jason and Will know each other, so Will trusts that the public key Jason gave him in person is the real one.[*] On the other hand, if Lisa wants to give Jason her public key, but Jason and Lisa have never met, there is no reason for Jason to believe that Lisa is not actually Mark. But, if we assume that Will knows Lisa, we can have Will use his private key to sign Lisa's public key. Then, when Jason gets the key, he can detect that Will, whom he trusts, is willing to vouch for Lisa's identity. These introductions are sometimes called a "web of trust."

In the real world, this third-party vouching is usually handled by a specially established certificate authority, such as VeriSign Corporation. Because VeriSign is a well-known organization with a well-known public key, keys verified and signed by VeriSign can be assumed to be trusted, at least to the extent that VeriSign received proper proof of the receiver's identity. VeriSign offers a number of classes of digital IDs, each with an increasing level of trust. You can get a Class 1 ID by simply filling out a form on the VeriSign web site and receiving an email. Higher classes are individually verified by VeriSign employees, using background checks and investigative services to verify identities.

When selecting a certificate authority, it is important to choose a firm with strong market presence. VeriSign certificates, for instance, are included in Netscape Navigator and Microsoft Internet Explorer, so virtually every user on the Internet will trust and accept them. The following firms provide certificate authority services:

- VeriSign (*http://www.verisign.com/*)
- Thawte Consulting (*http://www.thawte.com/*)
- Entrust Technologies (*http://www.entrust.com/*)
- Keywitness (*http://www.keywitness.ca/*)

---

[*] To be truthful, people almost never meet in dark alleys to exchange their full public keys. Instead, they exchange keys digitally (via email, perhaps) and in person simply compare a small fingerprint hash of the key.

For more abstract information about digital certificates, we recommend *Under-standing Digital Signatures* by Gail L. Grant (Mc-Graw Hill), which provides an excellent introduction to the subject suitable for programmers and nonprogrammers alike. For more on cryptography as it is related to Java, we recommend *Java Cryptography* by Jonathan Knudsen (O'Reilly).

Secure Sockets Layer (SSL)

The Secure Sockets Layer protocol, or SSL, sits between the application-level protocol (in this case HTTP) and the low-level transport protocol (for the Internet, almost exclusively TCP/IP). It handles the details of security management using public key cryptography to encrypt all client/server communication. SSL was introduced by Netscape with Netscape Navigator 1. It has since become the de facto standard for secure online communications and forms the basis of the Transport Layer Security (TLS) protocol currently under development by the Internet Engineering Task Force. For more information on TLS, see *http://www.ietf.org/ietf-tls*.

SSL Version 2.0, the version first to gain widespread acceptance, includes support for server certificates only. It provides authentication of the server, confidentiality, and integrity. Here's how it works:

1. A user connects to a secure site using the HTTPS (HTTP plus SSL) protocol. (You can detect sites using the HTTPS protocol because their URLs begin with *https:* instead of *http:*.)

2. The server signs its public key with its private key and sends it back to the browser.

3. The browser uses the server's public key to verify that the same person who signed the key actually owns it.

4. The browser checks to see whether a trusted certificate authority signed the key. If one didn't, the browser asks the user if the key can be trusted and proceeds as directed.

5. The client generates a symmetric (DES) key for the session, which is encrypted with the server's public key and sent back to the server. This new key is used to encrypt all subsequent transactions. The symmetric key is used because of the high computational cost of public key cryptosystems.

All this is completely transparent to servlets and servlet developers. You just need to obtain an appropriate server certificate, install it, and configure your server appropriately. Information transferred between servlets and clients is now encrypted. Voila, security!

SSL Client Authentication

Our security toolbox now includes strong encryption and strong server authentication, but only weak client authentication. Of course, using SSL 2.0 puts us in better shape because SSL-equipped servers can use the basic authentication methods discussed at the beginning of this chapter without concern for eavesdropping. We still don't have proof of client identity, however—after all, anybody could have guessed or gotten a hold of a client username and password.

SSL 3.0 fixes this problem by providing support for client certificates. These are the same type of certificates that servers use, but they are registered to clients instead. As of this writing, VeriSign claims to have distributed more than 750,000 client certificates. SSL 3.0 with client authentication works the same way as SSL 2.0, except that after the client has authenticated the server, the server requests the client's certificate. The client then sends its signed certificate, and the server performs the same authentication process as the client did, comparing the client certificate to a library of existing certificates (or simply storing the certificate to identify the user on a return visit). As a security precaution, many browsers require the client user to enter a password before they will send the certificate.

Once a client has been authenticated, the server can allow access to protected resources such as servlets or files just as with HTTP authentication. The whole process occurs transparently, without inconveniencing the user. It also provides an extra level of authentication because the server knows the client with a John Smith certificate really is John Smith (and it can know which John Smith it is by reading his unique certificate). The disadvantages of client certificates are that users must obtain and install signed certificates, servers must maintain a database of all accepted public keys, and servers must support SSL 3.0 in the first place. As of this writing, most do, including the Java Web Server.

Retrieving SSL Authentication Information

As with basic and digest authentication, all of this communication is transparent to servlets. It is sometimes possible, though, for a servlet to retrieve the relevant SSL authentication information. The java.security package has some basic support for manipulating digital certificates and signatures. To retrieve a client's digital information, however, a servlet has to rely on a server-specific implementation of the request's getAttribute() method. Example 8-6 (reprinted from Chapter 4) shows how to use getAttribute() to fetch the details of a client's certificates. Remember that this works only for the Java Web Server. Other servlet implementations, if they

include this functionality at all, are likely to do it in a slightly different way, although
we hope that they build on Java's standard signature support.

Example 8-6. Examining client certificates

```
import javax.security.cert.X509Certificate;

out.println("<PRE>");

// Display the cipher suite in use
String cipherSuite =
  (String) req.getAttribute("javax.net.ssl.cipher_suite");
out.println("Cipher Suite: " + cipherSuite);

// Display the client's certificates, if there are any
if (cipherSuite != null) {
  X509Certificate certChain[] =
    (X509Certificate[]) req.getAttribute("javax.net.ssl.peer_certificates");
  if (certChain != null) {
    for (int i = 0; i < certChain.length; i++) {
      out.println ("Client Certificate [" + i + "] = "
                      + certChain[i].toString());
    }
  }
}
out.println("</PRE>");
```

Here's the output we first saw in Chapter 4:

```
    Cipher Suite:  SSL_RSA_EXPORT_WITH_RC4_40_MD5
    Client Certificate [0] = [
      X.509v3 certificate,
      Subject is OID.1.2.840.113549.1.9.1=#160F6A68756E746572407367692E636F6D,
    CN=Jason Hunter, OU=Digital ID Class 1 - Netscape,
    OU="www.verisign.com/repository/CPS Incorp. by Ref.,LIAB.LTD(c)96",
    OU=VeriSign Class 1 CA - Individual Subscriber, O="VeriSign, Inc.",
    L=Internet
      Key:  algorithm = [RSA], exponent = 0x    010001, modulus =
        b35ed5e7 45fc5328 e3f5ce70 838cc25d 0a0efd41 df4d3e1b 64f70617 528546c8
        fae46995 9922a093 7a54584d d466bee7 e7b5c259 c7827489 6478e1a9 3a16d45f
      Validity  until
      Issuer is OU=VeriSign Class 1 CA - Individual Subscriber, O="VeriSign,
    Inc.",
    L=Internet
      Issuer signature used [MD5withRSA]
      Serial number =     20556dc0 9e31dfa4 ada6e10d 77954704
    ]
    Client Certificate [1] = [
      X.509v3 certificate,
      Subject is OU=VeriSign Class 1 CA - Individual Subscriber, O="VeriSign,
```

```
Inc.", L=Internet
  Key:  algorithm = [RSA], exponent = 0x    010001, modulus =
    b614a6cf 4dd0050d d8ca23d0 6faab429 92638e2c f86f96d7 2e9d764b 11b1368d
    57c9c3fd 1cc6bafe 1e08ba33 ca95eabe e35bcd06 a8b7791d 442aed73 f2b15283
    68107064 91d73e6b f9f75d9d 14439b6e 97459881 47d12dcb ddbb72d7 4c3f71aa
    e240f254 39bc16ee cf7cecba db3f6c2a b316b186 129dae93 34d5b8d5 d0f73ea9
  Validity until
  Issuer is OU=Class 1 Public Primary Certification Authority, O="VeriSign,
Inc.", C=US
  Issuer signature used [MD2withRSA]
  Serial number =    521f351d f2707e00 2bbeca59 8704d539
]
```

The first certificate is the user's public key. The second is VeriSign's signature that vouches for the authenticity of the first signature. Of course, the information from these certificate chains isn't particularly useful to the application programmer. In some applications, it is safe to simply assume that a user is authorized if she got past the SSL authentication phase. For others, the certificates can be picked apart using the `javax.security.cert.X509Certificate` class. More commonly, a web server allows you to assign a username to each certificate you tell it to accept. Servlets can then call `getRemoteUser()` to get a unique username. The latter solution works with almost all web servers.

Running Servlets Securely

CGI programs and C++-based plug-ins operate with relatively unfettered access to the server machine on which they execute (limited on Unix machines by the user account permissions of the web server process). This isn't so bad for an isolated programmer developing for a single web server, but it's a security nightmare for internet service providers (ISPs), corporations, schools, and everyone else running shared web servers.

For these sites, the problem isn't just protecting the server from malicious CGI programmers. The more troublesome problem is protecting from *careless* CGI programmers. There are dozens of well-known CGI programming mistakes that could let a malicious client gain unauthorized access to the server machine. One innocuous-looking but poorly written Perl `eval` function is all it takes. For an extensive list of CGI security gotchas, see Chapter 6 of The WWW Security FAQ at *http://www.w3.org/Security/Faq/www-security-faq.html.*

To better understand the situation, imagine you're an ISP and want to give your customers the ability to generate dynamic content using CGI programs. What can you do to protect yourself? Historically, ISPs have chosen one of three options:

Have blind faith in the customer.

He's a good guy and a smart programmer, and besides, we have his credit card number.

Educate the customer.

If he reads the WWW Security FAQ and passes a written test, we'll let him write CGI programs for our server.

Review all code.

Before we install any CGI program on the server, we'll have our expert review it and scan for security problems.

None of these approaches work very well. Having blind faith is just asking for trouble. Programmer education helps, but programmers are human and bound to make mistakes. As for code review, there's still no guarantees, plus it takes time and costs money to do the extra work.

Fortunately, with servlets there's another, better solution. Because servlets are written in Java, they can be forced to follow the rules of a security manager (or access controller with JDK 1.2) to greatly limit the server's exposure to risk, all with a minimal amount of human effort.

The Servlet Sandbox

Servlets built using JDK 1.1 generally operate with a security model called the "servlet sandbox." Under this model, servlets are either trusted and given open access to the server machine, or they're untrusted and have their access limited by a restrictive security manager. The model is very similar to the "applet sandbox," where untrusted applet code has limited access to the client machine.

What's a security manager? It's a class subclassed from `java.lang.SecurityManager` that is loaded by the Java environment to monitor all security-related operations: opening network connections, reading and writing files, exiting the program, and so on. Whenever an application, applet, or servlet performs an action that could cause a potential security breach, the environment queries the security manager to check its permissions. For a normal Java application, there is no security manager. When a web browser loads an untrusted applet over the network, however, it loads a very restrictive security manager before allowing the applet to execute.

Servlets can use the same technology, if the web server implements it. Local servlets can be trusted to run without a security manager, or with a fairly lenient one. For the Java Web Server 1.1, this is what happens when servlets are placed in the default servlet directory or another local source. Servlets loaded from a remote source, on the other hand, are by nature suspect and untrusted, so the Java Web

Server forces them to run in a very restrictive environment where they can't access the local file system, establish network connections, and so on.[*] All this logic is contained within the server and is invisible to the servlet, except that the servlet may see a `SecurityException` thrown when it tries to access a restricted resource. The servlet sandbox is a simple model, but it is already more potent than any other server extension technology to date.

Using digital signatures, it is possible for remotely loaded servlets to be trusted just like local servlets. Third-party servlets are often packaged using the Java Archive (JAR) file format. A JAR file collects a group of class files and other resources into a single archive for easy maintenance and fast download. Another nice feature of JAR files that is useful to servlets is that they can be digitally signed. This means that anyone with the public key for "Crazy Al's Servlet Shack" can verify that her copy of Al's Guestbook Servlet actually came from Al. On some servers, including the Java Web Server, these authenticated servlets can then be trusted and given extended access to the system.[†]

Fine-grained Control

This all-or-nothing approach to servlet permissions is useful, but it can be overly limiting. Consequently, some servlet engines have begun to explore a more fine-grained protection of server resources—for example, allowing a specific servlet to establish a network connection but not write to the server's file system. This fine-grained control is fairly awkward using the JDK 1.1 notion of a `SecurityManager` class and, therefore, isn't widely implemented, although it can be done, as the Java Web Server 1.1 proves.

The Java Web Server 1.1 includes eight permissions that can be granted to servlets:

Load servlet
Let the servlet load a named servlet.

Write files
Let the servlet write any file on the local file system.

Listen to socket
Allow the servlet to accept incoming socket (network) connections.

Link libraries
Allow the loading of native libraries, such as the JDBC-ODBC bridge.

---

[*] If you want a local servlet run in the restrictive environment, a workaround is to place them in your server's document root (such as *server_root/public_html*) and configure the server load them remotely from the same server.

[†] You can create your owned signed servlets using a certificate generated by the JDK's key management tools (*javakey* in JDK 1.1 or *keytool* and *jarsigner* in JDK 1.2). Alternately, you can obtain signed certificates from VeriSign or another certificate authority.

Read files

> Let the servlet read any file on the local file system.

Open remote socket

> Allow the servlet to connect to an external host.

Execute programs

> Permit the servlet to execute external programs on the server. This is useful for servlets that absolutely require access to some system utilities, but it is very dangerous: *rm* and *del* qualify as an external programs!

Access system properties

> Grant access to `java.lang.System` properties.

A screen shot of the Administration Tool configuration page that assigns these permissions is shown in Figure 8-3.

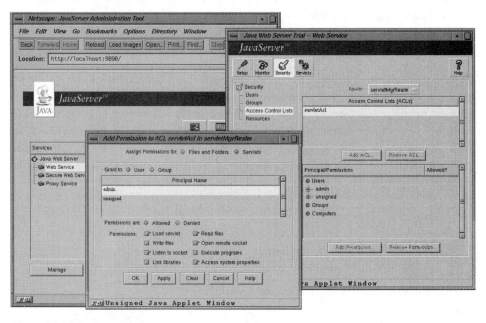

Figure 8-3. Eight permissions

Theoretically, any criterion can be used to determine what a servlet can or cannot do. It's possible for the security manager to base its permission-granting decision on any factor, including these:

The servlet itself

> For example, this servlet can read files and load native libraries but cannot write files.

The client user

> For instance, any servlet responding to a request from this client user can write files.

The client host

> For example, any servlet responding to a request from this machine can establish network connections.

Digital signatures

> For instance, any servlet in a JAR file signed by this entity has full reign on the server system.

Access Controllers

JDK 1.2 introduces a new extension to the security manager system: the access controller. The new architecture is quite similar to the "give particular servlets particular privileges" approach implemented by the Java Web Server 1.1, except that it applies to all JDK 1.2 programs and therefore makes fine-grained permission implementations much easier.

An access controller allows what might be called super-fine-grained permission control. Instead of granting a servlet the general ability to write files, with an access controller a servlet can be given the right to write to a single file—perfect for a counter servlet, for example. Or it can be given the right to read and write files only in the client user's home directory on the server—appropriate for a client/server application. With access controllers, servlets can be given the rights to do exactly what they need to do and nothing more.

Access controllers work by placing individual pieces of code, often identified by digital signatures, into particular virtual domains. Classes in these domains can be granted fine-grained permissions, such as the ability to read from the server's document root, write to a temporary directory, and accept socket connections. All permission policy decisions are managed by a single instance of the `java.security.AccessController` class. This class bases its policy decisions on a simple configuration file, easily managed using a graphical user interface.

Now, instead of relying on complicated custom security managers as the Java Web Server team had to do, a servlet engine need only add a few lines of code to use an access controller. So, while the Java Web Server is the only servlet implementation supporting fine-grained security as of early 1998, once JDK 1.2 becomes popular, it should be easy for other servlet engine implementers to add the same level of fine-grained access control. These implementations may already be available by the time you read this.

9

In this chapter:
- *Relational Databases*
- *The JDBC API*
- *Reusing Database Objects*
- *Transactions*
- *Advanced JDBC Techniques*

Database Connectivity

It's hard to find a professional web site today that doesn't have some sort of database connectivity. Webmasters have hooked online front ends to all manner of legacy systems, including package tracking and directory databases, as well as many newer systems like online messaging, storefronts, and search engines. But web-database interaction comes with a price: database-backed web sites can be difficult to develop and can often exact heavy performance penalties. Still, for many web sites, especially intranet applications, database connectivity is just too useful to let go. More and more, databases are driving the Web.

This chapter introduces relational databases, the Structured Query Language (SQL) used to manipulate those databases, and the Java database connectivity (JDBC) API itself. Servlets, with their enduring life cycle, and JDBC, a well-defined database-independent database connectivity API, are an elegant and efficient solution for webmasters who need to hook their web sites to back-end databases. In fact, both of your authors started working with servlets specifically because of this efficiency and elegance. Although elsewhere in the book we have assumed that you are familiar with Java, this chapter breaks that assumption and begins with a quick course in JDBC.

The biggest advantage for servlets with regard to database connectivity is that the servlet life cycle (explained in depth in Chapter 3, *The Servlet Life Cycle*) allows servlets to maintain open database connections. An existing connection can trim several seconds from a response time, compared to a CGI script that has to reestablish its connection for every invocation. Exactly how to maintain the database connection depends on the task at hand, and this chapter demonstrates several techniques appropriate for different tasks.

Another advantage of servlets over CGI and many other technologies is that JDBC is database-independent. A servlet written to access a Sybase database can, with a two-line modification or a change in a properties file, begin accessing an Oracle database (assuming none of the database calls it makes are vendor-specific). In fact, you should notice that the examples in this chapter are written to access a variety of different databases, including ODBC data sources (such as Microsoft Access), Oracle, and Sybase.

Relational Databases

In some earlier examples, we've seen servlets that used file storage on the local disk to store their persistent data. The use of a flat file is fine for a small amount of data, but it can quickly get out of control. As the amount of data grows, access times slow to a crawl. And just finding data can become quite a challenge: imagine storing the names, cities, and email addresses of all your customers in a text file. It works great for a company that is just starting out, but what happens when you have hundreds of thousands of customers and want to display a list of all your customers in Boston with email addresses ending in "aol.com"?

One of the best solutions to this problem is a Relational Database Management System (RDBMS). At the most basic level, an RDBMS organizes data into tables. These tables are organized into rows and columns, much like a spreadsheet. Particular rows and columns in a table can be related (hence the term "relational") to one or more rows and columns in another table.

One table in a relational database might contain information about customers, another might contain orders, and a third might contain information about individual items within an order. By including unique identifiers (say, customer numbers and order numbers), orders from the orders table can be linked to customer records and individual order components. Figure 9-1 shows how this might look if we drew it out on paper.

Data in the tables can be read, updated, appended, and deleted using the Structured Query Language, or SQL, sometimes also referred to as the Standard Query Language. Java's JDBC API introduced in JDK 1.1 uses a specific subset of SQL known as ANSI SQL-2 Entry Level. Unlike most programming languages, SQL is declarative: you say what you want, and the SQL interpreter gives it to you. Other languages, like C, C++, and Java, by contrast, are essentially procedural, in that you specify the steps required to perform a certain task. SQL, while not prohibitively complex, is also rather too broad a subject to cover in great (or, indeed, merely adequate) detail here. In order to make the rest of the examples in this chapter comprehensible, though, here's a brief tutorial.

The simplest and most common SQL expression is the SELECT statement, which queries the database and returns a set of rows that matches a set of search criteria.

Servlets in the Middle Tier

One common place for servlets, especially servlets that access a database, is in what's called the middle tier. A middle tier is something that helps connect one endpoint to another (an applet to a database, for example) and along the way adds a little something of its own.

The most compelling reason for putting a middle tier between a client and our ultimate date source is that software in the middle tier (commonly referred to as middleware) can include business logic. Business logic abstracts complicated low-level tasks (such as updating database tables) into high-level tasks (placing and order), making the whole operation simpler and safer.

Imagine a client application that places an order. Without middleware, the application has to connect directly to the database server that stores the order records and then change the database fields to reflect the order. If the database server changes in any way (by moving to a different machine, altering its internal table structure, or changing database vendors), the client may break. Even worse, if someone makes a minor change to the client (either intentionally or accidentally), it's possible for the database to record orders without first receiving payment or to reject perfectly valid entries.

Middleware uses business logic to abstract the ordering process. Middleware accepts information about the order (for example, name, address, item, quantity, credit card number), sanity-checks the information, verifies that the credit card is valid, and enters the information into the database. Should the database change, the middleware can be updated without any changes in the client. Even if the orders database is temporarily replaced with a simple flat file order log, the middleware can present the same appearance to the client.

Middleware can improve efficiency by spreading the processing load across several back-end servers (CPU servers, database servers, file servers, directory servers, etc.). Middleware can also make more efficient use of bandwidth: instead of having a client perform the back-and-forth communication with the server over what might be a slow network connection, the client can tell the middleware what it needs and the middleware can do the work using a fast network connection and probably pooled database connections.

On the Web, middle tiers are often implemented using servlets. Servlets provide a convenient way to connect clients built using HTML forms or applets to back-end servers. A client communicates its requirements to the servlet using HTTP, and the business logic in the servlet handles the request by connecting to the back-end server. (More information on applet-servlet communication is coming up in Chapter 10, *Applet-Servlet Communication.*)

Servlets sometimes use another middle tier to connect to a database. If a web browser sends an HTML form with order information to a servlet, that servlet may parse the information and make an RMI call to middleware on another machine that has the responsibility for handling all orders—from servlets as well as standalone programs. In these cases, what was once three tiers is now four tiers.

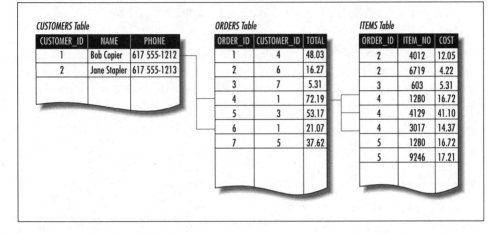

Figure 9-1. Related tables

For example, the following SELECT statement selects everything from the CUSTOMERS table:

```
SELECT * FROM CUSTOMERS
```

SQL keywords like SELECT and FROM and objects like CUSTOMERS are case insensitive but frequently written in uppercase. When run in Oracle's SQL*PLUS SQL interpreter, this query would produce something like the following output:

```
CUSTOMER_ID  NAME                          PHONE
-----------  ----------------------------  ---------------
1            Bob Copier                    617 555-1212
2            Janet Stapler                 617 555-1213
3            Joel Laptop                   508 555-7171
4            Larry Coffee                  212 555-6525
```

More advanced statements might restrict the query to particular columns or include some specific limiting criteria:

```
SELECT ORDER_ID, CUSTOMER_ID, TOTAL FROM ORDERS
WHERE ORDER_ID = 4
```

This statement selects the ORDER_ID, CUSTOMER_ID, and TOTAL columns from all records where the ORDER_ID field is equal to 4. Here's a possible result:

```
ORDER_ID CUSTOMER_ID    TOTAL
--------- ----------- ---------
        4           1    72.19
```

A SELECT statement can also link two or more tables based on the values of particular fields. This can be either a one-to-one relationship or, more typically, a one-to-many relation, such as one customer to several orders:

```
SELECT CUSTOMERS.NAME, ORDERS.TOTAL FROM CUSTOMERS, ORDERS
WHERE ORDERS.CUSTOMER_ID = CUSTOMERS.CUSTOMER_ID AND
ORDERS.ORDER_ID = 4
```

This statement connects (or, in database parlance, joins) the CUSTOMERS table with the ORDERS table via the CUSTOMER_ID field. Note that both tables have this field. The query returns information from both tables: the name of the customer who made order 4 and the total cost of that order. Here's some possible output:

```
NAME                                TOTAL
--------------------------------- ---------
Bob Copier                          72.19
```

SQL is also used to update the database. For example:

```
INSERT INTO CUSTOMERS (CUSTOMER_ID, NAME, PHONE)
   VALUES (5, "Bob Smith", "555 123-3456")
UPDATE CUSTOMERS SET NAME = "Robert Copier" WHERE CUSTOMER_ID = 1
DELETE FROM CUSTOMERS WHERE CUSTOMER_ID = 2
```

The first statement creates a new record in the CUSTOMERS table, filling in the CUSTOMER_ID, NAME, and PHONE fields with certain values. The second updates an existing record, changing the value of the NAME field for a specific customer. The last deletes any records with a CUSTOMER_ID of 2. Be very careful with all of these statements, especially DELETE. A DELETE statement without a WHERE clause will remove all the records in the table!

For a good primer on relational databases and SQL, we recommend *SQL for Dummies*, by Allen G. Taylor (IDG Books Worldwide).

The JDBC API

Previously, we've assumed that you have a general working knowledge of the various Java APIs. Because even experienced Java programmers may have had relatively little experience with databases, this section provides a general introduction to JDBC. If this is your first foray into the world of databases, we strongly recommend that you take a breather and find a book on general database and JDBC concepts. You may want to read *Database Programming with JDBC and Java,* by George Reese (O'Reilly), or *JDBC Database Access with Java,* by Graham Hamilton, Rick Cattell, and Maydene Fisher (Addison-Wesley). The official JDBC specification is also available online at *http://java.sun.com/products/jdbc.*

JDBC is a SQL-level API—one that allows you to execute SQL statements and retrieve the results, if any. The API itself is a set of interfaces and classes designed to perform actions against any database. Figure 9-2 shows how JDBC programs interact with databases.

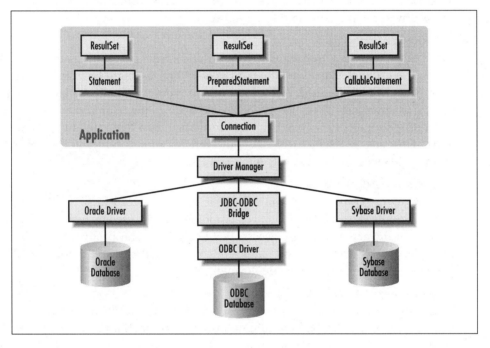

Figure 9-2. Java and the database

JDBC Drivers

The JDBC API, found in the `java.sql` package, contains only a few concrete classes. Much of the API is distributed as database-neutral interface classes that specify behavior without providing any implementation. The actual implementations are provided by third-party vendors.

An individual database system is accessed via a specific JDBC driver that implements the `java.sql.Driver` interface. Drivers exist for nearly all popular RDBMS systems, though few are available for free. Sun bundles a free JDBC-ODBC bridge driver with the JDK to allow access to standard ODBC data sources, such as a Microsoft Access database. However, Sun advises against using the bridge driver for anything other than development and very limited deployment. Servlet developers in particular should heed this warning because any problem in the JDBC-ODBC bridge driver's native code section can crash the entire server, not just your servlets.

JDBC drivers are available for most database platforms, from a number of vendors and in a number of different flavors. There are four driver categories:

Type 1-JDBC-ODBC Bridge Driver

Type 1 drivers use a bridge technology to connect a Java client to an ODBC database service. Sun's JDBC-ODBC bridge is the most common Type 1 driver. These drivers are implemented using native code.

Type 2-Native-API Partly-Java Driver

Type 2 drivers wrap a thin layer of Java around database-specific native code libraries. For Oracle databases, the native code libraries might be based on the OCI (Oracle Call Interface) libraries, which were originally designed for C/C++ programmers. Because Type 2 drivers are implemented using native code, in some cases they have better performance than their all-Java counterparts. They add an element of risk, however, because a defect in a driver's native code section can crash the entire server.

Type 3-Net-Protocol All-Java Driver

Type 3 drivers communicate via a generic network protocol to a piece of custom middleware. The middleware component might use any type of driver to provide the actual database access. WebLogic's Tengah product line is an example. These drivers are all Java, which makes them useful for applet deployment and safe for servlet deployment.

Type 4-Native-Protocol All-Java Driver

Type 4 drivers are the most direct of the lot. Written entirely in Java, Type 4 drivers understand database-specific networking protocols and can access the database directly without any additional software.

A list of currently available JDBC drivers can be found at *http://java.sun.com/products/jdbc/jdbc.drivers.html*.

Getting a Connection

The first step in using a JDBC driver to get a database connection involves loading the specific driver class into the application's JVM. This makes the driver available later, when we need it for opening the connection. An easy way to load the driver class is to use the `Class.forName()` method:

```
Class.forName("sun.jdbc.odbc.JdbcOdbcDriver");
```

When the driver is loaded into memory, it registers itself with the
`java.sql.DriverManager` class as an available database driver.

The next step is to ask the `DriverManager` class to open a connection to a given
database, where the database is specified by a specially formatted URL. The
method used to open the connection is `DriverManager.getConnection()`. It
returns a class that implements the `java.sql.Connection` interface:

```
Connection con =
    DriverManager.getConnection("jdbc:odbc:somedb", "user", "passwd");
```

A JDBC URL identifies an individual database in a driver-specific manner.
Different drivers may need different information in the URL to specify the host
database. JDBC URLs usually begin with *jdbc:subprotocol:subname*. For example,
the Oracle JDBC-Thin driver uses a URL of the form of
jdbc:oracle:thin:@dbhost:port:sid; the JDBC-ODBC bridge uses *jdbc:odbc:data-
sourcename;odbcoptions*.

During the call to `getConnection()`, the `DriverManager` object asks each registered driver if it recognizes the URL. If a driver says yes, the driver manager uses
that driver to create the `Connection` object. Here is a snippet of code a servlet
might use to load its database driver with the JDBC-ODBC bridge and create an
initial connection:

```
Connection con = null;
try {
  // Load (and therefore register) the JDBC-ODBC Bridge
  // Might throw a ClassNotFoundException
  Class.forName("sun.jdbc.odbc.JdbcOdbcDriver");

  // Get a connection to the database
  // Might throw an SQLException
  con = DriverManager.getConnection("jdbc:odbc:somedb", "user", "passwd");

  // The rest of the code goes here.
}
catch (ClassNotFoundException e) {
  // Handle an error loading the driver
}
catch (SQLException e) {
  // Handle an error getting the connection
}
finally {
  // Close the Connection to release the database resources immediately.
  try {
    if (con != null) con.close();
  }
  catch (SQLException ignored) { }
}
```

Executing SQL Queries

To really use a database, we need to have some way to execute queries. The simplest way to execute a query is to use the `java.sql.Statement` class. `Statement` objects are never instantiated directly; instead, a program calls the `createStatement()` method of `Connection` to obtain a new `Statement` object:

```
Statement stmt = con.createStatement();
```

A query that returns data can be executed using the `executeQuery()` method of `Statement`. This method executes the statement and returns a `java.sql.ResultSet` that encapsulates the retrieved data:

```
ResultSet rs = stmt.executeQuery("SELECT * FROM CUSTOMERS");
```

You can think of a `ResultSet` object as a representation of the query result returned one row at a time. You use the `next()` method of `ResultSet` to move from row to row. The `ResultSet` interface also boasts a multitude of methods designed for retrieving data from the current row. The `getString()` and `getObject()` methods are among the most frequently used for retrieving column values:

```
while(rs.next()) {
    String event = rs.getString("event");
    Object count = (Integer) rs.getObject("count");
}
```

You should know that the `ResultSet` is linked to its parent `Statement`. Therefore, if a `Statement` is closed or used to execute another query, any related `ResultSet` objects are closed automatically.

Example 9-1 shows a very simple servlet that uses the Oracle JDBC driver to perform a simple query, printing names and phone numbers for all employees listed in a database table. We assume that the database contains a table named `EMPLOYEES`, with at least two fields, `NAME` and `PHONE`.

Example 9-1. A JDBC-enabled servlet

```
import java.io.*;
import java.sql.*;
import javax.servlet.*;
import javax.servlet.http.*;

public class DBPhoneLookup extends HttpServlet {

  public void doGet(HttpServletRequest req, HttpServletResponse res)
                            throws ServletException, IOException {
    Connection con = null;
    Statement stmt = null;
```

Example 9-1. A JDBC-enabled servlet (continued)

```
    ResultSet rs = null;

    res.setContentType("text/html");
    PrintWriter out = res.getWriter();

    try {
      // Load (and therefore register) the Oracle Driver
      Class.forName("oracle.jdbc.driver.OracleDriver");

      // Get a Connection to the database
      con = DriverManager.getConnection(
        "jdbc:oracle:thin:dbhost:1528:ORCL", "user", "passwd");

      // Create a Statement object
      stmt = con.createStatement();

      // Execute an SQL query, get a ResultSet
      rs = stmt.executeQuery("SELECT NAME, PHONE FROM EMPLOYEES");

      // Display the result set as a list
      out.println("<HTML><HEAD><TITLE>Phonebook</TITLE></HEAD>");
      out.println("<BODY>");
      out.println("<UL>");
      while(rs.next()) {
        out.println("<LI>" + rs.getString("name") + " " + rs.getString("phone"));
      }
      out.println("</UL>");
      out.println("</BODY></HTML>");
    }
    catch(ClassNotFoundException e) {
      out.println("Couldn't load database driver: " + e.getMessage());
    }
    catch(SQLException e) {
      out.println("SQLException caught: " + e.getMessage());
    }
    finally {
      // Always close the database connection.
      try {
        if (con != null) con.close();
      }
      catch (SQLException ignored) { }
    }
  }
}
```

This is about as simple a database servlet as you are likely to see. All DBPhoneLookup does is connect to the database, run a query that retrieves the names and phone numbers of everyone in the employees table, and display the list to the user.

Handling SQL Exceptions

DBPhoneLookup encloses most of its code in a try/catch block. This block catches two exceptions: ClassNotFoundException and SQLException. The former is thrown by the Class.forName() method when the JDBC driver class can not be loaded. The latter is thrown by any JDBC method that has a problem. SQLException objects are just like any other exception type, with the additional feature that they can chain. The SQLException class defines an extra method, getNextException(), that allows the exception to encapsulate additional Exception objects. We didn't bother with this feature in the previous example, but here's how to use it:

```
catch (SQLException e) {
  out.println(e.getMessage());
  while((e = e.getNextException()) != null) {
    out.println(e.getMessage());
  }
}
```

This code displays the message from the first exception and then loops through all the remaining exceptions, outputting the error message associated with each one. In practice, the first exception will generally include the most relevant information.

Result Sets in Detail

Before we continue, we should take a closer look at the ResultSet interface and the related ResultSetMetaData interface. In Example 9-1, we knew what our query looked like, and we knew what we expected to get back, so we formatted the output appropriately. But, if we want to display the results of a query in an HTML table, it would nice to have some Java code that builds the table automatically from the ResultSet rather than having to write the same loop-and-display code over and over. As an added bonus, this kind of code makes it possible to change the contents of the table simply by changing the query.

The ResultSetMetaData interface provides a way for a program to learn about the underlying structure of a query result on the fly. We can use it to build an object that dynamically generates an HTML table from a ResultSet, as shown in

Example 9-2. Many Java HTML generation tools (such as WebLogic's htmlKona toolkit discussed in Chapter 5, *Sending HTML Information*) have a similar capability.

Example 9-2. A class to generate an HTML table from a ResultSet using ResultSetMetaData

```java
import java.sql.*;

public class HtmlResultSet {

  private ResultSet rs;

  public HtmlResultSet(ResultSet rs) {
    this.rs = rs;
  }

  public String toString() {  // can be called at most once
    StringBuffer out = new StringBuffer();
    // Start a table to display the result set
    out.append("<TABLE>\n");

    try {
      ResultSetMetaData rsmd = rs.getMetaData();

      int numcols = rsmd.getColumnCount();

      // Title the table with the result set's column labels
      out.append("<TR>");
      for (int i = 1; i <= numcols; i++) {
        out.append("<TH>" + rsmd.getColumnLabel(i));
      }
      out.append("</TR>\n");

      while(rs.next()) {
        out.append("<TR>"); // start a new row
        for (int i = 1; i <= numcols; i++) {
          out.append("<TD>"); // start a new data element
          Object obj = rs.getObject(i);
          if (obj != null)
            out.append(obj.toString());
          else
            out.append(" ");
        }
        out.append("</TR>\n");
      }

      // End the table
      out.append("</TABLE>\n");
    }
    catch (SQLException e) {
```

Example 9-2. A class to generate an HTML table from a ResultSet using ResultSetMetaData (continued)

```
        out.append("</TABLE><H1>ERROR:</H1> " + e.getMessage() + "\n");
    }

    return out.toString();
  }
} .
```

This example shows how to use two basic methods of `ResultSetMetaData`: `getColumnCount()` and `getColumnLabel()`. The first returns the number of columns in the `ResultSet`, while the second retrieves the name of a particular column in a result set based on its numerical index. Indexes in `ResultSet` objects follow the RDBMS standard rather than the C++/Java standard, which means they are numbered from 1 to n rather than from 0 to n-1.

This example also uses the `getObject()` method of `ResultSet` to retrieve the value of each column. All of the `getXXX()` methods work with column indexes as well as with column names. Accessing data this way is more efficient, and, with well-written SQL, is more portable. Here we use `getObject().toString()` instead of `getString()` to simplify the handling of `null` values, as discussed in the next section.

Table 9-1 shows the Java methods you can use to retrieve some common SQL data types from a database. No matter what the type, you can always use the `getObject()` method of `ResultSet`, in which case the type of the object returned is shown in the second column. You can also use a specific `getXXX()` method. These methods are shown in the third column, along with the Java data types they return. Remember that supported SQL data types vary from database to database.

Table 9-1. Methods to Retrieve Data from a ResultSet

SQL Data Type	Java Type Returned by getObject()	Recommended Alternative to getObject()
CHAR	String	String getString()
VARCHAR	String	String getString()
LONGVARCHAR	String	InputStream getAsciiStream() InputStream getUnicodeStream()
NUMERIC	java.math.BigDecimal	java.math.BigDecimal getBigDecimal()
DECIMAL	java.math.BigDecimal	java.math.BigDecimal getBigDecimal()
BIT	Boolean	boolean getBoolean()
TINYINT	Integer	byte getByte()

Table 9-1. Methods to Retrieve Data from a ResultSet (continued)

SQL Data Type	Java Type Returned by getObject()	Recommended Alternative to getObject()
SMALLINT	Integer	short getShort()
INTEGER	Integer	int getInt()
BIGINT	Long	long getLong()
REAL	Float	float getFloat()
FLOAT	Double	double getDouble()
DOUBLE	Double	double getDouble()
BINARY	byte[]	byte[] getBytes()
VARBINARY	byte[]	byte[] getBytes()
LONGVARBINARY	byte[]	InputStream getBinaryStream()
DATE	java.sql.Date	java.sql.Date getDate()
TIME	Java.sql.Time	java.sql.Time getTime()
TIMESTAMP	Java.sql.Timestamp	java.sql.Timestamp getTimestamp()

Handling Null Fields

Handling null database values with JDBC can be a little tricky. (A database field can be set to null to indicate that no value is present, in much the same way that a Java object can be set to null.) A method that doesn't return an object, like getInt(), has no way of indicating whether a column is null or whether it contains actual information. (Some drivers return a string that contains the text "null" when getString() is called on a null column!) Any special value like -1, might be a legitimate value. Therefore, JDBC includes the wasNull() method in ResultSet, which returns true or false depending on whether the last column read was a true database null. This means that you must read data from the ResultSet into a variable, call wasNull(), and proceed accordingly. It's not pretty, but it works. Here's an example:

```
int age = rs.getInt("age");
if (!rs.wasNull())
  out.println("Age: " + age);
```

Another way to check for null values is to use the getObject() method. If a column is null, getObject() always returns null. Compare this to the getString() method that has been known, in some implementations, to return the empty string if a column is `null`. Using `getObject()` eliminates the need to call `wasNull()` and leads to simpler code.

Updating the Database

Most database-enabled web sites need to do more than just perform queries. When a client submits an order or provides some kind of information, the data needs to be entered into the database. When you know you're executing a SQL UPDATE, INSERT, or DELETE statement and you know you don't expect a `ResultSet`, you can use the `executeUpdate()` method of `Statement`. It returns a count that indicates the number of rows modified by the statement. It's used like this:

```
int count =
  stmt.executeUpdate("DELETE FROM CUSTOMERS WHERE CUSTOMER_ID = 5");
```

If you are executing SQL that may return either a `ResultSet` or a count (say, if you're handling user-submitted SQL or building generic data-handling classes), use the generic `execute()` method of `Statement`. It returns a `boolean` whose value is `true` if the SQL statement produced one or more `ResultSet` objects or `false` if it resulted in an update count:

```
boolean b = stmt.execute(sql);
```

The `getResultSet()` and `getUpdateCount()` methods of `Statement` provide access to the results of the `execute()` method. Example 9-3 demonstrates the use of these methods with a new version of `HtmlResultSet`, named `HtmlSQLResult`, that creates an HTML table from any kind of SQL statement.

Example 9-3. A class to generate an HTML table from a ResultSet using the ResultSetMetaData

```
import java.sql.*;

public class HtmlSQLResult {
  private String sql;
  private Connection con;

  public HtmlSQLResult(String sql, Connection con) {
    this.sql = sql;
    this.con = con;
  }

  public String toString() {  // can be called at most once
    StringBuffer out = new StringBuffer();

    // Uncomment the following line to display the SQL command at start of table
    // out.append("Results of SQL Statement: " + sql + "<P>\n");
```

Example 9-3. A class to generate an HTML table from a ResultSet using the ResultSetMetaData

```java
try {
  Statement stmt = con.createStatement();

  if (stmt.execute(sql)) {
    // There's a ResultSet to be had
    ResultSet rs = stmt.getResultSet();
    out.append("<TABLE>\n");

    ResultSetMetaData rsmd = rs.getMetaData();

    int numcols = rsmd.getColumnCount();

    // Title the table with the result set's column labels
    out.append("<TR>");
    for (int i = 1; i <= numcols; i++)
      out.append("<TH>" + rsmd.getColumnLabel(i));
    out.append("</TR>\n");

    while(rs.next()) {
      out.append("<TR>");  // start a new row
      for(int i = 1; i <= numcols; i++) {
        out.append("<TD>");  // start a new data element
        Object obj = rs.getObject(i);
        if (obj != null)
          out.append(obj.toString());
        else
          out.append(" ");
        }
      out.append("</TR>\n");
    }

    // End the table
    out.append("</TABLE>\n");
  }
  else {
    // There's a count to be had
    out.append("<B>Records Affected:</B> " + stmt.getUpdateCount());
  }
}
catch (SQLException e) {
  out.append("</TABLE><H1>ERROR:</H1> " + e.getMessage());
}

return out.toString();
  }
}
```

This example uses `execute()` to execute whatever SQL statement is passed to the `HtmlSQLResult` constructor. Then, depending on the return value, it either calls `getResultSet()` or `getUpdateCount()`. Note that neither `getResultSet()` nor `getUpdateCount()` should be called more than once per query.

Using Prepared Statements

A `PreparedStatement` object is like a regular `Statement` object, in that it can be used to execute SQL statements. The important difference is that the SQL in a `PreparedStatement` is precompiled by the database for faster execution. Once a `PreparedStatement` has been compiled, it can still be customized by adjusting predefined parameters. Prepared statements are useful in applications that have to run the same general SQL command over and over.

Use the `prepareStatement(String)` method of `Connection` to create `PreparedStatement` objects. Use the ? character as a placeholder for values to be substituted later. For example:

```
PreparedStatement pstmt = con.prepareStatement(
    "INSERT INTO ORDERS (ORDER_ID, CUSTOMER_ID, TOTAL) VALUES (?,?,?)");

// Other code

pstmt.clearParameters();    // clear any previous parameter values
pstmt.setInt(1, 2);         // set ORDER_ID
pstmt.setInt(2, 4);         // set CUSTOMER_ID
pstmt.setDouble(3, 53.43);  // set TOTAL
pstmt.executeUpdate();      // execute the stored SQL
```

The `clearParameters()` method removes any previously defined parameter values, while the `setXXX()` methods are used to assign actual values to each of the placeholder question marks. Once you have assigned values for all the parameters, call `executeUpdate()` to execute the `PreparedStatement`.

The `PreparedStatement` class has an important application in conjunction with servlets. When loading user-submitted text into the database using `Statement` objects and dynamic SQL, you must be careful not to accidentally introduce any SQL control characters (such as " or ') without escaping them in the manner required by your database. With a database like Oracle that surrounds strings with single quotes, an attempt to insert `"John d'Artagan"` into the database results in this corrupted SQL:

```
INSERT INTO MUSKETEERS (NAME) VALUES ('John d'Artagan')
```

As you can see, the string terminates twice. One solution is to manually replace the single quote ' with two single quotes ' ', the Oracle escape sequence for one single quote. This solution, requires you to escape every character that your database treats as special—not an easy task and not consistent with writing platform-independent code. A far better solution is to use a `PreparedStatement` and pass the string using its `setString()` method, as shown below. The `PreparedStatement` automatically escapes the string as necessary for your database:

```
PreparedStatement pstmt = con.prepareStatement(
  "INSERT INTO MUSKETEERS (NAME) VALUES (?)");
pstmt.setString(1, "John d'Artagan");
pstmt.executeUpdate();
```

Reusing Database Objects

In the introduction, we mentioned that the servlet life cycle allows for extremely fast database access. After you've used JDBC for a short time, it will become evident that the major performance bottleneck often comes right at the beginning, when you are opening a database connection. This is rarely a problem for most applications and applets because they can afford a few seconds to create a `Connection` that is used for the life of the program. With servlets this bottleneck is more serious because we are creating and tearing down a new `Connection` for every page request. Luckily, the servlet life cycle allows us to reuse the same connection for multiple requests, even concurrent requests, as `Connection` objects are required to be thread safe.

Reusing Database Connections

A servlet can create one or more `Connection` objects in its `init()` method and reuse them in its `service()`, `doGet()`, and `doPost()` methods. To demonstrate, Example 9-4 shows the phone lookup servlet rewritten to create its `Connection` object in advance. It also uses the `HtmlSQLResult` class from Example 9-3 to display the results. Note that this servlet uses the Sybase JDBC driver.

Example 9-4. An improved directory servlet

```
import java.io.*;
import java.sql.*;
import javax.servlet.*;
import javax.servlet.http.*;

public class DBPhoneLookupReuse extends HttpServlet {

  private Connection con = null;

  public void init(ServletConfig config) throws ServletException {
    super.init(config);
    try {
```

Example 9-4. An improved directory servlet (continued)

```
    // Load (and therefore register) the Sybase driver
    Class.forName("com.sybase.jdbc.SybDriver");
    con = DriverManager.getConnection(
      "jdbc:sybase:Tds:dbhost:7678", "user", "passwd");
  }
  catch (ClassNotFoundException e) {
    throw new UnavailableException(this, "Couldn't load database driver");
  }
  catch (SQLException e) {
    throw new UnavailableException(this, "Couldn't get db connection");
  }
}

public void doGet(HttpServletRequest req, HttpServletResponse res)
                         throws ServletException, IOException {
  res.setContentType("text/html");
  PrintWriter out = res.getWriter();

  out.println("<HTML><HEAD><TITLE>Phonebook</TITLE></HEAD>");
  out.println("<BODY>");

  HtmlSQLResult result =
    new HtmlSQLResult("SELECT NAME, PHONE FROM EMPLOYEES", con);

  // Display the resulting output
  out.println("<H2>Employees:</H2>");
  out.println(result);
  out.println("</BODY></HTML>");
}

public void destroy() {
  // Clean up.
  try {
    if (con != null) con.close();
  }
  catch (SQLException ignored) { }
}
}
```

Reusing Prepared Statements

With a little care, you can speed servlet performance even more by creating other database-related objects ahead of time. The `PreparedStatement` object is an ideal candidate because it can precompile a SQL statement. This usually saves only a few milliseconds, but if your site gets a few hundred thousand hits a day, that can add up pretty quickly.

Note, however, that sharing objects other than connections poses a problem. Servlets must be thread safe, and accessing a `PreparedStatement` might require three or four method calls. If one thread calls the `clearParameters()` method of `PreparedStatement` right before another thread calls `execute()`, the results of `execute()` will be disastrous. Also, there's the limitation that a `Statement` can support only one query (and any associated result sets) at a time. The solution is to synchronize the sections of your code that use shared objects, as discussed in Chapter 3 and shown here:

```
synchronized (pstmt) {
  pstmt.clearParameters();
  pstmt.setInt(1, 2);
  pstmt.setInt(2, 4);
  pstmt.setDouble(3, 53.43);
  pstmt.executeUpdate();
}
```

Unfortunately, this solution is not without drawbacks. Entering a synchronization block on some platforms takes extra time, and synchronized objects can be used by only one thread at a time. However, some servlets already require a synchronization block, and in these cases the drawback is less of an issue. A good rule of thumb, then, is to create your connections ahead of time, along with any frequently used objects (such as `PreparedStatement` objects) that can be quickly used inside preexisting synchronization blocks.

For servlets written using the `SingleThreadModel` interface, these issues do not apply. On the other hand, you will have a number of copies of your servlet loaded at once, which could be just as detrimental to performance.

Transactions

So far, we have failed to mention one important feature of modern relational database systems: transactions. Most service-oriented web sites need to do more than run `SELECT` statements and insert single pieces of data. Let's look at an online banking application. To perform a transfer of $50,000 between accounts, your program needs to perform an operation that consists of two separate but related actions: credit one account and debit another. Now, imagine that for some reason or another, the SQL statement for the credit succeeds but the one for the debit fails. One account holder is $50,000 richer, but the other account has not been debited to match.

SQL failure is not the only potential problem. If another user checks the account balance in between the credit and the debit, he will see the original balance. The database is shown in an invalid state (more money is represented than actually exists). Granted, this kind of thing is unlikely to occur often, but in a universe of infinite possibilities, it will almost certainly happen sometime. This kind of problem is similar to the synchronization issues we discussed back in Chapter 3. This time, instead of concerning ourselves with the validity of data stored in a servlet, we are concerned with the validity of an underlying database. Simple synchronization is not enough to solve this problem: multiple servlets may be accessing the same database. For systems like banking software, chances are good that the database is being used by a number of entirely non-Java applications as well.

Sounds like a fairly tricky problem, right? Fortunately, it was a problem long before Java came along, so it has already been solved. Most major RDMBS systems support the concept of transactions. A *transaction* allows you to group multiple SQL statements together. Using a transaction-aware RDBMS, you can begin a transaction, perform any number of actions, and either *commit* the results to the database or *roll back* all of your SQL statements. If we build our online banking application with a transaction-based system, the credit will automatically be canceled if the debit fails.

A transaction is isolated from the rest of the database until finished. As far as the rest of the database is concerned, everything takes place at once (in other words, transactions are *atomic*). This means that other users accessing the database will always see a valid view of the data, although not necessarily an up-to-date view. If a user requests a report on widgets sold before your widget sales transaction is completed, the report will not include the most recent sale.

Using Transactions with JDBC

Transaction management with JDBC takes place via the `Connection` object. By default, new connections start out in auto-commit mode. This means that every SQL statement is executed as an individual transaction that is immediately committed to the database. To control commitment yourself, thereby allowing you to group SQL statements into transactions, you call `setAutoCommit(false)` on the `Connection` object. You can check the status of auto-commit with the `getAutoCommit()` method. Once you have completed all of your SQL statements, you call `commit()` to permanently record the transaction in the database. Or, if you encountered an error, you call `rollback()` to undo it.

Example 9-5 shows a servlet that uses transactions to do basic order processing. It assumes two tables in an ODBC database—INVENTORY (containing the product ID and amount in stock) and SHIPPING (containing a product ID, an order number, and the amount shipped). The servlet uses an unshown `chargeCard()` method that handles billing and throws an exception if the customer's credit card is invalid.

Example 9-5. Transaction-based order management

```java
import java.io.*;
import java.sql.*;
import javax.servlet.*;
import javax.servlet.http.*;

public class OrderHandler extends HttpServlet {

  public void doPost(HttpServletRequest req, HttpServletResponse res)
                               throws ServletException, IOException {
    res.setContentType("text/plain");
    PrintWriter out = res.getWriter();

    Connection con = null;
    try {
      Class.forName("sun.jdbc.odbc.JdbcOdbcDriver");
      con = DriverManager.getConnection("jdbc:odbc:ordersdb", "user", "passwd");

      // Turn on transactions
      con.setAutoCommit(false);

      Statement stmt = con.createStatement();
      stmt.executeUpdate(
        "UPDATE INVENTORY SET STOCK = (STOCK - 10) WHERE PRODUCTID = 7");
      stmt.executeUpdate(
        "UPDATE SHIPPING SET SHIPPED = (SHIPPED + 10) WHERE PRODUCTID = 7");

      chargeCard();  // method doesn't actually exist...

      con.commit();
      out.println("Order successful!  Thanks for your business!");
    }
    catch (Exception e) {
      // Any error is grounds for rollback
      try {
        con.rollback();
      }
      catch (SQLException ignored) { }
      out.println("Order failed. Please contact technical support.");
    }
    finally {
      // Clean up.
      try {
        if (con != null) con.close();
      }
      catch (SQLException ignored) { }
    }
  }
}
```

Here are a few notes on this example. First, the order transaction logic is in doPost() since the client's action is definitely not safely repeatable. Second, because the example demonstrates transaction logic more than servlet logic, the servlet simply assumes the user is buying 10 units of item 7, rather than bothering to actually parse a form for credit card and order information. Finally, as the servlet runs, any exception thrown during driver initialization, connecting to the database, executing SQL, or charging the credit card causes execution to jump to the catch() block, where the rollback() method is called, undoing all our work.

Optimized Transaction Processing

Note that in the previous example the Connection object was created inside the doPost() method, giving up the performance improvements we gained earlier in the chapter by moving the creation up to init(). This is done because transactions are linked to connections and, therefore, connections using transactions cannot be shared. Imagine what would happen if another invocation of this servlet invoked the commit() method when our order had reached only the second SQL statement. Our INVENTORY table would be short 10 units!

So, how do we use transactions without having to connect to the database every time a page is requested? There are several possibilities:

- Synchronize the doPost() method. This means that each instance of the servlet deals with only one request at a time. This works well for very low traffic sites, but it does slow things down for your users because every transaction has to finish before the next can start. If you need to perform database-intensive updates and inserts, the delay will probably be unacceptable.

- Leave things as they are, but create a new Connection object for each transaction. If you need to update data only once in every few thousand page requests, this might be the simplest route.

- Create a pool of Connection objects in the init() method and hand them out as needed, as shown in Figure 9-3. This is probably the most efficient way to handle the problem, if done right. It can, however, become very complicated very quickly without third-party support classes.

- Create a single Connection object in the init() method and have the servlet implement SingleThreadModel, so the web server creates a pool of servlet instances with a Connection for each, as shown in Figure 9-4. This has the same effect as synchronizing doPost(), but because the web server has a number of servlet instances to choose from, the performance hit for the user is not as great. This approach is easy to implement, but is less robust than using a separate connection pool because the servlet has no control over how many servlet instances are created and how many connections are used. When creating single-threaded database servlets, be especially sure to have the `destroy()` method close any open database connections.

- Implement session tracking in the servlet and use the `HttpSession` object to hold onto a `Connection` for each user. This allows you to go one step beyond the other solutions and extend a transaction across multiple page requests or even multiple servlets.

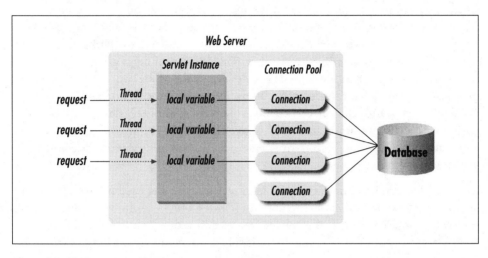

Figure 9-3. Servlets using a database connection pool

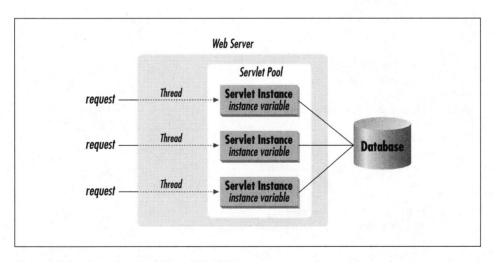

Figure 9-4. Servlets using SingleThreadModel for a server-managed connection pool

Connection Pooling

For a complicated servlet, creating a connection pool is the ideal approach. With a connection pool, we can duplicate only the resources we need to duplicate (that is, Connection objects), rather than the entire servlet. A connection pool can also intelligently manage the size of the pool and make sure each connection remains valid. A number of connection pool packages are currently available. Some, such as the DbConnectionBroker that is freely available from Java Exchange at *http://javaexchange.com*, work by creating an object that dispenses connections and connection IDs on request. Others, such as the pool drivers package available from WebLogic at *http://www.weblogic.com*, implement a new JDBC driver that handles a pool of connections to another JDBC driver. Using a pooling driver like this is the easiest way to implement connection pooling in your servlets. Pooling drivers, however, have a little more operational overhead than standard drivers because every JDBC class needs to be wrapped by another class. This is transparent to the programmer and won't make much of a difference with most Java applications—but with a high-performance, high-volume servlet application, every little performance gain helps.

Example 9-6 demonstrates a simple connection pooling system. A number of connections are created at startup and are handed out to methods as needed. If all the connections are in use, the servlet creates a new one. While our Connection-Pool class is fully functional, mission-critical deployments might benefit from one of the more complete third party packages.

Example 9-6. The ConnectionPool class

```
import java.sql.*;
import java.util.*;

public class ConnectionPool {
    private Hashtable connections;
    private int increment;
    private String dbURL, user, password;

    public ConnectionPool(String dbURL,
                          String user,
                          String password,
                          String driverClassName,
                          int initialConnections,
                          int increment)
          throws SQLException, ClassNotFoundException {

      // Load the specified driver class
      Class.forName(driverClassName);
```

Example 9-6. The ConnectionPool class (continued)

```
      this.dbURL = dbURL;
      this.user = user;
      this.password = password;
      this.increment = increment;

      connections = new Hashtable();

      // Put our pool of Connections in the Hashtable
      // The FALSE value indicates they're unused
      for(int i = 0; i < initialConnections; i++) {
        connections.put(DriverManager.getConnection(dbURL, user, password),
                        Boolean.FALSE);
      }
    }

  public Connection getConnection() throws SQLException {
    Connection con = null;

    Enumeration cons = connections.keys();

    synchronized (connnections) {
      while(cons.hasMoreElements()) {
        con = (Connection)cons.nextElement();

        Boolean b = (Boolean)connections.get(con);
        if (b == Boolean.FALSE) {
          // So we found an unused connection.
          // Test its integrity with a quick setAutoCommit(true) call.
          // For production use, more testing should be performed,
          // such as executing a simple query.
          try {
            con.setAutoCommit(true);
          }
          catch(SQLException e) {
            // Problem with the connection, replace it.
            con = DriverManager.getConnection(dbURL, user, password);
          }
          // Update the Hashtable to show this one's taken
          connections.put(con, Boolean.TRUE);
          // Return the connection
          return con;
        }
      }
    }

    // If we get here, there were no free connections.
    // We've got to make more.
    for(int i = 0; i < increment; i++) {
```

Example 9-6. The ConnectionPool class (continued)

```
        connections.put(DriverManager.getConnection(dbURL, user, password),
                        Boolean.FALSE);
    }

    // Recurse to get one of the new connections.
    return getConnection();
  }

  public void returnConnection(Connection returned) {
    Connection con;
    Enumeration cons = connections.keys();
    while (cons.hasMoreElements()) {
      con = (Connection)cons.nextElement();
      if (con == returned) {
        connections.put(con, Boolean.FALSE);
        break;
      }
    }
  }
}
```

The ConnectionPool class maintains a Hashtable, using Connection objects as keys and Boolean objects as stored values. The Boolean value indicates whether a connection is in use. A program calls the getConnection() method of ConnectionPool to be assigned a Connection object it can use; it calls returnConnection() to give the connection back to the pool. This is a fairly simple model of a connection pool. For deployment, you probably want something that does a better job of maintaining the quality of the pool and does more verification of integrity than a simple call to setAutoCommit().

Example 9-7 shows a revised version of the order processing servlet that uses the pooling class.

Example 9-7. Connection pooling transaction servlet

```
import java.io.*;
import java.sql.*;
import javax.servlet.*;
import javax.servlet.http.*;

public class OrderHandlerPool extends HttpServlet {
  private ConnectionPool pool;

  public void init(ServletConfig config) throws ServletException {
    super.init(config);
    try {
      pool = new ConnectionPool("jdbc:oracle:oci7:orders", "user", "passwd",
```

Example 9-7. Connection pooling transaction servlet (continued)

```
                              "oracle.jdbc.driver.OracleDriver", 10, 5);
    }
    catch (Exception e) {
      throw new UnavailableException(this, "Couldn't create connection pool");
    }
  }

  public void doPost(HttpServletRequest req, HttpServletResponse res)
                              throws ServletException, IOException {
    Connection con = null;

    res.setContentType("text/plain");
    PrintWriter out = res.getWriter();

    try {
      con = pool.getConnection();

      // Turn on transactions
      con.setAutoCommit(false);

      Statement stmt = con.createStatement();
      stmt.executeUpdate(
        "UPDATE INVENTORY SET STOCK = (STOCK − 10) WHERE PRODUCTID = 7");
      stmt.executeUpdate(
        "UPDATE SHIPPING SET SHIPPED = (SHIPPED + 10) WHERE PRODUCTID = 7");

      chargeCard();  // method doesn t actually exist...

      con.commit();
      out.println("Order successful!  Thanks for your business!");
    }
    catch (Exception e) {
      // Any error is grounds for rollback
      try {
        con.rollback();
      }
      catch (Exception ignored) { }
      out.println("Order failed. Please contact technical support.");
    }
    finally {
      if (con != null) pool.returnConnection(con);
    }
  }
}
```

Connections as Part of a Session

Session tracking, which we examined in detail back in Chapter 7, *Session Tracking*, gives us another way of handling transactions. Using sessions, we can create or allocate a dedicated database connection for individual users of a web site or intranet application. Example 9-8 demonstrates by showing a `ConnectionPer-Client` servlet that associates a unique `Connection` with each client `HttpSession`. It wraps the `Connection` with a `ConnectionHolder` that is responsible for managing the connection's life cycle.

Example 9-8. Associating a connection with a session

```
import java.io.*;
import java.sql.*;
import javax.servlet.*;
import javax.servlet.http.*;

class ConnectionHolder implements HttpSessionBindingListener {
  private Connection con = null;

  public ConnectionHolder(Connection con) {
    // Save the Connection
    this.con = con;
    try {
      con.setAutoCommit(false);  // transactions can extend between web pages!
    }
    catch(SQLException e) {
      // Perform error handling
    }
  }

  public Connection getConnection() {
    return con;  // return the cargo
  }

  public void valueBound(HttpSessionBindingEvent event) {
    // Do nothing when added to a Session
  }

  public void valueUnbound(HttpSessionBindingEvent event) {
    // Roll back changes when removed from a Session
    // (or when the Session expires)
    try {
      if (con != null) {
        con.rollback();  // abandon any uncomitted data
        con.close();
      }
    }
    catch (SQLException e) {
```

Example 9-8. Associating a connection with a session (continued)

```
      // Report it
    }
  }
}

/* Actual Servlet */

public class ConnectionPerClient extends HttpServlet {

  public void init(ServletConfig config) throws ServletException {
    super.init(config);
    try {
      Class.forName("oracle.jdbc.driver.OracleDriver");
    }
    catch (ClassNotFoundException e) {
      throw new UnavailableException(this, "Couldn't load OracleDriver");
    }
  }

  public void doGet(HttpServletRequest req, HttpServletResponse res)
                            throws ServletException, IOException {
    res.setContentType("text/plain");
    PrintWriter out = res.getWriter();

    HttpSession session = req.getSession(true);

    // Try getting the connection holder for this client
    ConnectionHolder holder =
      (ConnectionHolder) session.getValue("servletapp.connection");

    // Create (and store) a new connection and holder if necessary
    if (holder == null) {
      try {
        holder = new ConnectionHolder(DriverManager.getConnection(
          "jdbc:oracle:oci7:ordersdb", "user", "passwd"));
        session.putValue("servletapp.connection", holder);
      }
      catch (SQLException e) {
        getServletContext().log(e, "Couldn't get db connection");
      }
    }

    // Get the actual connection from the holder
    Connection con = holder.getConnection();

    // Now use the connection
    try {
      Statement stmt = con.createStatement();
```

Example 9-8. Associating a connection with a session (continued)

```
    stmt.executeUpdate(
      "UPDATE INVENTORY SET STOCK = (STOCK - 10) WHERE PRODUCTID = 7");
    stmt.executeUpdate(
      "UPDATE SHIPPING SET SHIPPED = (SHIPPED + 10) WHERE PRODUCTID = 7");

    // Charge the credit card and commit the transaction in another servlet
    res.sendRedirect(res.encodeRedirectUrl("/servlet/CreditCardHandler"));
  }
  catch (Exception e) {
    // Any error is grounds for rollback
    try {
      con.rollback();
      session.removeValue("servletapp.connection");
    }
    catch (Exception ignored) { }
    out.println("Order failed. Please contact technical support.");
  }
  }
}
```

Rather than directly binding a connection to the session, we've created a simple holder class that implements the `HttpSessionBindingListner` interface. We do this because database connections are the most limited resource in a JDBC application and we want to make sure that they will be released properly when no longer needed. The wrapper class also allows us to rollback any uncommitted changes. If a user leaves our hypothetical online shopping system before checking out, her transaction is rolled back when the session expires.

Storing connections in sessions requires careful analysis of your application's needs. Most low-end and mid-range database servers can max out at about 100 connections; desktop databases like Microsoft Access saturate even more quickly.

Advanced JDBC Techniques

Now that we've covered the basics, let's talk about a few advanced techniques that use servlets and JDBC. First, we'll examine how servlets can access stored database procedures. Then we'll look at how servlets can fetch complicated data types, such as binary data (images, applications, etc.), large quantities of text, or even executable database-manipulation code, from a database.

Stored Procedures

Most RDBMS systems include some sort of internal programming language. One example is Oracle's PL/SQL. These languages allow database developers to embed procedural application code directly within a database and then call that code from other applications. RDMBS programming languages are often well suited to performing certain database actions; many existing database installations have a number of useful stored procedures already written and ready to go. Most introductions to JDBC tend to skip over this topic, so we'll cover it here briefly.

The following code is an Oracle PL/SQL stored procedure. If it looks familiar, that's because it's from George Reese's *Database Programming with JDBC* (O'Reilly):

```
CREATE OR REPLACE PROCEDURE sp_interest
(id IN INTEGER
bal IN OUT FLOAT) IS
BEGIN
SELECT balance
INTO bal
FROM accounts
WHERE account_id = id;

bal := bal + bal * 0.03;

UPDATE accounts
SET balance = bal
WHERE account_id = id;

END;
```

This procedure executes a SQL statement, performs a calculation, and executes another SQL statement. It would be fairly simple to write the SQL to handle this (in fact, the transaction example earlier in this chapter does something similar), so why bother with this at all? There are several reasons:

- Stored procedures are precompiled in the RDBMS, so they run faster than dynamic SQL.

- Stored procedures execute entirely within the RDBMS, so they can perform multiple queries and updates without network traffic.

- Stored procedures allow you to write database manipulation code once and use it across multiple applications in multiple languages.

- Changes in the underlying table structures require changes only in the stored procedures that access them; applications using the database are unaffected.

- Many older databases already have a lot of code written as stored procedures, and it would be nice to be able to leverage that effort.

The Oracle PL/SQL procedure in our example takes an input value, in this case an account ID, and returns an updated balance. While each database has its own syntax for accessing stored procedures, JDBC creates a standardized escape sequence for accessing stored procedures using the `java.sql.CallableState-ment` class. The syntax for a procedure that doesn't return a result is `"{call` procedure_name(?,?)}". The syntax for a stored procedure that returns a result value is "{? = call procedure_name(?,?)}". The parameters inside the parentheses are optional.

Using the `CallableStatement` class is similar to using the `PreparedStatement` class:

```
CallableStatment cstmt = con.prepareCall("{call sp_interest(?,?)}");
cstmt.registerOutParameter(2, java.sql.Types.FLOAT);
cstmt.setInt(1, accountID);
cstmt.execute();
out.println("New Balance: " + cstmt.getFloat(2));
```

This code first creates a `CallableStatement` using the `prepareCall()` method of `Connection`. Because this stored procedure has an output parameter, it uses the `registerOutParameter()` method of `CallableStatement` to identify that parameter as an output parameter of type `FLOAT`. Finally, the code executes the stored procedure and uses the `getFloat()` method of `CallableStatement` to display the new balance. The get*XXX*() methods in `CallableStatement` interface are similar to those in the `ResultSet` interface.

Binaries and Books

Most databases support data types to handle text strings up to several gigabytes in size, as well as binary information like multimedia files. Different databases handle this kind of data in different ways, but the JDBC methods for retrieving it are standard. The `getAsciiStream()` method of `ResultSet` handles large text strings; `getBinaryStream()` works for large binary objects. Each of these methods returns an `InputStream`.

Support for large data types is one of the most common sources of JDBC problems. Make sure you test your drivers thoroughly, using the largest pieces of data your application will encounter. Oracle's JDBC driver is particularly prone to errors in this area.

Here's some code from a message board servlet that demonstrates reading a long ASCII string. We can assume that connections, statements, and so on have already been created:

```
try {
  ResultSet rs = stmt.executeQuery(
    "SELECT TITLE, SENDER, MESSAGE FROM MESSAGES WHERE MESSAGE_ID = 9");
  if (rs.next()) {
    out.println("<H1>" + rs.getString("title") + "</H1>");
    out.println("<B>From:</B> " + rs.getString("sender") + "<BR>");
    BufferedReader msgText = new BufferedReader(
      new InputStreamReader(rs.getAsciiStream("message")));
```

```
      while (msgText.ready()) {
        out.println(msgText.readLine());
      }
    }
  }
  catch (SQLException e) {
    // Report it
  }
```

While it is reading from the InputStream, this servlet doesn't get the value of any other columns in the result set. This is important because calling any other getXXX() method of ResultSet closes the InputStream.

Binary data can be retrieved in the same manner using the ResultSet.getBinaryStream(). In this case, we need to set the content type as appropriate and write the output as bytes. Example 9-9 shows a servlet that returns a GIF file loaded from a database.

Example 9-9. Reading a binary GIF image from a database

```
import java.io.*;
import java.sql.*;
import javax.servlet.*;
import javax.servlet.http.*;

public class DBGifReader extends HttpServlet {

  Connection con;

  public void init(ServletConfig config) throws ServletException {
    super.init(config);
    try {
      Class.forName("sun.jdbc.odbc.JdbcOdbcDriver");
      con = DriverManager.getConnection("jdbc:odbc:imagedb", "user", "passwd");
    }
    catch (ClassNotFoundException e) {
      throw new UnavailableException(this, "Couldn't load JdbcOdbcDriver");
    }
    catch (SQLException e) {
      throw new UnavailableException(this, "Couldn't get db connection");
    }
  }

  public void doGet(HttpServletRequest req, HttpServletResponse res)
                              throws ServletException, IOException {
    try {
      res.setContentType("image/gif");
      ServletOutputStream out = res.getOutputStream();
```

Example 9-9. Reading a binary GIF image from a database (continued)

```
Statement stmt = con.createStatement();
ResultSet rs = stmt.executeQuery(
  "SELECT IMAGE FROM PICTURES WHERE PID = " + req.getParameter("PID"));

if (rs.next()) {
  BufferedInputStream gifData =
    new BufferedInputStream(rs.getBinaryStream("image"));
  byte[] buf = new byte[4 * 1024];  // 4K buffer
  int len;
  while ((len = gifData.read(buf, 0, buf.length)) != -1) {
    out.write(buf, 0, len);
  }
}
else {
  res.sendError(res.SC_NOT_FOUND);
}
}
catch(SQLException e) {
// Report it
}
}
}
```

10

Applet-Servlet Communication

This chapter demonstrates several techniques by which applets can communicate with servlets. We're going to come at the topic from a slightly different angle than you might expect. Instead of assuming you have an applet and a servlet that need to communicate, we're going assume you have an applet that needs to talk to some entity on the server and explore why sometimes that entity should be a servlet.

To get the ball rolling, let's think about applets that need to communicate with the server. There are a number of good examples. Take a look at the administration applet that manages the Java Web Server. Think about how it works—it executes on the client, but it configures the server. To do this, the applet and the server need to be in near constant communication. As another example, take a look at one of the popular chat applets. One client says something, and all the rest see it. How does that work? They certainly don't communicate applet to applet. Instead, each applet posts its messages to a central server, and the server takes care of updating the other clients. Finally, imagine an applet that tracks the price of a set of stocks and offers continuous updates. How does the applet know the current stock prices, and, more importantly, how does it know when they change? The answer is that it talks with its server.

Communication Options

Our interest in stock trading has risen along with the Dow, so let's continue with this hypothetical stock tracking applet. We should warn you right now that this example will remain hypothetical. We'll use it solely as a reference point for discussing the issues involved in applet-server communication. But don't worry, there's plenty of code later in the chapter that demonstrates the techniques discussed here, just in somewhat simpler examples.

This stock tracking applet of ours needs to get a stock feed from some server machine. Assuming it's a normal, untrusted applet, there's just one choice: the machine from which it was downloaded. Any attempt to connect to another machine results in a `SecurityException`, so let's assume the applet gets a stock feed from the server machine from which it was downloaded.[*] The question remains: how can the applet and the server communicate?

Trusted and Untrusted Applets

When a Java applet is embedded in a web page, a browser can download it and execute it automatically. If you think about it, that's a very dangerous thing to do. So, to protect the client, JDK 1.0 assumed all applets were untrusted and ran them under the watch of a `SecurityManager` that severely limited what they could do. For example, the security manager made sure applets couldn't write to the user's file system, read certain system properties, accept incoming socket connections, or establish outgoing socket connections to any host but the origin server. This protected the client, but it limited the usefulness of applets.

Consequently, JDK 1.1 introduced the concept of trusted applets—applets that can operate like normal applications with full access to the client machine. For an applet to be trusted, it has to be digitally signed by a person or company the client trusts (as marked in the client's browser). The signature authenticates the applet's origin and guarantees integrity during the transfer, so the client knows the applet code hasn't been surreptitiously changed. This allowed for more productive applets, but it was an all-or-nothing approach.

To give the client more control, JDK 1.2 is introducing a fine-grained access control system. Under this new system, a digitally signed applet can be partially trusted, given certain abilities without being given free reign on the system. This promises to allow applets from unknown sources to be granted small privileges (such as writing to a single directory), without granting them the ability to wipe the client's hard drive. See Chapter 8, *Security*, for more information.

HTTP and Raw Socket Connections

Before JDK 1.1 and servlets, there were two options for applet-server communication:

- Have the applet establish an HTTP connection to a CGI program on the server machine. The applet acts like a browser and requests a page, parsing

---

[*] You may be wondering how the server machine itself got the stock feed. For the purposes of this example, it's magic.

the response for its own use. The applet can provide information using a query string or POST data and can receive information from the returned page.

- Have the applet establish a raw socket connection to a non-HTTP server running on the server machine. The non-HTTP server can listen to a particular port and communicate with the applet using whatever custom protocol they agree upon.

Each of these approaches has advantages and disadvantages. Having an applet make an HTTP connection to a CGI program works well for these reasons:

- It's easy to write. The applet can take advantage of the `java.net.URL` and `java.net.URLConnection` classes to manage the communication channel, and the CGI program can be written like any other.

- It works even for applets running behind a firewall. Most firewalls allow HTTP connections but disallow raw socket connections.

- It allows a Java applet to communicate with a program written in any language. The CGI program doesn't have to be written in Java. It can be in Perl, C, C++, or any other language.

- It works with applets written using JDK 1.0, so it works with all Java-enabled browsers.

- It allows secure communication. An applet can communicate with a secure server using the encrypted HTTPS (HTTP + SSL) protocol.

- The CGI program can be used by browsers as well as applets. In the case of our stock tracker example, the CGI program can do double duty, also acting as the back-end for an HTML form-based stock quote service. This makes it especially convenient for an applet to leverage existing CGI programs.

But the HTTP connection to a CGI program also has some problems:

- It's slow. Because of the HTTP request/response paradigm, the applet and the CGI program cannot communicate interactively. They have to reestablish a new communication channel for each request and response. Plus, there is the standard delay while the CGI program launches and initializes itself to handle a request.

- It usually requires requests to be formed as an awkward array of name/value pairs. For example, when our stock tracker applet asks for the daily high for Sun Microsystems' stock, it has to ask with an awkward query string like `"stock=sunw&query=dailyhi"`.

- It forces all responses to be formatted using some arbitrary, previously agreed-upon standard. For example, when our stock tracker applet receives the response that contains a stock's daily high price, it needs to know exactly how to parse the data. Does the returned price begin with a dollar sign? Does the response include the time when the high occurred? And if so, where is the time specified and in what format?

- Only the applet can initiate communication. The CGI program has to wait passively for the applet to request something before it can respond. If a stock price changes, the applet can find out only when it asks the right question.

An applet and server can also communicate by having the applet establish a socket connection to a non-HTTP server process. This provides the following advantages over the HTTP-based approach:

- It allows bidirectional, sustained communication. The applet and servlet can use the same socket (or even several sockets) to communicate interactively, sending messages back and forth. For security reasons, the applet must always initiate the connection by connecting to a server socket on the server machine, but after a socket connection has been established, either party can write to the socket at any time. This allows our stock tracker to receive stock price updates as soon as they are available.

- It allows a more efficient program to run on the server side. The non-HTTP server can be written to handle a request immediately without launching an external CGI program to do the work.

But a socket connection also has disadvantages versus the HTTP-based approach:

- It fails for applets running behind firewalls. Most firewalls don't allow raw socket connections, and thus they disallow this sort of applet-server communication. Therefore, this mechanism should be used only when an applet is guaranteed to never run on the far side of a firewall, such as for an intranet application.

- It can be fairly complicated to write the code that runs on the server. There must always be some process (such as a stock quote server) listening on a well-known port on the server machine. Developing such an application in Java is easier than in C++, but it is still nontrivial.

- It may require the development of a custom protocol. The applet and server need to define the protocol they use for the communication. While this protocol may be simpler and more efficient than HTTP, it often has to be specially developed.

- The non-HTTP server cannot be conveniently connected to by a web browser. Browsers speak HTTP; they cannot communicate with a non-HTTP server.

The standard historical approach has been for applets to use HTTP to connect to CGI programs on the server. It's easy, and it works for all types of browsers, even browsers running behind firewalls. The use of raw socket connections has generally been reserved for those situations where it's absolutely necessary, such as when the applet and server require bidirectional communication. And, even in those cases, it's often possible to use HTTP connections to simulate bidirectional communication in order to pass through firewalls, as we'll see in a later example.

Servlets and Object Serialization

The recent introduction of Java servlets and object serialization has given new life to these traditional applet-server communication techniques. Servlets are starting to replace slow-starting CGI programs, improving the performance of HTTP-based applet-server communication and making frequent applet-server communication feasible. While it's true in the general case that the applet and the servlet still have to take time to reestablish their connection for each request and response, the applet no longer has to wait as the server launches a CGI program to handle each of its repeated requests.

Java object serialization has simplified the issues involved with formatting responses. With both applets and servlets written in Java, it's only natural that they should communicate by exchanging Java objects. For example, when our hypothetical stock tracking applet asks our stock feed servlet the daily high value for Sun stock, it can receive the response as a serialized `StockPrice` object. From this, it can get the daily high value as a `float` and the time of the high value as a `Date`. It's convenient, and it provides easy type safety. But beware, object serialization works only with applets running inside browsers that support JDK 1.1 or later.

JDBC, RMI, and a Little CORBA

JDK 1.1 includes two additional features that have an impact on applet-server communication: JDBC and RMI. The JDBC (Java database connectivity) API, discussed in Chapter 9, *Database Connectivity*, allows a Java program to connect to a relational database on the same machine or on another machine. Java applets written to JDK 1.1 can use JDBC to communicate with a database on the server. This special-purpose communication doesn't generally require applet-servlet communication. However, it is often helpful for an applet (especially one written to JDK 1.0) to forgo connecting straight to the database (or to a pass-through proxy on the web server) and instead connect to a servlet that handles the database communication on the applet's behalf (as explained in the "Servlets in the Middle Tier" sidebar in Chapter 9). For example, an applet that wants to look up a person's address can connect to a servlet using HTTP, pass the name of the person using HTTP parameters, and then receive the address as either a specially formatted string or a serialized object. This use of applet-servlet communication tends to piggy-back on existing protocols like HTTP, so we aren't going to cover it in any more detail here.

The RMI (Remote Method Invocation) API allows an applet to invoke the methods of a Java object executing on the server machine, and, in some cases, it also allows the object on the server machine to invoke the methods of the applet. The advantages of RMI for applet-server communication are compelling:

- It allows applets and server objects to communicate using an elegant high-level, object-oriented paradigm. Requests can be made as method invocations, passing serialized object parameters if necessary. Responses can be received as serialized objects or even references to other remote objects. But to even use the words request and response shows we've been using HTTP too much! With RMI, there are no requests or responses, just method invocations. To go back to our stock tracker example, the applet can get the daily high for Sun stock by calling `sunw.getDailyHigh()`, where `sunw` is a Java object that exists on the server.

- It allows server objects to make callbacks to the methods of the applet. For example, with our stock tracking example, the server can notify interested applets that a stock price has changed by calling `applet.update(stock)`.

- It can be made to work through firewalls (though it doesn't like it, and current browsers don't support it very well). The RMI transport layer normally relies on direct socket connections to perform its work. When an applet executes behind a firewall, however, its socket connections fail. In this case, the RMI transport layer can automatically begin operating entirely within the HTTP protocol.[*] This is not without cost, though. The HTTP overhead affects performance, and the HTTP request/response paradigm cannot support callbacks.

The disadvantages of RMI are equally concerning:

- It's complicated. RMI communication uses special stub and skeleton classes for each remote object, and it requires a naming registry from which clients can obtain references to these remote objects.

- It's supported in few browsers. Of all the popular browsers available as of this writing, only Netscape Navigator 4 includes RMI support. Previous Netscape browser versions and all versions of Microsoft's Internet Explorer do not support RMI without installing a special plug-in.

- It can be used only by Java clients. The server object can't be shared by a web browser or even a C++ client.

---

[*] For a description of the system properties necessary for an RMI client application to poke through a firewall see John D. Mitchell's JavaWorld Java Tip 42 at *http://www.javaworld.com/javaworld/javatips/jw-javatip42.html.* (Unmentioned in the article but also important are the `socksProxySet`, `socksProxy-Host`, and `socksProxyPort` properties necessary for SOCKS-based proxies.) All these system properties should be set automatically by web browsers, but unfortunately few web browsers currently do this, leaving their applets with no way to determine the proper settings and no way to use RMI through a firewall.

For a more information on RMI programming, see *Java Network Programming*, by Elliotte Rusty Harold (O'Reilly) and *Java Distributed Computing*, by Jim Farley (O'Reilly).

CORBA (Common Object Request Broker Architecture) is a technology similar to RMI that enables communication between distributed objects written in various languages. With CORBA and its IIOP (Internet Inter-ORB Protocol) communication protocol, a C++ client can communicate with a Java servlet. Demonstrating this ability extends beyond the scope of this book. For more information, see *http://www.acl.lanl.gov/CORBA* and *http://java.sun.com/products/jdk/idl*.

The Hybrid Approach

Now that we've examined all the options, the question remains: how should our stock tracking applet communicate with its stock feed server? The answer is: it depends.

If we can guarantee that all our potential clients support it, RMI's elegance and power make it an ideal choice. But currently that's like assuming all your friends enjoy your Star Trek jokes. It can be true if you carefully choose your friends (or your clients), but it's generally not the case in the real world.

When RMI isn't available, the bidirectional capabilities of the non-HTTP socket connection make it look fairly attractive. Unfortunately, that bidirectional communication becomes nonexistent communication when the applet ends up on the far side of a firewall.

There's always the old workhorse, HTTP communication. It's straightforward to implement and works on every Java-enabled client. And if you can guarantee that the client supports JDK 1.1 (and this is easier to guarantee than that the client support RMI), you can use object serialization.

Perhaps the best solution is to use every solution, with servlets. Servlets make it possible to combine the HTTP, non-HTTP, and RMI applet-server communication techniques, supporting them all with a single servlet. That's right: one servlet, multiple access protocols. Why would anyone want to do this? Well, it's a handy technique when an applet wants to communicate using RMI or a non-HTTP protocol but needs to fallback to HTTP when necessary (such as when it finds itself behind a firewall). By using the same servlet to handle every client, the core server logic and the server state can be collected in one place. When you control your environment, of course, you can drop one or more of these protocols. But isn't it nice to know you don't have to?

Daytime Server

For a simple demonstration of each communication technique, we're going to write an applet that asks its server for the current time of day. The applet first uses an HTTP connection, then a non-HTTP socket connection, and finally an RMI connection. Of course, an applet can normally get the current time from the system on which it's running. To give this example an air of practicality, let's assume the applet needs an approximate time stamp for some event and cannot rely on the client machine to have a correctly set clock.

The Applet

We're going to be using the same example applet throughout this section. The skeleton code for this applet, `DaytimeApplet`, is shown in Example 10-1. Right now, the applet just creates a user interface where the times it retrieves can be displayed, as shown in Figure 10-1. As we proceed with this example, we'll implement its `getDateUsingHttpText()`, `getDateUsingHttpObject()`, `getDateUsingSocketText()`, `getDateUsingSocketObject()`, and `getDateUsingRMIObject()` methods. Note that the examples in this chapter use several JDK 1.0 methods that are deprecated in JDK 1.1. This is to maximize portability.

Example 10-1. DaytimeApplet, without all the good stuff

```
import java.applet.*;
import java.awt.*;
import java.io.*;
import java.util.*;

public class DaytimeApplet extends Applet {

  TextField httpText, httpObject, socketText, socketObject, RMIObject;
  Button refresh;

  public void init() {
    // Construct the user interface

    setLayout(new BorderLayout());

    // On the left create labels for the various communication
    // mechanisms
    Panel west = new Panel();
    west.setLayout(new GridLayout(5, 1));
    west.add(new Label("HTTP text: ", Label.RIGHT));
    west.add(new Label("HTTP object: ", Label.RIGHT));
    west.add(new Label("Socket text: ", Label.RIGHT));
    west.add(new Label("Socket object: ", Label.RIGHT));
    west.add(new Label("RMI object: ", Label.RIGHT));
```

Example 10-1. DaytimeApplet, without all the good stuff (continued)

```
    add("West", west);

    // On the right create text fields to display the retrieved time values
    Panel center = new Panel();
    center.setLayout(new GridLayout(5, 1));

    httpText = new TextField();
    httpText.setEditable(false);
    center.add(httpText);

    httpObject = new TextField();
    httpObject.setEditable(false);
    center.add(httpObject);

    socketText = new TextField();
    socketText.setEditable(false);
    center.add(socketText);

    socketObject = new TextField();
    socketObject.setEditable(false);
    center.add(socketObject);

    RMIObject = new TextField();
    RMIObject.setEditable(false);
    center.add(RMIObject);

    add("Center", center);

    // On the bottom create a button to update the times
    Panel south = new Panel();
    refresh = new Button("Refresh");
    south.add(refresh);
    add("South", south);
  }

public void start() {
  refresh();
}

private void refresh() {
  // Fetch and display the time values
  httpText.setText(getDateUsingHttpText());
  httpObject.setText(getDateUsingHttpObject());
  socketText.setText(getDateUsingSocketText());
  socketObject.setText(getDateUsingSocketObject());
  RMIObject.setText(getDateUsingRMIObject());
}
```

Example 10-1. DaytimeApplet, without all the good stuff (continued)

```
  private String getDateUsingHttpText() {
    // Retrieve the current time using an HTTP text-based connection
    return "unavailable";
  }

  private String getDateUsingHttpObject() {
    // Retrieve the current time using an HTTP object-based connection
    return "unavailable";
  }

  private String getDateUsingSocketText() {
    // Retrieve the current time using a non-HTTP text-based socket
    // connection
    return "unavailable";
  }

  private String getDateUsingSocketObject() {
    // Retrieve the current time using a non-HTTP object-based socket
    // connection
    return "unavailable";
  }

  private String getDateUsingRMIObject() {
    // Retrieve the current time using RMI communication
    return "unavailable";
  }

  public boolean handleEvent(Event event) {
    // When the refresh button is pushed, refresh the display
    // Use JDK 1.0 events for maximum portability
    switch (event.id) {
      case Event.ACTION_EVENT:
        if (event.target == refresh) {
          refresh();
          return true;
        }
    }
    return false;
  }
}
```

For this applet to be available for downloading to the client browser, it has to be placed under the server's document root, along with an HTML file referring to it. The HTML might look like this:

```
    <HTML>
    <HEAD><TITLE>Daytime Applet</TITLE></HEAD>
    <BODY>
```

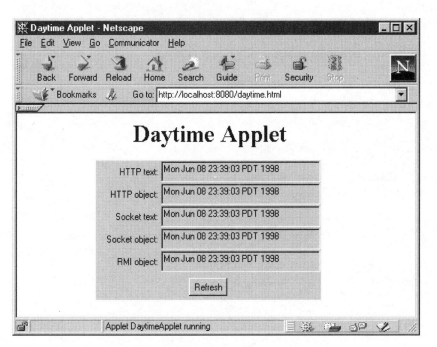

Figure 10-1. The DaytimeApplet user interface

```
<CENTER><H1>Daytime Applet</H1></CENTER>
<CENTER><APPLET CODE=DaytimeApplet CODEBASE=/ WIDTH=300 HEIGHT=180>
</APPLET></CENTER>
</BODY></HTML>
```

The CODEBASE parameter indicates the directory where the applet's class file has been placed. The parameter is relative to the document root, which for the Java Web Server is generally *server_root/public_html*. Assuming the HTML file was named *daytime.html*, this applet can be viewed at the URL *http://server:port/daytime.html*.

Text-based HTTP Communication

Let's start by implementing the lowest-common-denominator approach—text-based HTTP communication.

The servlet

For the DaytimeApplet to retrieve the current time from the server, it has to communicate with a servlet that returns the current time. Example 10-2 shows such a servlet. It responds to all GET and POST requests with a textual representation of the current time.

Example 10-2. The DaytimeServlet supporting basic HTTP access

```
import java.io.*;
import java.util.*;
import javax.servlet.*;
import javax.servlet.http.*;

public class DaytimeServlet extends HttpServlet {

  public Date getDate() {
    return new Date();
  }

  public void doGet(HttpServletRequest req, HttpServletResponse res)
                            throws ServletException, IOException {
    res.setContentType("text/plain");
    PrintWriter out = res.getWriter();
    out.println(getDate().toString());
  }

  public void doPost(HttpServletRequest req, HttpServletResponse res)
                            throws ServletException, IOException {
    doGet(req, res);
  }
}
```

This servlet's class files should be placed in the standard location for servlets, typically *server_root/servlets*. Once you place them there, they can be accessed by any web browser using the URL *http://server:port/servlet/DaytimeServlet*.

Back to the applet

Now, for our DaytimeApplet to access this servlet, it must behave just like a browser and make an HTTP connection to the servlet URL, as the implementation of getDateUsingHttpText() in Example 10-3 shows.

Example 10-3. DaytimeApplet getting the time using HTTP

```
import java.net.URL;                       // New addition
import com.oreilly.servlet.HttpMessage;  // A support class, shown later

  private String getDateUsingHttpText() {
    try {
      // Construct a URL referring to the servlet
      URL url = new URL(getCodeBase(), "/servlet/DaytimeServlet");
```

Example 10-3. DaytimeApplet getting the time using HTTP (continued)

```
    // Create a com.oreilly.servlet.HttpMessage to communicate with that URL
    HttpMessage msg = new HttpMessage(url);

    // Send a GET message to the servlet, with no query string
    // Get the response as an InputStream
    InputStream in = msg.sendGetMessage();

    // Wrap the InputStream with a DataInputStream
    DataInputStream result =
      new DataInputStream(new BufferedInputStream(in));

    // Read the first line of the response, which should be
    // a string representation of the current time
    String date = result.readLine();

    // Close the InputStream
    in.close();

    // Return the retrieved time
    return date;
  }
  catch (Exception e) {
    // If there was a problem, print to System.out
    // (typically the Java console) and return null
    e.printStackTrace();
    return null;
  }
}
```

This method retrieves the current time on the server using a text-based HTTP connection. First, it creates a URL object that refers to the DaytimeServlet running on the server. The server host and port for this URL come from the applet's own getCodeBase() method. This guarantees that it matches the host and port from which the applet was downloaded. Then, the method creates an HttpMessage object to communicate with that URL. This object does all the dirty work involved in making the connection. The applet asks it to make a GET request of the DaytimeServlet and then reads the response from the returned InputStream.

The code for HttpMessage is shown in Example 10-4. It is loosely modeled after the ServletMessage class written by Rod McChesney of Sun Microsystems.

Example 10-4. The HttpMessage support class

```
package com.oreilly.servlet;

import java.io.*;
```

Example 10-4. The HttpMessage support class (continued)

```java
import java.net.*;
import java.util.*;

public class HttpMessage {

  URL servlet = null;
  String args = null;

  public HttpMessage(URL servlet) {
    this.servlet = servlet;
  }

  // Performs a GET request to the previously given servlet
  // with no query string.
  public InputStream sendGetMessage() throws IOException {
    return sendGetMessage(null);
  }

  // Performs a GET request to the previously given servlet.
  // Builds a query string from the supplied Properties list.
  public InputStream sendGetMessage(Properties args) throws IOException {
    String argString = "";  // default

    if (args != null) {
      argString = "?" + toEncodedString(args);
    }
    URL url = new URL(servlet.toExternalForm() + argString);

    // Turn off caching
    URLConnection con = url.openConnection();
    con.setUseCaches(false);

    return con.getInputStream();
  }

  // Performs a POST request to the previously given servlet
  // with no query string.
  public InputStream sendPostMessage() throws IOException {
    return sendPostMessage(null);
  }

  // Performs a POST request to the previously given servlet.
  // Builds post data from the supplied Properties list.
  public InputStream sendPostMessage(Properties args) throws IOException {
    String argString = "";  // default
    if (args != null) {
      argString = toEncodedString(args);  // notice no "?"
    }
```

Example 10-4. The HttpMessage support class (continued)

```
    URLConnection con = servlet.openConnection();

    // Prepare for both input and output
    con.setDoInput(true);
    con.setDoOutput(true);

    // Turn off caching
    con.setUseCaches(false);

    // Work around a Netscape bug
    con.setRequestProperty("Content-Type",
                           "application/x-www-form-urlencoded");

    // Write the arguments as post data
    DataOutputStream out = new DataOutputStream(con.getOutputStream());
    out.writeBytes(argString);
    out.flush();
    out.close();

    return con.getInputStream();
  }

  // Converts a Properties list to a URL-encoded query string
  private String toEncodedString(Properties args) {
    StringBuffer buf = new StringBuffer();
    Enumeration names = args.propertyNames();
    while (names.hasMoreElements()) {
      String name = (String) names.nextElement();
      String value = args.getProperty(name);
      buf.append(URLEncoder.encode(name) + "=" + URLEncoder.encode(value));
      if (names.hasMoreElements()) buf.append("&");
    }
    return buf.toString();
  }
}
```

Some of you may have been expecting the HttpMessage class to establish a raw socket connection to the server and proceed to speak HTTP. This approach would certainly work, but it isn't necessary. The higher-level java.net.URL and java.net.URLConnection classes already provide this functionality in a convenient abstraction.

Let's do a quick walk-through of HttpMessage. HttpMessage is designed to communicate with just one URL, the URL given in its constructor. It can send multiple GET and/or POST requests to that URL, but it always communicates with just the one URL.

The code HttpMessage uses to send a GET message is fairly simple. First, sendGetMessage() creates a URL-encoded query string from the passed-in java.util.Properties list. Then, it appends this query string to the saved URL, creating a new URL object. At this point, it could elect to use this new URL (named url) to communicate with the servlet. A call to url.openStream() would return an InputStream that contains the response. But, unfortunately for our purposes, by default all connections made using a URL object are cached. We don't want this—we want the current time, not the time of the last request. So HttpMessage has to turn caching off.[*] The URL class doesn't directly support this low-level control, so HttpMessage gets the URL object's URLConnection and instructs it not to use caching. Finally, HttpMessage returns the URLConnection object's InputStream, which contains the servlet's response.

The code HttpMessage uses to send a POST request (sendPostMessage()) is similar. The major difference is that it directly writes the URL-encoded parameter information in the body of the request. This follows the protocol for how POST requests submit their information. The other difference is that HttpMessage manually sets the request's content type to "application/x-www-form-urlencoded". This should be set automatically by Java, but setting it manually works around a bug in some versions of Netscape's browser.

We should mention that HttpMessage is a general-purpose class for HTTP communication. It doesn't have to be used by applets, and it doesn't have to connect to servlets. It's usable by any Java client that needs to connect to an HTTP resource. It's included in the com.oreilly.servlet package, though, because it's often useful for applet-servlet communication.

For the HttpMessage class to be usable by applets, it has to be made available for downloading along with the applet classes. This means it must be placed in the proper location under the web server's document root. For the Java Web Server, this location is *server_root/public_html/com/oreilly/servlet*. We recommend you copy the class there from wherever you originally installed the com.oreilly.servlet package (probably *server_root/classes/com/oreilly/servlet*).

Note that HttpMessage as currently written does not provide a mechanism for an applet to either set or get the HTTP headers associated with its request and response. The URLConnection class, however, supports HTTP header access with its setRequestProperty() and getHeaderField() methods. You can add this functionality if you need it.

---

[*] Actually, we could leave it up to the servlet to turn caching off, by having it set its Pragma header to "no-cache". But it can't hurt to have it in the applet as well.

Now, with all this code working together, we have an applet that retrieves the current time from its server using text-based HTTP applet-servlet communication. If you try it yourself, you should see the "HTTP text" date filled in, while the rest of the dates are still marked "unavailable."

Object-based HTTP Communication

With a few modifications, we can have the `DaytimeApplet` receive the current time as a serialized `Date` object.

The servlet

For backward compatibility, let's change our `DaytimeServlet` to return a serialized `Date` only if the request asks for it by passing a `"format"` parameter with the value `"object"`. The code is given in Example 10-5.

Example 10-5. The DaytimeServlet using HTTP to serve an object

```java
import java.io.*;
import java.util.*;
import javax.servlet.*;
import javax.servlet.http.*;

public class DaytimeServlet extends HttpServlet {

  public Date getDate() {
    return new Date();
  }

  public void doGet(HttpServletRequest req, HttpServletResponse res)
                            throws ServletException, IOException {
    // If the client says "format=object" then
    // return the Date as a serialized object
    if ("object".equals(req.getParameter("format"))) {
      ObjectOutputStream out = new ObjectOutputStream(res.getOutputStream());
      out.writeObject(getDate());
    }
    // Otherwise send the Date as a normal string
    else {
      PrintWriter out = res.getWriter();
      out.println(getDate().toString());
    }
  }

  public void doPost(HttpServletRequest req, HttpServletResponse res)
                            throws ServletException, IOException {
    doGet(req, res);
```

Example 10-5. The DaytimeServlet using HTTP to serve an object (continued)

```
  }
}
```

As the code shows, sending a serialized Java object is quite simple. This technique can be used to send any primitive types and/or any Java objects that implement the `Serializable` interface, including a `Vector` that contains `Serializable` objects. Multiple objects can also be written to the same `ObjectOutputStream`, as long as the class receiving the objects reads them in the same order and casts them to the same types.

You may notice that the servlet didn't set the content type of the response to indicate it contained a serialized Java object. The reason is that currently there are no standard MIME types to represent serialized objects. This doesn't really matter, though. A content type acts solely as an indication to the client of how to handle or display the response. If an applet already assumes it's receiving a specific serialized Java object, everything works fine. Sometimes, though, it's useful to use a custom MIME type (specific to your application), so that a servlet can indicate to an applet the contents of its response.

The applet

The applet code to retrieve the serialized `Date` object is very similar to the code to retrieve plain text. The `getDateUsingHttpObject()` method is shown in Example 10-6.

Example 10-6. The DaytimeApplet using HTTP to retrieve an object

```
private String getDateUsingHttpObject() {
  try {
    // Construct a URL referring to the servlet
    URL url = new URL(getCodeBase(), "/servlet/DaytimeServlet");

    // Create a com.oreilly.servlet.HttpMessage to communicate with that URL
    HttpMessage msg = new HttpMessage(url);

    // Construct a Properties list to say format=object
    Properties props = new Properties();
    props.put("format", "object");

    // Send a GET message to the servlet, passing "props" as a query string
    // Get the response as an ObjectInputStream
    InputStream in = msg.sendGetMessage(props);
    ObjectInputStream result = new ObjectInputStream(in);

    // Read the Date object from the stream
    Object obj = result.readObject();
```

Example 10-6. The DaytimeApplet using HTTP to retrieve an object (continued)

```
    Date date = (Date)obj;

    // Return the string representation of the Date
    return date.toString();
  }
  catch (Exception e) {
    // If there was a problem, print to System.out
    // (typically the Java console) and return null
    e.printStackTrace();
    return null;
  }
}
```

There are two differences between this method and the getDateUsingHttp-Text() method. First, this method creates a Properties list to set the "format" parameter to the value "object". This tells DaytimeServlet to return a serialized object. Second, the new method reads the returned content as an Object, using an ObjectInputStream and its readObject() method.

If the class being serialized is not part of the Java Core API (and therefore isn't already available to the applet), it too has to be made available in the proper location under the web server's document root. An applet can always receive an object's serialized contents, but it needs to download its class file to fully reconstruct the object.

Now the applet can retrieve the current time using both text-based and object-based HTTP communication. If you try it yourself now (with a web browser or applet viewer that supports JDK 1.1), you should see both the "HTTP text" and "HTTP object" fields filled in.

Posting a serialized object

Before we go on, we should look at one more (hitherto unmentioned) method from the HttpMessage class: sendPostMessage(Serializable). This method helps an applet upload a serialized object to a servlet using the POST method. This object transfer isn't particularly useful to our daytime server example (and is kind of out of place here), but we mention it because it can come in handy when an applet needs to upload complicated data structures to its server. Example 10-7 contains the code for this method.

Example 10-7. Posting a serialized object

```
// Uploads a serialized object with a POST request.
// Sets the content type to java-internal/classname.
public InputStream sendPostMessage(Serializable obj) throws IOException {
```

Example 10-7. Posting a serialized object (continued)

```
URLConnection con = servlet.openConnection();

// Prepare for both input and output
con.setDoInput(true);
con.setDoOutput(true);

// Turn off caching
con.setUseCaches(false);

// Set the content type to be java-internal/classname
con.setRequestProperty("Content-Type",
                       "java-internal/" + obj.getClass().getName());

// Write the serialized object as post data
ObjectOutputStream out = new ObjectOutputStream(con.getOutputStream());
out.writeObject(obj);
out.flush();
out.close();

return con.getInputStream();
}
```

An applet uses `sendPostMessage(Serializable)` just as it uses `sendPostMes-sage(Properties)`. Here is the code for an applet that uploads any exceptions it encounters to a servlet:

```
catch (Exception e) {
  URL url = new URL(getCodeBase(), "/servlet/ExceptionLogger");
  HttpMessage msg = new HttpMessage(url);
  InputStream in = msg.sendPostMessage(e);
}
```

The servlet, meanwhile, receives the `Exception` in its `doPost()` method like this:

```
ObjectInputStream objin = new ObjectInputStream(req.getInputStream());
Object obj = objin.readObject();
Exception e = (Exception) obj;
```

The servlet can receive the type of the uploaded object as the subtype (second half) of the content type. Note that this `sendPostMessage(Serializable)` method uploads just one object at a time and uploads only serializable objects (that is, no primitive types).

Socket Communication

Now let's take a look at how an applet and servlet can communicate using non-HTTP socket communication.

The servlet

The servlet's role in this communication technique is that of a passive listener. Due to security restrictions, only the applet can initiate a socket connection. A servlet must be content to listen on a socket port and wait for an applet to connect. Generally speaking, a servlet should begin listening for applet connections in its `init()` method and stop listening in its `destroy()` method. In between, for every connection it receives, it should spawn a handler thread to communicate with the client.

With HTTP socket connections, these nitty-gritty details are managed by the web server. The server listens for incoming HTTP requests and dispatches them as appropriate, calling a servlet's `service()`, `doGet()`, or `doPost()` methods as necessary. But when a servlet opts not to use HTTP communication, the web server can't provide any help. The servlet acts, in essence, like its own server and thus has to manage the socket connections itself.

Okay, maybe we scared you a bit more than we had to there. The truth is that we can write a servlet superclass that abstracts away the details involved in managing socket connections. This class, which we call `DaemonHttpServlet`, can be extended by any servlet wanting to make itself available via non-HTTP socket communication.[*]

`DaemonHttpServlet` starts listening for client requests in its `init()` method and stops listening in its `destroy()` method. In between, for every connection it receives, it calls the abstract `handleClient(Socket)` method. This method should be implemented by any servlet that subclasses `DaemonHttpServlet`.

Example 10-8 shows how `DaytimeServlet` extends `DaemonHttpServlet` and implements `handleClient()` to make itself available via non-HTTP socket communication.

Example 10-8. The DaytimeServlet acting as a non-HTTP server

```
import java.io.*;
import java.net.*;
import java.util.*;
import javax.servlet.*;
import javax.servlet.http.*;

import com.oreilly.servlet.DaemonHttpServlet;
```

---

[*] The name "daemon" was chosen to refer to Unix daemons, programs that run in the background quietly handling certain events. And where did those programs get the "daemon" moniker? According to the *New Hacker's Dictionary*, it originally came "from the mythological meaning, (but was) later rationalized as the acronym 'Disk And Execution MONitor'".

Example 10-8. The DaytimeServlet acting as a non-HTTP server (continued)

```
public class DaytimeServlet extends DaemonHttpServlet {

  public Date getDate() {
    return new Date();
  }

  public void init(ServletConfig config) throws ServletException {
    // As before, if you override init() you have to call super.init()
    super.init(config);
  }

  public void doGet(HttpServletRequest req, HttpServletResponse res)
                              throws ServletException, IOException {
    // If the client says "format=object" then
    // send the Date as a serialized object
    if ("object".equals(req.getParameter("format"))) {
      ObjectOutputStream out = new ObjectOutputStream(res.getOutputStream());
      out.writeObject(getDate());
    }
    // Otherwise send the Date as a normal ASCII string
    else {
      PrintWriter out = res.getWriter();
      out.println(getDate().toString());
    }
  }

  public void doPost(HttpServletRequest req, HttpServletResponse res)
                              throws ServletException, IOException {
    doGet(req, res);
  }

  public void destroy() {
    // Now, unlike before, if you override destroy() you also have to call
    // super.destroy()
    super.destroy();
  }

  // Handle a client's socket connection by spawning a DaytimeConnection
  // thread.
  public void handleClient(Socket client) {
    new DaytimeConnection(this, client).start();
  }
}

class DaytimeConnection extends Thread {

  DaytimeServlet servlet;
  Socket client;
```

Example 10-8. The DaytimeServlet acting as a non-HTTP server (continued)

```java
DaytimeConnection(DaytimeServlet servlet, Socket client) {
  this.servlet = servlet;
  this.client = client;
  setPriority(NORM_PRIORITY - 1);
}

public void run() {
  try {
    // Read the first line sent by the client
    DataInputStream in = new DataInputStream(
                          new BufferedInputStream(
                          client.getInputStream()));
    String line = in.readLine();

    // If it was "object" then return the Date as a serialized object
    if ("object".equals(line)) {
      ObjectOutputStream out =
        new ObjectOutputStream(client.getOutputStream());
      out.writeObject(servlet.getDate());
      out.close();
    }
    // Otherwise, send the Date as a normal string
    else {
      // Wrap a PrintStream around the Socket's OutputStream
      PrintStream out = new PrintStream(client.getOutputStream());
      out.println(servlet.getDate().toString());
      out.close();
    }

    // Be sure to close the connection
    client.close();
  }
  catch (IOException e) {
    servlet.getServletContext()
      .log(e, "IOException while handling client request");
  }
  catch (Exception e) {
    servlet.getServletContext()
      .log("Exception while handling client request");
  }
}
}
```

The `DaytimeServlet` class remains largely unchanged from its previous form. The major difference is that it extends `DaemonHttpServlet` and implements a `handleClient(Socket)` method that spawns a new `DaytimeConnection` thread.

This DaytimeConnection instance bears the responsibility for handling a specific socket connection.

DaytimeConnection works as follows. When it is created, it saves a reference to the DaytimeServlet, so that it can call the servlet's getDate() method, and a reference to the Socket, so that it can communicate with the client. Daytime-Connection also sets its running priority to one less than normal, to indicate that this communication can wait if necessary while other threads perform more time-critical work.

Immediately after it creates the DaytimeConnection thread, DaytimeServlet starts the thread, causing its run() method to be called. In this method, the DaytimeConnection communicates with the client using some unnamed (but definitely not HTTP) protocol. It begins by reading the first line sent by the client. If the line is "object", it returns the current time as a serialized Date object. If the line is anything else, it returns the current time as a normal string. When it is done, it closes the connection.

The superclass

The low-level socket management is done in the DaemonHttpServlet class. Generally, this class can be used without modification, but it is useful to understand the internals. The code is shown in Example 10-9.

Example 10-9. The DaemonHttpServlet superclass

```
package com.oreilly.servlet;

import java.io.*;
import java.net.*;
import java.util.*;
import javax.servlet.*;
import javax.servlet.http.*;

public abstract class DaemonHttpServlet extends HttpServlet {

  protected int DEFAULT_PORT = 1313;  // not static or final
  private Thread daemonThread;

  public void init(ServletConfig config) throws ServletException {
    super.init(config);

    // Start a daemon thread
    try {
      daemonThread = new Daemon(this);
      daemonThread.start();
    }
    catch (Exception e) {
```

Example 10-9. The DaemonHttpServlet superclass (continued)

```
      getServletContext().log(e, "Problem starting socket server daemon thread");
    }
  }

  // Returns the socket port on which this servlet will listen.
  // A servlet can specify the port in three ways: by using the socketPort
  // init parameter, by setting the DEFAULT_PORT variable before calling
  // super.init(), or by overriding this method's implementation
  protected int getSocketPort() {
    try { return Integer.parseInt(getInitParameter("socketPort")); }
    catch (NumberFormatException e) { return DEFAULT_PORT; }
  }

  abstract public void handleClient(Socket client);

  public void destroy() {
    // Stop the daemon thread
    try {
      daemonThread.stop();
      daemonThread = null;
    }
    catch (Exception e) {
      getServletContext().log(e, "Problem stopping server socket daemon thread");
    }
  }
}

// This work is broken into a helper class so that subclasses of
// DaemonHttpServlet can define their own run() method without problems.

class Daemon extends Thread {

  private ServerSocket serverSocket;
  private DaemonHttpServlet servlet;

  public Daemon(DaemonHttpServlet servlet) {
    this.servlet = servlet;
  }

  public void run() {
    try {
      // Create a server socket to accept connections
      serverSocket = new ServerSocket(servlet.getSocketPort());
    }
    catch (Exception e) {
      servlet.getServletContext().log(e, "Problem establishing server socket");
      return;
    }
```

Example 10-9. The DaemonHttpServlet superclass (continued)

```
    try {
      while (true) {
        // As each connection comes in, call the servlet's handleClient().
        // Note this method is blocking. It's the servlet's responsibility
        // to spawn a handler thread for long-running connections.
        try {
          servlet.handleClient(serverSocket.accept());
        }
        catch (IOException ioe) {
          servlet.getServletContext()
            .log(ioe, "Problem accepting client's socket connection");
        }
      }
    }
    catch (ThreadDeath e) {
      // When the thread is killed, close the server socket
      try {
        serverSocket.close();
      }
      catch (IOException ioe) {
        servlet.getServletContext().log(ioe, "Problem closing server socket");
      }
    }
  }
}
```

The `init()` method of `DaemonHttpServlet` creates and starts a new `Daemon` thread that is in charge of listening for incoming connections. The `destroy()` method stops the thread. This makes it imperative that any servlet subclassing `DaemonHttpServlet` call `super.init(config)` and `super.destroy()` if the servlet implements its own `init()` and `destroy()` methods.

The `Daemon` thread begins by establishing a `ServerSocket` to listen on some specific socket port. Which socket port is determined with a call to the servlet's `getSocketPort()` method. The value returned is either the value of the init parameter `"socketPort"`, or, if that init parameter doesn't exist, the current value of the variable `DEFAULT_PORT`. A servlet may choose to override the `getSocketPort()` implementation if it so desires.

After establishing the `ServerSocket`, the `Daemon` thread waits for incoming requests with a call to `serverSocket.accept()`. This method is blocking—it stops this thread's execution until a client attaches to the server socket. When this happens, the `accept()` method returns a `Socket` object that the `Daemon` thread passes immediately to the servlet's `handleClient()` method. This `handle-Client()` method usually spawns a handler thread and returns immediately, leaving the `Daemon` thread ready to accept another connection.

The server socket clean-up is equally as important as its set-up. We have to be sure the server socket lives as long as the servlet, but no longer. To this end, the destroy() method of DaemonHttpServlet calls the Daemon thread's stop() method. This call doesn't immediately stop the Daemon thread, however. It just causes a ThreadDeath exception to be thrown in the Daemon thread at its current point of execution. The Daemon thread catches this exception and closes the server socket.

There are two caveats in writing a servlet that acts like a non-HTTP server. First, only one servlet at a time can listen to any particular socket port. This makes it vital that each daemon servlet choose its own socket port—by setting its socket-Port init parameter, setting the DEFAULT_PORT variable before calling super.init(config), or overriding getSocketPort() directly. Second, a daemon servlet must be loaded into its server and have its init() method called before it can accept incoming non-HTTP connections. Thus, you should either tell your server to load it at start-up or be sure it is always accessed via HTTP before it is accessed directly.

The applet

The applet code to connect to the servlet using non-HTTP communication, primarily the getDateUsingSocketText() and getDateUsingSocketObject() methods, is shown in Example 10-10.

Example 10-10. The DaytimeApplet getting the time using a socket connection

```
import java.net.Socket;                   // New addition

static final int DEFAULT_PORT = 1313;    // New addition

private int getSocketPort() {
  try { return Integer.parseInt(getParameter("socketPort")); }
  catch (NumberFormatException e) { return DEFAULT_PORT; }
}

private String getDateUsingSocketText() {
  InputStream in = null;
  try {
    // Establish a socket connection with the servlet
    Socket socket = new Socket(getCodeBase().getHost(), getSocketPort());

    // Print an empty line, indicating we want the time as plain text
    PrintStream out = new PrintStream(socket.getOutputStream());
    out.println();
    out.flush();

    // Read the first line of the response
```

Example 10-10. The DaytimeApplet getting the time using a socket connection (continued)

```
      // It should contain the current time
      in = socket.getInputStream();
      DataInputStream result =
        new DataInputStream(new BufferedInputStream(in));
      String date = result.readLine();

      // Return the retrieved string
      return date;
    }
    catch (Exception e) {
      // If there was a problem, print to System.out
      // (typically the Java console) and return null
      e.printStackTrace();
      return null;
    }
    finally {
      // Always close the connection
      // This code executes no matter how the try block completes
      if (in != null) {
        try { in.close(); }
        catch (IOException ignored) { }
      }
    }
  }

  private String getDateUsingSocketObject() {
    InputStream in = null;
    try {
      // Establish a socket connection with the servlet
      Socket socket = new Socket(getCodeBase().getHost(), getSocketPort());

      // Print a line saying "object", indicating we want the time as
      // a serialized Date object
      PrintStream out = new PrintStream(socket.getOutputStream());
      out.println("object");
      out.flush();

      // Create an ObjectInputStream to read the response
      in = socket.getInputStream();
      ObjectInputStream result =
        new ObjectInputStream(new BufferedInputStream(in));

      // Read an object, and cast it to be a Date
      Object obj = result.readObject();
      Date date = (Date)obj;

      // Return a string representation of the retrieved Date
      return date.toString();
```

Example 10-10. The DaytimeApplet getting the time using a socket connection (continued)

```
  }
  catch (Exception e) {
    // If there was a problem, print to System.out
    // (typically the Java console) and return null
    e.printStackTrace();
    return null;
  }
  finally {
    // Always close the connection
    // This code executes no matter how the try block completes
    if (in != null) {
      try { in.close(); }
      catch (IOException ignored) { }
    }
  }
}
```

For both these methods, the applet begins by creating a `Socket` that is used to communicate with the servlet. To do this, it needs to know both the host name and the port number on which the servlet is listening. Determining the host is easy—it has to be the same host from which it was downloaded, accessible with a call to `getCodeBase().getHost()`. The port is harder, as it depends entirely on the servlet to which this applet is connecting. This applet uses the `getSocket-Port()` method to make this determination. The implementation of `getSocketPort()` shown here returns the value of the applet's `socketPort` parameter, or (if that parameter isn't given) returns the value of the `DEFAULT_PORT` variable.

Once it has established a socket connection, the applet follows an unnamed protocol to communicate with the servlet. This protocol requires that the applet send one line to indicate whether it wants the current time as text or as an object. If the line says `"object"`, it receives an object. If it says anything else, it receives plain text. After sending this line, the applet can read the response as appropriate.

The applet and servlet could continue to communicate using this socket. That's one of the major advantages of not using HTTP communication. But, in this case, the applet got what it wanted and just needs to close the connection. It performs this close in a `finally` block. Putting the close here guarantees that the connection is closed whether the `try` throws an exception or not.

With the addition of these two methods our applet is nearly complete. If you run it now, you should see that all of the fields except "RMI object" contain dates.

RMI Communication

Earlier in this chapter, we pointed out that one of the reasons not to use RMI communication is that it's complicated. Although that's true, it's also true that with the help of another servlet superclass, the code required for a servlet to make itself available via RMI communication can be ridiculously simple. First, we'll lead you through the step-by-step instructions on how to make a servlet a remote object. Then, after you've seen how simple and easy that is, we'll explain all the work going on behind the scenes.

The servlet

To begin with, all RMI remote objects must implement a specific interface. This interface does two things: it declares which methods of the remote object are to be made available to remote clients, and it extends the `Remote` interface to indicate it's an interface for a remote object. For our `DaytimeServlet`, we can write the `DaytimeServer` interface shown in Example 10-11.

Example 10-11. The DaytimeServer interface

```
import java.util.Date;
import java.rmi.Remote;
import java.rmi.RemoteException;

public interface DaytimeServer extends Remote {
  public Date getDate() throws RemoteException;
}
```

This interface declares that our `DaytimeServlet` makes its `getDate()` method available to remote clients. Notice that the `getDate()` signature has been altered slightly—it now throws a `RemoteException`. Every method made available via RMI must declare that it throws this exception. Although the method itself may not throw the exception, it can be thrown by the system to indicate a network service failure.

The code for `DaytimeServlet` remains mostly unchanged from its original version. In fact, the only changes are that it now implements `DaytimeServer` and extends `com.oreilly.servlet.RemoteHttpServlet`, the superclass that allows this servlet to remain so unchanged. The servlet also implements a `destroy()` method that calls `super.destroy()`. It's true that this method is perfectly useless in this example, but it points out that any `destroy()` method implemented in a remote servlet must call `super.destroy()` to give the `RemoteHttpServlet` object's `destroy()` method a chance to terminate RMI communication. Example 10-12 shows the new `DaytimeServlet` code.

Example 10-12. The DaytimeServlet now supporting RMI access

```java
import java.io.*;
import java.net.*;
import java.util.*;
import javax.servlet.*;
import javax.servlet.http.*;

import com.oreilly.servlet.RemoteHttpServlet;        // New addition

public class DaytimeServlet extends RemoteHttpServlet  // New addition
                            implements DaytimeServer { // New addition

  // The single method from DaytimeServer
  // Note: the throws clause isn't necessary here
  public Date getDate() {
    return new Date();
  }

  public void init(ServletConfig config) throws ServletException {
    super.init(config);
    // Additional code could go here
  }

  public void doGet(HttpServletRequest req, HttpServletResponse res)
                          throws ServletException, IOException {
    // If the client says "format=object" then
    // send the Date as a serialized object
    if ("object".equals(req.getParameter("format"))) {
      ObjectOutputStream out = new ObjectOutputStream(res.getOutputStream());
      out.writeObject(getDate());
    }
    // Otherwise send the Date as a normal ASCII string
    else {
      PrintWriter out = res.getWriter();
      out.println(getDate().toString());
    }
  }

  public void doPost(HttpServletRequest req, HttpServletResponse res)
                           throws ServletException, IOException {
    doGet(req, res);
  }

  public void destroy() {
    // If you override destroy() you have to call super.destroy()
    super.destroy();
  }
}
```

So that's how to write a remote object servlet. We suggest you place such servlets directly in the server's classpath (*server_root/classes*) so they aren't reloaded, since reloading a remote object tends to cause unexpected results. Compiling a remote object servlet is the same as for every other servlet, with one additional step. After compiling the servlet source code, you now have to compile the servlet class with the RMI compiler *rmic*. The RMI compiler takes a remote object's class file and generates *stub* and *skeleton* versions of the class. These classes work behind the scenes to enable RMI communication. You don't need to worry about the details, but you should know that the stub helps the client invoke methods on the remote object and the skeleton helps the server handle those invocations.

Using *rmic* is similar to using *javac*. For this example you can compile `DaytimeServlet` with the following command:

```
% rmic DaytimeServlet
```

Notice that you provide *rmic* with a Java class name to compile, not a file. Thus, if the servlet to compile is part of a package it should be given to *rmic* as `package.name.ServletName`. The *rmic* program can take a classpath to search with the `-classpath` parameter, as well as a destination directory for the stub and skeleton files with the `-d` parameter.

After executing the above *rmic* command, you should see two new class files: *DaytimeServlet_Stub.class* and *DaytimeServlet_Skel.class*. We'll tell you what to do with these in just a minute. First, you should know that you don't have to rerun the RMI compiler every time you modify the remote servlet's code. This is because the stub and skeleton classes are built in terms of the servlet's interface, not its implementation of that interface. Accordingly, you need to regenerate them only when you modify the `DaytimeServer` interface (or your equivalent interface).

Now, for the final step in writing a remote servlet: copying a few class files to the server's document root, where they can be downloaded by an applet. There are two class files that need to be downloaded: the stub class *DaytimeServlet_Stub.class* and the remote interface class *DaytimeServer.class*. The client (in this case the applet) needs the stub class to perform its half of the RMI communication, and the stub class itself uses the remote interface class. Be aware that the servlet needs to use these classes, too, so copy them to the server's document root and leave them in the server's classpath.[*] Figure 10-2 shows where all the server files go.

---

[*] Managing multiple class files can become a serious headache during development. On a Unix system, you can use soft links to simplify the task. Or, on any system, you can implement a more general-purpose solution: change the server's classpath to include *server_root/public_html/classes*. Put the interface class and stub class in there. Then the server can find them in its new classpath and the applet's codebase can be set to */classes* to find them as well.

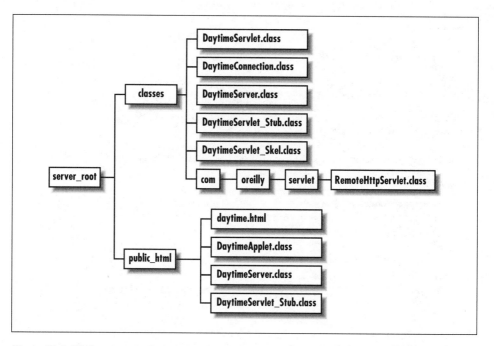

Figure 10-2. File locations for RMI communication

That's it! If you follow these instructions you should be able to get a remote servlet operating in short order. Now let's look at the `RemoteHttpServlet` class and see what's going on behind the scenes.

The superclass

A remote object needs to do two things to prepare itself for RMI communication: it needs to export itself and register itself. When a remote object exports itself, it begins listening on a port for incoming method invocation requests. When a remote object registers itself, it tells a registry server its name and port number, so that clients can locate it (essentially, find out its port number) and communicate with it. These two tasks are handled by the `RemoteHttpServlet` class, shown in Example 10-13.

Example 10-13. The RemoteHttpServlet superclass

```
package com.oreilly.servlet;

import java.io.*;
import java.net.*;
import java.rmi.*;
import java.rmi.server.*;
import java.rmi.registry.*;
```

Example 10-13. The RemoteHttpServlet superclass (continued)

```java
import java.util.*;
import javax.servlet.*;
import javax.servlet.http.*;

public abstract class RemoteHttpServlet extends HttpServlet
                                        implements Remote {

  protected Registry registry;

  public void init(ServletConfig config) throws ServletException {
    super.init(config);
    try {
      // Export ourself
      UnicastRemoteObject.exportObject(this);
      // Register ourself
      bind();
    }
    catch (RemoteException e) {
      getServletContext().log(e, "Problem binding to RMI registry");
    }
  }

  public void destroy() {
    // Unregister ourself
    unbind();
  }

  // Returns the name under which we are to be registered
  protected String getRegistryName() {
    // First name choice is the "registryName" init parameter
    String name = getInitParameter("registryName");
    if (name != null) return name;

    // Fallback choice is the name of this class
    return this.getClass().getName();
  }

  // Returns the port on which the registry server is listening
  // (or should be listening)
  protected int getRegistryPort() {
    // First port choice is the "registryPort" init parameter
    try { return Integer.parseInt(getInitParameter("registryPort")); }

    // Fallback choice is the default registry port (1099)
    catch (NumberFormatException e) { return Registry.REGISTRY_PORT; }
  }

  protected void bind() {
```

Example 10-13. The RemoteHttpServlet superclass (continued)

```
    // Try to find the appropriate registry already running
    try {
      registry = LocateRegistry.getRegistry(getRegistryPort());
      registry.list();  // Verify it's alive and well
    }
    catch (Exception e) {
      // Couldn't get a valid registry
      registry = null;
    }

    // If we couldn't find it, we need to create it.
    // (Equivalent to running "rmiregistry")
    if (registry == null) {
      try {
        registry = LocateRegistry.createRegistry(getRegistryPort());
      }
      catch (Exception e) {
        log("Could not get or create RMI registry on port " +
            getRegistryPort() + ": " + e.getMessage());
        return;
      }
    }

    // If we get here, we must have a valid registry.
    // Now register this servlet instance with that registry.
    // "Rebind" to replace any other objects using our name.
    try {
      registry.rebind(getRegistryName(), this);
    }
    catch (Exception e) {
      log("Could not bind to RMI registry: " + e.getMessage());
      return;
    }
  }

  protected void unbind() {
    try {
      if (registry != null) registry.unbind(getRegistryName());
    }
    catch (Exception e) {
      getServletContext().log(e, "Problem unbinding from RMI registry");
    }
  }
}
```

If you've ever used or read about RMI before, you've probably seen remote objects that extend the `java.rmi.server.UnicastRemoteObject` class. This is the standard—and, in fact, recommended—way to write a remote object. The

`RemoteHttpServlet` class, however, doesn't extend `UnicastRemoteObject`; it extends `HttpServlet`. As you may know, Java doesn't support multiple inheritance. This means that `RemoteHttpServlet` has to choose to extend *either* `UnicastRemoteObject` or `HttpServlet` even though it needs functionality from both classes. It's a difficult choice. Whichever class `RemoteHttpServlet` doesn't extend it has to basically reimplement on its own. In the end, we've extended `HttpServlet` because it's easier to rewrite the functionality of `UnicastRemote-Object` than that of `HttpServlet`.

This rewrite requires `RemoteHttpServlet` to do two things it wouldn't have to do if it extended `UnicastRemoteObject`. First, it must declare that it implements the `Remote` interface. All remote objects must implement this interface, but normally, by extending `UnicastRemoteObject`, a class gets this for free. Still, the price for going it alone isn't too bad, as the `Remote` interface doesn't actually define any methods. An object declares that it implements `Remote` solely to express its desire to be treated as a remote object.

The second thing `RemoteHttpServlet` has to do is manually export itself. Normally, this is performed automatically in the `UnicastRemoteObject()` constructor. But again, doing this without that constructor is not a problem. The `UnicastRemoteObject` class has a static `exportObject(Remote)` method that any `Remote` object can use to export itself. `RemoteHttpServlet` uses this method and exports itself with this single line:

```
UnicastRemoteObject.exportObject(this);
```

Those two steps, implementing `Remote` and exporting itself, are done by `Remote-HttpServlet` in lieu of extending `UnicastRemoteObject`.[*]

The rest of the `RemoteHttpServlet` code involves registering and unregistering itself with an RMI registry. As we said before, an RMI registry server acts as a location where clients can locate server objects. A remote object (server object) registers itself with the registry under a certain name. Clients can then go to the registry to look up the object by that name. To make itself available to clients then, our servlet has to find (or create) a registry server and register itself with that server under a specific name. In registry parlance, this is called *binding* to the

---

[*] To be absolutely correct, there is more we need to do. According to the `java.rmi.remote.Unicast-RemoteObject` documentation, "If `UnicastRemoteObject` is not extended, the implementation class must then assume the responsibility for the correct semantics of the `hashCode`, `equals`, and `toString` methods inherited from the `Object` class, so that they behave appropriately for remote objects." According to the `java.rmi.remote.RemoteRef` documentation, "These methods should guarantee that two remote object stubs that refer to the same remote object will have the same hash code (in order to support remote objects as keys in hash tables)." Implementing the mechanism to support this guarantee is fairly difficult and, we believe, not commonly necessary for applet-servlet communication; thus we've taken the liberty of shirking this responsibility with `RemoteHttpServlet`.

registry. `RemoteHttpServlet` performs this binding with its `bind()` method, called from within its `init()` method.

The `bind()` method uses two support methods, `getRegistryPort()` and `getRegistryName()`, to determine the port on which the servlet should be running and the name under which the servlet should be registered. With the current implementations, the port is fetched from the `registryPort` init parameter, or it defaults to 1099. The name is taken from the `registryName` init parameter or defaults to the servlet's class name—in this case, `DaytimeServlet`.

Let's step through the `bind()` method. It begins by using the following code to try to find an appropriate registry that is already running:

```
registry = LocateRegistry.getRegistry(getRegistryPort());
registry.list();
```

The first line attempts to get the registry running on the given port. The second asks the registry to list its currently registered objects. If both calls succeed, we have a valid registry. If either call throws an `Exception`, the `bind()` method determines there is no valid registry and creates one itself. It does this with the following line of code:

```
registry = LocateRegistry.createRegistry(getRegistryPort());
```

After this, the `bind()` method should have either found or created a registry server. If it failed in getting the registry and failed again in creating it, it returns and the servlet remains unregistered. `RemoteHttpServlet` next binds itself to the registry using this line of code:

```
registry.rebind(getRegistryName(), this);
```

It uses the `Registry.rebind()` method instead of the `Registry.bind()` method to indicate that this binding should replace any previous binding using our name. This binding persists until the servlet is destroyed, at which time the `destroy()` method of `RemoteHttpServlet` calls its `unbind()` method. The code `unbind()` uses to unbind from the registry is remarkably simple:

```
if (registry != null) registry.unbind(getRegistryName());
```

It simply asks the registry to unbind its name.

Please note that a remote servlet must be loaded into its server and have its `init()` method called before it is ready for RMI communication. Thus, just as with a daemon servlet, you should either tell your server to load it at start-up or be sure it is always accessed via HTTP before it is accessed directly.

Where to run the registry?

The commonly accepted way to run an RMI registry server is with the standalone Java program *rmiregistry*. We recommend, however, that you don't run *rmiregistry* and instead let the RemoteHttpServlet create the registry itself. It's easier and it's more efficient. The first servlet that needs the registry can create the registry. And, by starting the registry within a servlet, the registry runs using the same JVM as the servlet. That makes it possible to use just one JVM for the Java Web Server, all of its servlets (the remote objects), and the registry.

The applet

Now let's turn our attention from the server and focus it on the client. The code our DaytimeApplet uses to invoke the getDate() method of our new DaytimeServlet is shown in Example 10-14.

Example 10-14. The DaytimeApplet getting the time using RMI

```java
import java.rmi.*;           // New addition
import java.rmi.registry.*;  // New addition

private String getRegistryHost() {
  return getCodeBase().getHost();
}

private int getRegistryPort() {
  try { return Integer.parseInt(getParameter("registryPort")); }
  catch (NumberFormatException e) { return Registry.REGISTRY_PORT; }
}

private String getRegistryName() {
  String name = getParameter("registryName");
  if (name == null) {
    name = "DaytimeServlet";  // default
  }
  return name;
}

private String getDateUsingRMIObject() {
  try {
    Registry registry =
      LocateRegistry.getRegistry(getRegistryHost(), getRegistryPort());
    DaytimeServer daytime =
      (DaytimeServer)registry.lookup(getRegistryName());
    return daytime.getDate().toString();
```

Example 10-14. The DaytimeApplet getting the time using RMI (continued)

```
  }
  catch (ClassCastException e) {
    System.out.println("Retrieved object was not a DaytimeServer: " +
                       e.getMessage());
  }
  catch (NotBoundException e) {
    System.out.println(getRegistryName() + " not bound: " + e.getMessage());
  }
  catch (RemoteException e) {
    System.out.println("Hit remote exception: " + e.getMessage());
  }
  catch (Exception e) {
    System.out.println("Problem getting DaytimeServer reference: " +
                       e.getClass().getName() + ": " + e.getMessage());
  }
  return null;
}
```

The first three methods are support methods. `getRegistryHost()` returns the host on which the registry server should be running. This must always be the host from which the applet was downloaded. `getRegistryPort()` returns the port on which the registry server should be listening. It's normally the default registry port 1099, though it can be overridden with the `registryPort` parameter. `getRegistryName()` returns the name under which the servlet should have been registered. It defaults to `"DaytimeServlet"`, but it can be overridden with the `registryName` parameter.

The actual lookup of the remote servlet object and invocation of its `getDate()` method occur in these three lines of the `getDateUsingRMIObject()` method:

```
Registry registry =
  LocateRegistry.getRegistry(getRegistryHost(), getRegistryPort());
DaytimeServer daytime =
  (DaytimeServer)registry.lookup(getRegistryName());
return daytime.getDate().toString();
```

The first line locates the registry for the given host and the given port. The second line uses this registry to look up the remote object registered under the given name, in the process casting the object to a `DaytimeServer` object. The third line invokes this object's `getDate()` method and receives a serialized `Date` object in return. Then, in the same line, it returns the `String` representation of that `Date`.

The rest of the `getDateUsingRMIObject()` method handles the exceptions that could occur during these three lines. It catches a `ClassCastException` if the retrieved object is not a `DaytimeServer`, a `NotBoundException` if the registry has no object registered under the given name, and a `RemoteException` if there is a network service failure. It also catches a general `Exception`, in case there's some other problem.

You may be wondering why `DaytimeApplet` uses `Registry.lookup(String)` instead of `java.rmi.Naming.lookup(String)` to retrieve its reference to the remote servlet. There's really no reason—it's simply a matter of personal taste. It would work just as well to replace the first two lines in `getDateUsingRMIObject()` with the following code:

```
DaytimeServer daytime =
    (DaytimeServer)Naming.lookup("rmi://" + getRegistryHost() +
                                 ":" + getRegistryPort() +
                                 "/" + getRegistryName());
```

That's it for the fifth and final method of `DaytimeApplet`. Go ahead and run the applet now. Do you see every date field nicely filled in? You shouldn't. You should instead see empty values for the socket communication options. If you remember, we removed support for socket communication when we made `DaytimeServlet` a remote object. Now let's put socket communication back in.

A full-service servlet

What we need now is a single servlet that can make itself available via HTTP communication, non-HTTP socket communication, and RMI communication. A servlet of this sort can extend a new superclass, `com.oreilly.servlet.RemoteDaemonHttpServlet`, implementing the capabilities discussed so far for both an `RemoteHttpServlet` and a `DaemonHttpServlet`.

Here's the code that declares this full-service servlet:

```
import java.io.*;
import java.net.*;
import java.util.*;
import javax.servlet.*;
import javax.servlet.http.*;

import com.oreilly.servlet.RemoteDaemonHttpServlet;

public class DaytimeServlet extends RemoteDaemonHttpServlet
                            implements DaytimeServer {

  public Date getDate() {
    return new Date();
  }

  // The rest is unchanged
```

This code is almost the same as Example 10-8. It's basically that example rewritten to declare that it extends RemoteDaemonHttpServlet and that it implements DaytimeServer.

The code for the RemoteDaemonHttpServlet superclass also nearly matches the code for RemoteHttpServlet. There are just two changes: it extends Daemon-HttpServlet instead of HttpServlet, and its destroy() method first calls super.destroy():

```
package com.oreilly.servlet;

import java.io.*;
import java.net.*;
import java.rmi.*;
import java.rmi.server.*;
import java.rmi.registry.*;
import java.util.*;
import javax.servlet.*;
import javax.servlet.http.*;

public abstract class RemoteDaemonHttpServlet extends DaemonHttpServlet
                                              implements Remote {

  public void destroy() {
    super.destroy();
    unbind();
  }

  // The rest is unchanged
```

Now our DaytimeApplet can connect to this revised remote daemon servlet and produce the full and complete output shown earlier in Figure 10-1.

Chat Server

The daytime server example from the last section demonstrated the nuts and bolts of using each of the three communication techniques for applet-servlet communication. It didn't take advantage, though, of the persistence gains when using socket communication. Nor did it show off the simplicity of RMI communication or the elegance of RMI callbacks (where the servlet can invoke methods of the applet). It also didn't provide a compelling reason for why one servlet should support all the communication techniques—there was no state to maintain or complicated code base to collect in one location. So, before we end our discussion of applet-servlet communication, let's look at a more sophisticated example: a chat server, implemented as a servlet, that supports clients connecting via HTTP, non-HTTP sockets, and RMI.

We'll build this chat server using all three communication techniques so that it can take advantage of the best, most efficient solution for each client. For example, when the client supports RMI, the servlet can be treated as a remote object, and (where possible) it can treat the applet as a remote object, too. When the client doesn't support RMI but can support direct socket communication, the chat server can utilize socket persistence and communicate with the client using a non-HTTP socket protocol. And, of course, when all else fails, the chat server can fall back to using HTTP. It would rather not fall back because HTTP, being stateless, requires that the client poll for updates. But for many clients, HTTP is the only choice.

The chat server is implemented as a single class with a single instantiation because it has a large amount of associated state and a fair amount of code that would otherwise have to be repeated. To separate it into three classes, one for each protocol, would demand excessive interserver communication and replicate the core chat server code three times. Implementing the chat server as a servlet provides a simple way for one object to make itself available via all three communication techniques. By being an HTTP servlet, it has built-in HTTP support. And by extending the `RemoteDaemonHttpServlet` class, it can also easily gain support for non-HTTP socket and RMI communication.

Note that although you'll see the code in its entirety, we won't be fully explaining each and every line. To do so would extend this chapter beyond a reasonable length, assuming we aren't there already. Therefore, we'll explain the issues as they concern applet-servlet communication and rely on you to examine the code to understand all the details.

The Design

Figure 10-3 shows the chat applet in action. Notice that it uses a large `TextArea` component to display the running conversation, with a small `TextInput` component underneath where the user can post a new single-line message. As each contributor composes a message, it's sent to the chat server and distributed to the other chat clients in various ways.

HTTP chat clients post their messages to the server using the HTTP POST method. The applet takes the new message from the `TextInput` component when the user hits **Enter**, URL-encodes the message, and posts it to the servlet as a `message` parameter. It's all very straightforward. What is a bit more complicated is how an HTTP chat client manages to get the other clients' messages. It uses the HTTP GET method to receive each message, but it has a problem: it doesn't know when exactly there's a new message to get. This is the problem with a unidirectional request/response communication paradigm. The client has to either periodically poll for updates or simulate bidirectional communication by making a

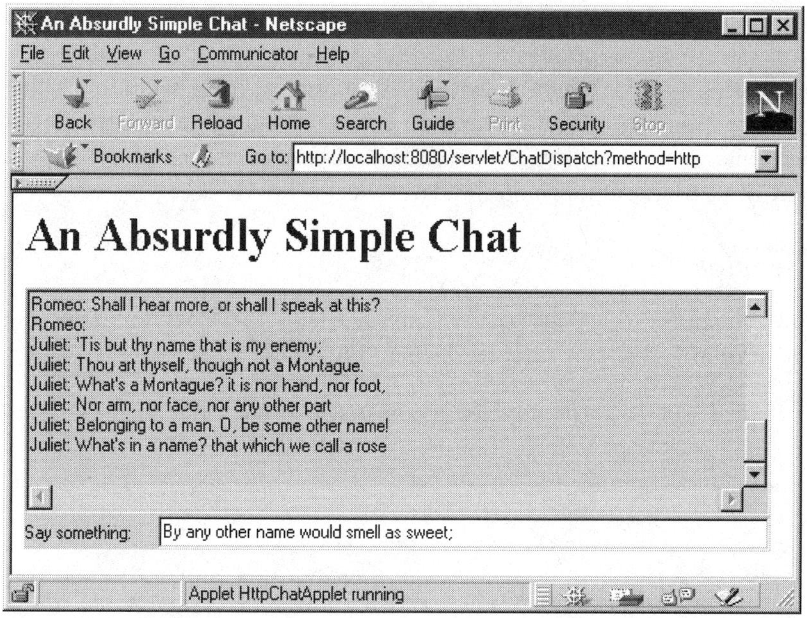

Figure 10-3. The chat applet in action

series of blocking GET requests. By that we mean the chat client initiates a GET request that blocks until the server decides it's time to return something. For our example, we implement this simulated bidirectional communication.

Socket chat clients, for the sake of convenience, post their messages to the server the same way HTTP chat clients do, with the HTTP POST method. They could post their messages using raw socket connections, but only with a marginal gain in efficiency that, at least in this case, doesn't outweigh the increased complexity. These socket clients, however, do use raw sockets to get messages from the other clients, replacing the simulated bidirectional communication with actual bidirectional communication. As each new message comes in to the servlet, it's sent right away from the servlet to the socket chat clients across plain-text socket connections.

RMI chat clients perform their POSTs and their GETs using method invocations. To post each new message, the applet simply calls the remote servlet's broadcastMessage(String) method. To get new messages, it has two options. It can call the servlet's blocking getNextMessage() method or, through the use of callbacks, it can ask the servlet to call its own setNextMessage(String) method every time there's a new message broadcast. We've chosen to use the callback option in our example.

In front of all these applets is a dispatch servlet. It lets the user choose the applet-servlet communication technique (HTTP, socket, or RMI) he wants to use and, based on his choice, generates a page that contains the appropriate applet. It's true that a single applet could be written to support all three techniques and auto-select between them based on its runtime environment, but to do that here would unnecessarily complicate our example. The dispatch servlet also tells the applet the name of its user, but more on that later.

The Servlet

The full listings for the ChatServer interface and the ChatServlet class that implements it are given in Example 10-15 and Example 10-16.

Example 10-15. The ChatServer interface, implemented by ChatServlet

```
import java.rmi.Remote;
import java.rmi.RemoteException;

public interface ChatServer extends Remote {
  public String getNextMessage() throws RemoteException;
  public void broadcastMessage(String message) throws RemoteException;

  public void addClient(ChatClient client) throws RemoteException;
  public void deleteClient(ChatClient client) throws RemoteException;
}
```

Example 10-16. A full-service chat server/servlet

```
import java.io.*;
import java.net.*;
import java.rmi.*;
import java.util.*;
import javax.servlet.*;
import javax.servlet.http.*;

import com.oreilly.servlet.RemoteDaemonHttpServlet;

public class ChatServlet extends RemoteDaemonHttpServlet
                        implements ChatServer {

  // source acts as the distributor of new messages
  MessageSource source = new MessageSource();

  // socketClients holds references to all the socket-connected clients
  Vector socketClients = new Vector();

  // rmiClients holds references to all the RMI clients
  Vector rmiClients = new Vector();
```

Example 10-16. A full-service chat server/servlet (continued)

```java
// doGet() returns the next message. It blocks until there is one.
public void doGet(HttpServletRequest req, HttpServletResponse res)
                              throws ServletException, IOException {
  res.setContentType("text/plain");
  PrintWriter out = res.getWriter();

  // Return the next message (blocking)
  out.println(getNextMessage());
}


// doPost() accepts a new message and broadcasts it to all
// the currently listening HTTP and socket clients.
public void doPost(HttpServletRequest req, HttpServletResponse res)
                              throws ServletException, IOException {
  // Accept the new message as the "message" parameter
  String message = req.getParameter("message");

  // Broadcast it to all listening clients
  if (message != null) broadcastMessage(message);

  // Set the status code to indicate there will be no response
  res.setStatus(res.SC_NO_CONTENT);
}


// getNextMessage() returns the next new message.
// It blocks until there is one.
public String getNextMessage() {
  // Create a message sink to wait for a new message from the
  // message source.
  return new MessageSink().getNextMessage(source);
}


// broadcastMessage() informs all currently listening clients that there
// is a new message. Causes all calls to getNextMessage() to unblock.
public void broadcastMessage(String message) {
  // Send the message to all the HTTP-connected clients by giving the
  // message to the message source
  source.sendMessage(message);

  // Directly send the message to all the socket-connected clients
  Enumeration enum = socketClients.elements();
  while (enum.hasMoreElements()) {
    Socket client = null;
    try {
      client = (Socket)enum.nextElement();
      PrintStream out = new PrintStream(client.getOutputStream());
      out.println(message);
    }
```

Example 10-16. A full-service chat server/servlet (continued)

```
        catch (IOException e) {
          // Problem with a client, close and remote it
          try {
            if (client != null) client.close();
          }
          catch (IOException ignored) { }
          socketClients.removeElement(client);
        }
      }

      // Directly send the message to all RMI clients
      enum = rmiClients.elements();
      while (enum.hasMoreElements()) {
        ChatClient chatClient = null;
        try {
          chatClient = (ChatClient)enum.nextElement();
          chatClient.setNextMessage(message);
        }
        catch (RemoteException e) {
          // Problem communicating with a client, remove it
          deleteClient(chatClient);
        }
      }
    }

    protected int getSocketPort() {
      // We listen on port 2428 (look at a phone to see why)
      return 2428;
    }

    public void handleClient(Socket client) {
      // We have a new socket client. Add it to our list.
      socketClients.addElement(client);
    }

    public void addClient(ChatClient client) {
      // We have a new RMI client. Add it to our list.
      rmiClients.addElement(client);
    }

    public void deleteClient(ChatClient client) {
      // Remote the specified client from our list.
      rmiClients.removeElement(client);
    }
  }


// MessageSource acts as the source for new messages.
// Clients interested in receiving new messages can
```

Example 10-16. A full-service chat server/servlet (continued)

```
// observe this object.
class MessageSource extends Observable {
  public void sendMessage(String message) {
    setChanged();
    notifyObservers(message);
  }
}


// MessageSink acts as the receiver of new messages.
// It listens to the source.
class MessageSink implements Observer {

  String message = null;  // set by update() and read by getNextMessage()

  // Called by the message source when it gets a new message
  synchronized public void update(Observable o, Object arg) {
    // Get the new message
    message = (String)arg;

    // Wake up our waiting thread
    notify();
  }

  // Gets the next message sent out from the message source
  synchronized public String getNextMessage(MessageSource source) {
    // Tell source we want to be told about new messages
    source.addObserver(this);

    // Wait until our update() method receives a message
    while (message == null) {
      try { wait(); } catch (Exception ignored) { }
    }

    // Tell source to stop telling us about new messages
    source.deleteObserver(this);

    // Now return the message we received
    // But first set the message instance variable to null
    // so update() and getNextMessage() can be called again.
    String messageCopy = message;
    message = null;
    return messageCopy;
  }
}
```

The `getNextMessage()` and `broadcastMessage(String message)` methods are most interesting portions of `ChatServlet`. The `getNextMessage()` method returns the next new message as it comes in, blocking until there is one. To enable this blocking, it uses the `MessageSource` and `MessageSink` classes. Without getting too deep into the details of these two classes, we'll just say this: the servlet constructs a new `MessageSink` and asks this sink to get the next message from the source. To accomplish this, the sink registers itself as an observer of source and calls `wait()` to block. When the source receives a new message, the sink (being an observer) is notified of the change with a call to its `update()` method. The sink's `update()` method saves the source's latest message in its `message` variable and then calls `notify()`. This causes its `getNextMessage()` method to unblock and return the message.

The `broadcastMessage()` method tells all listening clients when there's a new message. It notifies HTTP clients by sending the message to the `MessageSource`; other clients it notifies directly by looping through its client list. For each of its socket-connected clients, it prints the message to the client's socket. For each of its RMI clients, it calls the client's `setNextMessage(String)` method. This is the callback we've been talking about. If, at any point, there's a problem with a socket or RMI client, it removes that client from its list.

The two lists, `socketClients` and `rmiClients`, are populated as the servlet hears from clients. When a socket client connects, the servlet's `handle-Client(Socket)` method is called and the new client is added to the `socketClients` Vector. RMI clients have to add themselves to the list by invoking the servlet's `addClient(ChatClient)` method.

The `doGet()` and `doPost()` methods of `ChatServlet` are essentially thin wrappers around the `getNextMessage()` and `broadcastMessage()` methods. The `doGet()` wrapper is so thin you can almost see through it: `doGet()` sends as its response whatever `String` is returned by `getNextMessage()`. The `doPost()` wrapper is a bit less transparent. It extracts the posted message from the POST form data's `"message"` parameter, broadcasts the message by passing it to the `broadcastMessage()` method, and sets its response's status code to `SC_NO_CONTENT` to indicate there is no content in the response. In a sense, making a GET request is equivalent to calling `getNextMessage()`, and making a POST request is equivalent to calling `broadcastMessage()`.

Did you notice which socket port `ChatServlet` listens on? It's 2428. Overriding the `getSocketPort()` method as `ChatServlet` does is an easy way to set the socket port when you don't want to use an init parameter.

The HTTP Applet

The code for our first applet, the HTTP chat applet, is shown in Example 10-17.

Example 10-17. A chat client using HTTP communication

```java
import java.applet.*;
import java.awt.*;
import java.io.*;
import java.net.*;
import java.util.*;

import com.oreilly.servlet.HttpMessage;

public class HttpChatApplet extends Applet implements Runnable {

    TextArea text;
    Label label;
    TextField input;
    Thread thread;
    String user;

    public void init() {
        // Check if this applet was loaded directly from the filesystem.
        // If so, explain to the user that this applet needs to be loaded
        // from a server in order to communicate with that server's servlets.
        URL codebase = getCodeBase();
        if (!"http".equals(codebase.getProtocol())) {
            System.out.println();
            System.out.println("*** Whoops! ***");
            System.out.println("This applet must be loaded from a web server.");
            System.out.println("Please try again, this time fetching the HTML");
            System.out.println("file containing this servlet as");
            System.out.println("\"http://server:port/file.html\".");
            System.out.println();
            System.exit(1);  // Works only from appletviewer
                             // Browsers throw an exception and muddle on
        }

        // Get this user's name from an applet parameter set by the servlet
        // We could just ask the user, but this demonstrates a
        // form of servlet->applet communication.
        user = getParameter("user");
        if (user == null) user = "anonymous";

        // Set up the user interface...
        // On top, a large TextArea showing what everyone's saying.
        // Underneath, a labeled TextField to accept this user's input.
        text = new TextArea();
        text.setEditable(false);
```

Example 10-17. A chat client using HTTP communication (continued)

```java
    label = new Label("Say something: ");
    input = new TextField();
    input.setEditable(true);

    setLayout(new BorderLayout());
    Panel panel = new Panel();
    panel.setLayout(new BorderLayout());

    add("Center", text);
    add("South", panel);

    panel.add("West", label);
    panel.add("Center", input);
  }

  public void start() {
    thread = new Thread(this);
    thread.start();
  }

  String getNextMessage() {
    String nextMessage = null;
    while (nextMessage == null) {
      try {
        URL url = new URL(getCodeBase(), "/servlet/ChatServlet");
        HttpMessage msg = new HttpMessage(url);
        InputStream in = msg.sendGetMessage();
        DataInputStream data = new DataInputStream(
                           new BufferedInputStream(in));
        nextMessage = data.readLine();
      }
      catch (SocketException e) {
        // Can't connect to host, report it and wait before trying again
        System.out.println("Can't connect to host: " + e.getMessage());
        try { Thread.sleep(5000); } catch (InterruptedException ignored) { }
      }
      catch (FileNotFoundException e) {
        // Servlet doesn't exist, report it and wait before trying again
        System.out.println("Resource not found: " + e.getMessage());
        try { Thread.sleep(5000); } catch (InterruptedException ignored) { }
      }
      catch (Exception e) {
        // Some other problem, report it and wait before trying again
        System.out.println("General exception: " +
          e.getClass().getName() + ": " + e.getMessage());
        try { Thread.sleep(1000); } catch (InterruptedException ignored) { }
      }
    }
```

Example 10-17. A chat client using HTTP communication (continued)

```java
    return nextMessage + "\n";
  }

  public void run() {
    while (true) {
      text.appendText(getNextMessage());
    }
  }

  public void stop() {
    thread.stop();
    thread = null;
  }

  void broadcastMessage(String message) {
    message = user + ": " + message;  // Pre-pend the speaker's name
    try {
      URL url = new URL(getCodeBase(), "/servlet/ChatServlet");
      HttpMessage msg = new HttpMessage(url);
      Properties props = new Properties();
      props.put("message", message);
      msg.sendPostMessage(props);
    }
    catch (SocketException e) {
      // Can't connect to host, report it and abandon the broadcast
      System.out.println("Can't connect to host: " + e.getMessage());
    }
    catch (FileNotFoundException e) {
      // Servlet doesn't exist, report it and abandon the broadcast
      System.out.println("Resource not found: " + e.getMessage());
    }
    catch (Exception e) {
      // Some other problem, report it and abandon the broadcast
      System.out.println("General exception: " +
        e.getClass().getName() + ": " + e.getMessage());
    }
  }

  public boolean handleEvent(Event event) {
    switch (event.id) {
      case Event.ACTION_EVENT:
        if (event.target == input) {
          broadcastMessage(input.getText());
          input.setText("");
          return true;
        }
    }
    return false;
```

Example 10-17. A chat client using HTTP communication (continued)

```
  }
}
```

This applet has the same two workhorse methods as `ChatServlet`: `getNextMes-sage()` and `broadcastMessage()`. Its `getNextMessage()` method gets the next message from the servlet. It's called repeatedly to update the `TextArea`. It operates using an `HttpMessage` to make a GET request to the servlet, then interprets the first line of the response as the next new message. Its `broadcastMessage()` method sends a message to the servlet for distribution to the other clients. This method is called in the applet's `handleEvent()` method every time the user hits **Enter** in the `TextInput` component. It works similarly to `getNextMessage()`. It uses an `HttpMessage` to perform a POST request, passing the `TextInput`'s text as the `"message"` parameter, and it doesn't bother to read the response.

The Socket-Connecting Applet

The only difference between the socket-based `SocketChatApplet` and the HTTP-based `HttpChatApplet` is a redesigned `getNextMessage()` method. This method is shown in Example 10-18.

Example 10-18. A chat client using a raw socket connection

```java
static final int PORT = 2428;
DataInputStream serverStream;

String getNextMessage() {
  String nextMessage = null;
  while (nextMessage == null) {
    try {
      // Connect to the server if we haven't before
      if (serverStream == null) {
        Socket s = new Socket(getCodeBase().getHost(), PORT);
        serverStream = new DataInputStream(
                   new BufferedInputStream(
                   s.getInputStream())));
      }

      // Read a line
      nextMessage = serverStream.readLine();
    }
    catch (SocketException e) {
      // Can't connect to host, report it and wait before trying again
      System.out.println("Can't connect to host: " + e.getMessage());
      serverStream = null;
      try { Thread.sleep(5000); } catch (InterruptedException ignored) { }
    }
```

Example 10-18. A chat client using a raw socket connection (continued)

```
    catch (Exception e) {
      // Some other problem, report it and wait before trying again
      System.out.println("General exception: " +
        e.getClass().getName() + ": " + e.getMessage());
      try { Thread.sleep(1000); } catch (InterruptedException ignored) { }
    }
  }
  return nextMessage + "\n";
}
```

This method reads broadcast messages from a socket that's connected to the chat servlet. It uses a simple socket protocol: all content is plain text, one message per line. The first time this method is called, it establishes the socket connection and then uses the connection to get a `DataInputStream`, where it can read from the socket one line at a time. It reads the first line from this stream and returns the text as the next message. For each subsequent invocation, it reuses the same stream and simply returns the next line it reads. If there's ever a `SocketException`, it reestablishes the connection.

The RMI Applet

The code for the `ChatClient` interface is shown in Example 10-19; the RMI-based chat applet that implements it is shown in Example 10-20.

Example 10-19. The ChatClient interface, implemented by RMIChatApplet

```
import java.rmi.Remote;
import java.rmi.RemoteException;

public interface ChatClient extends Remote {
  public void setNextMessage(String message) throws RemoteException;
}
```

Example 10-20. A chat client using RMI communication

```
import java.applet.*;
import java.awt.*;
import java.io.*;
import java.net.*;
import java.rmi.*;
import java.rmi.registry.*;
import java.rmi.server.*;
import java.util.*;

public class RMIChatApplet extends Applet implements ChatClient {

  TextArea text;
```

Example 10-20. A chat client using RMI communication (continued)

```java
Label label;
TextField input;
Thread thread;
String user;

ChatServer chatServer;

private int getRegistryPort() {
  try { return Integer.parseInt(getParameter("port")); }
  catch (NumberFormatException ignored) { return Registry.REGISTRY_PORT; }
}

private String getRegistryName() {
  String name = getParameter("name");
  return (name == null ? "ChatServlet" : name);
}

// Returns a reference to the remote chat server/servlet
// Tries to exit if there's a problem.
private ChatServer getChatServer() {
  try {
    Registry registry =
      LocateRegistry.getRegistry(getCodeBase().getHost(), getRegistryPort());
    Object obj = registry.lookup(getRegistryName());
    return (ChatServer)obj;
  }
  catch (java.rmi.UnknownHostException e) {
    // Don't know the registry host, try to exit
    System.out.println("Host unknown in url: " + e.getMessage());
    System.exit(1);
  }
  catch (NotBoundException e) {
    // Can't find our object, try to exit
    System.out.println("Name not bound: " + e.getMessage());
    System.exit(1);
  }
  catch (ClassCastException e) {
    // The object wasn't a ChatServer, try to exit
    System.out.println(getRegistryName() + " was not a ChatServer:" +
                        e.getMessage());
    System.exit(1);
  }
  catch (RemoteException e) {
    // General RMI problem, try to exit
    System.out.println("Remote exception: " + e.getMessage());
    System.exit(1);
  }
  catch (Exception e) {
```

Example 10-20. A chat client using RMI communication (continued)

```
    // Some other problem, try to exit
    System.out.println("General exception: " +
      e.getClass().getName() + ": " + e.getMessage());
    System.exit(1);
  }
  return null;  // return null if the exit() doesn't work
}


// Add ourselves as a client of the chat server
// Notice there's no need for an RMI registry
private void registerWithChatServer(ChatServer server) {
  try {
    UnicastRemoteObject.exportObject(this);
    server.addClient(this);
  }
  catch (RemoteException e) {
    // General RMI problem, try to exit
    System.out.println("Remote exception: " + e.getMessage());
    System.exit(1);
  }
  catch (Exception e) {
    // Some other problem, try to exit
    System.out.println("General exception: " +
      e.getClass().getName() + ": " + e.getMessage());
    System.exit(1);
  }
}


public void init() {
  // Check if this applet was loaded directly from the filesystem.
  // If so, explain to the user that this applet needs to be loaded
  // from a server in order to communicate with that server's servlets.
  URL codebase = getCodeBase();
  if (!"http".equals(codebase.getProtocol())) {
    System.out.println();
    System.out.println("*** Whoops! ***");
    System.out.println("This applet must be loaded from a web server.");
    System.out.println("Please try again, this time fetching the HTML");
    System.out.println("file containing this servlet as");
    System.out.println("\"http://server:port/file.html\".");
    System.out.println();
    System.exit(1);  // Works only from appletviewer
                     // Browsers throw an exception and muddle on
  }

  // Get the remote chat server
  chatServer = getChatServer();
```

Example 10-20. A chat client using RMI communication (continued)

```
      // Register ourselves as one of its clients
      registerWithChatServer(chatServer);

      // Get this user's name from an applet parameter set by the dispatch servlet
      // We could just ask the user, but this demonstrates a
      // form of servlet->applet communication.
      user = getParameter("user");
      if (user == null) user = "anonymous";

      // Set up the user interface...
      // On top, a large TextArea showing what everyone's saying.
      // Underneath, a labeled TextField to accept this user's input.
      text = new TextArea();
      text.setEditable(false);
      label = new Label("Say something: ");
      input = new TextField();
      input.setEditable(true);

      setLayout(new BorderLayout());
      Panel panel = new Panel();
      panel.setLayout(new BorderLayout());

      add("Center", text);
      add("South", panel);

      panel.add("West", label);
      panel.add("Center", input);
    }

    String getNextMessage() {
      String nextMessage = null;
      while (nextMessage == null) {
        try {
          nextMessage = chatServer.getNextMessage();
        }
        catch (RemoteException e) {
          // Remote exception, report and wait before trying again
          System.out.println("Remote Exception:" + e.getMessage());
          try { Thread.sleep(1000); } catch (InterruptedException ignored) { }
        }
      }
      return nextMessage + "\n";
    }

    public void setNextMessage(String message) {
      text.appendText(message + "\n");
    }
```

Example 10-20. A chat client using RMI communication (continued)

```
  void broadcastMessage(String message) {
    message = user + ": " + message;   // Pre-pend the speaker's name
    try {
      chatServer.broadcastMessage(message);
    }
    catch (RemoteException e) {
      // Remote exception, report it and abandon the broadcast
      System.out.println("Remote exception: " + e.getMessage());
    }
    catch (Exception e) {
      // Some other exception, report it and abandon the broadcast
      System.out.println("General exception: " +
        e.getClass().getName() + ": " + e.getMessage());
    }
  }

  public boolean handleEvent(Event event) {
    switch (event.id) {
      case Event.ACTION_EVENT:
        if (event.target == input) {
          broadcastMessage(input.getText());
          input.setText("");
          return true;
        }
    }
    return false;
  }
}
```

This applet's `getNextMessage()` and `broadcastMessage()` implementations are as simple as any we've seen. They need only call the remote servlet's methods of the same name. But their simplicity comes with a cost: more complicated set-up code. Specifically, the `init()` method now has to call the lengthy (but by now understandable) `getChatServer()` method to obtain a reference to the remote chat servlet.

If you look closely at `RMIChatApplet`, you'll notice that it doesn't actually use its `getNextMessage()` method. Instead, it asks the servlet to call its `setNextMessage()` method each time there's a new message being broadcast. It makes this request in its `init()` method when it calls `registerWithChatServer(ChatServer)`. This method exports the applet as a remote object, then invokes the servlet's `addClient()` method passing a reference to itself. After this, the servlet's `broadcastMessage()` method sends a callback to the applet each time there's a new message.

If you try using callbacks on your own, don't forget the basics we covered earlier. You need to run the *rmic* RMI compiler on your remote applet to generate its stub and skeleton classes. And you need to be sure your server has the *RMIChatApplet_ Stub.class* and *ChatClient.class* files somewhere in its classpath.

The Dispatcher

Now, for this chapter's last code example, the `ChatDispatch` servlet is shown in Example 10-21. This servlet performs two duties. First, when this servlet is accessed without any request parameters, it prints a friendly welcome page asking the user which applet version he is interested in using, as shown in Figure 10-4. Second, when it's accessed with a request parameter, it prints a page that contains the appropriate applet, as you saw in Figure 10-3. Be aware that the URL used to access this dispatch servlet should contain the server's true name, not *localhost*, so as to avoid RMI security problems.

Example 10-21. The front door dispatch servlet

```
import java.io.*;
import javax.servlet.*;
import javax.servlet.http.*;

public class ChatDispatch extends HttpServlet {

  public void doGet(HttpServletRequest req, HttpServletResponse res)
                            throws IOException, ServletException {
    res.setContentType("text/html");

    if (!req.getParameterNames().hasMoreElements()) {
      // There were no request parameters. Print a welcome page.
      printWelcomePage(req, res);
    }
    else {
      // There was at least one request parameter.
      // Print a page containing the applet.
      printAppletPage(req, res);
    }
  }

  // The welcome page greets the reader and has a form where the user
  // can choose an applet-servlet communication method.
  private void printWelcomePage(HttpServletRequest req,
                                HttpServletResponse res)
                  throws IOException {
    PrintWriter out = res.getWriter();
    String me = req.getServletPath();

    out.println("<HTML>");
```

Example 10-21. The front door dispatch servlet (continued)

```
      out.println("<HEAD><TITLE>");
      out.println("Welcome to an Absurdly Simple Chat");
      out.println("</TITLE></HEAD>");
      out.println();
      out.println("<BODY>");
      out.println("<H1>Welcome to an Absurdly Simple Chat</H1>");
      out.println();
      out.println("Would you like to communicate via:");
      out.println("<UL>");
      out.println("  <LI><A HREF=\"" + me + "?method=http\">http</A>");
      out.println("  <LI><A HREF=\"" + me + "?method=socket\">socket</A>");
      out.println("  <LI><A HREF=\"" + me + "?method=rmi\">rmi</A>");
      out.println("</UL>");
      out.println("</BODY></HTML>");
  }


  // The applet page displays the chat applet.
  private void printAppletPage(HttpServletRequest req,
                               HttpServletResponse res)
                  throws IOException {
    PrintWriter out = res.getWriter();

    out.println("<HTML>");
    out.println("<HEAD><TITLE>An Absurdly Simple Chat</TITLE></HEAD>");
    out.println("<BODY>");
    out.println("<H1>An Absurdly Simple Chat</H1>");

    String method = req.getParameter("method");
    String user = req.getRemoteUser();
    String applet = null;

    if ("http".equals(method)) {
      applet = "HttpChatApplet";
    }
    else if ("socket".equals(method)) {
      applet = "SocketChatApplet";
    }
    else if ("rmi".equals(method)) {
      applet = "RMIChatApplet";
    }
    else {
      // No method given, or an invalid method given.
      // Explain to the user what we expect.
      out.println("Sorry, this servlet requires a <TT>method</TT> " +
                  "parameter with one of these values: " +
                  "http, socket, rmi");
      return;
    }
```

Example 10-21. The front door dispatch servlet (continued)

```
    // Print the HTML code to generate the applet.
    // Choose the applet code based on the method parameter.
    // Provide a user parameter if we know the remote user.
    out.println("<APPLET CODE=" + applet + " CODEBASE=/ " +
                "WIDTH=500 HEIGHT=170>");
    if (user != null)
      out.println("<PARAM NAME=user VALUE=\"" + user + "\">");
    out.println("</APPLET>");

    out.println("</BODY></HTML>");
  }
}
```

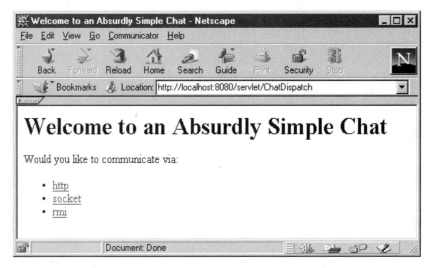

Figure 10-4. The chat dispatch welcome page

Nothing here should surprise you. In fact, we expect this code to appear refreshingly simple after the `ChatServlet` example. Still, this example does demonstrate one last form of applet-servlet communication: servlet-generated applet parameters. Using this technique, a servlet generates a page that contains an applet and passes information to the applet by manipulating the applet's <PARAM> tags. Any information the servlet wants to send to a new applet can be sent this way. In this example, the servlet sends the name returned by `req.getRemoteUser()`. In another example, a servlet could tell the applet its browser type by sending it the string returned by `req.getHeader("User-Agent")`. Or, to be more helpful, the servlet could use a database to determine the capabilities of the browser and tell the applet exactly what it needs to know. It could even tell the applet whether the browser supports RMI communication.

Interservlet Communication

Servlets running together in the same server have several ways to communicate with each other. There are three major reasons to use interservlet communication:

Direct servlet manipulation

A servlet can gain access to the other currently loaded servlets and perform some task on each. The servlet could, for example, periodically ask every servlet to write its state to disk to protect against server crashes.

Servlet reuse

One servlet can use another's abilities to perform a task. Think back to the ChatServlet from the previous chapter. It was written as a server for chat applets, but it could be reused (unchanged) by another servlet that needed to support an HTML-based chat interface.

Servlet collaboration

The most common, situation involves two or more servlets sharing state information. For example, a set of servlets managing an online store could share the store's product inventory count. Session tracking (see Chapter 7, *Session Tracking*) is a special case of servlet collaboration.

This chapter discusses why interservlet communication is useful and how it can be accomplished.

Servlet Manipulation

Direct servlet manipulation involves one servlet accessing the loaded servlets on its server and optionally performing some task on one or more of them. A servlet obtains information about other servlets through the ServletContext object. Use getServlet() to get a particular servlet:

```
public Servlet ServletContext.getServlet(String name) throws ServletException
```

This method returns the servlet of the given name, or null if the servlet is not found. The specified name can be the servlet's registered name (such as "file") or its class name (such as "com.sun.server.webserver.FileServlet"). The server maintains one servlet instance per name, so getServlet("file") returns a different servlet instance than getServlet("com.sun.server.webserver .FileServlet").[*] If the servlet implements SingleThreadModel, the server may return any instance of the servlet from the current pool. The server may—but isn't required to—load the named servlet and execute its init() method if it isn't already loaded. The Java Web Server does not perform this load. A Servlet-Exception is thrown if there is a problem during the load.

You can also get all of the servlets using getServlets():

```
public Enumeration ServletContext.getServlets()
```

This method returns an Enumeration of the Servlet objects loaded in the current ServletContext. Generally there's one servlet context per server, but for security or convenience, a server may decide to partition its servlets into separate contexts. The enumeration always includes the calling servlet itself. This method is deprecated in the Servlet API 2.0 in favor of getServletNames():

```
public Enumeration ServletContext.getServletNames()
```

This method returns an Enumeration of the names of the servlet objects loaded in the current ServletContext. The enumeration always includes the calling servlet itself. When used with getServlet(), this method can perform the same function as the deprecated getServlets(). The name returned can be a registered name (such as "file") or a class name (such as "com.sun.server .webserver.FileServlet"). This method was introduced in Version 2.0 of the Servlet API.

Casting the Servlet object returned by getServlet() or getServlets() to its specific subclass can, in some situations, throw a ClassCastException. For example, the following code sometimes works as expected and sometimes throws an exception:

```
MyServlet servlet = (MyServlet)getServletContext().getServlet("MyServlet");
```

The reason has to do with how a servlet can be automatically reloaded when its class file changes. As we explained in Chapter 3, *The Servlet Life Cycle*, a server uses a new ClassLoader each time it reloads a servlet. This has the interesting side effect that, when the MyServlet class is reloaded, it is actually a different version of MyServlet than the version used by other classes. Thus, although the returned

---

[*] getServlet("file") returns the instance that handles */servlet/file*, while getServlet("com.sun. server.webserver.FileServlet") returns the instance that handles */servlet/com.sun.server.webserver. FileServlet*.

class type is `MyServlet` and it's being cast to the type `MyServlet`, the cast is between different types (from two different class loaders) and the cast has to throw a `ClassCastException`. The same type mismatch can occur if the class performing the cast (that is, the servlet containing the above code) is reloaded. Why? Because its new `ClassLoader` won't find `MyServlet` using the primordial class loader and will load its own copy of `MyServlet`.

There are three possible workarounds. First, avoid casting the returned `Servlet` object and invoke its methods using reflection (a technique whereby a Java class can inspect and manipulate itself at runtime). Second, make sure that the servlet being cast is never reloaded. You can do this by moving the servlet out of the default servlet directory (usually *server_root/servlets*) and into the server's standard classpath (usually *server_root/classes*). The servlet performing the cast can remain in the *servlets* directory because its `ClassLoader` can find `MyServlet` using the primordial class loader. Third, cast the returned servlet to an interface that declares the pertinent methods and place the interface in the server's standard classpath where it won't be reloaded. Every class but the interface can remain in the *servlets* directory. Of course, in this case, the servlet must be changed to declare that it implements the interface.

Viewing the Currently Loaded Servlets

Example 11-1 uses these methods to display information about the currently loaded servlets, as shown in Figure 11-1.

Example 11-1. Checking out the currently loaded servlets

```
import java.io.*;
import java.util.*;
import javax.servlet.*;
import javax.servlet.http.*;

public class Loaded extends HttpServlet {

  public void doGet(HttpServletRequest req, HttpServletResponse res)
                          throws ServletException, IOException {
    res.setContentType("text/plain");
    PrintWriter out = res.getWriter();

    ServletContext context = getServletContext();
    Enumeration names = context.getServletNames();
    while (names.hasMoreElements()) {
      String name = (String)names.nextElement();
      Servlet servlet = context.getServlet(name);
      out.println("Servlet name: " + name);
      out.println("Servlet class: " + servlet.getClass().getName());
```

Example 11-1. Checking out the currently loaded servlets (continued)

```
        out.println("Servlet info: " + servlet.getServletInfo());
        out.println();
    }
  }
}
```

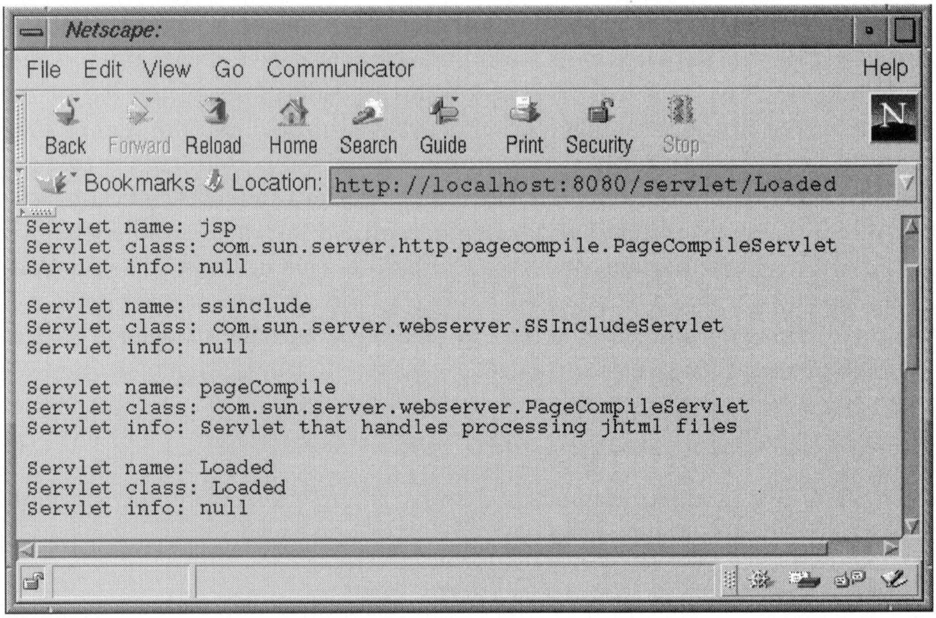

Figure 11-1. Output from the loaded servlet

There's nothing too surprising in this servlet. It retrieves its `ServletContext` to access the other servlets loaded in the server. Then it calls the context's `getServletNames()` method. This returns an `Enumeration` of `String` objects that the servlet iterates over in a `while` loop. For each name, it retrieves the corresponding `Servlet` object with a call to the context's `getServlet()` method. Then it prints three items of information about the servlet: its name, its class name, and its `getServletInfo()` text. Notice that if the `Loaded` servlet used the deprecated `getServlets()` method instead of `getServletNames()`, it would not have had access to the servlets' names.

Saving the State of the Currently Loaded Servlets

The next example demonstrates another use for these methods. It works like `Loaded`, except that it attempts to call each servlets' `saveState()` method, if it exists. This servlet could be run periodically (or be modified to spawn a thread that runs periodically) to guard against data loss in the event of a server crash. The code is in Example 11-2; the output is in Figure 11-2.

Example 11-2. Saving the state of all the currently loaded servlets

```java
import java.io.*;
import java.lang.reflect.*;
import java.util.*;
import javax.servlet.*;
import javax.servlet.http.*;

public class SaveState extends HttpServlet {

  public void doGet(HttpServletRequest req, HttpServletResponse res)
                              throws ServletException, IOException {
    res.setContentType("text/plain");
    PrintWriter out = res.getWriter();

    ServletContext context = getServletContext();
    Enumeration names = context.getServletNames();
    while (names.hasMoreElements()) {
      String name = (String)names.nextElement();
      Servlet servlet = context.getServlet(name);

      out.println("Trying to save the state of " + name + "...");
      out.flush();
      try {
        Method save = servlet.getClass().getMethod("saveState", null);
        save.invoke(servlet, null);
        out.println("Saved!");
      }
      catch (NoSuchMethodException e) {
        out.println("Not saved. This servlet has no saveState() method.");
      }
      catch (SecurityException e) {
        out.println("Not saved. SecurityException: " + e.getMessage());
      }
      catch (InvocationTargetException e) {
        out.print("Not saved. The saveState() method threw an exception: ");
        Throwable t = e.getTargetException();
        out.println(t.getClass().getName() + ": " + t.getMessage());
      }
      catch (Exception e) {
        out.println("Not saved. " + e.getClass().getName() + ": " +
                    e.getMessage());
      }

      out.println();
    }
```

Example 11-2. Saving the state of all the currently loaded servlets (continued)

```
  }

  public String getServletInfo() {
    return "Calls the saveState() method (if it exists) for all the " +
           "currently loaded servlets";
  }
}
```

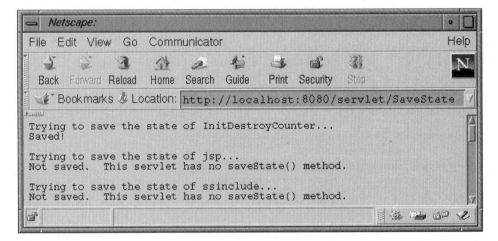

Figure 11-2. Output from the SaveState servlet

SaveState uses reflection to determine if a servlet has a public `saveState()` method and to invoke the method when it exists. If the invocation goes without a hitch, it prints "Saved!". If there's a problem, it reports the problem. Why does SaveState use reflection? Because otherwise it would have to cast each `Servlet` object to some class or interface that includes a `saveState()` method, and the code for each servlet would have to be modified to extend or implement that class or interface. Using reflection is an easier approach that doesn't require code modification. Reflection also avoids the `ClassCastException` problem noted earlier.

Servlet Reuse

Another use for interservlet communication is to allow one servlet to reuse the abilities (the public methods) of another servlet. The major challenge with servlet reuse is for the "user" servlet to obtain the proper instance of "usee" servlet when the usee servlet has not yet been loaded into the server.

The obvious solutions don't always work. `getServlet()` isn't guaranteed to load the named servlet on all servers; it may just return `null`. Directly creating a new instance of the usee servlet doesn't work either, as the newly created servlet doesn't have access to its own `ServletConfig` and `ServletContext` objects. Plus, the server would be using a different instance to handle client requests, leaving the new instance of the servlet without the right state information.

The solution is for the user servlet to ask the server to load the usee servlet, then call `getServlet()` to get a reference to it. Unfortunately, the Servlet API distinctly lacks any methods whereby a servlet can control the servlet life cycle, for itself or for other servlets. This is considered a security risk and is officially "left for future consideration."

Fortunately, there's a back door we can use today. A servlet can open an HTTP connection to the server in which it's running, ask for the unloaded servlet, and effectively force the server to load the servlet to handle the request. Then a call to `getServlet()` gets the proper instance.[*]

An Improved getServlet()

The `com.oreilly.servlet.ServletUtils` class has an improved `getServlet()` method that does just this. It returns the named servlet, loading it first via an HTTP request if necessary. The code is shown in Example 11-3.

Example 11-3. The code for an improved getServlet()

```
// Get the named servlet. Try loading it through an HTTP request if
// necessary. Returns null if there's a problem. Only loads HTTP
// servlets, of course.
public static Servlet getServlet(String name,
                                 ServletRequest req,
                                 ServletContext context) {
  try {
    // Try getting the servlet the old-fashioned way
    Servlet servlet = context.getServlet(name);
    if (servlet != null) return servlet;

    // If getServlet() returned null, we have to load it ourselves.
    // Do this by making an HTTP GET request to the servlet.
    // Use a raw socket connection so we can set a timeout.
    Socket socket = new Socket(req.getServerName(), req.getServerPort());
    socket.setSoTimeout(4000);  // wait up to 4 secs for a response
    PrintWriter out = new PrintWriter(socket.getOutputStream(), true);
    out.println("GET /servlet/" + name + " HTTP/1.0");  // the request
    out.println();
    try {
```

---

[*] Unfortunately, this technique does not work directly for servlets running within a secure web server because a secure server accepts only encrypted HTTPS connections.

Example 11-3. The code for an improved getServlet() (continued)

```
    socket.getInputStream().read();  // Even one byte means its loaded
  }
  catch (InterruptedIOException e) { /* timeout: ignore, hope for the best */ }
  out.close();

  // Try getting the servlet again.
  return context.getServlet(name);
  }
  catch (Exception e) {
  // If there's any problem, return null.
  return null;
  }
}
```

This `getServlet()` method uses a raw socket connection to perform the HTTP
GET request. This is so that it can set a time-out for how long it's willing to wait for
a response. The `URL` and `URLConnection` classes don't provide this ability. In this
case, the time-out is set to four seconds. If, after four seconds, the servlet hasn't
written any response, the `read()` method throws an `InterruptedIOException`
and the method continues. This time-out is necessary only for the special case
where a servlet spends a long time preparing its response and we don't want to
wait. It would appear this time-out could leave the loading servlet in an uninitial-
ized state, if its `init()` method were to take five seconds, for example. A well-
written server, however, should block in the `getServlet()` call until the servlet
has been fully initialized. Note that because this `ServletUtils.getServlet()`
method requires a `ServletRequest` parameter, it can be called only by methods
with access to a `ServletRequest`, such as `doGet()` and `doPost()`.

Reusing ChatServlet

An HTML-based chat servlet built around the abilities of last chapter's `Chat-`
`Servlet` is an excellent example of servlet reuse. This new servlet, called
`ChatPage`, wraps an HTML interface around the `getNextMessage()` and `broad-`
`castMessage()` methods of `ChatServlet`. The code is shown in Example 11-4,
while the output is shown in Figure 11-3.

Example 11-4. One servlet, ChatPage, reusing another servlet, ChatServlet

```
import java.io.*;
import java.util.*;
import javax.servlet.*;
import javax.servlet.http.*;

import com.oreilly.servlet.ServletUtils;
```

Example 11-4. One servlet, ChatPage, reusing another servlet, ChatServlet (continued)

```java
public class ChatPage extends HttpServlet implements Runnable {

  static final int MESSAGE_ARCHIVE_SIZE = 10;  // save the last 10 messages

  ChatServlet chat = null;  // the servlet to reuse
  String[] messages = new String[MESSAGE_ARCHIVE_SIZE];  // circular array
  int messageIndex = 0;  // index into the messages array
  Thread update = null;  // thread to update new messages

  // Gets new messages from the chat servlet and inserts them in
  // the messages' circular array.
  public void run() {
    while (true) {
      String message = chat.getNextMessage();
      synchronized (this) {
        messages[messageIndex] = message;
        messageIndex = (messageIndex + 1) % MESSAGE_ARCHIVE_SIZE;
      }
    }
  }

  // Prints the message archive (the 10 latest messages) and a text
  // field where the reader can input a new message.
  public void doGet(HttpServletRequest req, HttpServletResponse res)
                              throws ServletException, IOException {
    res.setContentType("text/html");
    PrintWriter out = res.getWriter();

    // Turn off caching, so the latest messages are always displayed.
    // (Works around a Netscape problem.)
    res.setHeader("Pragma", "no-cache");

    // For our first request, "chat" is null and we need to use
    // ServletUtils.getServlet() to get the ChatServlet instance.
    // Then we need to start another thread to listen for chat's
    // new messages.
    if (chat == null) {
      chat = (ChatServlet)ServletUtils.getServlet(
                "ChatServlet", req, getServletContext());
      if (chat != null) {
        update = new Thread(this);
        update.start();
      }
    }

    // Print a pretty header.
    out.println("<HTML><HEAD>");
    out.println("<TITLE>ChatPage</TITLE>");
```

Example 11-4. One servlet, ChatPage, reusing another servlet, ChatServlet (continued)

```
    out.println("</HEAD><BODY>");
    out.println("<CENTER><H1>Welcome to ChatPage!</H1></CENTER>");

    // Print the message archive, oldest first.
    // Synchronized so it doesn't change while we're printing it.
    synchronized (this) {
      out.println("<FONT SIZE=4>Recent messages:</FONT><P>");
      int i = messageIndex;
      do {
        String message = messages[i];
        if (message != null) out.println(message + "<P>");
        i = (i + 1) % MESSAGE_ARCHIVE_SIZE;
      } while (i != messageIndex);
    }

    // Print a button that gets new messages.
    out.println("<FORM METHOD=GET>");
    out.println("<INPUT TYPE=submit VALUE=\"Get New Messages\">");
    out.println("</FORM>");

    // Print a form where the reader can submit a new message.
    out.println("<HR>");
    out.println("<FORM METHOD=POST>");
    out.println("<FONT SIZE=4>Submit a message:</FONT>");
    out.println("<INPUT TYPE=text NAME=message>");
    out.println("</FORM>");

    // Print a pretty footer.
    out.println("<HR>");
    out.println("<CENTER><FONT SIZE=2><B>");
    out.println("Special thanks to ChatServlet for acting as our back-end");
    out.println("</B></FONT></CENTER>");
    out.println("</BODY></HTML>");
  }

  // Accepts messages for broadcast.
  public void doPost(HttpServletRequest req, HttpServletResponse res)
                          throws ServletException, IOException {
    // If our first request happens to be a POST, we need to set "chat"
    // and start our update thread just as we do for a GET request.
    if (chat == null) {
      chat = (ChatServlet)ServletUtils.getServlet(
                "ChatServlet", req, getServletContext());
      if (chat != null) {
        update = new Thread(this);
        update.start();
        Thread.currentThread().yield();  // let the run() method start
      }
```

Example 11-4. One servlet, ChatPage, reusing another servlet, ChatServlet (continued)

```
  }

  // Get the client's username. It's non-null only if ChatPage is
  // protected by client authentication.
  String user = req.getRemoteUser();
  if (user == null) user = "anonymous";

  // Get and broadcast the message.
  String message = req.getParameter("message");
  if (message != null && chat != null) {
    chat.broadcastMessage(user + ": " + message);
    Thread.currentThread().yield();  // let the message be broadcast
  }

  // Have doGet() print the updated message archive and the form.
  doGet(req, res);
}

// Stops the background thread.
public void destroy() {
  if (update != null)
    update.stop();
}

public String getServletInfo() {
  return "An HTML chat server front end, reusing ChatServlet";
}
}
```

The core logic for running the chat service remains in `ChatServlet`. `ChatPage` just uses the public methods of `ChatServlet` to present an alternative front end to the user. `ChatPage` gains access to the server's `ChatServlet` instance with the following line of code:

```
chat = (ChatServlet)ServletUtils.getServlet(
         "ChatServlet", req, getServletContext());
```

Remember that this cast can throw a `ClassCastException` if either `ChatServlet` or `ChatPage` was ever reloaded. To avoid this, put the class file for `ChatServlet` in the server's classpath. This ensures that `ChatServlet` isn't reloaded. (And what if `ChatPage` is reloaded? That won't be a problem as long as `ChatServlet` was loaded by the primordial class loader.) Not allowing `ChatServlet` to reload also guarantees that the background `update` thread of `ChatPage` won't find itself calling an old version of `ChatServlet`.

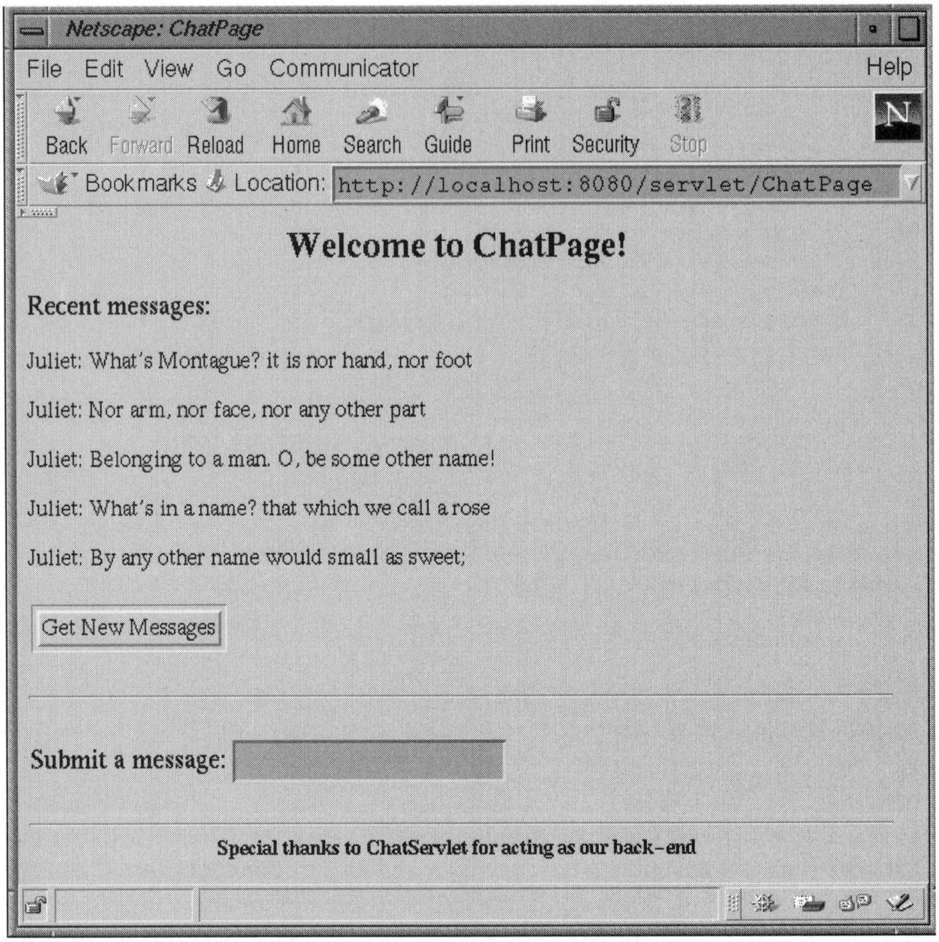

Figure 11-3. Another interface to ChatServlet

ChatPage uses the returned ChatServlet instance for its back end. It calls chat.getNextMessage() to fill its array of recent messages and chat.broadcastMessage() to broadcast each new message as it's entered by the user.

As often happens with servlet reuse, not everything fits together elegantly in this example. ChatServlet wasn't intended to be used by another servlet,[*] so ChatPage requires some extra code to work around some issues that could have been solved with a better back-end design. Specifically, the doPost() method has two points where the current thread yields to allow the update thread to proceed with its work. First, doPost() calls yield() after starting the update thread. This

---

[*] Honest! The examples from this chapter were dreamed up only after Chapter 10 had been written.

gives the new thread a chance to start listening for chat messages. Second, doPost() calls yield() after broadcasting its message. This gives the update thread a chance to receive the broadcasted message. Without these yields, the thread calling doPost() may broadcast the message before the update thread is able to receive the message, resulting in a response that doesn't include the latest message. (And even with the yields, it's possible this could happen anyway due to unfortunate thread scheduling.)

Servlet Collaboration

Sometimes servlets have to cooperate, usually by sharing some information. We call communication of this sort servlet collaboration. Collaborating servlets can pass the shared information directly from one servlet to another through method invocations, as shown earlier. This approach requires each servlet to know the other servlets with which it is collaborating—an unnecessary burden. There are several better techniques.

Collaboration Through the System Properties List

One simple way for servlets to share information is by using Java's system-wide Properties list, found in the java.lang.System class. This Properties list holds the standard system properties, such as java.version and path.separator, but it can also hold application-specific properties. Servlets can use the properties list to hold the information they need to share. A servlet can add (or change) a property by calling:

```
System.getProperties().put("key", "value");
```

That servlet, or another servlet running in the same JVM, can later get the value of the property by calling:

```
String value = System.getProperty("key");
```

The property can be removed by calling:

```
System.getProperties().remove("key");
```

It's best if the key for a property includes a prefix that contains the name of the servlet's package and the name of the collaboration group. For example, "com.oreilly.servlet.ShoppingCart".

The Properties class is intended to be String based, meaning that each key and value is supposed to be a String. This limitation, though, isn't commonly enforced and can (although it's quite a hack) be ignored by servlets that want to store and retrieve non-String objects. Such servlets can take advantage of the fact that the Properties class extends the Hashtable class, so the Properties list can (quite rudely) be treated as a `Hashtable` when storing keys and values. For example, a servlet can add or change a property object by calling:

```
System.getProperties().put(keyObject, valueObject);   // hack
```

It can retrieve the property object by calling:

```
SomeObject valueObject = (SomeObject)System.getProperties().get(keyObject);
```

It can remove the property object by calling:

```
System.getProperties().remove(keyObject);
```

This misuse of the `Properties` list causes the `getProperty()`, `list()` and `save()` methods of the `Properties` class to throw `ClassCastException` objects when they naturally—but erroneously—assume each key and value to be a `String`. For this reason, if there's *any* chance these methods might be called, you should instead use one of the techniques for servlet collaboration we describe later in the chapter. Also, remember the class files for `keyObject` and `valueObject` should be found in the server's classpath, not in the default servlet directory where they would be loaded, and perhaps reloaded, by the special servlet class loaders.

There are three more caveats to using the system `Properties` list for servlet collaboration: the information isn't naturally persistent between server restarts, the information can be viewed (and modified or deleted) by other classes executing in the servlet's JVM, and some servlet security managers may not grant servlets access to the system property list.

Using properties to sell burritos

Despite the stern warnings, servlet collaboration through the system-wide `Properties` list works well for servlets that are sharing insensitive, noncritical, easily replaceable information. As a fun example, imagine a set of servlets that sell burritos and share a "special of the day." An administrative servlet could set the special of the day using the following code:

```
System.getProperties().put("com.LaCostena.special.burrito", "Pollo Adobado");
System.getProperties().put("com.LaCostena.special.day", new Date());
```

Thereafter, every other servlet on the server can access the special and display it with code like this:

```
String burrito = System.getProperty("com.LaCostena.special.burrito");
Date day = (Date)System.getProperties().get("com.LaCostena.special.day");

DateFormat df = DateFormat.getDateInstance(DateFormat.SHORT);
String today = df.format(day);

out.println("Our burrito special today (" + today + ") is: " + burrito);
```

Faster image chaining

Servlets performing image effects in a servlet chain can boost their speed dramatically by using the system `Properties` list to pass their images. In Chapter 6, *Sending Multimedia Content*, we saw the standard method by which the servlets in a chain pass images from link to link. The first servlet takes an `Image` object, encodes it to a stream of bytes, and passes the bytes to the next servlet. The receiving servlet decodes the bytes back into the original `Image` object. The technique works fine, but it can be prohibitively slow for large images. An alternative solution is for the first servlet to save the `Image` object itself in the system-wide `Properties` list, then pass on a small unique key by which the next servlet in the chain can locate the `Image`. In a sense, the old approach works by shoving an entire elephant through the small portal between servlets. The new approach works by passing just the elephant's leash.

Example 11-5 demonstrates exactly how a servlet passes on a key to an `Image` object saved in the system `Properties` list.

Example 11-5. Passing an Image through the Properties list

```java
import java.awt.*;
import java.io.*;
import javax.servlet.*;
import javax.servlet.http.*;

public class ChainImageSource extends HttpServlet {

  int keynum = 0;   // used to create a unique key

  public void doGet(HttpServletRequest req, HttpServletResponse res)
                            throws ServletException, IOException {
    // Get an Image
    String imageFile = req.getRealPath("/system/images/serverduke.gif");
    Image image = Toolkit.getDefaultToolkit().getImage(imageFile);

    // Create a unique key under which to store the image
    String key = "com.oreilly.servlet.ChainImageSource." + keynum++;

    // Store the image in the system Properties list using that key
    System.getProperties().put(key, image);

    // Tell the next servlet to expect an image key
    res.setContentType("java-internal/image-key");

    PrintWriter out = res.getWriter();

    // Send the key
    out.println(key);
```

Example 11-5. Passing an Image through the Properties list (continued)

```
  }
}
```

Notice how the servlet generates its unique key. It prefixes the key with the string
`"com.oreilly.servlet.ChainImageSource"`, something no other servlet is
likely to use. Then it appends a different integer value for each image. Also notice
how this servlet uses the custom content type `"java-internal/image-key"` to
indicate that it's passing on an image key.

Example 11-6 shows the other half of this servlet chain—a servlet that uses the key
to fetch the original **Image** object.

Example 11-6. Fetching an image passed through the Properties list

```java
import java.awt.*;
import java.io.*;
import javax.servlet.*;
import javax.servlet.http.*;

public class ChainImageSink extends HttpServlet {

  public void doGet(HttpServletRequest req, HttpServletResponse res)
                            throws ServletException, IOException {

    // See what content type we're receiving
    String contentType = req.getContentType();

    Image image = null;

    // An "image/*" content type means to expect the image as an encoded
    // byte stream
    if (contentType != null && contentType.startsWith("image")) {
      // Receive the image bytes as shown in Chapter 6
    }

    // A "java-internal/image-key" content type means to expect a key
    else if ("java-internal/image-key".equals(contentType)) {
      // Read the first line of content to get the key
      String key = req.getReader().readLine();

      // Retrieve the Image stored under that key
      image = (Image)System.getProperties().get(key);

      // Always remove the Image, to avoid a memory leak
      System.getProperties().remove(key);
    }

    // Other content types cannot be handled
```

Example 11-6. Fetching an image passed through the Properties list (continued)

```
  else {
    throw new ServletException("Incoming content type must be " +
                    "\"image/*\" or \"java-internal/image-key\"");
  }

  // Proceed to use the image as appropriate...
  res.setContentType("text/plain");
  PrintWriter out = res.getWriter();
  out.println("Received the image: " + image);
  }
}
```

The most important thing to notice with this example is that the receiving servlet bears the responsibility of removing the Image from the system Properties list to avoid a potentially large memory leak.

This leash-passing technique works only when the source servlet can be absolutely sure its key is being sent to another servlet, not to a dumbfounded user who expected an image. This can be ensured if every chain has as its final servlet a special servlet whose sole purpose is to accept an image key and emit that Image's encoded byte stream.

Collaboration Through a Shared Object

Another way for servlets to share information is through a shared object. A shared object can hold the pool of shared information and make it available to each servlet as needed. In a sense, the system Properties list is a special case example of a shared object. By generalizing the technique into sharing any sort of object, however, a servlet is able to use whatever shared object best solves its particular problem.

Often the shared object incorporates a fair amount of business logic or rules for manipulating the object's data. This business logic protects the shared object's actual data by making it available only through well-defined methods. It can enforce data integrity, trigger events to handle certain conditions, and basically abstract lots of little data manipulations into a single method invocation. This capability isn't available with the Properties list.

There's one thing to watch out for when collaborating through a shared object: the garbage collector. It can reclaim the shared object if at any time the object isn't referenced by a loaded servlet. To keep the garbage collector at bay, it's wise for every servlet using a shared object to save a reference to the object.

Using a shared class to sell burritos

For an example of servlet collaboration through a shared object, let's look at how several servlets selling burritos can maintain a shared inventory of burrito ingredients. First, we need a shared burrito inventory class. This class is responsible for maintaining the ingredient count and making the count available through its public methods. An example burrito inventory class is shown in Example 11-7. You'll notice that this class is a singleton (a class that has just one instance). This makes it easy for every servlet sharing the class to maintain a reference to the same instance.

Example 11-7. A shared burrito inventory class

```java
public class BurritoInventory {

  // Protect the constructor, so no other class can call it
  private BurritoInventory() { }

  // Create the only instance, save it to a private static variable
  private static BurritoInventory instance = new BurritoInventory();

  // Make the static instance publicly available
  public static BurritoInventory getInstance() { return instance; }

  // How many "servings" of each item do we have?
  private int cheese = 0;
  private int rice = 0;
  private int beans = 0;
  private int chicken = 0;

  // Add to the inventory
  public void addCheese(int added) { cheese += added; }
  public void addRice(int added) { rice += added; }
  public void addBeans(int added) { beans += added; }
  public void addChicken(int added) { chicken += added; }

  // Called when it's time to make a burrito.
  // Returns true if there are enough ingredients to make the burrito,
  // false if not. Decrements the ingredient count when there are enough.
  synchronized public boolean makeBurrito() {
    // Burritos require one serving of each item
    if (cheese > 0 && rice > 0 && beans > 0 && chicken > 0) {
      cheese--; rice--; beans--; chicken--;
      return true;  // can make the burrito
    }
    else {
      // Could order more ingredients
      return false;  // cannot make the burrito
    }
```

Example 11-7. A shared burrito inventory class (continued)

```
    }
}
```

`BurritoInventory` maintains an inventory count for four burrito ingredients: cheese, rice, beans, and chicken. It holds the counts with private instance variables. For serious production use, information like these counts should probably be kept in an external database. Each ingredient's inventory count can be increased through the `addCheese()`, `addRice()`, `addBeans()`, and `addChicken()` methods. These methods might be called from a servlet accessed by the ingredient preparers throughout the day. All the counts are decreased together in the `makeBurrito()` method. This method checks that there are enough ingredients to make a full burrito. If there are, it decrements the ingredient count and returns `true`. If there aren't, it returns `false` (and, in an improved version, may choose to order more ingredients). The `makeBurrito()` method might be called by a servlet selling burritos over the Web, and perhaps also by a servlet communicating with the check-out cash register. Remember, the class file for `BurritoInventory` should be placed somewhere in the server's classpath (such as in *server_root/classes*), just like all the other non-servlet class files.

Example 11-8 shows how a servlet adds ingredients to the inventory.

Example 11-8. Adding ingredients to the shared inventory

```
import java.io.*;
import java.util.*;
import javax.servlet.*;
import javax.servlet.http.*;

public class BurritoInventoryProducer extends HttpServlet {

  // Get (and keep!) a reference to the shared BurritoInventory instance
  BurritoInventory inventory = BurritoInventory.getInstance();

  public void doGet(HttpServletRequest req, HttpServletResponse res)
                            throws ServletException, IOException {
    res.setContentType("text/html");
    PrintWriter out = res.getWriter();

    out.println("<HTML>");
    out.println("<HEAD><TITLE>Burrito Inventory Producer</TITLE></HEAD>");

    // Produce random amounts of each item
    Random random = new Random();

    int cheese = Math.abs(random.nextInt() % 10);
    int rice = Math.abs(random.nextInt() % 10);
```

Example 11-8. Adding ingredients to the shared inventory (continued)

```
    int beans = Math.abs(random.nextInt() % 10);
    int chicken = Math.abs(random.nextInt() % 10);

    // Add the items to the inventory
    inventory.addCheese(cheese);
    inventory.addRice(rice);
    inventory.addBeans(beans);
    inventory.addChicken(chicken);

    // Print the production results
    out.println("<BODY>");
    out.println("<H1>Added ingredients:</H1>");
    out.println("<PRE>");
    out.println("cheese: " + cheese);
    out.println("rice: " + rice);
    out.println("beans: " + beans);
    out.println("chicken: " + chicken);
    out.println("</PRE>");
    out.println("</BODY></HTML>");
  }
}
```

Every time this servlet is accessed, it produces a random amount of each ingredient (somewhere from zero to nine servings) and adds it to the inventory. Then this servlet prints the results of its work, as you can see in Figure 11-4.

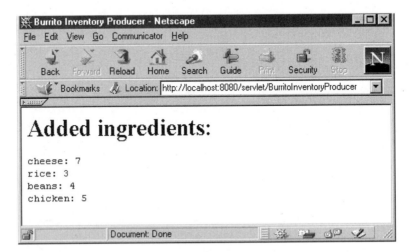

Figure 11-4. The output from BurritoInventoryProducer

The most important thing to note about this servlet is that it always keeps its reference to the shared `BurritoInventory` instance, preventing the garbage collector from reclaiming the instance as long as this servlet is loaded.

Example 11-9 shows how a servlet can consume the ingredients from the inventory.

Example 11-9. Consuming ingredients from the shared inventory

```
import java.io.*;
import javax.servlet.*;
import javax.servlet.http.*;

public class BurritoInventoryConsumer extends HttpServlet {

  // Get (and keep!) a reference to the shared BurritoInventory instance
  private BurritoInventory inventory = BurritoInventory.getInstance();

  public void doGet(HttpServletRequest req, HttpServletResponse res)
                              throws ServletException, IOException {
    res.setContentType("text/html");
    PrintWriter out = res.getWriter();

    out.println("<HTML>");
    out.println("<HEAD><TITLE>Burrito Inventory Consumer</TITLE></HEAD>");

    out.println("<BODY><BIG>");

    if (inventory.makeBurrito()) {
      out.println("Your burrito will be ready in a few minutes.");
    }
    else {
      out.println("We're low on ingredients.<BR>");
      out.println("Looks like you're gonna starve.");
    }

    out.println("</BIG></BODY></HTML>");
  }
}
```

This servlet calls the makeBurrito() method, telling the inventory it wants to make a burrito. This servlet doesn't have to (and, in fact, isn't allowed to) decrement the counts itself. This servlet saves its own reference to the BurritoInventory instance, making sure that even if BurritoInventoryProducer is unloaded, the BurritoInventory instance is still referenced and therefore protected from the garbage collector.

Using a servlet as the shared object

We should mention that it's possible for a servlet to act as the shared object. Using a shared servlet has the added advantage that the servlet can maintain its state using its init() and destroy() methods to load and save its state. Plus, a shared servlet can print its current state each time it's accessed. Example 11-10 shows the BurritoInventory class rewritten to be a servlet.

Example 11-10. The shared burrito inventory class, rewritten as a servlet

```java
import java.io.*;
import javax.servlet.*;
import javax.servlet.http.*;

public class BurritoInventoryServlet extends HttpServlet {

  // How many "servings" of each item do we have?
  private int cheese = 0;
  private int rice = 0;
  private int beans = 0;
  private int chicken = 0;

  // Add to the inventory as more servings are prepared.
  public void addCheese(int added) { cheese += added; }
  public void addRice(int added) { rice += added; }
  public void addBeans(int added) { beans += added; }
  public void addChicken(int added) { chicken += added; }

  // Called when it's time to make a burrito.
  // Returns true if there are enough ingredients to make the burrito,
  // false if not. Decrements the ingredient count when there are enough.
  synchronized public boolean makeBurrito() {
    // Burritos require one serving of each item
    if (cheese > 0 && rice > 0 && beans > 0 && chicken > 0) {
      cheese--; rice--; beans--; chicken--;
      return true;  // can make the burrito
    }
    else {
      // Could order more ingredients
      return false;  // cannot make the burrito
    }
  }

  // Display the current inventory count.
  public void doGet(HttpServletRequest req, HttpServletResponse res)
                              throws ServletException, IOException {
    res.setContentType("text/html");
    PrintWriter out = res.getWriter();

    out.println("<HTML><HEAD><TITLE>Current Ingredients</TITLE></HEAD>");
    out.println("<BODY>");
    out.println("<TABLE BORDER=1>");
    out.println("<TR><TH COLSPAN=2>Current ingredients:</TH></TR>");
    out.println("<TR><TD>Cheese:</TD><TD>" + cheese + "</TD></TR>");
```

Example 11-10. The shared burrito inventory class, rewriten as a servlet (continued)

```java
    out.println("<TR><TD>Rice:</TD><TD>" + rice + "</TD></TR>");
    out.println("<TR><TD>Beans:</TD><TD>" + beans + "</TD></TR>");
    out.println("<TR><TD>Chicken:</TD><TD>" + chicken + "</TD></TR>");
    out.println("</TABLE>");
    out.println("</BODY></HTML>");
  }

  // Load the stored inventory count
  public void init(ServletConfig config) throws ServletException {
    super.init(config);
    loadState();
  }

  public void loadState() {
    // Try to load the counts
    FileInputStream file = null;
    try {
      file = new FileInputStream("BurritoInventoryServlet.state");
      DataInputStream in = new DataInputStream(file);
      cheese = in.readInt();
      rice = in.readInt();
      beans = in.readInt();
      chicken = in.readInt();
      file.close();
      return;
    }
    catch (IOException ignored) {
      // Problem during read
    }
    finally {
      try { if (file != null) file.close(); }
      catch (IOException ignored) { }
    }
  }

  public void destroy() {
    saveState();
  }

  public void saveState() {
    // Try to save the counts
    FileOutputStream file = null;
    try {
      file = new FileOutputStream("BurritoInventoryServlet.state");
      DataOutputStream out = new DataOutputStream(file);
      out.writeInt(cheese);
      out.writeInt(rice);
      out.writeInt(beans);
```

Example 11-10. The shared burrito inventory class, rewriten as a servlet (continued)

```
        out.writeInt(chicken);
        return;
      }
      catch (IOException ignored) {
        // Problem during write
      }
      finally {
        try { if (file != null) file.close(); }
        catch (IOException ignored) { }
      }
    }
}
```

`BurritoInventoryServlet` is no longer a singleton: it's now a normal HTTP servlet. It defines an `init()` method that loads its state and a `destroy()` method that saves its state. It also defines a `doGet()` method that displays its state, as shown in Figure 11-5.

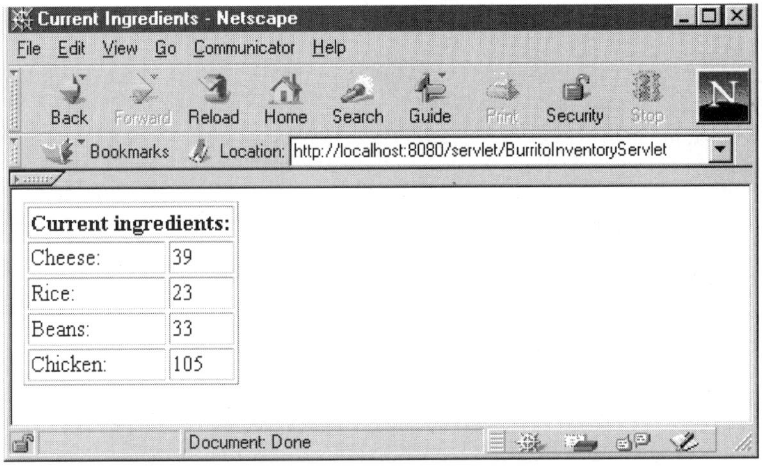

Figure 11-5. The output from BurritoInventoryServlet, showing its state

Remember that, even as a servlet, the *BurritoInventoryServlet.class* file should remain in the server's standard classpath to keep it from being reloaded.

The `BurritoInventoryProducer` and `BurritoInventoryConsumer` classes can get a reference to the `BurritoInventoryServlet` using the technique discussed earlier in this chapter for servlet reuse:

```
// Get the inventory servlet instance if we haven't before
if (inventory == null) {
  inventory = (BurritoInventoryServlet)ServletUtils.getServlet(
              "BurritoInventoryServlet", req, getServletContext());
```

```
      // If the load was unsuccessful, throw an exception
      if (inventory == null) {
        throw new ServletException(
                "Could not locate BurritoInventoryServlet");
      }
    }
```

Instead of calling `BurritoInventory.getInstance()`, the producer and consumer classes can ask the server for the `BurritoInventoryServlet` instance.

Collaboration Through Inheritance

Perhaps the easiest technique for servlet collaboration is through inheritance. Each servlet interested in collaborating can extend the same class and inherit the same shared information. This simplifies the code for the collaborating servlets and limits access to the shared information to the proper subclasses. The common superclass can hold a reference to the shared information, or it can hold the shared information itself.

Inheriting a shared reference

A common superclass can hold any number of references to shared business objects that are easily made available to its subclasses. Example 11-11 shows such a superclass, usable for our burrito inventory example.

Example 11-11. A superclass holding a reference to shared information

```
import javax.servlet.*;
import javax.servlet.http.*;

public class BurritoInventorySuperclass extends HttpServlet {
  protected static BurritoInventory inventory = new BurritoInventory();
}
```

This `BurritoInventorySuperclass` creates a new `BurritoInventory` instance. `BurritoInventoryProducer` and `BurritoInventoryConsumer` can then subclass `BurritoInventorySuperclass` and inherit a reference to this instance. The code for the revised `BurritoInventoryConsumer` is shown in Example 11-12 to clarify.

Example 11-12. Using an inherited business object

```
import java.io.*;
import javax.servlet.*;
import javax.servlet.http.*;

public class BurritoInventoryConsumer extends BurritoInventorySuperclass {
```

Example 11-12. Using an inherited business object (continued)

```
public void doGet(HttpServletRequest req, HttpServletResponse res)
                            throws ServletException, IOException {
  res.setContentType("text/html");
  PrintWriter out = res.getWriter();

  out.println("<HTML>");
  out.println("<HEAD><TITLE>Burrito Inventory Consumer</TITLE></HEAD>");

  out.println("<BODY><BIG>");

  if (inventory.makeBurrito()) {
    out.println("Your burrito will be ready in 3 minutes.");
  }
  else {
    out.println("We're low on ingredients.<BR>");
    out.println("Looks like you're gonna starve.");
  }

  out.println("</BIG></BODY></HTML>");
  }
}
```

The `BurritoInventory` class doesn't have to be a singleton anymore. The
subclasses naturally inherit the same instance. Again, the class file for `BurritoIn-`
`ventorySuperclass` should be put in the server's classpath to keep it from being
reloaded.

Inheriting the shared information

In addition to holding shared references, a common superclass can hold shared
information itself and optionally make it available through inherited business logic
methods. Example 11-13 shows `BurritoInventorySuperclass` rewritten using
this technique. It's essentially an alternate form of `BurritoInventoryServlet`.

Example 11-13. A superclass holding its own shared information

```
public class BurritoInventorySuperclass extends HttpServlet {

  // How many "servings" of each item do we have?
  private static int cheese = 0;
  private static int rice = 0;
  private static int beans = 0;
  private static int chicken = 0;

  // Add to the inventory as more servings are prepared.
```

Example 11-13. A superclass holding its own shared information (continued)

```
protected static void addCheese(int added) { cheese += added; }
protected static void addRice(int added) { rice += added; }
protected static void addBeans(int added) { beans += added; }
protected static void addChicken(int added) { chicken += added; }

// Called when it's time to make a burrito.
// Returns true if there are enough ingredients to make the burrito,
// false if not. Decrements the ingredient count when there are enough.
synchronized static protected boolean makeBurrito() {
    // ...etc...
}


// ...The rest matches BurritoInventoryServlet...
```

There are only two differences between this servlet superclass and `BurritoInventoryServlet`. First, all the variables and methods are now static. This guarantees that there's just one inventory kept for all the subclasses. Second, all the methods are now protected. This makes them available only to subclasses. By inheriting from a superclass that contains the shared information, `BurritoInventoryProducer` and `BurritoInventoryConsumer` can call the inventory methods directly. For example, `BurritoInventoryProducer` can add items to the inventory with this code:

```
// Add the items to the inventory
addCheese(cheese);
addRice(rice);
addBeans(beans);
addChicken(chicken);
```

`BurritoInventoryConsumer` can consume the ingredients with this code:

```
if (makeBurrito())
```

Recap

To summarize, there are three sorts of interservlet communication:

- Servlet manipulation, where one servlet directly invokes the methods of another. These servlets can get references to other servlets using `getServletNames()` and `getServlet(String name)`, but they must be careful not to use stale references to servlets that have been reloaded.

- Servlet reuse, where one servlet uses another's abilities for its own purposes. In some cases, this requires forcing a servlet load using a manual HTTP request. These servlets also have to be careful not to use stale references.

- Servlet collaboration, where cooperating servlets share information. Servlets can share information using the system properties list (saving strings or objects), using a shared object (a singleton found in the server's classpath), or using inheritance.

12

Internationalization

Despite its name, the World Wide Web has a long way to go before it can be considered to truly extend worldwide. Sure, physical wires carry web content to nearly every country across the globe. But to be considered a true worldwide resource, that web content has to be readable to the person receiving it—something that often doesn't occur with today's large number of English-only web pages.

The situation is starting to change, however. Many of the largest web sites have established areas designed for non-English languages. For example, the Netscape home page is available to English speakers at *http://home.netscape.com/index.html,* to French speakers at *http://home.netscape.com/fr/index.html,* and to speakers of a dozen other languages at a dozen other URLs.

Many web servers also support a transparent solution, where a single URL can be used to view the same content in several languages, with the language chosen based on the preferences of the client. For example, the Internet Movie Database home page at *http://us.imdb.com/index.html* can be read in English, German, or French. Which language you see depends on how you've configured your browser.* Although this technique creates the impression that a dynamic translation is occurring, in reality the server just has several specially named versions of the static document at its disposal.

While these techniques work well for static documents, they don't address the problem of how to internationalize and localize dynamic content. That's the topic of this chapter. Here we explore how servlets can use the internationalization capabilities added to JDK 1.1 to truly extend the Web worldwide.

---

* Many older browsers do not support language customization, however. For example, the feature is new in Netscape Navigator 4 and Microsoft Internet Explorer 4.

First, let's discuss terminology. Internationalization (a word that's often mercifully shortened to "i18n" because it begins with an "I", ends with an "n", and has 18 letters in between) is the task of making a program flexible enough to run in any locale. Localization (often shortened to "l10n") is the process of arranging for a program to run in a specific locale. This chapter, for the most part, covers servlet internationalization. We'll cover localization only in the case of dates, times, numbers, and other objects for which Java has built-in localization support.

Western European Languages

Let's begin with a look at how a servlet outputs a page written in a Western European language such as English, Spanish, German, French, Italian, Dutch, Norwegian, Finnish, or Swedish. As our example, we'll say "Hello World!" in Spanish, generating a page similar to the one shown in Figure 12-1.

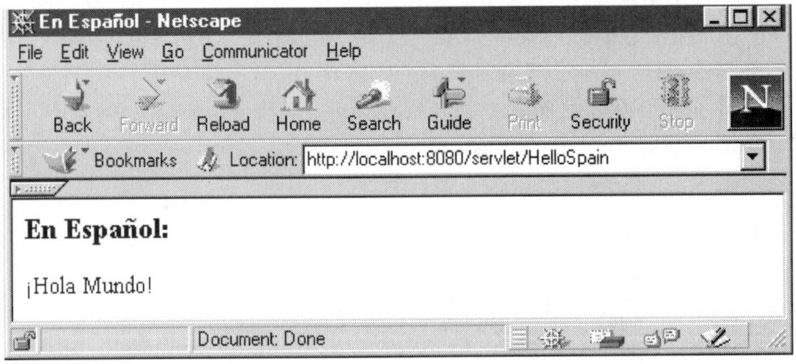

Figure 12-1. En Español: ¡Hola Mundo!

Notice the use of the special characters "ñ" and "¡". Characters such as these, while scarce in English, are prevalent in Western European languages. Servlets have two ways to generate these characters: with HTML character entities or Unicode escape sequences.

HTML Character Entities

HTML 2.0 introduced the ability for specific sequences of characters in an HTML page to be displayed as a single character. The sequences, called *character entities*, begin with an ampersand (&) and end with a semi-colon (;). Character entities can either be named or numbered. For example, the named character entity "ñ" represents "ñ", while "¡" represents "¡". A complete listing

of special characters and their names is given in Appendix D, *Character Entities.*
Example 12-1 shows a servlet that uses named entities to say hello in Spanish.

Example 12-1. Hello to Spanish speakers, using named character entities

```
import java.io.*;
import javax.servlet.*;
import javax.servlet.http.*;

public class HelloSpain extends HttpServlet {

  public void doGet(HttpServletRequest req, HttpServletResponse res)
                              throws ServletException, IOException {
    res.setContentType("text/html");
    PrintWriter out = res.getWriter();
    res.setHeader("Content-Language", "es");

    out.println("<HTML><HEAD><TITLE>En Espa&ntilde;ol</TITLE></HEAD>");
    out.println("<BODY>");
    out.println("<H3>En Espa&ntilde;ol:</H3>");
    out.println("&iexcl;Hola Mundo!");
    out.println("</BODY></HTML>");
  }
}
```

You may have noticed that, in addition to using character entities, this servlet sets its Content-Language header to the value "es". The Content-Language header is used to specify the language of the following entity body. In this case, the servlet uses the header to indicate to the client that the page is written in Spanish (Español). Most clients ignore this information, but it's polite to send it anyway. Languages are always represented using two-character lowercase abbreviations. For a complete listing, see the ISO-639 standard at *http://www.ics.uci.edu/pub/ietf/http/related/iso639.txt.*

Character entities can also be referenced by number. For example, "ñ" represents "ñ", and "¡" represents "¡". The number corresponds to the character's ISO-8859-1 (Latin-1) decimal value, which you will hear more about later in this chapter. A complete listing of the numeric values for character entities can also be found in Appendix D. Example 12-2 shows HelloSpain rewritten using numeric entities.

Example 12-2. Hello to Spanish speakers, using numbered character entities

```
import java.io.*;
import javax.servlet.*;
import javax.servlet.http.*;

public class HelloSpain extends HttpServlet {
```

Example 12-2. Hello to Spanish speakers, using numbered character entities (continued)

```
public void doGet(HttpServletRequest req, HttpServletResponse res)
                        throws ServletException, IOException {
  res.setContentType("text/html");
  PrintWriter out = res.getWriter();
  res.setHeader("Content-Language", "es");

  out.println("<HTML><HEAD><TITLE>En Espa&#241;ol</TITLE></HEAD>");
  out.println("<BODY>");
  out.println("<H3>En Espa&#241;ol:</H3>");
  out.println("&#161;Hola Mundo!");
  out.println("</BODY></HTML>");
  }
}
```

Unfortunately, there's one major problem with the use of character entities: they work only for HTML pages. If the servlet's output isn't HTML, the page looks something like Figure 12-2. To handle non-HTML output, we need to use Unicode escapes.

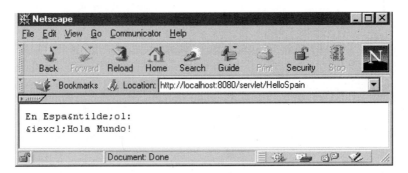

Figure 12-2. Not quite Spanish

Unicode Escapes

In Java, all characters, strings, and identifiers are internally composed of 16-bit (2-byte) Unicode characters. Unicode was established by the Unicode Consortium, which describes the standard as follows (see *http://www.unicode. org/unicode/standard/standard.html*):

> The Unicode Worldwide Character Standard is a character coding system designed to support the interchange, processing, and display of the written texts of the diverse languages of the modern world. In addition, it supports classical and historical texts of many written languages.
>
> In its current version (2.0), the Unicode standard contains 38,885 distinct coded characters derived from the Supported Scripts. These characters cover the prin-

cipal written languages of the Americas, Europe, the Middle East, Africa, India, Asia, and Pacifica.

For more information on Unicode see *http://www.unicode.org*. Also see *The Unicode Standard, Version 2.0* (Addison-Wesley).

Java's use of Unicode is very important to this chapter because it means a servlet can internally represent essentially any character in any commonly used written language. We can represent 16-bit Unicode characters in 7-bit US-ASCII source code using Unicode escapes of the form \u*xxxx*, where *xxxx* is a sequence of four hexadecimal digits. The Java compiler interprets each Unicode escape sequence as a single character.

Conveniently, and not coincidentally, the first 256 characters of Unicode (\u0000 to \u00ff) correspond to the 256 characters of ISO-8859-1 (Latin-1). Thus, the "ñ" character can be written as \u00f1 and the "¡" character can be written as \u00a1. A complete listing of the Unicode escape sequences for ISO-8859-1 characters is also included in Appendix D. Example 12-3 shows `HelloSpain` rewritten using Unicode escapes.

Example 12-3. Hello to Spanish speakers, using Unicode escapes

```
import java.io.*;
import javax.servlet.*;
import javax.servlet.http.*;

public class HelloSpain extends HttpServlet {

  public void doGet(HttpServletRequest req, HttpServletResponse res)
                             throws ServletException, IOException {
    res.setContentType("text/plain");
    PrintWriter out = res.getWriter();
    res.setHeader("Content-Language", "es");

    out.println("En Espa\u00f1ol:");
    out.println("\u00a1Hola Mundo!");
  }
}
```

The output from this servlet displays correctly when used as part of an HTML page or when used for plain-text output.

Conforming to Local Customs

Now we know how to use HTML character entities and Unicode escapes to display the characters in Western European languages. The question remains, what do we say with these languages? In general, this is a translation problem best left to a dedicated localization team. In some instances, however, Java provides some help.

For example, let's assume that in addition to saying "Hello World," we need our example servlet to tell the current time in a format naturally understood by the recipient. What could be a difficult formatting problem is actually quite easy because JDK 1.1 provides built-in support for localizing dynamic objects such as dates and times.

The trick is to use a `java.text.DateFormat` instance appropriate for the target audience. A `DateFormat` object can convert a `Date` to a correctly localized `String`. For example, a time stamp written in English as "February 16, 1998 12:36:18 PM PST" would be written in Spanish as "16 de febrero de 1998 12:36:18 GMT-08:00."

A `DateFormat` object is created using a factory method that accepts a formatting style (short, medium, long, full) and a `java.util.Locale` object that identifies the target audience (U.S. English, Mainland Chinese, etc.). The most common `Locale` constructor accepts two parameters: a two-character lowercase language abbreviation (as we saw earlier) and a two-character uppercase country code as defined by ISO-3166 (available at *http://www.chemie.fu-berlin.de/diverse/doc/ISO_3166.html*). An empty string for the country code indicates the default country for the language.

Example 12-4 shows the `HelloSpain` servlet using a `DateFormat` object to print the current time in a format naturally understood by a Spanish-speaking recipient.

Example 12-4. Hello to Spanish speakers, with the localized time

```
import java.io.*;
import java.text.*;
import java.util.*;
import javax.servlet.*;
import javax.servlet.http.*;

public class HelloSpain extends HttpServlet {

  public void doGet(HttpServletRequest req, HttpServletResponse res)
                            throws ServletException, IOException {
    res.setContentType("text/plain");
    PrintWriter out = res.getWriter();
    res.setHeader("Content-Language", "es");

    Locale locale = new Locale("es", "");
    DateFormat fmt = DateFormat.getDateTimeInstance(DateFormat.LONG,
                                                    DateFormat.LONG,
                                                    locale);
    fmt.setTimeZone(TimeZone.getDefault());
```

Example 12-4. Hello to Spanish speakers, with the localized time (continued)

```
    out.println("En Espa\u00f1ol:");
    out.println("\u00a1Hola Mundo!");
    out.println(fmt.format(new Date()));
  }
}
```

This servlet first creates a `Locale` that represents a generic Spanish environment. Then it uses that `Locale` to create a `DateFormat` instance that formats dates in Spanish. Next, it sets the time zone to the default time zone (the time zone of the server). The reason is that, by default, a `DateFormat` object formats its times to match the time zone in which it assumes the intended recipient is located, in this case Spain. Because this servlet can't be sure that's a correct assumption, it overrides the default and sets the time zone to match the server's. It would be better, of course, to set the time zone to accurately match the client's location, but that's not currently possible without additional user-provided information. Finally, after saying its "Hello World," this servlet prints the correctly formatted date and time. The output is shown in Figure 12-3.

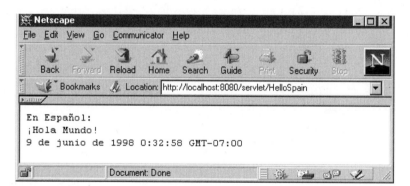

Figure 12-3. Hola Tiempo

This example provides just a glimpse of the dynamic formatting capabilities of Java. If you're interested in more complicated formatting, there are several other classes in the `java.text` package you may find useful. Look especially at those that extend `java.text.Format`.

Non-Western European Languages

Let's continue now with a look at how a servlet outputs a page written in a non-Western European language, such as Russian, Japanese, Chinese, Korean, or Hebrew. To understand how to work with these languages, we must first understand how things work behind the scenes of our previous examples.

Charsets

Let's begin looking at the situation from the perspective of the browser. Imagine having the browser's job. You make an HTTP request to some URL and receive a response. That response, in the basest terms, is nothing more than a long sequence of bytes. How do you know how to display that response?

A common way, and in fact the default way, is to assume that every byte represents one of 256 possible characters and to further assume that the character a byte represents can be determined by looking up the byte value in some table. The default table is specified by the ISO-8859-1 standard, also called Latin-1. It contains byte-to-character mappings for the characters most commonly used in Western European languages. So, by default, you (acting as the browser) can receive a sequence of bytes and convert them to a sequence of Western European characters.

Now what do you do if you want to receive text that isn't written in a Western European language? You have to take the long sequence of bytes in the response and interpret it differently, using some other byte-sequence to character mapping. Technically put, you need to use a different *charset*.* There are an infinite number of potential charsets. Fortunately, there are only a few dozen that are commonly used.

Some charsets use single-byte characters in a fashion similar to ISO-8859-1, though with a different byte-to-character mapping. For example, ISO-8859-5 defines a byte-to-character mapping for the characters of the Cyrillic (Russian) alphabet, while ISO-8859-8 defines a mapping for the Hebrew alphabet.†

Other charsets use multibyte characters, where it may take more than one byte to represent a single character. This is most common with languages that contain thousands of characters, such as Chinese, Japanese, and Korean—often referred to collectively as CJK. Charsets used to display these languages include Big5 (Chinese), Shift_JIS (Japanese), and EUC-KR (Korean). A table listing languages and their corresponding charsets can be found in Appendix E, *Charsets*.

What this boils down to is that if you (as the browser again) know the charset in which the response was encoded, you can determine how to interpret the bytes you receive. Just one question remains: how can you determine the charset? You can do it in one of two ways. First, you can require your user to tell you the charset. With Netscape Navigator 3, this is done through **Options | Document Encoding**;

---

* A charset (a byte-sequence to character mapping) is not the same as a character set (a set of characters). See RFC 2278 at *http://www.ietf.org/rfc/rfc2278.txt* for a full explanation.

† It's useful to note that, for nearly all charsets, the byte values between 0 and 127 decimal represent the standard US-ASCII characters, allowing English text to be added to a page written in nearly any language.

with Netscape Navigator 4, it is done through **View | Encoding**. With Microsoft Internet Explorer 4, it's done through **View | Fonts**. This approach often requires the user to try a few charsets until the display makes sense. The second possibility is that the server (or servlet) specifies the charset in the `Content-Type` header you receive. For example, the following `Content-Type` value:

```
text/html; charset=Shift_JIS
```

indicates that the charset is Shift_JIS. Unfortunately, a few older browsers can be confused by the inclusion of a charset in the `Content-Type` header.

Writing Encoded Output

Now that we understand charsets from the perspective of the browser, it's time to return to the perspective of the servlet. A servlet's role is to do the following:

1. Choose a charset and set it for the servlet

2. Get a `PrintWriter` for that charset

3. Output characters that can be displayed using that charset

Example 12-5 demonstrates with a servlet that says "Hello World" and displays the current date and time in Japanese. A screen shot is shown in Figure 12-4.

Example 12-5. Hello to Japanese speakers

```java
import java.io.*;
import java.text.*;
import java.util.*;
import javax.servlet.*;
import javax.servlet.http.*;

public class HelloJapan extends HttpServlet {

  public void doGet(HttpServletRequest req, HttpServletResponse res)
                            throws ServletException, IOException {
    res.setContentType("text/plain; charset=Shift_JIS");
    PrintWriter out = res.getWriter();
    res.setHeader("Content-Language", "ja");

    Locale locale = new Locale("ja", "");
    DateFormat full = DateFormat.getDateTimeInstance(DateFormat.LONG,
                                                     DateFormat.LONG,
                                                     locale);
    out.println("In Japanese:");
    out.println("\u4eca\u65e5\u306f\u4e16\u754c");  // Hello World
    out.println(full.format(new Date()));
  }
}
```

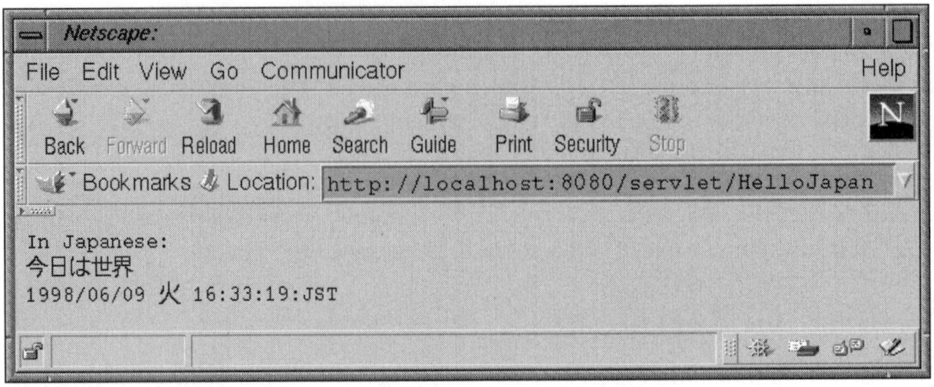

Figure 12-4. A Japanese Hello

This servlet starts by setting the content type to `"text/plain"` and the charset to `"Shift_JIS"`. Then it calls `res.getWriter()` just like always—except in this case the `PrintWriter` it receives is special. This `PrintWriter` encodes all the servlet's output in the Shift_JIS charset because that charset is specified in the `Content-Type` header. This second line is therefore equivalent to the following:

```
PrintWriter out = new PrintWriter(
    new OutputStreamWriter(res.getOutputStream(), "Shift_JIS"), true);
```

Note that the call to `res.getWriter()` may throw an `UnsupportedEncodingException` if the charset is not recognized by Java[*] or an `IllegalStateException` if `getOutputStream()` has been called already on this request.

The servlet next creates a `Locale` with the language `"ja"` to represent a generic Japanese environment and then creates a `DateFormat` to match. Finally, it prints the equivalent of "Hello World" in Japanese, using Unicode escapes for the characters, and outputs the current date and time.

For this servlet to work, your server's classpath must include the `sun.io.CharToByte*` converter classes or their equivalent. On some platforms, these are not always included by default. Also, for the Japanese glyphs (or glyphs from other languages) to display correctly in the browser, the browser has to support the charset and have access to the necessary fonts to display the charset.

For more information on the internationalization capabilities of Netscape Navigator, see *http://home.netscape.com/eng/intl/index.html*. For more information on the capabilities of Microsoft Internet Explorer, see *http://www.microsoft.com/ie/intlhome.htm*.

---

[*] With some early versions of Java, it may in some situations erroneously throw an `IllegalArgument-Exception` if the charset is not recognized.

Reading and Writing Encoded Output

It can often be prohibitively slow to enter hundreds or thousands of Unicode escapes manually in Java source files. An easier option is to read localized text from an encoded file. For example, let's assume the "Hello World" Japanese text we want to output is saved by someone on the localization team in a file named *HelloWorld.ISO-2022-JP*, using the ISO-2022-JP encoding to make things more interesting. A servlet can read this file and send the content to the browser using the Shift_JIS encoding, as shown in Example 12-6.

Example 12-6. Sending localized output read from a file

```
import java.io.*;
import java.text.*;
import java.util.*;
import javax.servlet.*;
import javax.servlet.http.*;

public class HelloJapanReader extends HttpServlet {

  public void doGet(HttpServletRequest req, HttpServletResponse res)
                            throws ServletException, IOException {
    res.setContentType("text/plain; charset=Shift_JIS");
    PrintWriter out = res.getWriter();
    res.setHeader("Content-Language", "ja");

    Locale locale = new Locale("ja", "");
    DateFormat full = DateFormat.getDateTimeInstance(DateFormat.LONG,
                                          DateFormat.LONG,
                                          locale);
    out.println("In Japanese:");

    try {
      FileInputStream fis =
        new FileInputStream(req.getRealPath("/HelloWorld.ISO-2022-JP"));
      InputStreamReader isr = new InputStreamReader(fis, "ISO-2022-JP");
      BufferedReader reader = new BufferedReader(isr);
      String line = null;
      while ((line = reader.readLine()) != null) {
        out.println(line);
      }
    }
    catch (FileNotFoundException e) {
      // No Hello for you
    }

    out.println(full.format(new Date()));
  }
}
```

This servlet is essentially a character encoding converter. It reads the *HelloWorld.ISO-2022-JP* text encoded with ISO-2022-JP and internally converts it to Unicode. Then, it outputs the same text by converting from Unicode to Shift_JIS.

Multiple Languages

Now it's time to push the envelope a little and attempt something that has only recently become possible. Let's write a servlet that includes several languages on the same page. In a sense, we have already written such a servlet. Our last example, HelloJapan, included both English and Japanese text. It should be observed, however, that this is a special case. Adding English text to a page is almost always possible, due to the convenient fact that nearly all charsets include the 128 U.S.-ASCII characters. In the more general case, when the text on a page contains a mix of languages and none of the previously mentioned charsets contains all the necessary characters, we require an alternate technique.

UCS-2 and UTF-8

The best way to generate a page containing multiple languages is to output 16-bit Unicode characters to the client. There are two common ways to do this: UCS-2 and UTF-8. UCS-2 (Universal Character Set, 2-byte form) sends Unicode characters in what could be called their natural format, two bytes per character. All characters, including US-ASCII characters, require two bytes. UTF-8 (UCS Transformation Format, 8-bit form) is a variable-length encoding. With UTF-8, a Unicode character is transformed into a 1-, 2-, or 3-byte representation. In general, UTF-8 tends to be more efficient than UCS-2 because it can encode a character from the US-ASCII charset using just 1 byte. For this reason, the use of UTF-8 on the Web far exceeds UCS-2. For more information on UTF-8, see RFC 2279 at *http://www.ietf.org/rfc/rfc2279.txt.*

Before we proceed, you should know that support for UTF-8 is just beginning to appear on the Web. Netscape first added support for the UTF-8 encoding in Netscape Navigator 4, and Microsoft first added support in Internet Explorer 4.

Writing UTF-8

Example 12-7 shows a servlet that uses the UTF-8 encoding to say "Hello World!" and tell the current time (in the local time zone) in English, Spanish, Japanese,

Chinese, Korean, and Russian. A screen shot of the servlet's output is shown in Figure 12-5.

Example 12-7. A servlet version of the Rosetta Stone

```java
import java.io.*;
import java.text.*;
import java.util.*;
import javax.servlet.*;
import javax.servlet.http.*;

import com.oreilly.servlet.ServletUtils;

public class HelloRosetta extends HttpServlet {

  public void doGet(HttpServletRequest req, HttpServletResponse res)
                            throws ServletException, IOException {
    Locale locale;
    DateFormat full;

    try {
      res.setContentType("text/plain; charset=UTF-8");
      PrintWriter out = res.getWriter();

      locale = new Locale("en", "US");
      full = DateFormat.getDateTimeInstance(DateFormat.LONG,
                                            DateFormat.LONG,
                                            locale);
      out.println("In English appropriate for the US:");
      out.println("Hello World!");
      out.println(full.format(new Date()));
      out.println();

      locale = new Locale("es", "");
      full = DateFormat.getDateTimeInstance(DateFormat.LONG,
                                            DateFormat.LONG,
                                            locale);
      out.println("En Espa\u00f1ol:");
      out.println("\u00a1Hola Mundo!");
      out.println(full.format(new Date()));
      out.println();

      locale = new Locale("ja", "");
      full = DateFormat.getDateTimeInstance(DateFormat.LONG,
                                            DateFormat.LONG,
                                            locale);
      out.println("In Japanese:");
      out.println("\u4eca\u65e5\u306f\u4e16\u754c");
      out.println(full.format(new Date()));
```

Example 12-7. A servlet version of the Rosetta Stone (continued)

```
        out.println();

        locale = new Locale("zh", "");
        full = DateFormat.getDateTimeInstance(DateFormat.LONG,
                                              DateFormat.LONG,
                                              locale);
      out.println("In Chinese:");
      out.println("\u4f60\u597d\u4e16\u754c");
      out.println(full.format(new Date()));
      out.println();

        locale = new Locale("ko", "");
        full = DateFormat.getDateTimeInstance(DateFormat.LONG,
                                              DateFormat.LONG,
                                              locale);
      out.println("In Korean:");
      out.println("\uc548\ub155\ud558\uc138\uc694\uc138\uacc4");
      out.println(full.format(new Date()));
      out.println();

        locale = new Locale("ru", "");
        full = DateFormat.getDateTimeInstance(DateFormat.LONG,
                                              DateFormat.LONG,
                                              locale);
      out.println("In Russian (Cyrillic):");
      out.print("\u0417\u0434\u0440\u0430\u0432\u0441\u0442");
      out.println("\u0432\u0443\u0439, \u041c\u0438\u0440");
      out.println(full.format(new Date()));
      out.println();
    }
    catch (Exception e) {
      log(ServletUtils.getStackTraceAsString(e));
    }
  }
}
```

For this servlet to work as written, your server must support JDK 1.1.6 or later. Earlier versions of Java throw an `UnsupportedEncodingException` when trying to get the `PrintWriter`, and the page is left blank. The problem is a missing charset alias. Java has had support for the UTF-8 encoding since JDK 1.1 was first introduced. Unfortunately, the JDK used the name "UTF8" for the encoding, while browsers expect the name "UTF-8." So, who's right? It wasn't clear until early 1998, when the IANA (Internet Assigned Numbers Authority) declared "UTF-8" to be the preferred name. (See *http://www.isi.edu/in-notes/iana/assignments/character-sets.*) Shortly thereafter, JDK 1.1.6 added "UTF-8" as an alternate alias for the

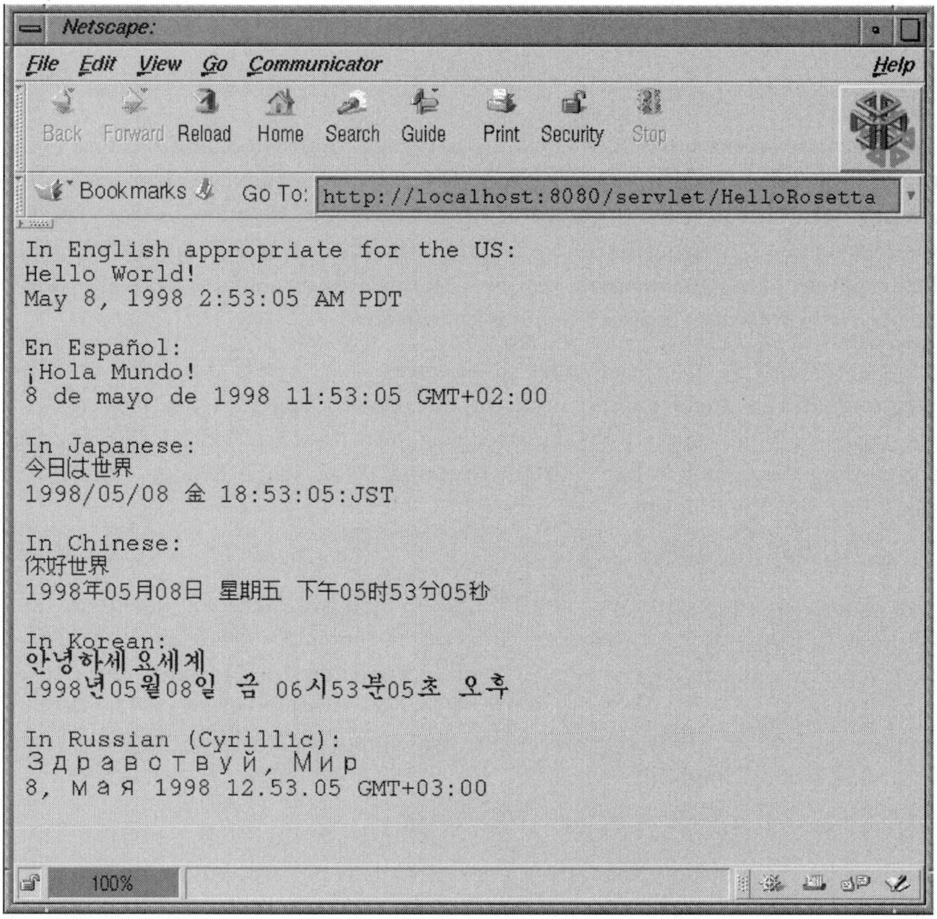
Netscape:
File Edit View Go Communicator Help
Back Forward Reload Home Search Guide Print Security Stop
Bookmarks Go To: http://localhost:8080/servlet/HelloRosetta
In English appropriate for the US:
Hello World!
May 8, 1998 2:53:05 AM PDT
En Español:
¡Hola Mundo!
8 de mayo de 1998 11:53:05 GMT+02:00
In Japanese:
今日は世界
1998/05/08 金 18:53:05:JST
In Chinese:
你好世界
1998年05月08日 星期五 下午05时53分05秒
In Korean:
안녕하세요세계
1998년05월08일 금 06시53분05초 오후
In Russian (Cyrillic):
Здравствуй, Мир
8, мая 1998 12.53.05 GMT+03:00
100%

Figure 12-5. A true hello world

"UTF8" encoding. For maximum portability across Java versions, you can use the "UTF8" name directly with the following code:

```
res.setContentType("text/html; charset=UTF-8");
PrintWriter out = new PrintWriter(
  new OutputStreamWriter(res.getOutputStream(), "UTF8"), true);
```

Also, your client must support the UTF-8 encoding and have access to all the necessary fonts. Otherwise, some of your output is likely to appear garbled.

Dynamic Language Negotiation

Now let's push the envelope yet a little farther (perhaps off the edge of the table) with a servlet that tailors its output to match the language preferences of the client. This allows the same URL to serve its content to readers across the globe in their native tongues.

Language Preferences

There are two ways a servlet can know the language preferences of the client. First, the browser can send the information as part of its request. Newer browsers, such as Netscape Navigator 4 and Microsoft Internet Explorer 4, allow users to specify their preferred languages. With Netscape Navigator 4, this is done under **Edit | Preferences | Navigator | Languages**. With Microsoft Internet Explorer 4, it's done under **View | Internet Options | General | Languages**.

A browser sends the user's language preferences to the server using the Accept-Language HTTP header. The value of this header specifies the language or languages that the client prefers to receive. Note that the HTTP specification allows this preference to be ignored. An Accept-Language header value looks something like the following:

```
en, es, de, ja, zh-TW
```

This indicates the client user reads English, Spanish, German, Japanese, and Chinese appropriate for Taiwan. By convention, languages are listed in order of preference. Each language may also include a *q-value* that indicates, on a scale from 0.0 to 1.0, an estimate of the user's preference for that language. The default q-value is 1.0 (maximum preference). An Accept-Language header value including q-values looks like this:

```
en, es;q=0.8, de;q=0.7, ja;q=0.3, zh-TW;q=0.1
```

This header value means essentially the same thing as the previous example.

The second way a servlet can know the language preferences of the client is by asking. For example, a servlet might generate a form that asks which language the client prefers. Thereafter, it can remember and use the answer, perhaps using the session tracking techniques discussed in Chapter 7, *Session Tracking*.

Charset Preferences

In addition to an Accept-Language HTTP header, a browser may send an Accept-Charset header that tells the server which charsets it understands. An Accept-Charset header value may look something like this:

```
iso-8859-1, utf-8
```

This indicates the browser understands ISO-8859-1 and UTF-8. If the Accept-Charset isn't sent or if its value contains an asterisk (*), it can be assumed the client accepts all charsets. Note that the current usefulness of this header is limited: few browsers yet send the header, and those browsers that do tend to send a value that contains an asterisk.

Resource Bundles

Using `Accept-Language` (and, in some cases, `Accept-Charset`), a servlet can determine the language in which it will speak to each client. But how can a servlet efficiently manage several localized versions of a page? One answer is to use Java's built-in support for resource bundles.

A resource bundle holds a set of localized resources appropriate for a given locale. For example, a resource bundle for the French locale might contain a French translation of all the phrases output by a servlet. Then, when the servlet determines it wants to speak French, it can load that resource bundle and use the stored phrases. All resource bundles extend `java.util.ResourceBundle`. A servlet can load a resource bundle using the static method `ResourceBundle.getBundle()`:

```
public static final
    ResourceBundle ResourceBundle.getBundle(String bundleName, Locale locale)
```

A servlet can pull phrases from a resource bundle using the `getString()` method of `ResourceBundle`:

```
public final String ResourceBundle.getString(String key)
```

A resource bundle can be created in several ways. For servlets, the most useful technique is to put a special properties file in the server's classpath that contains the translated phrases. The file should be specially named according to the pattern *bundlename_language.properties* or *bundlename_language_country.properties*. For example, use *Messages_fr.properties* for a French bundle or *Messages_zh_TW.properties* for a Chinese/Taiwan bundle. The file should contain US-ASCII characters in the following format:

```
name1=value1
name2=value2
...
```

Each line may also contain whitespace and Unicode escapes. The information in this file can be loaded automatically by the `getBundle()` method.

Writing To Each His Own

Example 12-8 demonstrates the use of `Accept-Language`, `Accept-Charset`, and resource bundles with a servlet that says "Hello World" to each client in that client's own preferred language. Here's a sample resource bundle properties file for English, which you would store in *HelloBabel_en.properties* somewhere in the server's classpath (such as *server_root/classes*):

```
greeting=Hello world
```

And here's a resource bundle for Japanese, to be stored in *HelloBabel_ja.properties*:

```
greeting=\u4eca\u65e5\u306f\u4e16\u754c
```

This `HelloBabel` servlet uses the `com.oreilly.servlet.LocaleNegotiator` class that contains the black box logic to determine which `Locale`, charset, and `ResourceBundle` should be used. Its code is shown in the next section.

Example 12-8. A servlet version of the Tower of Babel

```
import java.io.*;
import java.util.*;
import java.text.*;
import javax.servlet.*;
import javax.servlet.http.*;

import com.oreilly.servlet.LocaleNegotiator;
import com.oreilly.servlet.ServletUtils;

public class HelloBabel extends HttpServlet {

  public void doGet(HttpServletRequest req, HttpServletResponse res)
                          throws ServletException, IOException {
    try {
      String bundleName = "HelloBabel";
      String acceptLanguage = req.getHeader("Accept-Language");
      String acceptCharset = req.getHeader("Accept-Charset");

      LocaleNegotiator negotiator =
        new LocaleNegotiator(bundleName, acceptLanguage, acceptCharset);

      Locale locale = negotiator.getLocale();
      String charset = negotiator.getCharset();
      ResourceBundle bundle = negotiator.getBundle();  // may be null

      res.setContentType("text/plain; charset=" + charset);
      res.setHeader("Content-Language", locale.getLanguage());
      res.setHeader("Vary", "Accept-Language");

      PrintWriter out = res.getWriter();

      DateFormat fmt = DateFormat.getDateTimeInstance(DateFormat.LONG,
                                                DateFormat.LONG,
                                                locale);
      if (bundle != null) {
        out.println("In " + locale.getDisplayLanguage() + ":");
```

Example 12-8. A servlet version of the Tower of Babel (continued)

```
        out.println(bundle.getString("greeting"));
        out.println(fmt.format(new Date()));
      }
      else {
        out.println("Bundle could not be found.");
      }
    }
    catch (Exception e) {
      log(ServletUtils.getStackTraceAsString(e));
    }
  }
}
```

This servlet begins by setting the name of the bundle it wants to use, and then it retrieves its Accept-Language and Accept-Charset headers. It creates a LocaleNegotiator, passing in this information, and quickly asks the negotiator which Locale, charset, and ResourceBundle it is to use. Note that a servlet may ignore the returned charset in favor of the UTF-8 encoding. Just remember, UTF-8 is not as widely supported as the charsets normally returned by LocaleNegotiator. Next, the servlet sets its headers: its Content-Type header specifies the charset, Content-Language specifies the locale's language, and the Vary header indicates to the client (if by some chance it should care) that this servlet can vary its output based on the client's Accept-Language header.

Once the headers are set, the servlet generates its output. It first gets a Print-Writer to match the charset. Then it says—in the default language, usually English—which language the greeting is to be in. Next, it retrieves and outputs the appropriate greeting from the resource bundle. And lastly, it prints the date and time appropriate to the client's locale. If the resource bundle is null, as happens when there are no resource bundles to match the client's preferences, the servlet simply reports that no bundle could be found.

The LocaleNegotiator Class

The code for LocaleNegotiator is shown in Example 12-9. Its helper class, LocaleToCharsetMap, is shown in Example 12-10. If you are happy to treat the locale negotiator as a black box, feel free to skip this section.

LocaleNegotiator works by scanning through the client's language preferences looking for any language for which there is a corresponding resource bundle. Once it finds a correspondence, it uses LocaleToCharsetMap to determine the charset. If there's any problem, it tries to fall back to U.S. English. The logic ignores the client's charset preferences.

The most complicated aspect of the `LocaleNegotiator` code is having to deal
with the unfortunate behavior of `ResourceBundle.getBundle()`. The
`getBundle()` method attempts to act intelligently. If it can't find a resource
bundle that is an exact match to the specified locale, it tries to find a close match.
The problem, for our purposes, is that `getBundle()` considers the resource
bundle for the default locale to be a close match. Thus, as we loop through client
languages, it's difficult to determine when we have an exact resource bundle
match and when we don't. The workaround is to first fetch the ultimate fallback
resource bundle, then use that reference later to determine when there is an exact
match. This logic is encapsulated in the `getBundleNoFallback()` method.

Example 12-9. The LocaleNegotiator class

```
package com.oreilly.servlet;

import java.io.*;
import java.util.*;

import com.oreilly.servlet.LocaleToCharsetMap;

public class LocaleNegotiator {

  private ResourceBundle chosenBundle;
  private Locale chosenLocale;
  private String chosenCharset;

  public LocaleNegotiator(String bundleName,
                          String languages,
                          String charsets) {

    // Specify default values:
    //   English language, ISO-8859-1 (Latin-1) charset, English bundle
    Locale defaultLocale = new Locale("en", "US");
    String defaultCharset = "ISO-8859-1";
    ResourceBundle defaultBundle = null;
    try {
      defaultBundle = ResourceBundle.getBundle(bundleName, defaultLocale);
    }
    catch (MissingResourceException e) {
      // No default bundle was found. Flying without a net.
    }

    // If the client didn't specify acceptable languages, we can keep
    // the defaults.
    if (languages == null) {
      chosenLocale = defaultLocale;
      chosenCharset = defaultCharset;
      chosenBundle = defaultBundle;
```

Example 12-9. The LocaleNegotiator class (continued)

```
      return;  // quick exit
    }

    // Use a tokenizer to separate acceptable languages
    StringTokenizer tokenizer = new StringTokenizer(languages, ",");

    while (tokenizer.hasMoreTokens()) {
      // Get the next acceptable language.
      // (The language can look something like "en; qvalue=0.91")
      String lang = tokenizer.nextToken();

      // Get the locale for that language
      Locale loc = getLocaleForLanguage(lang);

      // Get the bundle for this locale. Don't let the search fallback
      // to match other languages!
      ResourceBundle bundle = getBundleNoFallback(bundleName, loc);

      // The returned bundle is null if there's no match. In that case
      // we can't use this language since the servlet can't speak it.
      if (bundle == null) continue;  // on to the next language

      // Find a charset we can use to display that locale's language.
      String charset = getCharsetForLocale(loc, charsets);

      // The returned charset is null if there's no match. In that case
      // we can't use this language since the servlet can't encode it.
      if (charset == null) continue;  // on to the next language

      // If we get here, there are no problems with this language.
      chosenLocale = loc;
      chosenBundle = bundle;
      chosenCharset = charset;
      return;  // we're done
    }

    // No matches, so we let the defaults stand
    chosenLocale = defaultLocale;
    chosenCharset = defaultCharset;
    chosenBundle = defaultBundle;
  }

  public ResourceBundle getBundle() {
    return chosenBundle;
  }

  public Locale getLocale() {
    return chosenLocale;
```

Example 12-9. The LocaleNegotiator class (continued)

```java
  }

  public String getCharset() {
    return chosenCharset;
  }

  private Locale getLocaleForLanguage(String lang) {
    Locale loc;
    int semi, dash;

    // Cut off any q-value that might come after a semi-colon
    if ((semi = lang.indexOf(';')) != -1) {
      lang = lang.substring(0, semi);
    }

    // Trim any whitespace
    lang = lang.trim();

    // Create a Locale from the language. A dash may separate the
    // language from the country.
    if ((dash = lang.indexOf('-')) == -1) {
      loc = new Locale(lang, "");   // No dash, no country
    }
    else {
      loc = new Locale(lang.substring(0, dash), lang.substring(dash+1));
    }

    return loc;
  }

  private ResourceBundle getBundleNoFallback(String bundleName, Locale loc) {

    // First get the fallback bundle -- the bundle that will be selected
    // if getBundle() can't find a direct match. This bundle can be
    // compared to the bundles returned by later calls to getBundle() in
    // order to detect when getBundle() finds a direct match.
    ResourceBundle fallback = null;
    try {
      fallback =
        ResourceBundle.getBundle(bundleName, new Locale("bogus", ""));
    }
    catch (MissingResourceException e) {
      // No fallback bundle was found.
    }

    try {
      // Get the bundle for the specified locale
      ResourceBundle bundle = ResourceBundle.getBundle(bundleName, loc);
```

Example 12-9. The LocaleNegotiator class (continued)

```
        // Is the bundle different than our fallback bundle?
        if (bundle != fallback) {
          // We have a real match!
          return bundle;
        }
        // So the bundle is the same as our fallback bundle.
        // We can still have a match, but only if our locale's language
        // matches the default locale's language.
        else if (bundle == fallback &&
                loc.getLanguage().equals(Locale.getDefault().getLanguage())) {
          // Another way to match
          return bundle;
        }
        else {
          // No match, keep looking
        }
      }
      catch (MissingResourceException e) {
        // No bundle available for this locale
      }

      return null;  // no match
  }

  protected String getCharsetForLocale(Locale loc, String charsets) {
    // Note: This method ignores the client-specified charsets
    return LocaleToCharsetMap.getCharset(loc);
  }
}
```

Example 12-10. The LocaleToCharsetMap class

```
package com.oreilly.servlet;

import java.util.*;

public class LocaleToCharsetMap {

  private static Hashtable map;

  static {
    map = new Hashtable();

    map.put("ar", "ISO-8859-6");
    map.put("be", "ISO-8859-5");
    map.put("bg", "ISO-8859-5");
    map.put("ca", "ISO-8859-1");
```

Example 12-10. The LocaleToCharsetMap class (continued)

```
    map.put("cs", "ISO-8859-2");
    map.put("da", "ISO-8859-1");
    map.put("de", "ISO-8859-1");
    map.put("el", "ISO-8859-7");
    map.put("en", "ISO-8859-1");
    map.put("es", "ISO-8859-1");
    map.put("et", "ISO-8859-1");
    map.put("fi", "ISO-8859-1");
    map.put("fr", "ISO-8859-1");
    map.put("he", "ISO-8859-8");
    map.put("hr", "ISO-8859-2");
    map.put("hu", "ISO-8859-2");
    map.put("is", "ISO-8859-1");
    map.put("it", "ISO-8859-1");
    map.put("iw", "ISO-8859-8");
    map.put("ja", "Shift_JIS");
    map.put("ko", "EUC-KR");        // Requires JDK 1.1.6
    map.put("lt", "ISO-8859-2");
    map.put("lv", "ISO-8859-2");
    map.put("mk", "ISO-8859-5");
    map.put("nl", "ISO-8859-1");
    map.put("no", "ISO-8859-1");
    map.put("pl", "ISO-8859-2");
    map.put("pt", "ISO-8859-1");
    map.put("ro", "ISO-8859-2");
    map.put("ru", "ISO-8859-5");
    map.put("sh", "ISO-8859-5");
    map.put("sk", "ISO-8859-2");
    map.put("sl", "ISO-8859-2");
    map.put("sq", "ISO-8859-2");
    map.put("sr", "ISO-8859-5");
    map.put("sv", "ISO-8859-1");
    map.put("tr", "ISO-8859-9");
    map.put("uk", "ISO-8859-5");
    map.put("zh", "GB2312");
    map.put("zh_TW", "Big5");
  }

  public static String getCharset(Locale loc) {
    String charset;

    // Try for a full name match (may include country)
    charset = (String) map.get(loc.toString());
    if (charset != null) return charset;

    // If a full name didn't match, try just the language
    charset = (String) map.get(loc.getLanguage());
    return charset;  // may be null
```

Example 12-10. The LocaleToCharsetMap class (continued)

```
  }
}
```

Future Directions

In the future, you can expect to see improved internationalization support in the Servlet API and in Java itself. Some likely areas for improvement are these:

- Support for additional charsets, especially those charsets that are commonly used on the Web.

- New classes that help an application support multiple languages at the same time. These classes will make it easier for servlets to present information to the user using one language, while using another language for administrative tasks such as logging.

- New classes that support language negotiation using a list of multiple locales. These classes will act in a similar fashion to `LocaleNegotiator`.

HTML Forms

Managing HTML forms requires a little extra work and a few special tricks when you're dealing with localized content. To understand the problem, imagine this situation. An HTML form is sent as part of a Japanese page. It asks the user for his name, which he enters as a string of Japanese characters. How is that name submitted to the servlet? And, more importantly, how can the servlet read it?

The answer to the first question is that all HTML form data is sent as a sequence of bytes. Those bytes are an encoded representation of the original characters. With Western European languages, the encoding is the default, ISO-8859-1, with one byte per character. For other languages, there can be other encodings. Browsers tend to encode form data using the same encoding that was applied to the page containing the form. Thus, if the Japanese page mentioned was encoded using Shift_JIS, the submitted form data would also be encoded using Shift_JIS. Note, however, that if the page did not specify a charset and the user had to manually choose Shift_JIS encoding for viewing, many browsers stubbornly submit the form data using ISO-8859-1.* Generally, the encoded byte string contains a large number of special bytes that have to be URL-encoded. For example, if we assume the Japanese form sends the user's name using a GET request, the resulting URL might look like this:

---

* For more information on the internationalization of HTML and HTML forms, see RFC 2070 at *http: //www.ietf.org/rfc/rfc2070.txt.*

```
http://server:port/servlet/NameHandler?name=%8CK%8C%B4%90%B3%8E%9F
```

The answer to the second question, how can a servlet read the submitted information, is a bit more complicated. A servlet has two choices. First, a servlet can leave the form data in its raw encoded format, treating it essentially like a sequence of bytes—with each byte awkwardly stored as a character in the parameter string. This tactic is useful only if the servlet does not need to manipulate the data and can be sure that the data is output only to the same user using the same charset. Alternatively, a servlet can convert the form data from its native encoded format to a Java-friendly Unicode string. This allows the servlet to freely manipulate the text and output the text using alternate charsets. There is one problem with this plan, however. Browsers currently provide no information to indicate which encoding was used on the form data. Browsers may provide that information in the future (using the `Content-Type` header in a POST, most likely), but for now, the servlet is left responsible for tracking that information.

The Hidden Charset

The commonly accepted technique for tracking the charset of submitted form data is to use a hidden charset form field.[*] Its value should be set to the charset of the page in which it is contained. Then, any servlet receiving the form can read the value of the charset field and know how to decode the submitted form data.

Example 12-11 demonstrates this technique with a form generator that sets the charset to match the charset of the page. Here's an English resource bundle that might accompanying the servlet, stored as *CharsetForm_en.properties*:

```
title=CharsetForm
header=<H1>Charset Form</H1>
prompt=Enter text:
```

And here's a Japanese resource, to be stored as *CharsetForm_ja.properties*:

```
title=CharsetForm
header=<H1>\u6587\u5b57\u30bb\u30c3\u30c8\u30fb\u30d5\u30a9\u30fc\u30e0</H1>
prompt=\u30c6\u30ad\u30b9\u30c8\u3092\u5165\u529b\u3057\u3066\u304f\u3060\
\u3055\u3044
```

A screen shot of the Japanese version is shown in Figure 12-6.

Example 12-11. Saving the charset in a hidden form field

```
import java.io.*;
import java.util.*;
import javax.servlet.*;
```

---

[*] Hidden form fields, if you remember, were first discussed in Chapter 7, where they were used for session tracking.

Example 12-11. Saving the charset in a hidden form field (continued)

```java
import javax.servlet.http.*;

import com.oreilly.servlet.LocaleNegotiator;
import com.oreilly.servlet.ServletUtils;

public class CharsetForm extends HttpServlet {

  public void doGet(HttpServletRequest req, HttpServletResponse res)
                              throws ServletException, IOException {
    try {
      String bundleName = "CharsetForm";
      String acceptLanguage = req.getHeader("Accept-Language");
      String acceptCharset = req.getHeader("Accept-Charset");

      LocaleNegotiator negotiator =
        new LocaleNegotiator(bundleName, acceptLanguage, acceptCharset);

      Locale locale = negotiator.getLocale();
      String charset = negotiator.getCharset();
      ResourceBundle bundle = negotiator.getBundle();  // may be null

      res.setContentType("text/html; charset=" + charset);
      res.setHeader("Content-Language", locale.getLanguage());
      res.setHeader("Vary", "Accept-Language");

      PrintWriter out = res.getWriter();

      if (bundle != null) {
        out.println("<HTML><HEAD><TITLE>");
        out.println(bundle.getString("title"));
        out.println("</TITLE></HEAD>");
        out.println("<BODY>");
        out.println(bundle.getString("header"));
        out.println("<FORM ACTION=/servlet/CharsetAction METHOD=get>");
        out.println("<INPUT TYPE=hidden NAME=charset value=" + charset + ">");
        out.println(bundle.getString("prompt"));
        out.println("<INPUT TYPE=text NAME=text>");
        out.println("</FORM>");
        out.println("</BODY></HTML>");
      }
      else {
        out.println("Bundle could not be found.");
      }
    }
    catch (Exception e) {
      log(ServletUtils.getStackTraceAsString(e));
    }
```

Example 12-11. Saving the charset in a hidden form field (continued)

```
  }
}
```

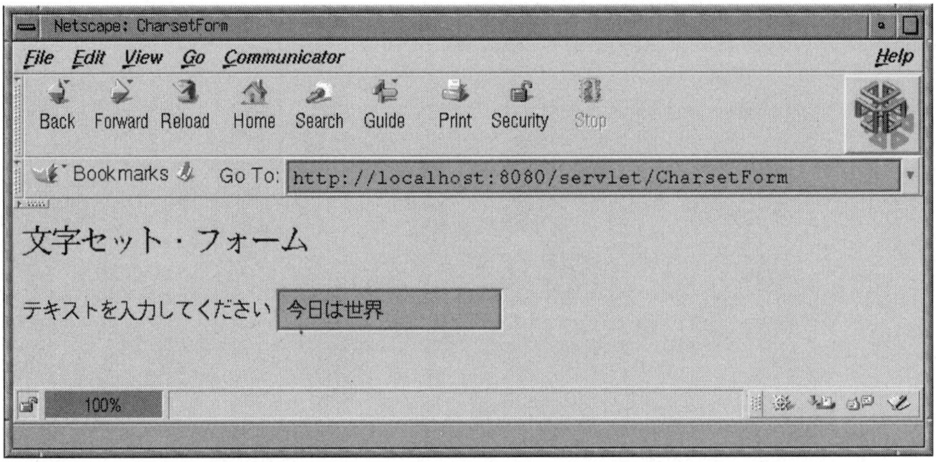

Figure 12-6. A Japanese form, with the user entering text

The servlet responsible for handling the submitted form is shown in Example 12-12. This servlet reads the submitted text and converts it to Unicode, then outputs the characters using the UTF-8 encoding. As a bonus, it also displays the received string as a Unicode escape string, showing what you would have to enter in a Java source file or resource bundle to create the same output. This lets the servlet act as a web-based native charset to Unicode string translator. Sample output is shown in Figure 12-7.

Example 12-12. Receiving the charset in a hidden form field

```java
import java.io.*;
import java.text.*;
import java.util.*;
import javax.servlet.*;
import javax.servlet.http.*;

public class CharsetAction extends HttpServlet {

  public void doGet(HttpServletRequest req, HttpServletResponse res)
                            throws ServletException, IOException {
    try {
      res.setContentType("text/plain; charset=UTF-8");
      PrintWriter out = res.getWriter();

      String charset = req.getParameter("charset");
```

Example 12-12. Receiving the charset in a hidden form field (continued)

```
    // Get the text parameter
    String text = req.getParameter("text");

    // Now convert it from an array of bytes to an array of characters.
    // Do this using the charset that was sent as a hidden field.
    // Here we bother to read only the first line.
    BufferedReader reader = new BufferedReader(
      new InputStreamReader(new StringBufferInputStream(text), charset));
    text = reader.readLine();

    out.println("Received charset: " + charset);
    out.println("Received text: " + text);
    out.println("Received text (escaped): " + toUnicodeEscapeString(text));
  }
  catch (Exception e) {
    e.printStackTrace();
  }
}

public void doPost(HttpServletRequest req, HttpServletResponse res)
                              throws ServletException, IOException {
  doGet(req, res);
}

private static String toUnicodeEscapeString(String str) {
  // Modeled after the code in java.util.Properties.save()
  StringBuffer buf = new StringBuffer();
  int len = str.length();
  char ch;
  for (int i = 0; i < len; i++) {
    ch = str.charAt(i);
    switch (ch) {
      case '\\': buf.append("\\\\"); break;
      case '\t': buf.append("\\t"); break;
      case '\n': buf.append("\\n"); break;
      case '\r': buf.append("\\r"); break;

      default:
        if (ch >= ' ' && ch <= 127) {
          buf.append(ch);
        }
        else {
          buf.append('\\');
          buf.append('u');
          buf.append(toHex((ch >> 12) & 0xF));
          buf.append(toHex((ch >>  8) & 0xF));
          buf.append(toHex((ch >>  4) & 0xF));
```

Example 12-12. Receiving the charset in a hidden form field (continued)

```
            buf.append(toHex((ch >>  0) & 0xF));
        }
      }
    }
    return buf.toString();
  }

  private static char toHex(int nibble) {
    return hexDigit[(nibble & 0xF)];
  }

  private static char[] hexDigit = {
    '0','1','2','3','4','5','6','7','8','9','a','b','c','d','e','f'
  };
}
```

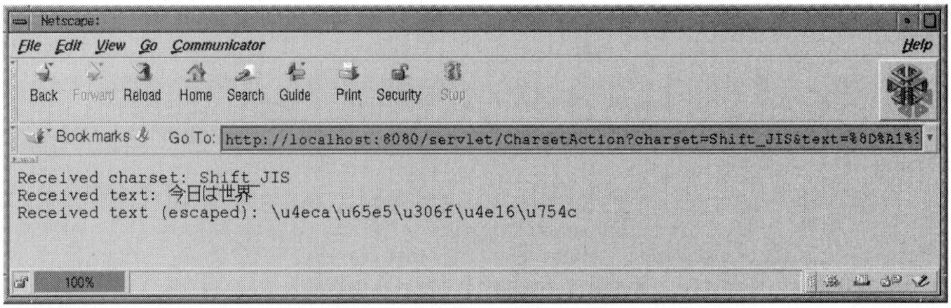

Figure 12-7. Handling a Japanese form

The most interesting part of this servlet is the bit that receives and converts the submitted text.

```
String text = req.getParameter("text");
BufferedReader reader = new BufferedReader(
  new InputStreamReader(new StringBufferInputStream(text), charset));
text = reader.readLine();
```

The first line receives the text in its raw format. Although it's stored as a `String`, it's not a true `String`. Each character in the `String` stores one byte of the encoded text. The second and third lines wrap the text with a `StringBufferInputStream`, an `InputStreamReader`, and a `BufferedReader`. The decoding happens with the `InputStreamReader`, whose constructor accepts the encoding specified by the charset field. Finally, the `BufferedReader` wraps around the `InputStreamReader` for convenience. This lets us receive the text one line at a time, as shown in the fourth line.

Receiving Multilingual Input

We need to discuss one more aspect of internationalization: receiving multilingual input. It's actually quite simple for a servlet to receive multilingual character data. The `ServletRequest.getReader()` method handles the task automatically. It returns a `BufferedReader` specially built to read the character encoding of the input data. For example, if the `Content-Type` of the servlet's input is `"text/html; charset=Shift_JIS"`, the `BufferedReader` is one that reads Shift_JIS characters.

Because `getReader()` works automatically, it means our `Deblink` servlet and other chained servlets found throughout the book are already multilingual friendly. No matter what charset is used for the content they receive, they always read the input characters correctly using `getReader()`.

Example 12-13 shows another servlet that uses `getReader()`. This servlet is designed to be the last servlet in a chain. It uses `getReader()` to read its input as character data, then outputs the characters using the UTF-8 encoding.

Example 12-13. UTF-8 encoder

```
import java.io.*;
import javax.servlet.*;
import javax.servlet.http.*;

public class UTF8 extends HttpServlet {

  public void doGet(HttpServletRequest req, HttpServletResponse res)
                          throws ServletException, IOException {
    try {
      // Get a reader to read the incoming data
      BufferedReader reader = req.getReader();

      // Get a writer to write the data in UTF-8
      res.setContentType("text/html; charset=UTF-8");
      PrintWriter out = res.getWriter();

      // Read and write 4K chars at a time
      // (Far more efficient than reading and writing a line at a time)
      char[] buf = new char[4 * 1024];  // 4Kchar buffer
      int len;
      while ((len = reader.read(buf, 0, buf.length)) != -1) {
        out.write(buf, 0, len);
      }
    }
    catch (Exception e) {
      getServletContext().log(e, "Problem filtering page to UTF-8");
    }
```

Example 12-13. UTF-8 encoder (continued)

```
  }

  public void doPost(HttpServletRequest req, HttpServletResponse res)
                        throws ServletException, IOException {
    doGet(req, res);
  }
}
```

Sometimes it's useful for a servlet to determine the charset of its input. For this you can use the getCharacterEncoding() method of ServletRequest, introduced in the Servlet API 2.0. Note that this method does not exist in the Java Web Server 1.1.x implementation of ServletRequest, as the method was added between the release of the Java Web Server 1.1 and the official Servlet API 2.0 release with JSDK 2.0. For maximum portability you can do what getReader() does and fetch the request's content type using getContentType(). Any charset information can be found in the content type following the "charset=" tag.

In this chapter:
- *Parsing Parameters*
- *Sending Email*
- *Using Regular Expressions*
- *Executing Programs*
- *Using Native Methods*
- *Acting as an RMI Client*
- *Debugging*
- *Performance Tuning*

13

Odds and Ends

Every house has a junk drawer—a drawer loaded to the brim with odds and ends that don't exactly fit into any organized drawer and yet can't be thrown away because when they're needed they're really needed. This chapter is like that drawer. It holds a whole slew of useful servlet examples and tips that don't really fit anywhere else. Included are servlets that parse parameters, send email, execute programs, use regular expression engines, use native methods, and act as RMI clients. There's also a demonstration of basic debugging techniques, along with some suggestions for servlet performance tuning.

Parsing Parameters

If you've tried your hand at writing your own servlets as you've read through this book, you've probably noticed how awkward it can be to get and parse request parameters, especially when the parameters have to be converted to some non-`String` format. For example, let's assume you want to fetch the `count` parameter and get its value as an `int`. Furthermore, let's assume you want to handle error conditions by calling `handleNoCount()` if `count` isn't given and `handleMal-formedCount()` if `count` cannot be parsed as an integer. To do this using the standard Servlet API requires the following code:

```
int count;

String param = req.getParameter("count");
if (param == null || param.length() == 0) {
  handleNoCount();
}
else {
  try {
    count = Integer.parseInt(param);
```

```
    }
  catch (NumberFormatException e) {
    handleMalformedCount();
  }
}
```

Does this look like any code you've written? It's not very pretty, is it? A better solution is to hand off the responsibility for getting and parsing parameters to a utility class. The com.oreilly.servlet.ParameterParser class is just such a class. By using ParameterParser, we can rewrite the previous code to be more elegant:

```
int count;

ParameterParser parser = new ParameterParser(req);
try {
  count = parser.getIntParameter("count");
}
catch (NumberFormatException e) {
  handleMalformedCount();
}
catch (ParameterNotFoundException e) {
  handleNoCount();
}
```

The parameter parser's getIntParameter() method returns the specified parameter's value as an int. It throws a NumberFormatException if the parameter cannot be converted to an int and a ParameterNotFoundException if the parameter isn't part of the request. It also throws ParameterNotFoundException if the parameter had a value of the empty string. This often happens with form submissions for text fields when nothing is entered, something that for all intents and purposes should be treated the same as a missing parameter.

If it's enough that a servlet use a default value if there's a problem with a parameter, as is often the case, the code can be simplified even further:

```
ParameterParser parser = new ParameterParser(req);
int count = parser.getIntParameter("count", 0);
```

This second version of getIntParameter() takes a default value of 0 that is returned in lieu of throwing an exception.

ParameterParser Code

The ParameterParser class contains more than a dozen methods that return request parameters—two for each of Java's native types. It also has two getStringParameter() methods in case you want to get the parameter in its raw

String format. The code for `ParameterParser` is provided in Example 13-1;
`ParameterNotFoundException` is in Example 13-2.

Example 13-1. The ParameterParser class

```
package com.oreilly.servlet;

import java.io.*;
import javax.servlet.*;

public class ParameterParser {

  private ServletRequest req;

  public ParameterParser(ServletRequest req) {
    this.req = req;
  }

  public String getStringParameter(String name)
      throws ParameterNotFoundException {
    // Use getParameterValues() to avoid the once-deprecated getParameter()
    String[] values = req.getParameterValues(name);
    if (values == null)
      throw new ParameterNotFoundException(name + " not found");
    else if (values[0].length() == 0)
      throw new ParameterNotFoundException(name + " was empty");
    else
      return values[0];  // ignore multiple field values
  }

  public String getStringParameter(String name, String def) {
    try { return getStringParameter(name); }
    catch (Exception e) { return def; }
  }

  public boolean getBooleanParameter(String name)
      throws ParameterNotFoundException {
    return new Boolean(getStringParameter(name)).booleanValue();
  }

  public boolean getBooleanParameter(String name, boolean def) {
    try { return getBooleanParameter(name); }
    catch (Exception e) { return def; }
  }

  public byte getByteParameter(String name)
      throws ParameterNotFoundException, NumberFormatException {
    return Byte.parseByte(getStringParameter(name));
  }
```

Example 13-1. The ParameterParser class (continued)

```java
public byte getByteParameter(String name, byte def) {
  try { return getByteParameter(name); }
  catch (Exception e) { return def; }
}

public char getCharParameter(String name)
    throws ParameterNotFoundException {
  String param = getStringParameter(name);
  if (param.length() == 0)  // shouldn't be possible
    throw new ParameterNotFoundException(name + " is empty string");
  else
    return (param.charAt(0));
}

public char getCharParameter(String name, char def) {
  try { return getCharParameter(name); }
  catch (Exception e) { return def; }
}

public double getDoubleParameter(String name)
    throws ParameterNotFoundException, NumberFormatException {
  return new Double(getStringParameter(name)).doubleValue();
}

public double getDoubleParameter(String name, double def) {
  try { return getDoubleParameter(name); }
  catch (Exception e) { return def; }
}

public float getFloatParameter(String name)
    throws ParameterNotFoundException, NumberFormatException {
  return new Float(getStringParameter(name)).floatValue();
}

public float getFloatParameter(String name, float def) {
  try { return getFloatParameter(name); }
  catch (Exception e) { return def; }
}

public int getIntParameter(String name)
    throws ParameterNotFoundException, NumberFormatException {
  return Integer.parseInt(getStringParameter(name));
}

public int getIntParameter(String name, int def) {
  try { return getIntParameter(name); }
  catch (Exception e) { return def; }
```

Example 13-1. The ParameterParser class (continued)

```
  }

  public long getLongParameter(String name)
      throws ParameterNotFoundException, NumberFormatException {
    return Long.parseLong(getStringParameter(name));
  }

  public long getLongParameter(String name, long def) {
    try { return getLongParameter(name); }
    catch (Exception e) { return def; }
  }

  public short getShortParameter(String name)
      throws ParameterNotFoundException, NumberFormatException {
    return Short.parseShort(getStringParameter(name));
  }

  public short getShortParameter(String name, short def) {
    try { return getShortParameter(name); }
    catch (Exception e) { return def; }
  }
}
```

Example 13-2. The ParameterNotFoundException class

```
package com.oreilly.servlet;

public class ParameterNotFoundException extends Exception {

  public ParameterNotFoundException() {
    super();
  }

  public ParameterNotFoundException(String s) {
    super(s);
  }
}
```

Sending Email

Sometimes it's necessary, or just convenient, for a servlet to fire off an email message. For example, imagine a servlet that receives data from a user feedback form. The servlet might want to send the feedback data to a mailing list of interested parties. Or imagine a servlet that encounters an unexpected problem and knows to send an email page to its administrator asking for help.

A servlet has four choices for sending email:

- It can manage the details itself—establishing a raw socket connection to a mail server and speaking a low-level mail transport protocol, usually the so-called Simple Mail Transfer Protocol (SMTP).

- It can run on external command-line email program, if the server system has such a program.

- It can use the new JavaMail API, designed to support complicated mail handling, filing, and processing (see *http://java.sun.com/products/javamail*).

- It can use one of the many freely available mail classes that abstracts the details of sending email into simple, convenient method calls.

For most servlets, we recommend the final approach for its simplicity.

Using sun.net.smtp.SmtpClient

For the purposes of this example, we'll demonstrate a servlet that uses the `sun.net.smtp.SmtpClient` class. It's conveniently provided with Sun's JDK and most JVMs descended from it, but we should warn you that it's unsupported and subject to change (though it hasn't changed since JDK 1.0). Using it is simple:

1. Call `SmtpClient smtp = new SmtpClient()`. Optionally, pass the constructor the name of a host to use as the mail server, which replaces the default of *localhost*. Most Unix machines can act as SMTP mail servers.

2. Call `smtp.from(fromAddress)`, specifying the address of the sender. The address doesn't have to be valid.

3. Call `smtp.to(toAddress)`, specifying the address of the receiver.

4. Call `PrintStream msg = smtp.startMessage()` to get an output stream for the message.

5. Write any mail headers to the `PrintStream`. For example, `"Subject: Customer feedback"`. The headers should conform to the format given in RFC 822 at *http://www.ietf.org/rfc/rfc822.txt*. The basic syntax is `"name: value"`.

6. Write the body of the mail message to the `PrintStream`.

7. Call `smtp.closeServer()` to close the connection to the server and send the message.

Emailing Form Data

Example 13-3 shows a servlet that emails the form data it receives to a mailing list. Notice the extensive use of the `ParameterParser` class.

Example 13-3. Sending mail from a servlet

```
import java.io.*;
import java.util.*;
import javax.servlet.*;
import javax.servlet.http.*;

import com.oreilly.servlet.ParameterParser;
import com.oreilly.servlet.ServletUtils;

import sun.net.smtp.SmtpClient;

public class MailServlet extends HttpServlet {

  static final String FROM = "MailServlet";
  static final String TO = "feedback-folks@attentive-company.com";

  public void doGet(HttpServletRequest req, HttpServletResponse res)
                            throws ServletException, IOException {
    res.setContentType("text/plain");
    PrintWriter out = res.getWriter();

    ParameterParser parser = new ParameterParser(req);
    String from = parser.getStringParameter("from", FROM);
    String to = parser.getStringParameter("to", TO);

    try {
      SmtpClient smtp = new SmtpClient();  // assume localhost
      smtp.from(from);
      smtp.to(to);
      PrintStream msg = smtp.startMessage();

      msg.println("To: " + to);  // so mailers will display the To: address
      msg.println("Subject: Customer feedback");
      msg.println();

      Enumeration enum = req.getParameterNames();
      while (enum.hasMoreElements()) {
        String name = (String)enum.nextElement();
        if (name.equals("to") || name.equals("from")) continue;  // Skip to/from
        String value = parser.getStringParameter(name, null);
        msg.println(name + " = " + value);
      }
```

Example 13-3. Sending mail from a servlet (continued)

```
      msg.println();
      msg.println("---");
      msg.println("Sent by " + HttpUtils.getRequestURL(req));

      smtp.closeServer();

      out.println("Thanks for the submission...");
    }
    catch (IOException e) {
      out.println("There was a problem handling the submission...");
      getServletContext().log(e, "There was a problem sending email");
    }
  }
}
```

This servlet first determines the "from" and "to" addresses for the message. The default values are set in the FROM and TO variables, although a submitted form can include (probably hidden) fields that specify alternate from and to addresses. The servlet then begins an SMTP email message. It connects to the local host and addresses the message. Next, it sets its headers and fills the body with the form data, ignoring the to and from variables. Finally, it sends the message and thanks the user for the submission. If there's a problem, it informs the user and logs the exception.

Using Regular Expressions

If you're a servlet programmer with a background in Perl-based CGI scripting and you're still smitten with Perl's regular expression capabilities, this section is for you. Here we show how to use Perl 5 regular expressions from within Java. For those of you who are unfamiliar with regular expressions, they are a mechanism for allowing extremely advanced string manipulation with minimal code. Regular expressions are wonderfully explained in all their glory in the book *Mastering Regular Expressions* by Jeffrey E. F. Friedl (O'Reilly).

With all the classes and capabilities Sun has added in JDK 1.1 and JDK 1.2, one feature still absent is a regular expression engine. Ah, well, not to worry. As with most Java features, if you can't get it from Sun, a third-party vendor is probably offering what you need at a reasonable price.

Several companies offer full-featured regular expression engines. One of the first was Thought, Inc., which developed VanillaSearch. It's available for trial download and purchase at *http://www.thoughtinc.com*. More recently, Original Reusable Objects, Inc. has come out with a product called OROMatcher (along with a utility package built using OROMatcher called PerlTools). These products are available for download at *http://www.oroinc.com*. A binary license to use OROMatcher and PerlTools is being offered absolutely free. Support, source, and "mere" redistribution (that is, as added value to an IDE) cost extra.

Improving Deblink with Regular Expressions

To demonstrate the use of regular expressions, let's use OROMatcher and Perl-Tools to rewrite the `Deblink` servlet originally shown in Chapter 2, *HTTP Servlet Basics*. As you may recall, `Deblink` acted as a filter to remove the `<BLINK>` and `</BLINK>` tags from HTML pages. The original `Deblink` code is shown in Example 13-4 to help refresh your memory.

Example 13-4. The original Deblink

```
import java.io.*;
import javax.servlet.*;
import javax.servlet.http.*;

public class Deblink extends HttpServlet {

  public void doGet(HttpServletRequest req, HttpServletResponse res)
                              throws ServletException, IOException {

    String contentType = req.getContentType();  // get the incoming type
    if (contentType == null) return;  // nothing incoming, nothing to do
    res.setContentType(contentType);  // set outgoing type to be incoming type

    PrintWriter out = res.getWriter();

    BufferedReader in = req.getReader();

    String line = null;
    while ((line = in.readLine()) != null) {
      line = replace(line, "<BLINK>", "");
      line = replace(line, "</BLINK>", "");
      out.println(line);
    }
  }

  public void doPost(HttpServletRequest req, HttpServletResponse res)
                              throws ServletException, IOException {
    doGet(req, res);
  }

  private String replace(String line, String oldString, String newString) {
    int index = 0;
    while ((index = line.indexOf(oldString, index)) >= 0) {
      // Replace the old string with the new string (inefficiently)
```

Example 13-4. The original Deblink (continued)

```
      line = line.substring(0, index) +
            newString +
            line.substring(index + oldString.length());
      index += newString.length();
    }
    return line;
  }
}
```

As we pointed out in Chapter 2, this version of `Deblink` has one serious limitation: it's case sensitive. It won't remove <blink>, </blink>, <Blink>, or </Blink>. Sure, we could enumerate inside `Deblink` all the case combinations that should be removed, but regular expressions provide a much simpler alternative.

With a single regular expression, we can rewrite `Deblink` to remove the opening and closing blink tags, no matter how they are capitalized. The regular expression we'll use is `"</?blink>"`. This matches both <blink> and </blink>. (The ? character means the previous character is optional.) With a case-insensitive mask set, this expression also matches <BLINK>, </Blink>, and even <bLINK>. Any occurrence of this regular expression can be replaced with the empty string, to completely deblink an HTML page. The rewritten `Deblink` code appears in Example 13-5.

Example 13-5. Deblink rewritten using regular expressions

```
import java.io.*;
import javax.servlet.*;
import javax.servlet.http.*;

import com.oroinc.text.perl.*;  // PerlTools package

public class Deblink extends HttpServlet {

  Perl5Util perl = new Perl5Util();

  public void doGet(HttpServletRequest req, HttpServletResponse res)
                              throws ServletException, IOException {

    String contentType = req.getContentType();  // get the incoming type
    if (contentType == null) return;  // nothing incoming, nothing to do
    res.setContentType(contentType);  // set outgoing type to be incoming type

    PrintWriter out = res.getWriter();

    BufferedReader in = req.getReader();
```

Example 13-5. Deblink rewritten using regular expressions (continued)

```
    try {
      String line = null;
      while ((line = in.readLine()) != null) {
        if (perl.match("#</?blink>#i", line))
          line = perl.substitute("s#</?blink>##ig", line);
        out.println(line);
      }
    }
    catch(MalformedPerl5PatternException e) { // only thrown during development
      log("Problem compiling a regular expression: " + e.getMessage());
    }
  }

  public void doPost(HttpServletRequest req, HttpServletResponse res)
                          throws ServletException, IOException {
    doGet(req, res);
  }
}
```

The most important lines of this servlet are the lines that replace our
`"</?blink>"` expression with the empty string:

```
    if (perl.match("#</?blink>#i", line))
      line = perl.substitute("s#</?blink>##ig", line);
```

The first line does a case-insensitive search for the regular expression `</?blink>`.
The syntax is exactly like Perl. It may look slightly unfamiliar, though, because we
chose to use hash marks instead of slashes to avoid having to escape the slash
that's part of the expression (which would result in `"/<\\/?blink>/i"`). The
trailing `"i"` indicates the regular expression is case insensitive.

The second line substitutes all occurrences of the regular expression with the
empty string. This line alone would accomplish the same as both lines together,
but it's more efficient to do the check first. The syntax is also identical to Perl. The
text between the first pair of hashes is the regular expression to search for. The
text between the second pair is the replacement text. The trailing `"g"` indicates
that all occurrences should be replaced (the default is one replacement per line).

For more information on what can be done with regular expressions in Java, see
the documentation that comes with each of the third-party products.

Executing Programs

Sometimes a servlet needs to execute an external program. This is generally
important in situations where an external program offers functionality that isn't
easily available from within Java. For example, a servlet could call an external

program to perform an image manipulation or to check the status of the server. Launching an external program raises a number of security concerns. For this reason, it's an action that can be taken only by servlets running with a fairly lenient security manager—specifically, a security manager that grants permission for the servlet to call the `exec()` method of `java.lang.Runtime`.

Finger

The *finger* program queries a (possibly remote) computer for a list of currently logged in users. It's available on virtually all Unix systems and some Windows NT machines with networking capabilities. The *finger* program works by connecting to a finger daemon (usually named *fingerd*) that listens on port 79. *finger* makes its request of *fingerd* using a custom "finger" protocol, and *fingerd* replies with the appropriate information. Most Unix systems run *fingerd*, though many security-conscious administrators turn it off to limit information that could be used for break-in attempts. It's still fairly rare to find *fingerd* on Windows systems. Run without any arguments, *finger* reports all users of the local machine. The local machine must be running *fingerd*. Here's an example:

```
% finger
Login    Name                    TTY Idle When        Office
jhunter  Jason Hunter            q0   3:13 Thu 12:13
ktaylor  Kristi Taylor           q1        Thu 12:18
```

Run with a username as an argument, *finger* reports on just that user:

```
% finger jhunter
Login name: jhunter                   In real life: Jason Hunter
Directory: /usr/people/jhunter        Shell: /bin/tcsh
On since Jan  1 12:13:28 on ttyq0 from :0.0
3 hours 13 minutes Idle Time
On since Jan  1 12:13:30 on ttyq2 from :0.0
```

Run with a hostname as an argument, *finger* reports all the users of the specified host. The remote host must be running *fingerd*:

```
% finger @deimos
Login    Name                    TTY Idle When        Office
bday     Bill Day                q0   17d Mon 10:45
```

And, of course, run with a username and hostname, *finger* reports on the specified user on the specified host:

```
% finger bday@deimos
[deimos.engr.sgi.com]
Login name: bday                      In real life: Bill Day
Directory: /usr/people/bday           Shell: /bin/tcsh
On since Dec 15 10:45:22 on ttyq0 from :0.0
17 days Idle Time
```

Executing the Finger Command

Let's assume that a servlet wants access to the information retrieved by *finger*. It has two options: it can establish a socket connection to *fingerd* and make a request for information just like any other finger client, or it can execute the command-line *finger* program to make the connection on its behalf and read the information from *finger*'s output. We'll show the second technique here.[*]

Example 13-6 shows how a servlet can execute the *finger* command to see who's logged into the local machine. It reads the command's output and prints it to its output stream.

Example 13-6. Executing the finger command from a servlet

```java
import java.io.*;
import java.util.*;
import javax.servlet.*;
import javax.servlet.http.*;

import com.oreilly.servlet.ServletUtils;

public class Finger extends HttpServlet {

  public void doGet(HttpServletRequest req, HttpServletResponse res)
                              throws ServletException, IOException {
    res.setContentType("text/plain");
    PrintWriter out = res.getWriter();

    String command = "finger";

    Runtime runtime = Runtime.getRuntime();
    Process process = null;
    try {
      process = runtime.exec(command);
      DataInputStream in = new DataInputStream(process.getInputStream());

      // Read and print the output
      String line = null;
      while ((line = in.readLine()) != null) {
        out.println(line);
      }
    }
    catch (Exception e) {
      out.println("Problem with finger: " +
                  ServletUtils.getStackTraceAsString(e));
```

---

[*] If you're interested in the code necessary to connect to *fingerd*, see the `FingerServlet` example provided with the Java Web Server.

Example 13-6. Executing the finger command from a servlet (continued)

```
      }
    }
  }
```

This servlet uses the `exec()` command just like any other Java class would. It executes the *finger* command, then reads and prints the output. If there's a problem, the servlet catches an exception and prints the stack trace to the user. This servlet assumes the `finger` command exists in the default search path. If that isn't the case, change the `command` string to specify the path where *finger* can be found.

We should point out that, although Java is executing native code when it executes the *finger* program, it doesn't open itself up to the risks that normally exist when executing native code. The reason is that the *finger* program executes as a separate process. It can crash or be killed without impacting the server executing the servlet.

Executing Finger with Arguments

Now let's assume we want to pass an argument to the *finger* command. The usage is slightly different. `exec()` takes either a single string that specifies a command or an array of strings that specifies a command and the arguments to pass to that command. To run *finger jhunter* the code looks like Example 13-7.

Example 13-7. Adding a parameter to the executed command

```java
import java.io.*;
import java.util.*;
import javax.servlet.*;
import javax.servlet.http.*;

import com.oreilly.servlet.ServletUtils;

public class Finger extends HttpServlet {

  public void doGet(HttpServletRequest req, HttpServletResponse res)
                          throws ServletException, IOException {
    res.setContentType("text/plain");
    PrintWriter out = res.getWriter();

    String[] command = { "finger", "jhunter" };  // Only change!

    Runtime runtime = Runtime.getRuntime();
    Process process = null;
    try {
      process = runtime.exec(command);
```

Example 13-7. Adding a parameter to the executed command (continued)

```
    BufferedReader in =
    new BufferedReader(new InputStreamReader(process.getInputStream()));

    // Read and print the output
    String line = null;
    while ((line = in.readLine()) != null) {
      out.println(line);
    }
  }
  catch (Exception e) {
    out.println("Problem with finger: " +
              ServletUtils.getStackTraceAsString(e));
  }
 }
}
```

The command variable is now the string array {"finger", "jhunter"}. The command would not work as the single string "finger jhunter".

Executing Finger with Redirected Output

Finally, let's assume we want to redirect the output from our *finger* command. We may want to redirect the output to a file for later use, as in *finger jhunter > /tmp/jhunter*. Or we may want to redirect the output to the *grep* program to remove any references to some user, as in *finger | grep -v jhunter*.

This task is harder than it may appear. If the command variable is set to the string "finger | grep -v jhunter", Java treats this string as the name of as a single program—one that it most assuredly won't find. If the command variable is set to the string array "{"finger", "|", "grep", "-v", "jhunter"}", Java executes the *finger* command and pass it the next four strings as parameters, no doubt thoroughly confusing *finger*.

The solution requires an understanding that redirection is a feature of the shell. The shell is the program into which you normally type commands. On Unix the most common shells are *csh, tcsh, bash,* and *sh*. On Windows 95, the shell is usually *command.com*. On Windows NT, the shell is either *command.com* or *cmd.exe*.

Instead of executing *finger* directly, we can execute a shell and tell it the command string we want run. That string can contain the *finger* command and any sort of redirection. The shell can parse the command and correctly recognize and perform the redirection. The exact command needed to execute a shell and program depends on the shell and thus on the operating system. This technique therefore necessarily limits the platform independence of the servlets that use it.

On a Unix system, the following `command` variable asks *csh* to execute the command *finger | grep -v jhunter*:

```
String[] command = { "/bin/csh", "-c", "finger | grep -v jhunter" };
```

The program Java executes is */bin/csh*. *csh* is passed two arguments: *-c*, which asks the shell to execute the next parameter, and *finger | grep -v jhunter*, which is executed by the shell.

On a Windows system, the `command` variable looks like this:

```
String[] command = { "command.com", "/c", "finger | grep -v jhunter" };
```

The */c* argument for *command.com* works the same way *-c* did for *csh* and, yes, the *.com* suffix is necessary. Windows NT users should note that using *cmd.exe* is problematic because it redirects its output to a new window instead of to the Java runtime that spawned it. In fact, even launching the Java Web Server from a *cmd.exe* shell can cause the *command.com* command to fail.

Using Native Methods

Despite Sun's push for 100% Pure Java, native code still has its place. You need native code to do things that Java (and external programs launched by Java) cannot do: locking files, accessing user IDs, accessing shared memory, sending faxes, and so on. Native code is also useful when accessing legacy data through non-Java gateways. Last, in situations where every last bit of performance is vital, native code libraries can give a servlet a big boost.

Native code, however, should not be used except when absolutely necessary, since if the native code run by a servlet goes south, the entire server goes down with it! The security protections in Java can't protect the server from native code crashes. For this reason, it's wise not to use the native JDBC-ODBC bridge from a servlet because many ODBC drivers seem to have problems with multithreaded access. Native code also limits the platform independence of a servlet. While this may not matter for custom-built servlets tied to a particular server, it's something to remember.

How a servlet accesses native methods depends on the web server and JVM in which it's running. To take a risk and speak in broad generalities, let us say that you can pretty much expect your web server and JVM to support the standard Java Native Interface (JNI). Using JNI is fairly involved, and even a basic introduction extends beyond the scope of this chapter. For a tutorial on JNI, see the upcoming *Java Native Methods,* by Alligator Descartes (O'Reilly).

When using JNI with servlets, remember these things:

- Only the most liberal server security managers allow a servlet to execute native code.

- There is a common JVM bug that doesn't allow native code to be loaded by a class that was loaded with a custom class loader (such as the class loader that loads servlets from the default servlet directory). Servlets using native code may therefore need to reside in the server's classpath (*server_root/classes*).

- The directory where the shared library (or dynamic load library or DLL) that contains the native code is placed depends on the web server and JVM. Some servers have specific locations where they look for shared libraries. For example, the Java Web Server looks in *server_root\lib* on Windows and *server_root/lib/sparc/solaris* on Solaris. If the server doesn't provide a specific shared library directory, try placing the library in a JVM-specific location such as *jdk_root\bin* or under *jdk_root/lib*, or try an operating system-specific location such as *windows_root\system32* or */usr/lib*.

Acting as an RMI Client

In Chapter 10, *Applet-Servlet Communication*, we saw how a servlet can act as an RMI server. Here we turn the tables and see a servlet acting as an RMI client. By taking the role of an RMI client, a servlet can leverage the services of other servers to accomplish its task, coordinate its efforts with other servers or servlets on those servers, and/or act as an proxy on behalf of applets that can't communicate with RMI servers themselves.

Example 13-8 shows `DaytimeClientServlet`, a servlet that gets the current time of day from the `DaytimeServlet` RMI server shown in Chapter 10.

Example 13-8. A servlet as an RMI client

```
import java.io.*;
import java.rmi.*;
import java.rmi.registry.*;
import javax.servlet.*;
import javax.servlet.http.*;

public class DaytimeClientServlet extends HttpServlet {

  DaytimeServer daytime;

  // Returns a reference to a DaytimeServer or null if there was a problem.
  protected DaytimeServer getDaytimeServer() {
    // Set the security manager if it hasn't been done already.
    // Provides protection from a malicious DaytimeServer stub.
    if (System.getSecurityManager() == null) {
      System.setSecurityManager(new RMISecurityManager());
```

Example 13-8. A servlet as an RMI client (continued)

```
    }

    try {
      Registry registry =
        LocateRegistry.getRegistry(getRegistryHost(), getRegistryPort());
      return (DaytimeServer)registry.lookup(getRegistryName());
    }
    catch (Exception e) {
      getServletContext().log(e, "Problem getting DaytimeServer reference");
      return null;
    }
  }

  private String getRegistryName() {
    String name = getInitParameter("registryName");
    return (name == null ? "DaytimeServlet" : name);
  }

  private String getRegistryHost() {
    // Return either the hostname given by "registryHost" or
    // if no name was given return null to imply localhost
    return getInitParameter("registryHost");
  }

  private int getRegistryPort() {
    try { return Integer.parseInt(getInitParameter("registryPort")); }
    catch (NumberFormatException e) { return Registry.REGISTRY_PORT; }
  }

  public void doGet(HttpServletRequest req, HttpServletResponse res)
                                 throws ServletException, IOException {
    res.setContentType("text/plain");
    PrintWriter out = res.getWriter();

    // Get a daytime object if we haven't before
    if (daytime == null) {
      daytime = getDaytimeServer();
      if (daytime == null) {
        // Couldn't get it, so report we're unavailable.
        throw new UnavailableException(this, "Could not locate daytime");
      }
    }

    // Get and print the current time on the (possibly remote) daytime host
    out.println(daytime.getDate().toString());
  }
}
```

This servlet should remind you of the applet you saw in Chapter 10. Both servlets and applets perform the same basic steps to access an RMI server. They both locate a registry using a hostname and port number, then use that registry to look up a reference to the remote object. The only significant difference is that a servlet must first ensure it's running under the protection of a default security manager. Every RMI client has to have a security manager in place to protect itself from hostile remotely loaded stubs. An applet is guaranteed to run under an applet security manager, so this step isn't necessary. A servlet, however, can operate without a default security manager, so before acting as an RMI client it may need to assign one.

Debugging

The testing/debugging phase is one of the hardest aspects of developing servlets. Servlets tend to involve a large amount of client/server interaction, making errors likely—but hard to reproduce. It can also be hard to track down the cause of nonobvious errors because servlets don't work well with standard debuggers, since they run inside a heavily multithreaded and generally complex web server. Here are a few hints and suggestions that may aid you in your debugging.

Check the Logs

When you first think there might be a problem, check the logs. Most servers output an error log where you can find a list of all the errors observed by the server and an event log where you can find a list of interesting servlet events. The event log may also hold the messages logged by servlets through the `log()` method, but not always.

Note that many servers buffer their output to these logs to improve performance. When hunting down a problem, you may want to stop this buffering (usually by reducing the server's buffer size to 0 bytes), so you can see problems as they occur. Be sure to reset the buffer size to a reasonable value afterward.

Output Extra Information

If you don't see an indication of the problem in the server's logs, try having your servlet log extra information with the `log()` method. As you've seen in examples elsewhere in this book, we habitually log stack traces and other error situations. During debugging, you can add a few temporary `log()` commands as a poor man's debugger, to get a general idea of the code execution path and the values of the servlet's variables. Sometimes it's convenient to leave the `log()` commands in a servlet surrounded by `if` clauses so they trigger only when a specific `debug` init parameter is set to `true`.

Extracting the extra information from the server's logs can at times be unwieldy. To make the temporary debugging information easier to find, you can have a servlet output its debug information to the client (through the `PrintWriter`) or to a console on the server (through `System.out`). Not all servers have a console associated with a servlet's `System.out`; some redirect the output to a file instead.

Use a Standard Debugger

It's also possible to use a standard debugger to track down servlet problems, although exactly how might not be intuitively obvious. After all, you can't debug a servlet directly because servlets aren't standalone programs. Servlets are server extensions, and, as such, they need to run inside a server.

Fortunately, Sun provides a simple "servlet runner" server perfect for debugging servlets. This servlet runner acts as a small all-Java web server that is simpler and more lightweight than the Java Web Server—it handles only HTTP requests for servlets, and it doesn't even serve files. You'll find the servlet runner packaged as part of the Java Servlet Development Kit (JSDK), available from *http://jserv.java.sun.com*.

The servlet runner can be executed from the command line as the *servletrunner* shell script on a Unix system or the *servletrunner.exe* program on Windows. What *servletrunner* does is set the classpath to include the appropriate classes and then execute *java sun.servlet.http.HttpServer*. The `HttpServer` class contains the `main()` method that listens for incoming requests for servlets. By default, it listens on port 8080.

To debug a servlet, we can debug `sun.servlet.http.HttpServer`, then watch as `HttpServer` executes servlets in response to HTTP requests we make from a browser. This is very similar to how applets are debugged. The difference is that with applets, the actual program being debugged is `sun.applet.AppletViewer`. Most debuggers hide this detail by automatically knowing how to debug applets. Until they do the same for servlets, you have to help your debugger by doing the following:

1. Set your debugger's classpath so that it can find `sun.servlet.http.Http-Server` and associated classes.

2. Set your debugger's classpath so that it can also find your servlets and support classes, typically *server_root/servlets* and *server_root/classes*. You normally wouldn't want *server_root/servlets* in your classpath because it disables servlet reloading. This inclusion, however, is useful for debugging. It allows your debugger to set breakpoints in a servlet before the custom servlet loader in `HttpServer` loads the servlet.

Once you have set the proper classpath, start debugging `sun.servlet.http.HttpServer`. You can set breakpoints in whatever servlet you're interested in debugging, then use a web browser to make a request to the `HttpServer` for the given servlet (*http://localhost:8080/servlet/ServletToDebug*). You should see execution stop at your breakpoints.

Use a Third-Party Tool

Third-party tools promise to bring new capabilities and ease of use to the task of servlet debugging. LiveSoftware, maker of the popular JRun servlet plug-in, was the first company to market a tool for servlet debugging. The product, named ServletDebugger, is designed to help programmatically test and debug a servlet. ServletDebugger doesn't require using `HttpServer` or a browser to make a request. Instead, you use a set of classes to write a small stub class that prepares and executes a servlet request. The stub specifies everything: the servlet's init parameters, the request's HTTP headers, and the request's parameters. Servlet-Debugger is fairly straightforward and is well suited to automated testing. The largest drawback is that it takes extra effort to properly prepare a realistic request. ServletDebugger is available from *http://www.livesoftware.com.*

You can expect additional third-party debugging tools to become available as servlets become more popular.

Examine the Client Request

Sometimes when a servlet doesn't behave as expected, it's useful to look at the raw HTTP request to which it's responding. If you're familiar with the structure of HTTP, you can read the request and see exactly where a servlet might get confused.[*] One way to see the raw request is to replace the web server process with a custom server application that prints out everything it receives. Example 13-9 shows such a server.

Example 13-9. Catching a client request

```
import java.io.*;
import java.net.*;
import java.util.*;

public class SocketWatch {

  private static void printUsage() {
```

---

[*] Of course, if you're not familiar with the structure of HTTP, it may be you who are getting confused. In that case, we recommend reading the HTTP primer in Chapter 2 and the book *Web Client Programming* by Clinton Wong (O'Reilly).

Example 13-9. Catching a client request (continued)

```java
    System.out.println("usage: java SocketWatch port");
  }

  public static void main(String[] args) {
    if (args.length < 1) {
      printUsage();
      return;
    }

    // The first argument is the port to listen on
    int port;
    try {
      port = Integer.parseInt(args[0]);
    }
    catch (NumberFormatException e) {
      printUsage();
      return;
    }

    try {
      // Establish a server socket to accept client connections
      // As each connection comes in, pass it to a handler thread
      ServerSocket ss = new ServerSocket(port);
      while (true) {
        Socket request = ss.accept();
        new HandlerThread(request).start();
      }
    }
    catch (Exception e) {
      e.printStackTrace();
    }
  }
}

class HandlerThread extends Thread {

  Socket s;

  public HandlerThread(Socket s) {
    this.s = s;
  }

  public void run() {
    try {
      // Print each byte as it comes in from the socket
      InputStream in = s.getInputStream();
      byte[] bytes = new byte[1];
      while ((in.read(bytes)) != -1) {
```

Example 13-9. Catching a client request (continued)

```
      System.out.print((char)bytes[0]);
    }
  }
  catch (Exception e) {
    e.printStackTrace();
  }
  }
}
```

You can start this server listening on port 8080 by typing *java SocketWatch 8080* in a shell. Note that two applications can't listen to the same socket at the same time, so you should first make sure there's no other server listening on your chosen port. Once you have the server running, you can make HTTP requests to it as if it were a normal web server. For example, you can use a web browser to surf to *http://localhost:8080*. When SocketWatch receives the browser's HTTP request, it sends the request to its standard out for your examination. The browser, meanwhile, is likely to be busy waiting for a response that will never come. You can end its wait by hitting the **Stop** button.

Here is some sample output from SocketWatch that shows the details of a GET request made to *http://localhost:8080*:

```
GET / HTTP/1.0
Connection: Keep-Alive
User-Agent: Mozilla/3.03C-SGI (X11; I; IRIX 6.2 IP22)
Pragma: no-cache
Host: localhost:8080
Accept: image/gif, image/x-xbitmap, image/jpeg, image/pjpeg, */*
Cookie: jwssessionid=USN1RLIAAAAABQDGPM5QAAA
```

Create a Custom Client Request

In addition to catching and examining a client's HTTP request, you may find it useful to create your own HTTP request. You can do this by connecting to the server socket on which the web server is listening, then manually entering a properly structured HTTP request. To establish the connection, you can use the *telnet* program, available on all Unix machines and most Windows machines with networking. The *telnet* program accepts as arguments the host and port number to which it should connect. Once you're connected, you can make a request that looks like what you saw in the last section. Fortunately, your request can be far simpler—all you need to specify is the first line, saying what to get, and the last line, which must be an empty line that indicates the end of the request. For example:

```
% telnet localhost 8080
```

```
Trying 127.0.0.1...
Connected to localhost.
Escape character is '^]'.
GET /servlet/ParameterSnoop?name=value HTTP/1.0

HTTP/1.1 200 OK
Server: JavaWebServer/1.1.1
Content-Type: text/plain
Connection: close
Date: Sun, 12 Apr 1998 20:29:06 GMT

Query String:
name=value

Request Parameters:
name (0): value
Connection closed by foreign host.
```

As is too often the case, Windows behaves a little differently than you'd like. The default Windows *telnet.exe* program misformats many web server responses because it doesn't understand that on the Web, a line feed should be treated the same as a line feed and carriage return. In lieu of *telnet.exe,* Windows programmers can use the better-behaved Java program shown in Example 13-10.

Example 13-10. Another way to connect to a web server

```java
import java.io.*;
import java.net.*;
import java.util.*;

public class HttpClient {

  private static void printUsage() {
    System.out.println("usage: java HttpClient host port");
  }

  public static void main(String[] args) {
    if (args.length < 2) {
      printUsage();
      return;
    }

    // Host is the first parameter, port is the second
    String host = args[0];
    int port;
    try {
      port = Integer.parseInt(args[1]);
    }
    catch (NumberFormatException e) {
```

Example 13-10. Another way to connect to a web server (continued)

```
      printUsage();
      return;
    }

    try {
      // Open a socket to the server
      Socket s = new Socket(host, port);

      // Start a thread to send keyboard input to the server
      new KeyboardInputManager(System.in, s).start();

      // Now print everything we receive from the socket
      BufferedReader in =
        new BufferedReader(new InputStreamReader(s.getInputStream()));
      String line;
      while ((line = in.readLine()) != null) {
        System.out.println(line);
      }
    }
    catch (Exception e) {
      e.printStackTrace();
    }
  }
}

class KeyboardInputManager extends Thread {

  InputStream in;
  Socket s;

  public KeyboardInputManager(InputStream in, Socket s) {
    this.in = in;
    this.s = s;
    setPriority(MIN_PRIORITY);  // socket reads should have a higher priority
                                // Wish I could use a select() !
    setDaemon(true);  // let the app die even when this thread is running
  }

  public void run() {
    try {
      BufferedReader keyb = new BufferedReader(new InputStreamReader(in));
      PrintWriter server = new PrintWriter(s.getOutputStream());

      String line;
      System.out.println("Connected... Type your manual HTTP request");
      System.out.println("-----------------------------------------");
      while ((line = keyb.readLine()) != null) {
        server.print(line);
```

Example 13-10. Another way to connect to a web server (continued)

```
        server.print("\r\n");  // HTTP lines end with \r\n
        server.flush();
      }
    }
    catch (Exception e) {
      e.printStackTrace();
    }
  }
}
```

This `HttpClient` program operates similarly to `telnet`:

```
% java HttpClient localhost 8080
Connected... Type your manual HTTP request
-------------------------------------------
GET / HTTP/1.0

HTTP/1.1 200 OK
Server: JavaWebServer/1.1.1
Content-Length: 1999
Content-Type: text/html
Last-Modified: Mon, 12 Jan 1998 08:26:20 GMT
Date: Wed, 08 Apr 1998 23:41:50 GMT

<html>
  <head>
    <title>Java(TM) Web Server Default Page</title>
  </head>
  ...
```

Some Final Tips

If all the advice so far hasn't helped track down your bug, here are some final tips on servlet debugging:

- Use `System.getProperty("java.class.path")` from your servlet to help debug classpath problems. Because servlets are often run from web servers with embedded JVMs, it can be hard at times to identify exactly what classpath the JVM is searching. The property `"java.class.path"` will tell you.

- Be aware that *server_root/classes* doesn't reload and that *server_root/servlets* probably does.

- Ask a browser to show the raw content of the page it is displaying. This can help identify formatting problems. It's usually an option under the **View** menu.

- Make sure the browser isn't caching a previous request's output by forcing a full reload of the page. With Netscape Navigator, use **Shift-Reload**; with Internet Explorer use **Shift-Refresh**.

- Verify that your servlet's `init()` method takes a `ServletConfig` parameter and calls `super.init(config)` right away.

Performance Tuning

Performance tuning servlets requires a slightly different mindset than performance tuning normal Java applications or applets. The reason is that the JVM running the servlets is expected to simultaneously handle dozens, if not hundreds, of threads, each executing a servlet. These coexisting servlets have to share the resources of the JVM in a way that normal applications do not. The traditional performance-tuning tricks still apply, of course, but they have a different impact when used in a heavily multithreaded system. What follows are some of the tricks that have the largest special impact on servlet developers.

Go Forth, but Don't Prosper

Avoid the unnecessary creation of objects. This has always been good advice—creating unnecessary objects wastes memory and wastes a fair amount of time as the objects are created. With servlets, it's even better advice. All but the most recent JVMs have a global object heap that must be locked for each new memory allocation. While any servlet is creating a new object or allocating additional memory, no other servlet can do so.

Don't Append by Concatenation

Avoid concatenating several strings together. Use the `append()` method of `StringBuffer` instead. This too has always been good advice, but with servlets it's particularly tempting to write code like this to prepare a string for later output:

```
String output;
output += "<TITLE>";
output += "Hello, " + user;
output += "</TITLE>";
```

Although this code looks nice and neat, when it runs it executes as if written roughly as follows, with a new `StringBuffer` and new `String` created on each line:

```
String output;
output = new StringBuffer().append("<TITLE>").toString();
output = new StringBuffer(output).append("Hello, ").toString();
```

```
output = new StringBuffer(output).append(user).toString();
output = new StringBuffer(output).append("</TITLE>").toString();
```

When efficiency counts, rewrite the original code to look like the following, so just one `StringBuffer` and one `String` are created:

```
StringBuffer buf = new StringBuffer();
buf.append("<TITLE>");
buf.append("Hello, ").append(user);
buf.append("</TITLE);
output = buf.toString();
```

Note that using an array of bytes is even more efficient.

Limit Synchronization

Synchronize whenever necessary, but no more. Every synchronized block in a servlet slows the servlet's response time. Because the same servlet instance may handle multiple concurrent requests, it must, of course, take care to protect its class and instance variables with synchronized blocks. All the time one request thread is in a servlet's synchronized block, however, no other thread can enter the block. Therefore, it's generally best to keep these blocks as small as possible.

You should also take a look at the worst-case result of thread contention. If the worst case is bearable (as with the counter example from Chapter 3, *The Servlet Life Cycle*), you can consider removing synchronization blocks entirely. Also consider using the `SingleThreadModel` tag interface, where the server manages a pool of servlet instances to guarantee each instance is used at most by one thread at a time. Servlets that implement `SingleThreadModel` don't need to synchronize access to their instance variables.

Buffer Your Input and Output

Buffer your input and your output, all your storage files, any streams loaded from a database, and so on. This almost always improves performance, but the improvement can be especially profound with servlets. The reason is that reading and writing one unit at a time can slow down the entire server due to the frequent context switches that have to be made. Fortunately, you generally don't need to buffer when writing to a servlet's `PrintWriter` or `ServletOutputStream` or when reading from a servlet's `BufferedReader` or `ServletInputStream`. Most server implementations already buffer these streams.

A

Servlet API Quick
Reference

The `javax.servlet` package is the core of the Servlet API. It includes the basic `Servlet` interface, which all servlets must implement in one form or another, and an abstract `GenericServlet` class for developing basic servlets. This package also includes classes for communication with the host server and client (`Servlet-Request` and `ServletResponse`) and communicating with the client (`ServletInputStream` and `ServletOutputStream`). The class hierarchy of the `javax.servlet` package is shown in Figure A-1. Servlets should confine themselves to the classes in this package in situations where the underlying protocol is unknown.

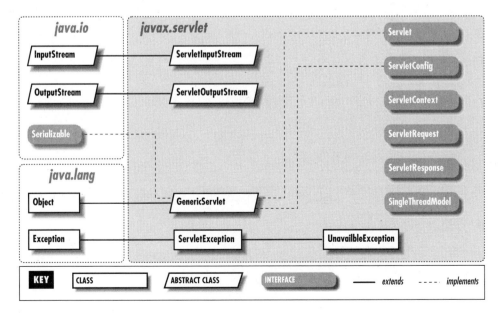

Figure A-1. The javax.servlet package

GenericServlet

Synopsis

Class Name:	`javax.servlet.GenericServlet`
Superclass:	`java.lang.Object`
Immediate Subclasses:	`javax.servlet.http.HttpServlet`
Interfaces Implemented:	`javax.servlet.Servlet,`
	`javax.servlet.ServletConfig,`
	`java.io.Serializable`
Availability:	Servlet API 1.0 and later

Description

GenericServlet provides a basic implementation of the Servlet interface for protocol-independent servlets. As a convenience, it also implements the Servlet-Config interface. Most servlet developers subclass this class or HttpServlet, rather than implement the Servlet interface directly.

GenericServlet includes basic versions of the init() and destroy() methods, which perform basic setup and cleanup tasks, such as managing the server's ServletConfig object. It's good form for a servlet that overrides one of these methods to call the superclass version of the method. GenericServlet also includes a log() method that provides easy access to the logging functions from ServletContext.

The service() method is declared as abstract and must be overridden. Well written servlets also override getServletInfo().

Class Summary

```
public abstract class GenericServlet
  implements Servlet, ServletConfig, java.io.Serializable {
  // Constructors
  public GenericServlet();

  // Instance Methods
  public void destroy();
  public String getInitParameter(String name);
  public Enumeration getInitParameterNames();
  public ServletConfig getServletConfig();
  public ServletContext getServletContext();
  public String getServletInfo();
  public void init(ServletConfig config) throws ServletException;
  public void log(String msg);
```

```
    public abstract void service(ServletRequest req, ServletResponse res)
      throws ServletException, IOException;
}
```

Constructors

GenericServlet()

public GenericServlet()

Description

The default `GenericServlet` constructor does no work. Any servlet initialization tasks should be performed in `init()`, rather than in the constructor.

Instance Methods

destroy()

public void destroy()

Description

Called by the server before unloading the servlet. The default implementation logs the servlet's destruction in the server log file using the `log()` method. A servlet can override this method to save its state, free its resources, etc.

getInitParameter()

public String getInitParameter(String name)

Description

Returns the value of the named servlet initialization parameter or `null` if no matching parameter is found. From the `ServletConfig` interface.

getInitParameterNames()

public Enumeration getInitParameterNames()

Description

Returns all the servlet's init parameter names as an `Enumeration` of `String` objects or an empty `Enumeration` if no parameters exist. From the `ServletConfig` interface.

getServletConfig()

public ServletConfig getServletConfig()

Description

Returns the servlet's `ServletConfig` object. In practice, this method is rarely called by a `GenericServlet` because all of the `ServletConfig` methods are duplicated internally.

getServletContext()

```
public ServletContext getServletContext()
```

Description

Returns the servlet's `ServletContext` object. From the `ServletConfig` interface.

getServletInfo()

```
public String getServletInfo()
```

Description

Returns a programmer-defined `String` that describes the servlet. A servlet should override this method and provide a customized identity string (e.g., "Al's Message Board Servlet v1.21"), but it is not required.

init()

```
public void init(ServletConfig config) throws ServletException
```

Description

Called by the server after the servlet is first loaded and before the servlet's `service()` method is called. The default implementation of `init()` logs the servlet's initialization and stores the `ServletConfig` object for use by the methods in the `ServletConfig` interface. A servlet can override this method to perform additional one-time setup, creation of resources, etc. A servlet should always call the superclass implementation of `init()` using `super.init(config)` before executing any custom initialization code.

log()

```
public void log(String msg)
```

Description

Writes the given message to a servlet log, usually an event log file. Both the output format and location are server-specific.

service()

```
public abstract void service(ServletRequest req, ServletResponse res)
    throws ServletException, IOException
```

Description

Called to handle a single client request. A servlet receives request information via a `ServletRequest` object and sends data back to the client via a `ServletResponse` object. This is the only method that must be overridden when extending `GenericServlet`. Because multiple service requests may execute concurrently, the `service()` method must be thread safe, unless the servlet also implements the `SingleThreadModel` interface.

Servlet

Synopsis

Interface Name: `javax.servlet.Servlet`
Super-interface: None
Immediate Subinterfaces: None
Implemented By: `javax.servlet.GenericServlet`
Availability: Servlet API 1.0 and later

Description

All servlets implement the `Servlet` interface, either directly or by subclassing the `GenericServlet` or `HttpServlet` class. Most servlet developers find it easier to subclass one of the two existing servlet classes than to implement this interface directly. The interface declares the basic servlet functionality—initializing a servlet, handling a client request, and destroying a servlet.

Interface Declaration

```
public interface Servlet {
  // Methods
  public abstract void destroy();
  public abstract ServletConfig getServletConfig();
  public abstract String getServletInfo();
  public abstract void init(ServletConfig config) throws ServletException;
  public abstract void service(ServletRequest req, ServletResponse res)
    throws ServletException, IOException;
}
```

Methods

destroy()

```
public abstract void destroy()
```

Description

Called when the server is preparing to unload a servlet. Used to clean up any outstanding resources (database connections, threads, file handles and so forth). The servlet programmer is responsible for making sure that any requests currently executing are allowed to finish.

getServletConfig()

```
public abstract ServletConfig getServletConfig()
```

Description

Returns the `ServletConfig` object passed to the `init()` method.

getServletInfo()

> public abstract String getServletInfo()

> *Description*

> Returns a programmer-defined String that describes the servlet.

init()

> public abstract void init(ServletConfig config) throws ServletException

> *Description*

> Called by the server when the servlet is first loaded. The init() method should store the ServletConfig object for retrieval by getServlet-Config(). When using either GenericServlet or HttpServlet, the default init() implementation handles this task. This method can also be used to perform any one-time actions required by the servlet, such as creating database connections. It is guaranteed to finish before any client requests are accepted.

service()

> public abstract void service(ServletRequest req, ServletResponse res)
>   throws ServletException, IOException

> *Description*

> Called to handle a single client request. A servlet receives request information via the ServletRequest object and sends data back to the client via the ServletResponse object.

ServletConfig

Synopsis

Interface Name:	javax.servlet.ServletConfig
Superinterface:	None
Immediate Subinterfaces:	None
Implemented By:	javax.servlet.GenericServlet
Availability:	Servlet API 1.0 and later

Description

Servers use ServletConfig objects to pass initialization and context information to servlets. The initialization information generally consists of a series of initialization parameters (*init parameters*) and a ServletContext object, which provides information about the server environment. A servlet can implement Servlet-

Config to allow easy access to init parameters and context information, as GenericServlet does.

Interface Declaration

```
public interface ServletConfig {
  // Methods
  public abstract String getInitParameter(String name);
  public abstract Enumeration getInitParameterNames();
  public abstract ServletContext getServletContext();
}
```

Methods

getInitParameter()

public abstract String getInitParameter(String name)

Description

Returns the value of the named servlet initialization parameter or null if no matching parameter is found.

getInitParameterNames()

public abstract Enumeration getInitParameterNames()

Description

Returns the names of all the servlet's initialization parameters as an Enumeration of String objects or an empty Enumeration if no parameters exist.

getServletContext()

public abstract ServletContext getServletContext()

Description

Returns the ServletContext object for this servlet, allowing interaction with the server.

ServletContext

Synopsis

Interface Name:	javax.servlet.ServletContext
Superinterface:	None
Immediate Subinterfaces:	None
Implemented By:	None
Availability:	Servlet API 1.0 and later

Description

The ServletContext interface defines a set of methods that can be used to communicate with the server in a non-request-specific manner. This includes finding path information, accessing other servlets running on the server, and writing to the server log file. Different virtual servers may return different servlet contexts.

Interface Declaration

```
public interface ServletContext {
  // Methods
  public abstract Object getAttribute(String name);
  public abstract String getMimeType(String file);
  public abstract String getRealPath(String path);
  public abstract String getServerInfo();
  public abstract Servlet getServlet(String name) throws ServletException;
  public abstract Enumeration getServletNames();            // New in 2.0
  public abstract Enumeration getServlets();                // Deprecated
  public abstract void log(Exception exception, String msg); // New in 2.0
  public abstract void log(String msg);
}
```

Methods

getAttribute()

```
public abstract Object getAttribute(String name)
```

Description

Returns the value of the named server attribute as an Object or null if the attribute does not exist. The attributes are server-dependent and allow web servers to provide servlets with information above and beyond that provided for by the base Servlet API. Attribute names should follow the same convention as package names. The package names java.* and javax.* are reserved for use by the Java Software division of Sun Microsystems (formerly known as JavaSoft), and com.sun.* is reserved for use by Sun Microsystems. See your server's documentation for a list of its attributes. Remember that servlets relying on server-specific attributes are not portable.

getMimeType()

```
public abstract String getMimeType(String file)
```

Description

Returns the MIME type of the given file or null if it is not known. Some implementations return "text/plain" if the specified file does not exist.

Common MIME types are "text/html", "text/plain", "image/gif", and "image/jpeg".

getRealPath()

```
public abstract String getRealPath(String path)
```

Description

Returns the real file system path of any given "virtual path" or null if the translation cannot be performed. If the given path is "/", the method returns the document root for the servlet. If the given path is the same as the one returned by getPathInfo(), the method returns the same real path as would be returned by getPathTranslated(). There is no CGI counterpart.

getServerInfo()

```
public abstract String getServerInfo()
```

Description

Returns the name and version of the server software, separated by a forward slash (/). The value is the same as the CGI variable SERVER_SOFTWARE.

getServlet()

```
public abstract Servlet getServlet(String name) throws ServletException
```

Description

Returns the loaded servlet matching the given name or null if the servlet is not found. The specified name can be the servlet's registered name (e.g., "file") or class name (e.g., "com.sun.server.webserver.FileServlet"). The server maintains one servlet instance per name, so getServlet("file") returns a different servlet instance than get-Servlet("com.sun.server.webserver.FileServlet"). If the servlet implements SingleThreadModel, the server may return any instance of the servlet from the current pool. The server may—but is not required to—load the named servlet and execute its init() method if it was not already loaded. A ServletException is thrown if there is a problem during the load.

getServletNames()

```
public abstract Enumeration getServletNames()
```

Description

Returns an Enumeration of the names of the servlet objects loaded in this context. When used with getServlet(String name), it can replace the deprecated getServlets(). This method was introduced in the Servlet API 2.0.

`getServlets()`

> `public abstract Enumeration getServlets() throws ServletException`

> *Description*

>> Returns an `Enumeration` of the `Servlet` objects loaded in this context. This method was deprecated in the Servlet API 2.0 in favor of `getServletNames()`.

`log()`

> `public abstract void log(Exception exception, String msg)`

> *Description*

>> Writes an exception's stack trace and a given message to a servlet log, usually an event log file. Both output format and location are server-specific. Notice the non-standard placement of the optional `Exception` parameter as the first parameter instead of the last. This method was introduced in the Servlet API 2.0.

> `public abstract void log(String msg)`

> *Description*

>> Writes the given message to a servlet log, usually an event log file. Both the output format and location are server-specific.

ServletException

Synopsis

Class Name:	`javax.servlet.ServletException`
Superclass:	`java.lang.Exception`
Immediate Subclasses:	`javax.servlet.UnavailableException`
Interfaces Implemented:	None
Availability:	Servlet API 1.0 and later

Description

A generic exception thrown by servlets encountering difficulties.

Class Summary

```
public class ServletException extends java.lang.Exception {
  // Constructors
  public ServletException();                          // New in 2.0
  public ServletException(String msg);
}
```

Constructors

ServletException()

```
public ServletException()
public ServletException(String msg)
```

Description

> Constructs a new ServletException, with an optional descriptive message. If a message is specified, it can be retrieved by calling getMessage() and is usually included in server logs and user error messages.

ServletInputStream

Synopsis

Class Name:	javax.servlet.ServletInputStream
Superclass:	java.io.InputStream
Immediate Subclasses:	None
Interfaces Implemented:	None
Availability:	Servlet API 1.0 and later

Description

Provides an input stream for reading binary data from a client request, including an efficient readLine() method for reading data one line at a time. A Servlet-InputStream is returned by the getInputStream() method of ServletRequest. A servlet that filters binary output from other sources generally gets its input via this stream.

Class Summary

```
public abstract class ServletInputStream extends java.io.InputStream {
  // Constructors
  protected ServletInputStream();

  // Instance Methods
  public int readLine(byte b[], int off, int len) throws IOException;
}
```

Constructors

ServletInputStream()

```
protected ServletInputStream()
```

Description

> The default constructor does nothing. Because servlets rarely, if ever, create their own input streams, it can be safely ignored.

Instance Methods

readLine()

```
public int readLine(byte b[], int off, int len) throws IOException
```

Description

> Reads bytes from the input stream into the byte array b, starting at an offset in the array given by off. It stops reading when it encounters an '\n' or it has read len number of bytes. The ending '\n' character is read into the buffer as well. Returns the number of bytes read, or –1 if the end of the stream is reached.

ServletOutputStream

Synopsis

Class Name:	`javax.servlet.ServletOutputStream`
Superclass:	`java.io.OutputStream`
Immediate Subclasses:	None
Interfaces Implemented:	None
Availability:	Servlet API 1.0 and later

Description

Provides an output stream for sending binary data back to a client. A servlet obtains a `ServletOutputStream` object from the `getOutputStream()` method of `ServletResponse`. Although it includes a range of `print()` and `println()` methods for sending text or HTML, the `ServletOutputStream` has been superseded by `PrintWriter`. It should be used only for sending binary data or with early servlet implementations built on the Servlet API 1.0.

If you subclass `ServletOutputStream`, you must provide an implementation of the `write(int)` method.

Class Summary

```
public abstract class ServletOutputStream extends java.io.OutputStream {
    // Constructors
    protected ServletOutputStream();

    // Instance Methods
```

```
    public void print(boolean b) throws IOException;
    public void print(char c) throws IOException;
    public void print(double d) throws IOException;
    public void print(float f) throws IOException;
    public void print(int i) throws IOException;
    public void print(long l) throws IOException;
    public void print(String s) throws IOException;
    public void println() throws IOException;
    public void println(boolean b) throws IOException;
    public void println(char c) throws IOException;
    public void println(double d) throws IOException;
    public void println(float f) throws IOException;
    public void println(int i) throws IOException;
    public void println(long l) throws IOException;
    public void println(String s) throws IOException;
}
```

Constructors

ServletOutputStream()

```
    protected ServletOutputStream()
```

Description

The default constructor does nothing.

Instance Methods

print()

```
    public void print(boolean b) throws IOException
    public void print(char c) throws IOException
    public void print(double d) throws IOException
    public void print(float f) throws IOException
    public void print(int i) throws IOException
    public void print(long l) throws IOException
    public void print(String s) throws IOException
```

Description

Writes the given data to the client, without a trailing carriage return/line feed (CRLF).

println()

```
    public void println() throws IOException
    public void println(boolean b) throws IOException
    public void println(char c) throws IOException
    public void println(double d) throws IOException
    public void println(float f) throws IOException
    public void println(int i) throws IOException
    public void println(long l) throws IOException
    public void println(String s) throws IOException
```

Description

Writes the given data to the client, with a trailing CRLF. The method with no parameters simply writes a CRLF.

ServletRequest

Synopsis

Interface Name: `javax.servlet.ServletRequest`
Superinterface: None
Immediate Subinterfaces: `javax.servlet.http.HttpServletRequest`
Implemented By: None
Availability: Servlet API 1.0 and later

Description

A `ServletRequest` object encapsulates information about a single client request, including request parameters, implementation-specific attributes, and an input stream for reading binary data from the request body. `ServletRequest` can be subclassed to provide additional protocol-specific information. `HttpServlet-Request`, for instance, includes methods to manipulate HTTP headers.

Interface Declaration

```
public interface ServletRequest {
  // Methods
  public abstract Object getAttribute(String name);
  public abstract String getCharacterEncoding();               // New in 2.0
  public abstract int getContentLength();
  public abstract String getContentType();
  public abstract ServletInputStream getInputStream() throws IOException;
  public abstract String getParameter(String name);
  public abstract Enumeration getParameterNames();
  public abstract String[] getParameterValues(String name);
  public abstract String getProtocol();
  public abstract BufferedReader getReader() throws IOException;// New in 2.0
  public abstract String getRealPath(String path);
  public abstract String getRemoteAddr();
  public abstract String getRemoteHost();
  public abstract String getScheme();
  public abstract String getServerName();
  public abstract int getServerPort();
}
```

Methods

getAttribute()

```
public abstract Object getAttribute(String name)
```

Description

Returns the value of the named server-specific attribute as an Object, or null if the server does not support the named request attribute. Servers may use this method to provide servlets with custom information about a request. Attributes should follow the same conventions as package names, with the package names java.* and javax.* reserved for use by the Java Software division of Sun Microsystems (formerly known as JavaSoft), and com.sun.* reserved for use by Sun Microsystems. Remember that servlets that rely on server-specific request attributes are non-portable.

getCharacterEncoding()

```
public abstract String getCharacterEncoding()
```

Description

Returns the charset encoding for the servlet's input stream, or null if not known. This method was introduced in the Servlet API 2.0. It does not exist in the Java Web Server 1.1.x.

getContentLength()

```
public abstract int getContentLength()
```

Description

Returns the length, in bytes, of the content being sent via the input stream, or -1 if the length is not known (such as when there is no data). Equivalent to the CGI variable CONTENT_LENGTH.

getContentType()

```
public abstract String getContentType()
```

Description

Returns the media type of the content being sent via the input stream or null if the type is not known or there is no data. The same as the CGI variable CONTENT_TYPE.

getInputStream()

```
public abstract ServletInputStream getInputStream() throws IOException
```

Description

Retrieves the input stream as a ServletInputStream object. Servlet-InputStream is a direct subclass of InputStream and can be treated identically to a normal InputStream, with the added ability to efficiently read input a line at a time into an array of bytes. This method should be

used for reading binary input. It throws an `IllegalStateException` if
`getReader()` has been called before on the request. The `IllegalState-`
`Exception` does not need to be explicitly caught.

getParameter()

> `public abstract String getParameter(String name)`

> *Description*
>
> Returns the value of the named parameter as a `String`. Returns `null` if
> the parameter does not exist, or an empty string if the parameter exists
> but without a value. The value is guaranteed to be in its normal, decoded
> form. If the parameter has multiple values, the value returned is server
> dependent. If there is any chance that a parameter has more than one
> value, you should use the `getParameterValues()` method instead. If the
> parameter information came in as encoded POST data, it may not be
> available if the POST data has already been manually read using the
> `getReader()` or `getInputStream()` methods. This method was depre-
> cated momentarily in favor of `getParameterValues()`, but thanks to an
> overwhelming flood of support from the developer community, it has been
> restored in the Servlet API 2.0.

getParameterNames()

> `public abstract Enumeration getParameterNames()`

> *Description*
>
> Returns all the parameter names as an `Enumeration` of `String` objects. It
> returns an empty `Enumeration` if the servlet has no parameters.

getParameterValues()

> `public abstract String[] getParameterValues(String name)`

> *Description*
>
> Returns all the values of the named parameter as an array of `String`
> objects, or `null` if the parameter does not exist. A single value is returned
> in an array of length 1.

getProtocol()

> `public abstract String getProtocol()`

> *Description*
>
> Returns the name and version of the protocol used by the request as a
> string of the form *protocol/major-version.minor-version*. Equiva-
> lent to the CGI variable `SERVER_PROTOCOL`.

getReader()

> `public abstract BufferedReader getReader() throws IOException`

Description

This method retrieves the input stream as a `BufferedReader` object, which should be used for reading character-based input, since the reader translates charsets as appropriate. This method throws an `IllegalState-Exception` if `getInputStream()` has been called before on this same request. It throws an `UnsupportedEncodingException` if the character encoding of the input is unsupported or unknown. This method was introduced in the Servlet API 2.0.

getRealPath()

`public abstract String getRealPath(String path)`

Description

Returns the real file system path of any given "virtual path" or `null` if the translation cannot be performed. If the given path is `"/"` it returns the document root for the server. If the given path is the same as the one returned by `getPathInfo()`, it returns the same real path as would be returned by `getPathTranslated()`. There is no CGI counterpart.

getRemoteAddr()

`public abstract String getRemoteAddr()`

Description

Returns the IP address of the client machine as a `String`. This information comes from the socket connecting the server to the client, so the remote address may be that of a proxy server. It is the same as the CGI variable REMOTE_ADDR.

getRemoteHost()

`public abstract String getRemoteHost()`

Description

Returns the name of the client host. This comes from the socket connecting the server to the client and may be the name of a proxy server. It is the same as the CGI variable REMOTE_HOST.

getScheme()

`public abstract String getScheme()`

Description

This method returns the scheme used to make this request. Examples include `"http"`, `"https"`, and `"ftp"`, as well as the newer Java-specific schemes `"jdbc"` and `"rmi"`.

getServerName()

`public abstract String getServerName()`

Description

> Returns the name of the server that received the request. It is an attribute
> of the `ServletRequest` because it can change for different requests if the
> server has more than one name (a situation that might arise if one server
> is hosting more than one web site). Equivalent to the CGI variable
> `SERVER_NAME`.

getServerPort()

```
public abstract int getServerPort()
```

Description

> Returns the port number on which this request was received. The same as
> the CGI variable `SERVER_PORT`.

ServletResponse

Synopsis

Interface Name:	`javax.servlet.ServletResponse`
Superinterface:	None
Immediate Subinterfaces:	`javax.servlet.http.HttpServletResponse`
Interfaces Implemented:	None
Availability:	Servlet API 1.0 and later

Description

Servlets use `ServletResponse` objects to send MIME encoded data back to the
client. The servlet engine creates this object and passes it to the servlet's
`service()` method. To send binary data, use the `ServletOutputStream`
returned by `getOutputStream()`. To send character data, use the `PrintWriter`
returned by `getWriter()`. You can explicitly set the output's MIME type using the
`setContentType()` method. If you elect to set this manually, do so before calling
`getWriter()`, as `getWriter()` consults the content type to determine which
charset to use. Consult RFC 2045 at *http://www.ietf.org/rfc/rfc2045.txt* for more information on MIME.

Interface Declaration

```
public interface ServletResponse {
    // Methods
    public abstract String getCharacterEncoding();              // New in 2.0
    public abstract ServletOutputStream getOutputStream() throws IOException;
    public abstract PrintWriter getWriter() throws IOException;  // New in 2.0
    public abstract void setContentLength(int len);
```

```
        public abstract void setContentType(String type);
    }
```

Methods

`getCharacterEncoding()`

```
public abstract String getCharacterEncoding()
```

Description

Returns the charset encoding used for this MIME body. This is the charset specified by the assigned content type or `"ISO-8859-1"` if no charset has been specified. This method was introduced in the Servlet API 2.0.

`getOutputStream()`

```
public abstract ServletOutputStream getOutputStream() throws IOException
```

Description

Returns a `ServletOutputStream` for writing binary (byte-at-a-time) response data. No encoding is performed. Throws an `IllegalState-Exception` if `getWriter()` has already been called on this response.

`getWriter()`

```
public abstract PrintWriter getWriter() throws IOException
```

Description

Returns a `PrintWriter` for writing character-based response data. The writer encodes the characters according to whatever charset is given in the content type. If no charset is specified in the content type, as is generally the case, the writer uses the ISO-8859-1 (Latin-1) encoding appropriate for Western European languages. Throws an `IllegalStateException` if `getOutputStream()` has already been called on this response, and an `UnsupportedEncodingException` if the encoding of the output stream is unsupported or unknown. This method was introduced in the Servlet API 2.0.

`setContentLength()`

```
public abstract void setContentLength(int len)
```

Description

Sets the length of the content being returned by the server. In HTTP servlets, it sets the HTTP `Content-Length` header. HTTP servlets use this method to enable persistent connections and help client progress monitors, so its use is optional.

`setContentType()`

```
public abstract void setContentType(String type)
```

Description

This method sets the content type of the response to be the specified type. In HTTP servlets, it sets the `Content-Type` HTTP header.

SingleThreadModel

Synopsis

Interface Name: `javax.servlet.SingleThreadModel`
Superinterface: None
Immediate Subinterfaces   None
Implemented By: None
Availability: New as of Servlet API 2.0; found in JSDK 2.0, JWS 1.1

Description

`SingleThreadModel` is a tag interface with no methods. If a servlet implements this interface, the server ensures that each instance of the servlet handles only one service request at a time. Servers implement this functionality by maintaining a pool of servlet instances and dispatching incoming requests to free servlets within the pool. `SingleThreadModel` provides easy thread safety, but at the cost of increased resource requirements as more servlet instances are loaded at any given time.

Interface Declaration

```
public interface SingleThreadModel {
}
```

UnavailableException

Synopsis

Class Name: `javax.servlet.UnavailableException`
Superclass: `javax.servlet.ServletException`
Immediate Subclasses: None
Interfaces Implemented: None
Availability: Servlet API 1.0 and later

Description

A servlet can throw an `UnavailableException` at any time to indicate that it is not available to service client requests. There are two types of unavailability: permanent (where some corrective action must be taken on the server) and temporary. A servlet is temporarily unavailable if some system-wide problem momentarily prevents it from servicing requests. This may include network troubles or a crashed or overloaded database server. To mark a servlet as temporarily unavailable, specify a duration (in seconds) when constructing the exception. Well-written servers check back after this time. Servlet implementations are not required to treat temporary and permanent unavailability differently.

Servers generally provide clients with polite error messages when handling requests for unavailable servlets. For example, the Java Web Server returns a 404 (Unavailable) message.

Class Summary

```
public class UnavailableException extends ServletException {
  // Constructors
  public UnavailableException(int seconds, Servlet servlet, String msg);
  public UnavailableException(Servlet servlet, String msg);

  // Instance Methods
  public Servlet getServlet();
  public int getUnavailableSeconds();
  public boolean isPermanent();
}
```

Constructors

UnavailableException()

```
public UnavailableException(int seconds, Servlet servlet, String msg)
public UnavailableException(Servlet servlet, String msg)
```

Description

Constructs an `UnavailableException` with a given explanatory message. You can optionally specify a period of unavailability, given in seconds. If no time estimate can be made, a nonpositive value can be passed to the constructor, indicating permanent unavailability. Notice the nonstandard placement of the optional `seconds` parameter as the first parameter instead of the last. This may be changed in an upcoming release.

Instance Methods

getServlet()

```
public Servlet getServlet()
```

Description

Returns the servlet that threw this exception.

getUnavailableSeconds()

```
public int getUnavailableSeconds()
```

Description

Returns the number of seconds for which this servlet will be unavailable. A negative number indicates permanent unavailability. No attempt is made to compensate for the time elapsed since the exception was thrown.

isPermanent()

```
public boolean isPermanent()
```

Description

Returns `true` if the servlet is unavailable indefinitely, `false` otherwise.

B

HTTP Servlet API Quick Reference

The `javax.servlet.http` package allows development of servlets that support the HTTP protocol. While the core functionality in the `javax.servlet` package provides everything necessary for web development, the specialized classes in this package automate many otherwise tedious tasks. For example, the abstract `HttpServlet` class includes support for different HTTP request methods and headers. The `HttpServletRequest` and `HttpServletResponse` interfaces allow additional direct interaction with the web server, while `HttpSession` provides built-in session tracking functionality. The `Cookie` class allows you to quickly set up and process HTTP cookies, and the `HttpUtils` class does the same for query strings. Figure B-1 shows the class hierarchy of the `javax.servlet.http` package.

Cookie

Synopsis

Class Name:	`javax.servlet.http.Cookie`
Superclass:	`java.lang.Object`
Immediate Subclasses:	None
Interfaces Implemented:	`java.lang.Cloneable`
Availability:	New as of Servlet API 2.0; found in JSDK 2.0, JWS 1.1; an earlier version previously in `sun.*` hierarchy

Description

The `Cookie` class provides an easy way for servlets to read, create, and manipulate HTTP-style cookies, which allow servlets to store small amounts of data on the

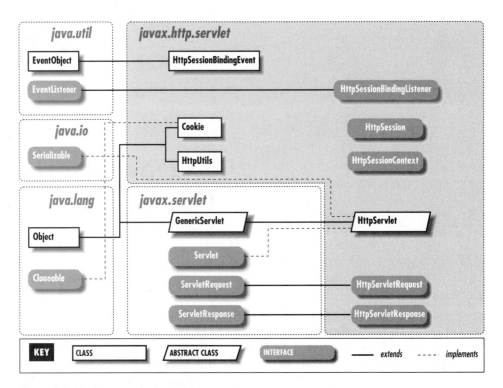

Figure B-1. The javax.servlet.http package

client. Cookies are generally used for session tracking or storing small amounts of user-specific configuration information. For more information, consult Chapter 7, *Session Tracking*.

A servlet uses the getCookies() method of HttpServletRequest to retrieve cookies submitted as part of a client request. The addCookie() method of HttpServletResponse sends a new cookie to the browser. Because cookies are set using HTTP headers, addCookie() must be called before any output is sent to the client.

The original Servlet API 1.0 lacked this Cookie class, although the Java Web Server included a Sun-specific sun.servlet.util.Cookie class that worked in roughly the same manner. The only significant difference is that the retrieval and creation methods were static components of the Cookie class itself, rather than being part of the HttpServletRequest and HttpServletResponse interfaces.

Class Summary

```
public class Cookie implements java.lang.Cloneable {
    // Constructors
```

```
    public Cookie(String name, String value);

    // Instance Methods
    public Object clone();
    public String getComment();
    public String getDomain();
    public int getMaxAge();
    public String getName();
    public String getPath();
    public boolean getSecure();
    public String getValue();
    public int getVersion();
    public void setComment(String purpose);
    public void setDomain(String pattern);
    public void setMaxAge(int expiry);
    public void setPath(String uri);
    public void setSecure(boolean flag);
    public void setValue(String newValue);
    public void setVersion(int v);
}
```

Constructors

Cookie()

public Cookie(String name, String value)
Description

Constructs a new cookie with an initial name and value. The rules for valid names and values are given in Netscape's Cookie Specification and RFC 2109.

Instance Methods

clone()

public Object clone()
Description

Overrides the standard clone() method to return a copy of this object (a duplicate cookie).

getComment()

public String getComment()
Description

Returns the comment associated with the cookie.

getDomain()

public String getDomain()
Description

Returns the domain limitation associated with this cookie.

getMaxAge()

public int getMaxAge()

Description

Returns the maximum age allowed for this cookie.

getPath()

public String getPath()

Description

Returns the path limitation for this servlet.

getSecure()

public boolean getSecure()

Description

Returns true if this cookie requires a secure connection, false otherwise.

getName()

public String getName()

Description

Returns the name of this cookie.

getValue()

public String getValue()

Description

Returns the value of this cookie, in string format.

getVersion()

public int getVersion()

Description

Returns the version of this cookie.

setComment()

public void setComment(String purpose)

Description

Sets the comment field of the cookie. A comment describes the intended purpose of a cookie. A web browser may choose to display this text to the user. Comments are not supported by Version 0 cookies.

setDomain()

public void setDomain(String pattern)

Description

Specifies a domain restriction pattern. A domain pattern specifies the servers that should see a cookie. By default, cookies are returned only to the host that saved them. Specifying a domain name pattern overrides this. The pattern must begin with a dot and must contain at least two dots. A pattern matches only one entry beyond the initial dot. For example, ".foo.com" is valid and matches *www.foo.com* and *upload.foo.com* but not *www.upload.foo.com*. For details on domain patterns, see Netscape's Cookie Specification and RFC 2109.

setMaxAge()

```
public void setMaxAge(int expiry)
```

Description

Specifies the maximum age of the cookie in seconds before it expires. A negative value indicates the default, that the cookie should expire when the browser exits. A zero value tells the browser to delete the cookie immediately.

setPath()

```
public void setPath(String uri)
```

Description

Specifies a path for the cookie, which is the subset of URIs to which a cookie should be sent. By default, cookies are sent to the page that set the cookie and to all the pages in that directory or under that directory. For example, if */servlet/CookieMonster* sets a cookie, the default path is "/servlet". That path indicates the cookie should be sent to */servlet/Elmo* and to */servlet/subdir/BigBird*—but not to the */Oscar.html* servlet alias or to any CGI programs under */cgi-bin*. A path set to "/" causes a cookie to be sent to all the pages on a server. A cookie's path must be such that it includes the servlet that set the cookie.

setSecure()

```
public void setSecure(boolean flag)
```

Description

The secure flag indicates whether the cookie should be sent only over a secure channel, such as SSL. This value defaults to `false`.

setValue()

```
public void setValue(String newValue)
```

Description

Assigns a new value to a cookie. With Version 0 cookies, values should not contain the following: whitespace, brackets and parentheses, equals signs, commas, double quotes, slashes, question marks, at signs, colons, and semicolons. Empty values may not behave the same way on all browsers.

setVersion()

```
public void setVersion(int v)
```

Description

Servlets can send and receive cookies formatted to match either Netscape persistent cookies (Version 0) or the newer, somewhat experimental, RFC 2109 cookies (Version 1). Newly constructed cookies default to Version 0 to maximize interoperability.

HttpServlet

Synopsis

Class Name: `javax.servlet.http.HttpServlet`
Superclass: `javax.servlet.GenericServlet`
Immediate Subclasses: None
Interfaces Implemented: `javax.servlet.Servlet,`
                                    `java.io.Serializable`
Availability: Servlet API 1.0 and later

Description

`HttpServlet` is an abstract class that serves as a framework for developing HTTP (World Wide Web) servlets. The public `service()` method dispatches requests to an HTTP-specific, protected `service()` method. You may either extend the HTTP-specific `service()` method (which is then used to handle all types of HTTP requests) or leave the default service method alone and allow it to dispatch requests to particular handler functions for each HTTP submission type: `doGet()`, `doPost()`, and so on. Because the default HTTP servlet implementation handles dispatching to these methods, if you override the protected `service()` method, you must either handle the dispatching manually or not use the handler functions for HTTP request methods.

Class Summary

```
public abstract class HttpServlet extends javax.servlet.GenericServlet
  implements javax.servlet.Servlet, java.io.Serializable {
  // Constructors
  public HttpServlet();

  // Public Instance Methods
  public void service(ServletRequest req, ServletResponse res)
    throws ServletException, IOException;

  // Protected Instance Methods
  protected void doDelete(HttpServletRequest req, HttpServletResponse res)
    throws ServletException, IOException;                    // New in 2.0
```

```
        protected void doGet(HttpServletRequest req, HttpServletResponse res)
          throws ServletException, IOException;
        protected void doOptions(HttpServletRequest req, HttpServletResponse res)
          throws ServletException, IOException;                    // New in 2.0
        protected void doPost(HttpServletRequest req,  HttpServletResponse res)
          throws ServletException, IOException;
        protected void doPut(HttpServletRequest req, HttpServletResponse res)
          throws ServletException, IOException;                    // New in 2.0
        protected void doTrace(HttpServletRequest req, HttpServletResponse res)
          throws ServletException, IOException;                    // New in 2.0
        protected long getLastModified(HttpServletRequest req);
        protected void service(HttpServletRequest req, HttpServletResponse res)
          throws ServletException, IOException;
    }
```

Constructors

HttpServlet()

public HttpServlet()

Description

> The default constructor does nothing. Because you cannot be sure of how
> and when classes will be loaded, it is not advisable to override this
> constructor to perform startup tasks. Use init() instead.

Public Instance Methods

service()

public void service(ServletRequest req, ServletResponse res)
  throws ServletException, IOException

Description

> This service() method handles dispatching requests to the protected,
> HTTP-specific service() method and cannot be overridden without
> disabling dispatching to the do*XXX*() methods.

Protected Instance Methods

doDelete()

protected void doDelete(HttpServletRequest req, HttpServletResponse res)
  throws ServletException, IOException

Description

> The default service() implementation in HttpServlet dispatches all
> HTTP DELETE requests to this method. Servlets implement this method to
> handle DELETE requests. The default implementation returns an HTTP
> BAD_REQUEST error. This method was introduced in the Servlet API 2.0.

doGet()

```
protected void doGet(HttpServletRequest req, HttpServletResponse res)
   throws ServletException, IOException
```
Description

The default `service()` implementation in `HttpServlet` dispatches all HTTP GET requests to this method. Servlets implement this method to handle GET requests. The default implementation returns an HTTP BAD_ REQUEST error.

doPost()

```
protected void doPost(HttpServletRequest req, HttpServletResponse res)
   throws ServletException, IOException
```
Description

The default `service()` implementation in `HttpServlet` dispatches all HTTP POST requests to this method. Servlets implement this method to handle POST requests. The default implementation returns an HTTP BAD_REQUEST error.

doPut()

```
protected void doPut(HttpServletRequest req, HttpServletResponse res)
   throws ServletException, IOException
```
Description

The default `service()` implementation in `HttpServlet` dispatches all HTTP PUT requests to this method. Servlets implement this method to handle PUT requests. The default implementation returns an HTTP BAD_ REQUEST error. See RFC 2068 at *http://www.ietf.org/rfc/rfc2068.txt* for more on HTTP PUT requests. This method was introduced in the Servlet API 2.0.

doOptions()

```
protected void doOptions(HttpServletRequest req, HttpServletResponse res)
   throws ServletException, IOException
```
Description

The default `service()` implementation in `HttpServlet` dispatches all HTTP OPTIONS requests to this method. The default implementation determines which options are supported and returns an appropriate header. For example, if a servlet overrides `doGet()` and `doPost()`, the browser is informed that GET, POST, HEAD, TRACE, and OPTIONS are supported. There is almost never any reason to override this method. This method was introduced in the Servlet API 2.0.

doTrace()

```
protected void doTrace(HttpServletRequest req, HttpServletResponse res)
   throws ServletException, IOException
```

Description

> The default `service()` implementation in `HttpServlet` dispatches all HTTP TRACE requests to this method. The default implementation returns a message listing all of the headers sent in the TRACE request. There is almost never any reason to override this method. This method was introduced in the Servlet API 2.0.

getLastModified()

> `protected long getLastModified(HttpServletRequest req)`
>
> *Description*
>
> Returns the date and time (expressed as milliseconds since midnight, January 1, 1970 GMT) that the content produced by the servlet was last modified. Negative values indicate that the time is not known. The default implementation returns −1. Called by servers in support of conditional HTTP GET requests. See Chapter 4, *Retrieving Information*, for more information.

service()

> `protected void service(HttpServletRequest req, HttpServletResponse res)`
>   `throws ServletException, IOException`
>
> *Description*
>
> The public `service()` method dispatches requests to this `service()` method. This method handles dispatching requests to `doGet()`, `doPost()`, and the other handler functions based on the type of request. If this method is overridden, no handlers are called.

HttpServletRequest

Synopsis

Interface Name:	`javax.servlet.http.HttpServletRequest`
Superinterface:	`javax.servlet.ServletRequest`
Immediate Subinterfaces:	None
Implemented By:	None
Availability:	Servlet API 1.0 and later

Description

`HttpServletRequest` extends the basic `ServletRequest` class, providing additional functionality for HTTP (World Wide Web) servlets. It includes support for cookies and session tracking and access to HTTP header information. `HttpServletRequest` also parses incoming HTTP form data and stores it as servlet parameters.

The server passes an `HttpServletRequest` object to the service method of an `HttpServlet`.

Certain methods in this interface have suffered from documentation and implementation inconsistencies. Discrepancies have been noted where possible.

Interface Declaration

```
public interface HttpServletRequest extends javax.servlet.ServletRequest {
  // Methods
  public abstract String getAuthType();
  public abstract Cookie[] getCookies();                        // New in 2.0
  public abstract long getDateHeader(String name);
  public abstract String getHeader(String name);
  public abstract Enumeration getHeaderNames();
  public abstract int getIntHeader(String name);
  public abstract String getMethod();
  public abstract String getPathInfo();
  public abstract String getPathTranslated();
  public abstract String getQueryString();
  public abstract String getRemoteUser();
  public abstract String getRequestedSessionId();              // New in 2.0
  public abstract String getRequestURI();
  public abstract String getServletPath();
  public abstract HttpSession getSession(boolean create);      // New in 2.0
  public abstract boolean isRequestedSessionIdFromCookie();    // New in 2.0
  public abstract boolean isRequestedSessionIdFromUrl();       // New in 2.0
  public abstract boolean isRequestedSessionIdValid();         // New in 2.0
}
```

Methods

getAuthType()

public abstract String getAuthType()

Description

> Returns the servlet's authentication scheme or `null` if the servlet was not protected by an access control mechanism. Possible schemes are `"BASIC"`, `"DIGEST"`, and `"SSL"`. Same as the CGI variable AUTH_TYPE.

getCookies()

public abstract Cookie[] getCookies()

Description

> Returns an array of `Cookie` objects that contains all the cookies sent by the browser as part of the request or `null` if no cookies were sent. This method was introduced in the Servlet API 2.0.

getDateHeader()

public abstract long getDateHeader(String name)

Description

> Returns the value of the named header as a `long` value that represents a `Date` (the number of milliseconds since midnight, January 1, 1970, GMT) or −1 if the header was not sent as part of the request. The name is case insensitive. Throws an `IllegalArgumentException` when called on a header whose value cannot be converted to a `Date`. This method is useful for handling headers like `Last-Modified` and `If-Modified-Since`.

getHeader()

> `public abstract String getHeader(String name)`
>
> *Description*
>
> Returns the value of the named header as a `String` or `null` if the header was not sent as part of the request. The name is case insensitive. This method can retrieve all header types.

getHeaderNames()

> `public abstract Enumeration getHeaderNames()`
>
> *Description*
>
> Returns the names of all the headers a servlet can access as an `Enumeration` of `Strings` or an empty `Enumeration` if there were no headers. Some servlet implementations may not allow headers to be accessed in this way, in which case this method returns `null`.

getIntHeader()

> `public abstract int getIntHeader(String name)`
>
> *Description*
>
> Returns the value of the named header as an `int` or −1 if the header was not sent as part of the request. The name is case insensitive. Throws a `NumberFormatException` when called on a header with a value that cannot be converted to an `int`.

getMethod()

> `public abstract String getMethod()`
>
> *Description*
>
> Returns the HTTP method used to make the request. Example methods include `"GET"`, `"POST"`, and `"HEAD"`. The same as the CGI variable `REQUEST_METHOD`. The `HttpServlet` implementation of `service()` uses this method when dispatching requests.

getPathInfo()

> `public abstract String getPathInfo()`
>
> *Description*
>
> Returns the extra path information associated with the request or `null` if none was provided. The same as the CGI variable `PATH_INFO`.

getPathTranslated()

public abstract String getPathTranslated()

Description

Returns the extra path information translated to a file system path or null if there was no extra path information. The path returned does not necessarily point to an existing file or directory. The same as the CGI variable PATH_TRANSLATED. This method has been known to not function properly in some servlet runners.

getQueryString()

public abstract String getQueryString()

Description

Returns the query string from the request's URL. This value is the same as the CGI variable QUERY_STRING. Because HttpServletRequest parses this string into a set of servlet parameters available through getParameter(), most servlets can ignore this method.

getRemoteUser()

public abstract String getRemoteUser()

Description

Returns the name of the user making the request as a String or null if access to the servlet was not restricted. The same as the CGI variable REMOTE_USER. This generally requires that the user has logged in using HTTP authentication. There is no comparable method to directly retrieve the remote user's password.

getRequestedSessionId()

public abstract String getRequestedSessionId()

Description

This method returns the session ID specified by the client. This may not be the actual session identifier currently in use—for example, if the session expired before the request occurred, the server creates a new session ID and uses that one instead. This method was introduced in the Servlet API 2.0.

getRequestURI()

public abstract String getRequestURI()

Description

Returns the Universal Resource Identifier (URI) of the request. This is the resource requested by the client in the first line of its HTTP request, with the query string removed. For normal HTTP servlets, the request URI is the request URL minus the scheme, host, port, and query string but including extra path information. Early versions of the Servlet API defined and implemented this method in different ways. When writing code that depends on this method, make sure you know what you're actually getting.

getServletPath()

public abstract String getServletPath()

Description

Returns the part of the URI that refers to the servlet. It does not include any extra path information or the query string. This is the same as the CGI variable SCRIPT_NAME.

getSession()

public abstract HttpSession getSession(boolean create)

Description

Returns the current session associated with the user making the request. If the user has no current valid session, this method creates one if create is true or returns null if create is false. To ensure the session is properly maintained, this method should be called at least once before any output is written to the response. Servlets not using session tracking may ignore this method. This method was introduced in the Servlet API 2.0.

isRequestedSessionIdFromCookie()

public abstract boolean isRequestedSessionIdFromCookie()

Description

Returns true if the client submitted a session identifier via a cookie, false otherwise. This method was introduced in the Servlet API 2.0.

isRequestedSessionIdFromUrl()

public abstract boolean isRequestedSessionIdFromUrl()

Description

Returns true if the requested session ID was submitted via a rewritten URL, false otherwise. This method was introduced in the Servlet API 2.0.

isRequestedSessionIdValid()

public abstract boolean isRequestedSessionIdValid()

Description

Returns true if the session requested by the client is a valid session and is therefore the session currently in use. For new sessions and expired sessions, it returns false. This method was introduced in the Servlet API 2.0.

HttpServletResponse

Synopsis

Interface Name: `javax.servlet.http.HttpServletResponse`
Superinterface: `javax.servlet.ServletResponse`
Immediate Subinterfaces: None
Implemented By: None
Availability: Servlet API 1.0 and later

Description

`HttpServletResponse` extends the `ServletResponse` class to allow manipulation of HTTP protocol-specific data, including response headers and status codes. It also defines a series of constants that represent various HTTP status codes and includes helper functions for session tracking operations.

Interface Declaration

```
public interface HttpServletResponse extends javax.servlet.ServletResponse {
// Constants
public static final int SC_ACCEPTED;
public static final int SC_BAD_GATEWAY;
public static final int SC_BAD_REQUEST;
public static final int SC_CONFLICT;
public static final int SC_CREATED;
public static final int SC_CONTINUE;                          // New in 2.0
public static final int SC_FORBIDDEN;
public static final int SC_GATEWAY_TIMEOUT;                   // New in 2.0
public static final int SC_GONE;                             // New in 2.0
public static final int SC_HTTP_VERSION_NOT_SUPPORTED;       // New in 2.0
public static final int SC_INTERNAL_SERVER_ERROR;
public static final int SC_LENGTH_REQUIRED;                  // New in 2.0
public static final int SC_METHOD_NOT_ALLOWED;               // New in 2.0
public static final int SC_MOVED_PERMANENTLY;
public static final int SC_MOVED_TEMPORARILY;
public static final int SC_MULTIPLE_CHOICES;                 // New in 2.0
public static final int SC_NO_CONTENT;
public static final int SC_NON_AUTHORITATIVE_INFORMATION;    // New in 2.0
public static final int SC_NOT_ACCEPTABLE;                   // New in 2.0
public static final int SC_NOT_FOUND;
public static final int SC_NOT_IMPLEMENTED;
public static final int SC_NOT_MODIFIED;
public static final int SC_OK;
public static final int SC_PARTIAL_CONTENT;                  // New in 2.0
public static final int SC_PAYMENT_REQUIRED;                 // New in 2.0
public static final int SC_PRECONDITION_FAILED;              // New in 2.0
public static final int SC_PROXY_AUTHENTICATION_REQUIRED;    // New in 2.0
```

```
    public static final int SC_REQUEST_ENTITY_TOO_LARGE;        // New in 2.0
    public static final int SC_REQUEST_TIMEOUT;                 // New in 2.0
    public static final int SC_REQUEST_URI_TOO_LONG;            // New in 2.0
    public static final int SC_RESET_CONTENT;                   // New in 2.0
    public static final int SC_SEE_OTHER;                       // New in 2.0
    public static final int SC_SERVICE_UNAVAILABLE;
    public static final int SC_SWITCHING_PROTOCOLS;             // New in 2.0
    public static final int SC_UNAUTHORIZED;
    public static final int SC_UNSUPPORTED_MEDIA_TYPE;          // New in 2.0
    public static final int SC_USE_PROXY;                       // New in 2.0

    // Methods
    public abstract void addCookie(Cookie cookie);             // New in 2.0
    public abstract boolean containsHeader(String name);
    public abstract String encodeRedirectUrl(String url);      // New in 2.0
    public abstract String encodeUrl(String url);              // New in 2.0
    public abstract void sendError(int sc) throws IOException;
    public abstract void sendError(int sc, String msg) throws IOException;
    public abstract void sendRedirect(String location) throws IOException;
    public abstract void setDateHeader(String name, long date);
    public abstract void setHeader(String name, String value);
    public abstract void setIntHeader(String name, int value);
    public abstract void setStatus(int sc);
    public abstract void setStatus(int sc, String sm);
}
```

Constants

Appendix C, *HTTP Status Codes*, contains complete descriptions of all the SC_*XXX* status codes.

Methods

addCookie()

```
public abstract void addCookie(Cookie cookie)
```
Description

> Adds the specified cookie to the response. Additional cookies can be added with repeated calls to addCookie(). Because cookies are sent using HTTP headers, they should be added to the response before sending any content. Browsers are required to accept only 20 cookies per site, 300 total per user, and they can limit each cookie's size to 4096 bytes.

containsHeader()

```
public abstract boolean containsHeader(String name)
```
Description

> Returns true if the named header has already been set, false if not.

encodeRedirectUrl()

```
public abstract String encodeRedirectUrl(String url)
```
Description

> Returns the specified URL encoded (rewritten) to include the session ID.
> If encoding is not needed or not supported, the method leaves the URL
> unchanged. The rules used to decide when and how to encode a URL are
> server-specific. This method may use different rules than `encodeUrl()`.
> To enable session tracking, all URLs passed to the `sendRedirect()`
> method should be run through this method. Note that this method
> employs a different capitalization scheme than `getRequestURL()` and
> `getRequestURI()`.

encodeUrl()

```
public abstract String encodeUrl(String url)
```
Description

> Returns the specified URL encoded (rewritten) to include the session ID.
> If encoding is not needed or not supported, the method leaves the URL
> unchanged. The rules used to decide when and how to encode a URL are
> server-specific. To enable session tracking, all URLs emitted by a servlet
> should be run through this method. Note that this method employs a
> different capitalization scheme than `getRequestURL()` and
> `getRequestURI()`.

sendError()

```
public abstract void sendError(int sc) throws IOException
public abstract void sendError(int sc, String msg) throws IOException
```
Description

> These methods are similar to `setStatus()`, except that they are used
> when the status code indicates an error during the handling of the
> request. A server may give these methods different treatment than
> `setStatus()`. This method should be called before sending any content.

sendRedirect()

```
public abstract void sendRedirect(String location) throws IOException
```
Description

> Redirects the response to the specified location, automatically setting the
> status code and `Location` header. The location must be an absolute URL,
> (including `"http://"`). The default implementaion also writes a short
> response body that contains a hyperlink to the location, to support
> browers without redirect capabilities. Consequently, do not write your own
> response body when using this method.

setDateHeader()

```
public abstract void setDateHeader(String name, long date)
```

Description

Sets the value of the named header as a `String` specifying a particular date and time. The method accepts the date value as a `long` that represents the number of milliseconds since midnight, January 1, 1970, GMT. If the header has already been set, the new value overwrites the previous one.

setHeader()

```
public abstract void setHeader(String name, String value)
```
Description

Sets the value of the named header as a `String`. The name is case insensitive (as with all header-related methods). If the header has already been set, the new value overwrites the previous one. This method can set any header type. Headers should always be set before sending any content.

setIntHeader()

```
public abstract void setIntHeader(String name, int value)
```
Description

Sets the value of the named header as an `int`. If the header has already been set, the new value overwrites the previous one.

setStatus()

```
public abstract void setStatus(int sc)
public abstract void setStatus(int sc, String sm)
```
Description

Sets the HTTP status code. The code can be specified using a numeric value or by using the `SC_XXX` codes defined within `HttpServletResponse`. You can optionally specify a custom error message; otherwise, the server uses the default message for that code, if any. The status should be set before sending any content.

HttpSession

Synopsis

Interface Name:	`javax.servlet.http.HttpSession`
Superinterface:	None
Immediate Subinterfaces:	None
Implemented By:	None
Availability:	New as of the Servlet API 2.0; found in JSDK 2.0, JWS 1.1

Description

The HttpSession interface provides a mechanism for identifying return visitors to a web site. For a detailed introduction to session tracking, see Chapter 7. The HttpSession interface itself allows servlets to view and manipulate session-specific information, such as creation time and the unique session identifier. It also includes methods to bind objects to the session for later retrieval, allowing "shopping cart" and other applications to hold onto data between connections without resorting to databases or other extra-servlet resources.

A servlet obtains an HttpSession object from the getSession() method of HttpServletRequest. Specific session behavior, such as the amount of idle time before a session is destroyed, depends on the server.

While any object can be bound to a session, lots of high-traffic servlets binding large objects to their sessions will impose a heavy resource burden on the server. With most implementations, this can be alleviated by binding only objects that implement the java.io.Serializable interface (this includes all of the data type objects in the core Java API). Some servers have the ability to write Serializable objects to disk to save memory. Unserializable objects, such as java.sql.Connection, must be retained in memory.

Interface Declaration

```
public interface HttpSession {
  // Methods
  public abstract long getCreationTime();
  public abstract String getId();
  public abstract long getLastAccessedTime();
  public abstract HttpSessionContext getSessionContext();
  public abstract Object getValue(String name);
  public abstract String[] getValueNames();
  public abstract void invalidate();
  public abstract boolean isNew();
  public abstract void putValue(String name, Object value);
  public abstract void removeValue(String name);
}
```

Methods

getCreationTime()

```
public abstract long getCreationTime()
```
Description

> Returns the time at which the session was created, as a long representing the number of milliseconds since midnight, January 1, 1970, GMT. Throws an IllegalStateException if the session is invalid.

getId()

```
public abstract String getId()
```
Description

Returns the unique String identifier assigned to this session. The structure of the ID is implementation dependent. For example, a Java Web Server ID might be something like HT04D1QAAAAABQDGPM5QAAA. Throws an IllegalStateException if the session is invalid.

getLastAccessTime()

```
public abstract long getLastAccessedTime()
```
Description

Returns the time at which the client last sent a request associated with this session, as a long representing the number of milliseconds since midnight, January 1, 1970, GMT. Throws an IllegalStateException if the session is invalid.

getSessionContext()

```
public abstract HttpSessionContext getSessionContext()
```
Description

Returns the context in which the session is bound. See HttpSessionContext for more information. Throws an IllegalStateException if the session is invalid.

getValue()

```
public abstract Object getValue(String name)
```
Description

Returns the object bound in the session under the specified name or null if there is no matching binding. Throws an IllegalStateException if the session is invalid.

getValueNames()

```
public abstract String[] getValueNames()
```
Description

Returns an array containing the names of all objects bound to this session or an empty (zero length) array if there are no bindings. Throws an IllegalStateException if the session is invalid. Note that unlike most similar methods (getParameterNames(), getInitParameterNames(), getServletNames(), etc.), this method does not return an Enumeration. (No, we don't know why either.)

invalidate()

```
public abstract void invalidate()
```

Description

Causes the session to be immediately invalidated. All objects stored in the session are unbound. Throws an `IllegalStateException` if the session is already invalid.

isNew()

`public abstract boolean isNew()`

Description

Returns whether the session is new. A session is considered new if it has been created by the server but the client has not yet acknowledged joining the session. For example, if a server supports only cookie-based sessions and a client has completely disabled the use of cookies, calls to `getSession()` always return new sessions. Throws an `IllegalState-Exception` if the session is invalid.

putValue()

`public abstract void putValue(String name, Object value)`

Description

Binds the specified object value under the specified name in the session. Any existing binding with the same name is replaced. Throws an `Ille-galStateException` if the session is invalid.

removeValue()

`public abstract void removeValue(String name)`

Description

Removes the object bound to the specified name or does nothing if there is no binding. Throws an `IllegalStateException` if the session is invalid.

HttpSessionBindingEvent

Synopsis

Class Name:	`javax.servlet.http.HttpSession-BindingEvent`
Superclass:	`java.util.EventObject`
Immediate Subclasses:	None
Interfaces Implemented:	None
Availability:	New as of the Servlet API 2.0; found in JSDK 2.0, JWS 1.1

Description

An `HttpSessionBindingEvent` is passed to an `HttpSessionBindingListener` when the listener object is bound to or unbound from a session.

Class Summary

```
public class HttpSessionBindingEvent extends java.util.EventObject {
  // Constructors
  public HttpSessionBindingEvent(HttpSession session, String name);

  // Instance Methods
  public String getName();
  public HttpSession getSession();
}
```

Constructors

HttpSessionBindingEvent()

public HttpSessionBindingEvent(HttpSession session, String name)
Description

Constructs a new `HttpSessionBindingEvent` using the session being bound and the name that this object is being assigned (this is the same name passed to the `putValue()` method of `HttpSession`). Servlet programmers should never need to use this constructor.

Instance Methods

getName()

public String getName()
Description

Returns the name this object has been assigned within the session.

getSession()

public HttpSession getSession()
Description

Returns the session this object is being bound to or unbound from.

HttpSessionBindingListener

Synopsis

Interface Name:	`javax.servlet.http.HttpSession-` `BindingListener`
Superinterface:	`java.util.EventListener`

Immediate Subinterfaces:	None
Implemented By:	None
Availability:	New as of the Servlet API 2.0; found in JSDK 2.0, JWS 1.1

Description

An object that implements `HttpSessionBindingListener` is notified via calls to `valueBound()` and `valueUnbound()` when it is bound to or unbound from an `HttpSession`. Among other things, this interface allows orderly cleanup session-specific resources, such as database connections.

Interface Declaration

```
public interface HttpSessionBindingListener extends java.util.EventListener {
  // Methods
  public abstract void valueBound(HttpSessionBindingEvent event);
  public abstract void valueUnbound(HttpSessionBindingEvent event);
}
```

Methods

valueBound()

```
public abstract void valueBound(HttpSessionBindingEvent event)
```
Description
> Called when the listener is bound to a session.

valueUnbound()

```
public abstract void valueUnbound(HttpSessionBindingEvent event)
```
Description
> Called when the listener is unbound from a session (including at session destruction).

HttpSessionContext

Synopsis

Interface Name:	`javax.servlet.http.HttpSessionContext`
Superinterface:	None
Immediate Subinterfaces:	None
Implemented By:	None
Availability:	New as of the Servlet API 2.0; found in JSDK 2.0, JWS 1.1

Description

`HttpSessionContext` provides access to all of the currently active sessions on the server. This can be useful for servlets that weed out inactive sessions, display statistics, or otherwise share information. A servlet obtains an `HttpSessionContext` object from the `getSessionContext()` method of `HttpSession`.

Interface Declaration

```
public interface HttpSessionContext {
  // Methods
  public abstract Enumeration getIds();
  public abstract HttpSession getSession(String sessionId);
}
```

Methods

getIds()

```
public abstract Enumeration getIds()
```
Description

Returns an `Enumeration` that contains the session IDs for all the currently valid sessions in this context. It returns an empty `Enumeration` if there are no valid sessions. The session IDs returned by `getIds()` should be held as a server secret because any client with knowledge of another client's session ID can, with a forged cookie or URL, join the second client's session.

getSession()

```
public abstract HttpSession getSession(String sessionId)
```
Description

Returns the session associated with the given session identifier. A list of valid session IDs can be obtained from the `getIds()` method.

HttpUtils

Synopsis

Class Name:	`javax.servlet.http.HttpUtils`
Superclass:	`java.lang.Object`
Immediate Subclasses:	None
Interfaces Implemented:	None
Availability:	Servlet API 1.0 and later

Description

A container object for a handful of potentially useful HTTP-oriented methods.

Class Summary

```
public class HttpUtils {
  // Constructors
  public HttpUtils();

  // Class Methods
  public static StringBuffer getRequestURL(HttpServletRequest req);
  public static Hashtable parsePostData(int len, ServletInputStream in);
  public static Hashtable parseQueryString(String s);
}
```

Constructors

HttpUtils()

```
public HttpUtils()
```
Description

The default constructor does nothing.

Class Methods

getRequestURL()

```
public static StringBuffer getRequestURL(HttpServletRequest req)
```
Description

Reconstitutes the request URL based on information available in the HttpServletRequest object. Returns a `StringBuffer` that includes the scheme, server name, server port, and extra path information. The reconstituted URL should look almost identical to the URL used by the client. This method can be used for error reporting, redirecting, and URL creation. For applications that need to uniquely identify particular servlets, the `getRequestURI()` method of `HttpServletRequest` is generally a better choice.

parsePostData()

```
public static Hashtable parsePostData(int len, ServletInputStream in)
```
Description

Parses `len` characters of parameter data from a `ServletInputStream` (usually sent as part of a POST operation). Throws an `IllegalArgumentException` if the parameter data is invalid. Most servlets use `getParameterNames()`, `getParameter()`, and `getParameterValues()` instead of this method.

parseQueryString()

```
public static Hashtable parseQueryString(String s)
```
Description

Returns a `Hashtable` where the hashtable keys are the parameter names taken from the query string and each hashtable value is a `String` array that contains the parameter's decoded value(s). Throws an `IllegalArgumentException` if the query string is invalid. Most servlets use `getParameterNames()`, `getParameter()`, and `getParameterValues()` instead. It is not safe to use both.

C

HTTP Status Codes

HTTP status codes are grouped as shown in Table C-1.

Table C-1. HTTP Status Code Groupings

Code Range	Response Meaning
100-199	Informational
200-299	Client request successful
300-399	Client request redirected, further action necessary
400-499	Client request incomplete
500-599	Server error

Table C-2 lists the HTTP status code constants defined by the `HttpServlet-Request` interface and used as parameters to its `setStatus()` and `sendError()` methods. The version number in the last column refers to the HTTP protocol version that first defined the status code. The Servlet API 2.0 added constants for HTTP Version 1.1 status codes. Note that HTTP 1.1 status codes require an HTTP 1.1-compliant browser.

For more information on HTTP, see *Web Client Programming* by Clinton Wong (O'Reilly). The proposed HTTP/1.1 specification is available in RFC 2068 at *http://www.ietf.org/rfc/rfc2068.txt.*

Table C-2. HTTP Status Code Constants

Constant	Code	Default Message	Meaning	HTTP Version
SC_CONTINUE	100	Continue	The server has received the initial part of the request, and the client can continue with the remainder of its request.	1.1
SC_SWITCHING_ PROTOCOLS	101	Switching Protocols	The server is willing to comply with the client's request to switch protocols to the one specified in the request's Upgrade header. This might include switching to a newer HTTP version.	1.1
SC_OK	200	OK	The client's request was successful and the server's response contains the requested data. This is the default status code.	1.0
SC_CREATED	201	Created	A resource has been created on the server, presumably in response to a client request. The response body should include the URL(s) where the new resource can be found, with the most specific URL set in the Location header. If the resource cannot be created immediately, an SC_ACCEPTED status code should be returned instead.	1.0
SC_ACCEPTED	202	Accepted	The request has been accepted for processing but has not yet completed. The server should describe the current status of the request in the response body. The server is under no obligation to act on or complete the request.	1.0
SC_NON_ AUTHORITATIVE_ INFORMATION	203	Non-Authorita-tive Infor-mation	The HTTP response headers came from a local or third-party source, rather than the original server. Normal servlets have no reason to use this status code.	1.1
SC_NO_CONTENT	204	No Content	The request succeeded but there was no new response body to return. Browsers receiving this code should retain their current document view. This is a useful code for a servlet to use when it accepts data from a form but wants the browser view to stay at the form, as it avoids the "Document contains no data" error message.	1.0

Table C-2. HTTP Status Code Constants (continued)

Constant	Code	Default Message	Meaning	HTTP Version
SC_RESET_ CONTENT	205	Reset Content	The request succeeded and the browser should reset (reload) the current document view. This is a useful code for a servlet to use when it accepts data from a form and wants the form redisplayed in a fresh state.	1.1
SC_PARTIAL_ CONTENT	206	Partial Content	The server has completed a partial GET request and returned the portion of the document specified in the client's Range header.	1.1
SC_MULTIPLE_ CHOICES	300	Multiple Choices	The requested URL refers to more than one resource. For example, the URL may refer to a document translated into many languages. The response body should explain the client's options in a format appropriate for the response content type. The server can suggest a choice with the Location header.	1.1
SC_MOVED_ PERMANENTLY	301	Moved Perma- nently	The requested resource has permanently moved to a new location and future references should use the new URL in their requests. The new location is given by the Location header. Most browsers automatically access the new location.	1.0
SC_MOVED_ TEMPORARILY	302	Moved Tempo- rarily	The requested resource has temporarily moved to another location, but future references should still use the original URL to access the resource. The new location is given by the Location header. Most browsers automatically access the new location.	1.0
SC_SEE_OTHER	303	See Other	The requested resource processed the request but the client should get its response by performing a GET on the URL specified in the Location header. This code is useful for a servlet that wants to receive POST data then redirect the client to another resource for the response.	1.1

Table C-2. HTTP Status Code Constants (continued)

Constant	Code	Default Message	Meaning	HTTP Version
SC_NOT_ MODIFIED	304	Not Modified	The requested document has not changed since the date specified in the request's If-Modified-Since header. Normal servlets should not need to use this status code. They implement getLast-Modified() instead.	1.0
SC_USE_PROXY	305	Use Proxy	The requested resource must be accessed via the proxy given in the Location header.	1.1
SC_BAD_REQUEST	400	Bad Request	The server could not understand the request, probably due to a syntax error.	1.0
SC_ UNAUTHORIZED	401	Unauthorized	The request lacked proper authorization. Used in conjunction with the WWW-Authenticate and Authorization headers.	1.0
SC_PAYMENT_ REQUIRED	402	Payment Required	Reserved for future use. Proposals exist to use this code in conjunction with a Charge-To header, but this has not been standardized as of press time.	1.1
SC_FORBIDDEN	403	Forbidden	The request was understood, but the server is not willing to fulfill it. The server can explain the reason for its unwillingness in the response body.	1.0
SC_NOT_FOUND	404	Not Found	The requested resource was not found or is not available.	1.0
SC_METHOD_NOT_ ALLOWED	405	Method Not Allowed	The method used by the client is not supported by this URL. The methods that are supported must be listed in the response's Allow header.	1.1
SC_NOT_ ACCEPTABLE	406	Not Acceptable	The requested resource exists, but not in a format acceptable to the client (as indicated by the Accept header(s) in the request).	1.1
SC_PROXY_ AUTHENTICATION _REQUIRED	407	Proxy Authentication Required	The proxy server needs authorization before it can proceed. Used with the Proxy-Authenticate header. Normal servlets should not need to use this status code.	1.1

Table C-2. HTTP Status Code Constants (continued)

Constant	Code	Default Message	Meaning	HTTP Version
SC_REQUEST_ TIMEOUT	408	Request Timeout	The client did not completely finish its request within the time that the server was willing to listen.	1.1
SC_CONFLICT	409	Conflict	The request could not be completed because it conflicted with another request or the server's configuration. This code is most likely to occur with HTTP PUT requests, where the file being put is under revision control and the new version conflicts with some previous changes. The server can send a description of the conflict in the response body.	1.0
SC_GONE	410	Gone	The resource is no longer available at this server, and no alternate address is known. This code should be used only when the resource has been permanently removed. Normal servlets have no reason to use this status code.	1.1
SC_LENGTH_ REQUIRED	411	Length Required	The server will not accept the request without a `Content-Length` header.	1.1
SC_ PRECONDITION_ FAILED	412	Precondition Failed	A precondition specified by one or more `If...` headers in the request evaluated to false.	1.1
SC_REQUEST_ ENTITY_TOO_ LARGE	413	Request Entity Too Large	The server will not process the request because the request content is too large. If this limitation is temporary, the server can include a `Retry-After` header.	1.1
SC_REQUEST_ URI_TOO_LONG	414	Request-URI Too Long	The server will not process the request because the request URI is longer than the server is willing to interpret. This can occur when a client has accidentally converted a POST request into a GET request. Normal servlets have no reason to use this status code.	1.1
SC_ UNSUPPORTED_ MEDIA_TYPE	415	Unsupported Media Type	The server will not process the request because the request body is in a format unsupported by the requested resource.	1.1

Table C-2. HTTP Status Code Constants (continued)

Constant	Code	Default Message	Meaning	HTTP Version
SC_INTERNAL_ SERVER_ERROR	500	Internal Server Error	An unexpected error occurred inside the server that prevented it from fulfilling the request.	1.0
SC_NOT_ IMPLEMENTED	501	Not Imple- mented	The server does not support the functionality needed to fulfill the request.	1.0
SC_BAD_GATEWAY	502	Bad Gateway	A server acting as a gateway or proxy did not receive a valid response from an upstream server.	1.0
SC_SERVICE_ UNAVAILABLE	503	Service Unavail- able	The service (server) is temporarily unavailable but should be restored in the future. If the server knows when it will be available again, a `Retry-After` header may also be supplied.	1.0
SC_GATEWAY_ TIMEOUT	504	Gateway Timeout	A server acting as a gateway or proxy did not receive a valid response from an upstream server during the time it was prepared to wait.	1.1
SC_HTTP_ VERSION_NOT_ SUPPORTED	505	HTTP Version Not Supported	The server does not support the version of the HTTP protocol used in the request. The response body should specify the protocols supported by the server. Normal servlets should not need to use this status code.	1.1

D

Character Entities

Table D-1 lists the various Unicode escapes, HTML numeric entities, and HTML named entities for all printable ISO-8859-1 (Latin-1) characters.

The numeric and named entities may be used within HTML pages; they are converted to symbols by web browsers. Unicode escapes may be used within servlet code; they are interpreted by the Java compiler. For example, a pound sign (£) can be embedded in an HTML page as "£" or "£". It can be embedded directly in Java code as "\u00A3".

Not every HTML character entity is universally supported. The Support column indicates its level of support. An "S" value means the numeric and named entity values for the symbol are part of the HTML standard. A "P" indicates the entity values are proposed standards—not part of the HTML standard but in most cases widely supported. An "N" in the column indicates the entity values are nonstandard and poorly supported. For these symbols, it's often best to use Unicode escapes.

Table D-1. Character Entities

Unicode Escape	Numeric Entity	Named Entity	Symbol	Description	Support
\u0009	&#009;		\t	Horizontal tab	S
\u000A	&#010;		\n	Line feed	S
\u000D	&#013;		\r	Carriage return	S
\u0020	&#032;			Space	S
\u0021	&#033;		!	Exclamation point	S
\u0022	&#034;	&quot;	"	Quotation mark	S
\u0023	&#035;		#	Hash mark	S
\u0024	&#036;		$	Dollar sign	S

Table D-1. Character Entities (continued)

Unicode Escape	Numeric Entity	Named Entity	Symbol	Description	Support
\u0025	&#037;		%	Percent sign	S
\u0026	&#038;	&amp;	&	Ampersand	S
\u0027	&#039;		'	Apostrophe	S
\u0028	&#040;		(	Left parenthesis	S
\u0029	&#041;		)	Right parenthesis	S
\u002A	&#042;		*	Asterisk	S
\u002B	&#043;		+	Plus sign	S
\u002C	&#044;		,	Comma	S
\u002D	&#045;		–	Hyphen	S
\u002E	&#046;		.	Period	S
\u002F	&#047;		/	Slash	S
\u0030-\u0039	0-9		0-9	Digits 0-9	S
\u003A	&#058;		:	Colon	S
\u003B	&#059;		;	Semicolon	S
\u003C	&#060;	&lt;	<	Less than	S
\u003D	&#061;		=	Equal sign	S
\u003E	&#062;	&gt;	>	Greater than	S
\u003F	&#063;		?	Question mark	S
\u0040	&#064;		@	Commercial "at" sign	S
\u0041-\u005A	A-Z		A-Z	Letters A-Z	S
\u005B	&#091;		[	Left square bracket	S
\u005C	&#092;		\	Backslash	S
\u005D	&#093;		]	Right square bracket	S
\u005E	&#094;		^	Caret	S
\u005F	&#095;		_	Underscore	S
\u0060	&#096;		`	Grave accent	S
\u0061-\u007A	a-z		a-z	Letters a-z	S
\u007B	&#123;		{	Left curly brace	S
\u007C	|		|	Vertical bar	S
\u007D	&#125;		}	Right curly brace	S
\u007E	&#126;		~	Tilde	S
\u0082	&#130;		,		N
\u0083	&#131;		*f*	Florin	N

Table D-1. Character Entities (continued)

Unicode Escape	Numeric Entity	Named Entity	Symbol	Description	Support
\u0084	&#132;		″	Right double quote	N
\u0085	&#133;		…	Ellipsis	N
\u0086	&#134;		†	Dagger	N
\u0087	&#135;		‡	Double dagger	N
\u0088	&#136;		ˆ	Circumflex	N
\u0089	&#137;		‰	Permil	N
\u008A	&#138;		Š	Capital S, caron	N
\u008B	&#139;		<	Less than sign	N
\u008C	&#140;		Œ	Capital OE ligature	N
\u0091	&#145;		`	Left single quote	N
\u0092	&#146;		′	Right single quote	N
\u0093	&#147;		″	Left double quote	N
\u0094	&#148;		″	Right double quote	N
\u0095	&#149;		•	Bullet	N
\u0096	&#150;		–	En dash	N
\u0097	&#151;		—	Em dash	N
\u0098	&#152;		~	Tilde	N
\u0099	&#153;		™	Trademark	N
\u009A	&#154;		š	Small s, caron	N
\u009B	&#155;		>	Greater than sign	N
\u009C	&#156;		œ	Small oe ligature	N
\u009F	&#159;		Ÿ	Capital Y, umlaut	N
\u00A0				Nonbreaking space	P
\u00A1	&#161;	&iexcl;	¡	Inverted exclamation point	P
\u00A2	&#162;	&cent;	¢	Cent sign	P
\u00A3	&#163;	&pound;	£	Pound sign	P
\u00A4	&#164;	&curren;	¤	General currency sign	P
\u00A5	&#165;	&yen;	¥	Yen sign	P
\u00A6	&#166;	&brvbar;			Broken vertical bar	P
\u00A7	&#167;	&sect;	§	Section sign	P
\u00A8	&#168;	&uml;	¨	Umlaut	P
\u00A9	&#169;	&copy;	©	Copyright	P
\u00AA	&#170;	&ordf;	ª	Feminine ordinal	P
\u00AB	&#171;	&laquo;	«	Left angle quote	P

Table D-1. Character Entities (continued)

Unicode Escape	Numeric Entity	Named Entity	Symbol	Description	Support
\u00AC	&#172;	&not;	¬	Not sign	P
\u00AD	&#173;	&shy;	-	Soft hyphen	P
\u00AE	&#174;	&reg;	®	Registered trademark	P
\u00AF	&#175;	&macr;	¯	Macron accent	P
\u00B0	&#176;	&deg;	°	Degree sign	P
\u00B1	&#177;	&plusmn;	±	Plus or minus	P
\u00B2	&#178;	&sup2;	^{2}	Superscript 2	P
\u00B3	&#179;	&sup3;	^{3}	Superscript 3	P
\u00B4	&#180;	&acute;	´	Acute accent	P
\u00B5	&#181;	&micro;	µ	Micro sign (Greek mu)	P
\u00B6	&#182;	&para;	¶	Paragraph sign	P
\u00B7	&#183;	&middot;	·	Middle dot	P
\u00B8	&#184;	&cedil;	¸	Cedilla	P
\u00B9	&#185;	&sup1;	^{1}	Superscript 1	P
\u00BA	&#186;	&ordm;	º	Masculine ordinal	P
\u00BB	&#187;	&raquo;	»	Right angle quote	P
\u00BC	&#188;	&frac14;	¼	Fraction one-fourth	P
\u00BD	&#189;	&frac12;	½	Fraction one-half	P
\u00BE	&#190;	&frac34;	¾	Fraction three-fourths	P
\u00BF	&#191;	&iquest;	¿	Inverted question mark	P
\u00C0	&#192;	&Agrave;	À	Capital A, grave accent	S
\u00C1	&#193;	&Aacute;	Á	Capital A, acute accent	S
\u00C2	&#194;	&Acirc;	Â	Capital A, circumflex accent	S
\u00C3	&#195;	&Atilde;	Ã	Capital A, tilde	S
\u00C4	&#196;	&Auml;	Ä	Capital A, umlaut	S
\u00C5	&#197;	&Aring;	Å	Capital A, ring	S
\u00C6	&#198;	&AElig;	Æ	Capital AE ligature	S
\u00C7	&#199;	&Ccedil;	Ç	Capital C, cedilla	S
\u00C8	&#200;	&Egrave;	È	Capital E, grave accent	S
\u00C9	&#201;	&Eacute;	É	Capital E, acute accent	S
\u00CA	&#202;	&Ecirc;	Ê	Capital E, circumflex accent	S
\u00CB	&#203;	&Euml;	Ë	Capital E, umlaut	S
\u00CC	&#204;	&Igrave;	Ì	Capital I, grave accent	S

Table D-1. Character Entities (continued)

Unicode Escape	Numeric Entity	Named Entity	Symbol	Description	Support
\u00CD	&#205;	&Iacute;	Í	Capital I, acute accent	S
\u00CE	&#206;	&Icirc;	Î	Capital I, circumflex accent	S
\u00CF	&#207;	&Iuml;	Ï	Capital I, umlaut	S
\u00D0	&#208;	&ETH;	Ð	Capital eth, Icelandic	S
\u00D1	&#209;	&Ntilde;	Ñ	Capital N, tilde	S
\u00D2	&#210;	&Ograve;	Ò	Capital O, grave accent	S
\u00D3	&#211;	&Oacute;	Ó	Capital O, acute accent	S
\u00D4	&#212;	&Ocirc;	Ô	Capital O, circumflex accent	S
\u00D5	&#213;	&Otilde;	Õ	Capital O, tilde	S
\u00D6	&#214;	&Ouml;	Ö	Capital O, umlaut	S
\u00D7	&#215;	&times;	×	Multiply sign	P
\u00D8	&#216;	&Oslash;	Ø	Capital O, slash	S
\u00D9	&#217;	&Ugrave;	Ù	Capital U, grave accent	S
\u00DA	&#218;	&Uacute;	Ú	Capital U, acute accent	S
\u00DB	&#219;	&Ucirc;	Û	Capital U, circumflex accent	S
\u00DC	&#220;	&Uuml;	Ü	Capital U, umlaut	S
\u00DD	&#221;	&Yacute;	Ý	Capital Y, acute accent	S
\u00DE	&#222;	&THORN;	Þ	Capital thorn, Icelandic	S
\u00DF	&#223;	&szlig;	ß	Small sz ligature, German	S
\u00E0	&#224;	&agrave;	à	Small a, grave accent	S
\u00E1	&#225;	&aacute;	á	Small a, acute accent	S
\u00E2	&#226;	&acirc;	â	Small a, circumflex accent	S
\u00E3	&#227;	&atilde;	ã	Small a, tilde	S
\u00E4	&#228;	&auml;	ä	Small a, umlaut	S
\u00E5	&#229;	&aring;	å	Small a, ring	S
\u00E6	&#230;	&aelig;	æ	Small ae ligature	S
\u00E7	&#231;	&ccedil;	ç	Small c, cedilla	S
\u00E8	&#232;	&egrave;	è	Small e, grave accent	S
\u00E9	&#233;	&eacute;	é	Small e, acute accent	S
\u00EA	&#234;	&ecirc;	ê	Small e, circumflex accent	S
\u00EB	&#235;	&euml;	ë	Small e, umlaut	S
\u00EC	&#236;	&igrave;	ì	Small i, grave accent	S
\u00ED	&#237;	&iacute;	í	Small i, acute accent	S

Table D-1. Character Entities (continued)

Unicode Escape	Numeric Entity	Named Entity	Symbol	Description	Support
\u00EE	&#238;	&icirc;	î	Small i, circumflex accent	S
\u00EF	&#239;	&iuml;	ï	Small i, umlaut	S
\u00F0	&#240;	&eth;	ð	Small eth, Icelandic	S
\u00F1	&#241;	&ntilde;	ñ	Small n, tilde	S
\u00F2	&#242;	&ograve;	ò	Small o, grave accent	S
\u00F3	&#243;	&oacute;	ó	Small o, acute accent	S
\u00F4	&#244;	&ocirc;	ô	Small o, circumflex accent	S
\u00F5	&#245;	&otilde;	õ	Small o, tilde	S
\u00F6	&#246;	&ouml;	ö	Small o, umlaut	S
\u00F7	&#247;	&divide;	÷	Division sign	P
\u00F8	&#248;	&oslash;	ø	Small o, slash	S
\u00F9	&#249;	&ugrave;	ù	Small u, grave accent	S
\u00FA	&#250;	&uacute;	ú	Small u, acute accent	S
\u00FB	&#251;	&ucirc;	û	Small u, circumflex accent	S
\u00FC	&#252;	&uuml;	ü	Small u, umlaut	S
\u00FD	&#253;	&yacute;	ý	Small y, acute accent	S
\u00FE	&#254;	&thorn;	þ	Small thorn, Icelandic	S
\u00FF	&#255;	&yuml;	ÿ	Small y, umlaut	S

E

Charsets

Table E-1 lists the suggested charset(s) for a number of languages. Charsets are used by servlets that generate multilingual output; they determine which character encoding a servlet's `PrintWriter` is to use. By default, the `PrintWriter` uses the ISO-8859-1 (Latin-1) charset, appropriate for most Western European languages. To specify an alternate charset, the charset value must be passed to the `setContentType()` method before the servlet retrieves its `PrintWriter`. For example:

```
res.setContentType("text/html; charset=Shift_JIS");  // A Japanese charset
PrintWriter out = res.getWriter();  // Writes Shift_JIS Japanese
```

Note that not all web browsers support all charsets or have the fonts available to represent all characters, although at minimum all clients support ISO-8859-1. Also, the UTF-8 charset can represent all Unicode characters and may be assumed a viable alternative for all languages.

Table E-1. Suggested Charsets

Language	Language Code	Suggested Charsets
Albanian	sq	ISO-8859-2
Arabic	ar	ISO-8859-6
Bulgarian	bg	ISO-8859-5
Byelorussian	be	ISO-8859-5
Catalan (Spanish)	ca	ISO-8859-1
Chinese (Simplified/Mainland)	zh	GB2312
Chinese (Traditional/Taiwan)	zh (country TW)	Big5
Croatian	hr	ISO-8859-2
Czech	cs	ISO-8859-2
Danish	da	ISO-8859-1

Table E-1. Suggested Charsets (continued)

Language	Language Code	Suggested Charsets
Dutch	nl	ISO-8859-1
English	en	ISO-8859-1
Estonian	et	ISO-8859-1
Finnish	fi	ISO-8859-1
French	fr	ISO-8859-1
German	de	ISO-8859-1
Greek	el	ISO-8859-7
Hebrew	he (formerly iw)	ISO-8859-8
Hungarian	hu	ISO-8859-2
Icelandic	is	ISO-8859-1
Italian	it	ISO-8859-1
Japanese	ja	Shift_JIS, ISO-2022-JP, EUC-JP[a]
Korean	ko	EUC-KR[b]
Latvian, Lettish	lv	ISO-8859-2
Lithuanian	lt	ISO-8859-2
Macedonian	mk	ISO-8859-5
Norwegian	no	ISO-8859-1
Polish	pl	ISO-8859-2
Portuguese	pt	ISO-8859-1
Romanian	ro	ISO-8859-2
Russian	ru	ISO-8859-5, KOI8-R
Serbian	sr	ISO-8859-5, KOI8-R
Serbo-Croatian	sh	ISO-8859-5, ISO-8859-2, KOI8-R
Slovak	sk	ISO-8859-2
Slovenian	sl	ISO-8859-2
Spanish	es	ISO-8859-1
Swedish	sv	ISO-8859-1
Turkish	tr	ISO-8859-9
Ukranian	uk	ISO-8859-5, KOI8-R

[a] First supported in JDK 1.1.6. Earlier versions of the JDK know the EUC-JP character set by the name EUCJIS, so for portability you can set the character set to EUC-JP and manually construct an EUCJIS `PrintWriter`.

[b] First supported in JDK 1.1.6. Earlier versions of the JDK know the EUC-KR character set by the name KSC_5601, so for portability you can set the character set to EUC-KR and manually construct a KSC_5601 `PrintWriter`.

Index

About the Authors

Jason Hunter is a Java consultant, speaker, instructor, and author. Jason graduated summa cum laude from Willamette University (Salem, Oregon) in 1995 with a degree in Computer Science. After graduation, he worked at Silicon Graphics in Mountain View, California, for several years, where he was responsible for developing (and breaking) all sorts of web technologies. He currently works as the Chief Technology Officer of a Silicon Valley startup, K&A Software, where he specializes in Java training and consulting, with an emphasis on servlets. Jason also writes columns for *JavaWorld*.

Jason began programming in Java in the summer of 1995 and has concentrated on servlets and related server-extension technologies since December 1996. If by some miracle you don't find him at work, he's probably out hiking in the mountains.

William "Will" Crawford got involved with web development back in 1995. He has worked at the Children's Hospital Informatics Program in Boston, where he helped develop the first web-based electronic medical record system and was involved in some of the first uses of Java at the enterprise level. He has consulted on Intranet development projects for, among others, Children's Hospital, Massachusetts General Hospital, Brigham and Women's Hospital, the Boston Anesthesia Education Foundation, and Harvard Medical Center.

Will currently heads the product development team at Invantage, Inc., a Cambridge, Massachusetts, startup developing Java-based Intranet tools for the pharmaceutical industry. In his spare time, he is an avid amateur photographer, writer, and pursuer of a Bachelor's of Economics at Yale University.

Colophon

Our look is the result of reader comments, our own experimentation, and feedback from distribution channels. Distinctive covers complement our distinctive approach to technical topics, breathing personality and life into potentially dry subjects.

The image on the cover of *Java Servlet Programming* is a copper teakettle.

The cover was designed by Hanna Dyer using a series design by Edie Freedman. The image was photographed by Kevin Thomas and manipulated in Adobe Photoshop by Michael Snow. The cover layout was produced with QuarkXPress 3.3 using the

Bodoni Black font from URW Software and Bodoni BT Bold Italic from Bitstream. The inside layout was designed by Nancy Priest.

Text was produced in FrameMaker 5.5 using a template implemented by Mike Sierra. The heading font is Bodoni BT; the text font is New Baskerville. The illustrations that appear in the book were created in Macromedia Freehand 8 and Adobe Photoshop 5 by Robert Romano.

Paula Carroll was the production editor for *Java Servlet Programming*; Benchmark Productions provided editorial and production services.

Whenever possible, our books use RepKover™, a durable and flexible lay-flat binding. If the pagecount exceeds RepKover's limit, perfect binding is used.

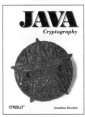

Java

Java Examples in a Nutshell

By David Flanagan
1st Edition September 1997
414 pages, ISBN 1-56592-371-5

From the author of *Java in a Nutshell*, this companion book is chock full of practical real-world programming examples to help novice Java programmers and experts alike explore what's possible with Java 1.1. If you learn best by example, this is the book for you.

Java Threads, Second Edition

By Scott Oaks and Henry Wong
2nd Edition January 1999
336 pages, ISBN 1-56592-418-5

Revised and expanded to cover Java 2, *Java Threads, 2nd Edition*, shows you how to take full advantage of Java's thread facilities: where to use threads to increase efficiency, how to use them effectively, and how to avoid common mistakes. It thoroughly covers the Thread and ThreadGroup classes, the Runnable interface, and the language's synchronized operator. The book pays special attention to threading issues with Swing, as well as problems like deadlock, race condition, and starvation to help you write code without hidden bugs.

Java Language Reference, Second Edition

By Mark Grand
2nd Edition July 1997
492 pages, ISBN 1-56592-326-X

This book helps you understand the subtle nuances of Java—from the definition of data types to the syntax of expressions and control structures—so you can ensure your programs run exactly as expected. The second edition covers the new language features that have been added in Java 1.1, such as inner classes, class literals, and instance initializers.

Java Fundamental Classes Reference

By Mark Grand & Jonathan Knudsen
1st Edition May 1997
1114 pages, ISBN 1-56592-241-7

The *Java Fundamental Classes Reference* provides complete reference documentation on the core Java 1.1 classes that comprise the *java.lang, java.io, java.net, java.util, java.text, java.math, java.lang.reflect*, and *java.util.zip* packages. Part of O'Reilly's Java documentation series, this edition describes Version 1.1 of the Java Development Kit. It includes easy-to-use reference material and provides lots of sample code to help you learn by example.

Java Distributed Computing

By Jim Farley
1st Edition January 1998
384 pages, ISBN 1-56592-206-9

Java Distributed Computing offers a general introduction to distributed computing, meaning programs that run on two or more systems. It focuses primarily on how to structure and write distributed applications and, therefore, discusses issues like designing protocols, security, working with databases, and dealing with low bandwidth situations.

Java Network Programming

By Elliotte Rusty Harold
1st Edition February 1997
442 pages, ISBN 1-56592-227-1

The network is the soul of Java. Most of what is new and exciting about Java centers around the potential for new kinds of dynamic, networked applications. *Java Network Programming* teaches you to work with Sockets, write network clients and servers, and gives you an advanced look at the new areas like multicasting, using the server API, and RMI. Covers Java 1.1.

Web Programming

CGI Programming on the World Wide Web

By Shishir Gundavaram
1st Edition March 1996
450 pages, ISBN 1-56592-168-2

This book offers a comprehensive explanation of CGI and related techniques for people who hold on to the dream of providing their own information servers on the Web. It starts at the beginning, explaining the value of CGI and how it works, then moves swiftly into the subtle details of programming.

Dynamic HTML: The Definitive Reference

By Danny Goodman
1st Edition July 1998
1088 pages, ISBN 1-56592-494-0

Dynamic HTML: The Definitive Reference is an indispensable compendium for Web content developers. It contains complete reference material for all of the HTML tags, CSS style attributes, browser document objects, and JavaScript objects supported by the various standards and the latest versions of Netscape Navigator and Microsoft Internet Explorer.

Frontier: The Definitive Guide

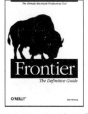

By Matt Neuburg
1st Edition February 1998
618 pages, 1-56592-383-9

This definitive guide is the first book devoted exclusively to teaching and documenting Userland Frontier, a powerful scripting environment for web site management and system level scripting. Packed with examples, advice, tricks, and tips, Frontier: The Definitive Guide teaches you Frontier from the ground up. Learn how to automate repetitive processes, control remote computers across a network, beef up your web site by generating hundreds of related web pages automatically, and more. Covers Frontier 4.2.3 for the Macintosh.

JavaScript: The Definitive Guide, 3rd Edition

By David Flanagan & Dan Shafer
3rd Edition June 1998
800 pages, ISBN 1-56592-392-8

This third edition of the definitive reference to JavaScript covers the latest version of the language, JavaScript 1.2, as supported by Netscape Navigator 4.0. JavaScript, which is being standardized under the name ECMAScript, is a scripting language that can be embedded directly in HTML to give web pages programming-language capabilities.

Learning VBScript

By Paul Lomax
1st Edition July 1997
616 pages, includes CD-ROM
ISBN 1-56592-247-6

This definitive guide shows web developers how to take full advantage of client-side scripting with the VBScript language. In addition to basic language features, it covers the Internet Explorer object model and discusses techniques for client-side scripting, like adding ActiveX controls to a web page or validating data before sending to the server. Includes CD-ROM with over 170 code samples.

Web Client Programming with Perl

By Clinton Wong
1st Edition March 1997
228 pages, ISBN 1-56592-214-X

Web Client Programming with Perl shows you how to extend scripting skills to the Web. This book teaches you the basics of how browsers communicate with servers and how to write your own customized web clients to automate common tasks. It is intended for those who are motivated to develop software that offers a more flexible and dynamic response than a standard web browser.

O'REILLY®

TO ORDER: **800-998-9938** • **order@oreilly.com** • **http://www.oreilly.com/**
OUR PRODUCTS ARE AVAILABLE AT A BOOKSTORE OR SOFTWARE STORE NEAR YOU.
FOR INFORMATION: **800-998-9938** • **707-829-0515** • **info@oreilly.com**

How to stay in touch with O'Reilly

1. Visit Our Award-Winning Web Site

http://www.oreilly.com/

★ "Top 100 Sites on the Web" —*PC Magazine*
★ "Top 5% Web sites" —*Point Communications*
★ "3-Star site" —*The McKinley Group*

Our web site contains a library of comprehensive product information (including book excerpts and tables of contents), downloadable software, background articles, interviews with technology leaders, links to relevant sites, book cover art, and more. File us in your Bookmarks or Hotlist!

2. Join Our Email Mailing Lists

New Product Releases

To receive automatic email with brief descriptions of all new O'Reilly products as they are released, send email to:
listproc@online.oreilly.com
Put the following information in the first line of your message (*not* in the Subject field):
subscribe oreilly-news

O'Reilly Events

If you'd also like us to send information about trade show events, special promotions, and other O'Reilly events, send email to:
listproc@online.oreilly.com
Put the following information in the first line of your message (*not* in the Subject field):
subscribe oreilly-events

3. Get Examples from Our Books via FTP

There are two ways to access an archive of example files from our books:

Regular FTP

- ftp to:
  ftp.oreilly.com
  (login: anonymous
  password: your email address)
- Point your web browser to:
  ftp://ftp.oreilly.com/

FTPMAIL

- Send an email message to:
  ftpmail@online.oreilly.com
  (Write "help" in the message body)

4. Contact Us via Email

order@oreilly.com
To place a book or software order online. Good for North American and international customers.

subscriptions@oreilly.com
To place an order for any of our newsletters or periodicals.

books@oreilly.com
General questions about any of our books.

software@oreilly.com
For general questions and product information about our software. Check out O'Reilly Software Online at **http://software.oreilly.com/** for software and technical support information. Registered O'Reilly software users send your questions to: **website-support@oreilly.com**

cs@oreilly.com
For answers to problems regarding your order or our products.

booktech@oreilly.com
For book content technical questions or corrections.

proposals@oreilly.com
To submit new book or software proposals to our editors and product managers.

international@oreilly.com
For information about our international distributors or translation queries. For a list of our distributors outside of North America check out:
http://www.oreilly.com/www/order/country.html

O'Reilly & Associates, Inc.
101 Morris Street, Sebastopol, CA 95472 USA
TEL   707-829-0515 or 800-998-9938
          (6am to 5pm PST)
FAX   707-829-0104

O'REILLY®

TO ORDER: **800-998-9938** • **order@oreilly.com** • **http://www.oreilly.com/**
OUR PRODUCTS ARE AVAILABLE AT A BOOKSTORE OR SOFTWARE STORE NEAR YOU.
FOR INFORMATION: **800-998-9938** • **707-829-0515** • **info@oreilly.com**

Titles from O'Reilly

International Distributors

UK, EUROPE, MIDDLE EAST AND AFRICA (EXCEPT FRANCE, GERMANY, AUSTRIA, SWITZERLAND, LUXEMBOURG, LIECHTENSTEIN, AND EASTERN EUROPE)

INQUIRIES
O'Reilly UK Limited
4 Castle Street
Farnham
Surrey, GU9 7HS
United Kingdom
Telephone: 44-1252-711776
Fax: 44-1252-734211
Email: josette@oreilly.com

ORDERS
Wiley Distribution Services Ltd.
1 Oldlands Way
Bognor Regis
West Sussex PO22 9SA
United Kingdom
Telephone: 44-1243-779777
Fax: 44-1243-820250
Email: cs-books@wiley.co.uk

FRANCE

ORDERS
GEODIF
61, Bd Saint-Germain
75240 Paris Cedex 05, France
Tel: 33-1-44-41-46-16 (French books)
Tel: 33-1-44-41-11-87 (English books)
Fax: 33-1-44-41-11-44
Email: distribution@eyrolles.com

INQUIRIES
Éditions O'Reilly
18 rue Séguier
75006 Paris, France
Tel: 33-1-40-51-52-30
Fax: 33-1-40-51-52-31
Email: france@editions-oreilly.fr

GERMANY, SWITZERLAND, AUSTRIA, EASTERN EUROPE, LUXEMBOURG, AND LIECHTENSTEIN

INQUIRIES & ORDERS
O'Reilly Verlag
Balthasarstr. 81
D-50670 Köln
Germany
Telephone: 49-221-973160-91
Fax: 49-221-973160-8
Email: anfragen@oreilly.de (inquiries)
Email: order@oreilly.de (orders)

CANADA (FRENCH LANGUAGE BOOKS)
Les Éditions Flammarion ltée
375, Avenue Laurier Ouest
Montréal (Québec) H2V 2K3
Tel: 00-1-514-277-8807
Fax: 00-1-514-278-2085
Email: info@flammarion.qc.ca

HONG KONG
City Discount Subscription Service, Ltd.
Unit D, 3rd Floor, Yan's Tower
27 Wong Chuk Hang Road
Aberdeen, Hong Kong
Tel: 852-2580-3539
Fax: 852-2580-6463
Email: citydis@ppn.com.hk

KOREA
Hanbit Media, Inc.
Sonyoung Bldg. 202
Yeksam-dong 736-36
Kangnam-ku
Seoul, Korea
Tel: 822-554-9610
Fax: 822-556-0363
Email: hant93@chollian.dacom.co.kr

PHILIPPINES
Mutual Books, Inc.
429-D Shaw Boulevard
Mandaluyong City, Metro
Manila, Philippines
Tel: 632-725-7538
Fax: 632-721-3056
Email: mbikikog@mnl.sequel.net

TAIWAN
O'Reilly Taiwan
No. 3, Lane 131
Hang-Chow South Road
Section 1, Taipei, Taiwan
Tel: 886-2-23968990
Fax: 886-2-23968916
Email: benh@oreilly.com

CHINA
O'Reilly Beijing
Room 2410
160, FuXingMenNeiDaJie
XiCheng District
Beijing, China PR 100031
Tel: 86-10-86631006
Fax: 86-10-86631007
Email: frederic@oreilly.com

INDIA
Computer Bookshop (India) Pvt. Ltd.
190 Dr. D.N. Road, Fort
Bombay 400 001 India
Tel: 91-22-207-0989
Fax: 91-22-262-3551
Email: cbsbom@giasbm01.vsnl.net.in

JAPAN
O'Reilly Japan, Inc.
Kiyoshige Building 2F
12-Bancho, Sanei-cho
Shinjuku-ku
Tokyo 160-0008 Japan
Tel: 81-3-3356-5227
Fax: 81-3-3356-5261
Email: japan@oreilly.com

ALL OTHER ASIAN COUNTRIES
O'Reilly & Associates, Inc.
101 Morris Street
Sebastopol, CA 95472 USA
Tel: 707-829-0515
Fax: 707-829-0104
Email: order@oreilly.com

AUSTRALIA
WoodsLane Pty., Ltd.
7/5 Vuko Place
Warriewood NSW 2102
Australia
Tel: 61-2-9970-5111
Fax: 61-2-9970-5002
Email: info@woodslane.com.au

NEW ZEALAND
Woodslane New Zealand, Ltd.
21 Cooks Street (P.O. Box 575)
Waganui, New Zealand
Tel: 64-6-347-6543
Fax: 64-6-345-4840
Email: info@woodslane.com.au

LATIN AMERICA
McGraw-Hill Interamericana
Editores, S.A. de C.V.
Cedro No. 512
Col. Atlampa
06450, Mexico, D.F.
Tel: 52-5-547-6777
Fax: 52-5-547-3336
Email: mcgraw-hill@infosel.net.mx

O'REILLY®

O'REILLY™

O'Reilly & Associates, Inc.
101 Morris Street
Sebastopol, CA 95472-9902
1-800-998-9938

Visit us online at:
http://www.ora.com/
orders@ora.com

O'REILLY WOULD LIKE TO HEAR FROM YOU

Which book did this card come from?

_____

Where did you buy this book?
- ❏ Bookstore
- ❏ Direct from O'Reilly
- ❏ Bundled with hardware/software
- ❏ Computer Store
- ❏ Class/seminar
- ❏ Other _____

What operating system do you use?
- ❏ UNIX
- ❏ Windows NT
- ❏ Macintosh
- ❏ PC(Windows/DOS)
- ❏ Other _____

What is your job description?
- ❏ System Administrator
- ❏ Network Administrator
- ❏ Web Developer
- ❏ Programmer
- ❏ Educator/Teacher
- ❏ Other _____

❏ Please send me O'Reilly's catalog, containing a complete listing of O'Reilly books and software.

Name _____ Company/Organization _____

Address _____

City _____ State _____ Zip/Postal Code _____ Country _____

Telephone _____ Internet or other email address (specify network) _____

Nineteenth century wood engraving
of a bear from the O'Reilly &
Associates Nutshell Handbook®
Using & Managing UUCP.

POST CARD

||||||

BUSINESS REPLY MAIL
FIRST CLASS MAIL   PERMIT NO. 80   SEBASTOPOL, CA

Postage will be paid by addressee

O'Reilly & Associates, Inc.
101 Morris Street
Sebastopol, CA 95472-9902

||I||ıı|ı|ı|ıı|ıı|ıı|ı|ı|ı||ı|ı|ı|ıı||ıııı|ı|ı||ı|